MW01073719

SELECTED LOGIC PAPERS

SELECTED LOGIC PAPERS

ENLARGED EDITION

W. V. QUINE

HARVARD UNIVERSITY PRESS
Cambridge, Massachusetts
London, England
1995

Printed in the United States of America

Library of Congress Cataloging-in-Publication Data

Quine, W. V. (Willard Van Orman)
Selected logic papers / W.V. Quine. — Enlarged ed.
p. cm.
Includes bibliographical references and index.
ISBN 0-674-79836-8. — ISBN 0-674-79837-6 (pbk.)
1. Logic, Symbolic and mathematical. I. Title.
B945.Q53S45 1995
511'.3—dc20 94-28372
CIP

TO MY SON

Douglas

PREFACE TO THE ENLARGED EDITION

The twenty-three papers that comprised the first edition are retained here, unchanged except for insertion of a somber note on page 223. Eight more papers, XXIV–XXXI, are added.

I would have happily included nine further papers, if I had not already reprinted them in my other volumes of collected papers. Three of them—"The Variable," "Truth and Disquotation," and "Algebraic Logic and Predicate Functors"—were included in the enlarged second edition of *The Ways of Paradox and Other Essays* (Harvard, 1976), when I had not foreseen an enlarged edition of *Selected Logic Papers.* Five others—"Lewis Carroll's Logic," "Grades of Discriminability," "Kurt Gödel," "On the Limits of Decision," and "Predicates, Terms, and Classes"—appeared in *Theories and Things* (Harvard, 1981).

The ninth and most conspicuous omission is "New Foundations for Mathematical Logic" (1937). It was reprinted in *From a Logical Point of View* (Harvard, 1953), before I had thought of a separate volume of logic papers. That eleven-page paper was my most influential contribution to the field, but it would seem excessive to reprint it again here, for *From a Logical Point of View* has been abundantly disseminated and is still available in paperback.

W. V. Q.

Boston, Mass.
September 1994

PREFACE

This volume assembles twenty-three of my papers on mathematical logic, 1934–1960. Twelve of them were published in the *Journal of Symbolic Logic,* nine elsewhere, two nowhere. All are technical. Still, apart from part of paper X, the collection is self-contained: points presupposed in one paper are covered in others.

The papers were chosen with a view less to chronology than to present interest and utility. Ones whose substance has gone into my books were omitted.

The papers are arranged by subject. The first gives history; the second surveys the field. The next three deal with elementary theories of integers or, what is in a way the same, of strings of signs. Then come seven papers on axiomatic set theory. One of these, from 1936, plays variations on Zermelo's system. The second bases everything on inclusion and abstraction. The third develops a deviant definition of ordered pair boasting certain virtues. The next three relate variously to the set theories of my "New foundations" and *Mathematical Logic,* and the last deals with Frege's.

The remaining papers comprise four on truth functions, or Boolean algebra, and seven on quantification. One truth-functional topic treated is the simplification problem, dear to computer engineers; another is completeness. Two of the quantification papers make the proofs of undecidability and the Löwenheim-Skolem theorem easier to follow than usual. Others develop streamlined deductive techniques. One paper shows how to reduce predicates to a single dyadic one. A final paper translates quantification into a notation without variables.

Twenty-three of my papers, including some of the present lot, were privately reprinted by offset in 1963 on Dr. Dagfinn Føllesdal's initiative and with my hearty approval, for the use of his pupils and mine. In the light of that operation I came to see that there was a place for an edited and published assortment on a larger scale. For his part in thus sparking the present volume, as well as a more discursive volume that Random House is bringing out simultaneously under the title *The Ways of Paradox,* I am grateful to Dr. Føllesdal.

The assembling and editing of the two books occupied the fifth of my five good months as Fellow of the Center for Advanced Studies at Wesleyan University. I am grateful to the administration of the Center for generous support and to the staff for cheerful assistance.

I thank the ten editors and publishers by whose permission various of my papers are reprinted in this volume. For the particulars see the bottom of the first page of each paper.

W. V. Q.

Harvard, Mass.
August 1965

Contents

SELECTED LOGIC PAPERS

I

Whitehead and the Rise of Modern Logic

1

"Algebra," for centuries, meant numerical algebra: arithmetic formulated with help of variables. Complex numbers came as an extension, but an extension still of number, arithmetically motivated; not as a departure from number. During the short period from 1843 to 1847, then, three utterly non-numerical theories came to be created in the partial image of numerical algebra: Sir William Rowan Hamilton's theory of quaternions, Hermann Grassmann's theory of extension (*Ausdehnungslehre*), and George Boole's algebra of logic. Mathematicians began to recognize that there was no necessary connection between the algebraic type of approach and the numerical type of subject matter, and indeed that the algorithmic laws of an algebra might fruitfully be studied in abstraction from all subject matter. Benjamin Peirce's *Linear Associative Algebras* (1870), a generalization of Hamilton's quaternion theory, was explicitly a comparative study of certain uninterpreted algebras. Thus it was that a wide new field came to be cleared which is today undergoing intensive cultivation under the name of abstract algebra.

Reprinted from P. A. Schilpp, ed., *The Philosophy of Alfred North Whitehead* (Library of Living Philosophers, 1941) by permission of Professor Schilpp. The Library of Living Philosophers is now handled by the Open Court Publishing Co., La Salle, Ill. The end of the second paragraph of the paper as here presented is new.

It was as a pioneer in this field that Whitehead wrote his first book, *A Treatise on Universal Algebra* (1898). In Book I of this work he undertook to characterize such algebraic notions as equivalence, addition, and multiplication along lines general enough to suit any algebra, irrespective of the more special laws of the algebra and irrespective of the interpretation. The laws:

$$x + y = y + x, \quad (x + y) + z = x + (y + z), \quad x(y + z) = xy + xz,$$

e.g., he regarded as common to algebras generally; whereas algebras might differ in point of various other laws, including:

$$xy = yx, \qquad (xy)z = x(yz), \qquad x + x = x.$$

Algebras violating the law '$x + x = x$' he called *numerical*, and classified in turn into *species* substantially as follows. Some algebras allow multiplication only between elements belonging to appropriately related *manifolds;* and an algebra is of nth species if n manifolds have to be thus distinguished.

The projected second volume of *Universal Algebra*, which never appeared, was to deal with *linear* algebras, or algebras of first species. The existing Volume I is concerned, in the last five of its seven Books, with algebras of higher species. This portion of the work constitutes a detailed investigation of the calculus of extension founded by Grassmann. Book II of the volume deals with a non-numerical algebra, namely the Boolean algebra of logic. This Book will concern us to the exclusion of the five succeeding Books. But meanwhile there is an aspect of Book I that calls for discussion: the general doctrine of equivalence.

Whitehead regarded '=' as expressing a relation of equivalence, short of identity. His defense was that laws such as '$x + y = y + x$' would otherwise, like '$z = z$', makes no assertion at all. This reasoning, which hints strongly of Wittgenstein's more recent polemic against identity,[1] loses its force if we attend closely to the distinction between notation and subject matter. Let us tentatively suppose, contrary to Whitehead as of 1898, that '$x + y = y + x$' does hold as a genuine identity; i.e., that the order of summands is wholly immaterial. A notation of addition more suggestive than '$x + y$', then, would consist in simply superimposing 'x' and 'y' in the manner of a monogram. This notation quite properly refrains from suggesting any order of summands; and there ceases to be any analogue of '$x + y = y + x$', the nearest approach being of the

[1] Paragraph 5·5303.

vacuous type '$z = z$'. Now the one objection to this procedure is the expense of casting monograms; and thus it is that we revert to a linear notation which imposes an arbitrary notational order on summands. The printer foists upon us a redundant notation, issuing in synonyms. One and the same sum can now be expressed in two ways, '$x + y$' and '$y + x$'. The law '$x + y = y + x$' comes to be needed as a means of neutralizing this excess of notation over subject matter. The law thus preserves a consequential role, even with '=' construed in the strict sense of identity.

It is not easy to imagine a notation capable of absorbing various other laws, e.g., '$x(y + z) = xy + xz$', in the manner in which the monogram notation absorbed '$x + y = y + x$'; nor is it easy to imagine a notation capable even of absorbing '$x + y = y + x$' and yet leaving '$x + x = x$' unprejudiced. For most purposes, notations teeming with synonyms are forced upon us by circumstances yet more compelling than the cost of monograms. Hence the utility of the identity concept.

Continuing his discussion of equivalence ('='), Whitehead pointed out that an equivalence formula or equation implies replaceability of the one side by the other in all algebraic contexts, whereas this does not hold for certain non-algebraic contexts. In the differential calculus, e.g., we cannot assert that if $x^3 = 8$ then $dx^3/dx = d8/dx$; for dx^3/dx is $3x^2$ (hence 12 where $x^3 = 8$) whereas $d8/dx$ is 0. This was no doubt further ground for his construing '=' as meaning something short of identity; for if x^3 *is* simply 8, so that dx^3/dx and $d8/dx$ are d/dx of one and the same thing, then surely $dx^3/dx = d8/dx$.

As is now known, however, this apparent anomaly calls for no departure from the strict identity relation. It is functions or relations, not numbers, that have derivatives. The expression 'dx^3/dx', which may for logical purposes be rendered more clearly in the fashion '$D\,\lambda_x(x^3)$', designates the derivative not of the number x^3 but of a relation $\lambda_x(x^3)$—the relation "cube of."[2] Likewise '$d8/dx$' or '$D\,\lambda_x 8$' designates the derivative not of the number 8 but of the relation $\lambda_x 8$—the relation that 8 bears to everything.[3] The 'x' of '$\lambda_x(x^3)$' and similar contexts is a so-called bound (or apparent) variable, a relative pronoun in effect, having no relevance beyond

[2] Cf. §8 below. For the logical definition of the derivative see my *Mathematical Logic*, 279.

[3] Incidentally dx^3/dx or $D\lambda_x(x^3)$ is itself not a number, $3x^2$, but a relation in turn, viz. $\lambda_x(3x^2)$—"triple of square of"; and $d8/dx$ or $D\lambda_x 8$ is not 0 but $\lambda_x 0$.

the immediate 'λ' context. Both '$\lambda_x(x^3)$' and '$\lambda_x 8$' are constants referring to fixed relations, and they are quite unaffected by special numerical hypotheses such as '$x^3 = 8$'.

Whitehead's version of '=' as equivalence-in-diversity does not reappear in his later work. Hinted in the contrast which he drew on this early occasion between algebra and the differential calculus, still, there is this sound characterization of an algebra: its terms are constructed from one another without any binding of variables.

2

The elements of the Boolean algebra are classes. The product xy is construed as the class whose members are the common members of the class x and y, and the sum $x + y$ is construed as the class obtained by pooling the members of x and y.[4] A further notion is that of the *complement* $\bar{x}$, whose members comprise everything except the members of x. Finally there is the empty class 0, and the exhaustive class 1. Equations constructed of these materials admit of an algorithm which is rather like that of the familiar numerical algebra, but simpler.

The algebra is subject, as Schröder showed in 1877,[5] to a neat principle of *duality:* every law remains true when 'plus' is switched with 'times' and '0' with '1'. Another important principle is that of *development*, which goes back to Boole: any function $f(x)$ of the algebra is expressible as a sum $ax + b\bar{x}$, wherein the coefficients a and b are respectively $f(1)$ and $f(0)$; likewise any function $f(x, y)$ is expressible as a sum:

$$axy + b\bar{x}y + cx\bar{y} + d\bar{x}\bar{y}, \tag{1}$$

wherein the coefficients are respectively $f(1, 1)$, $f(0, 1)$, $f(1, 0)$, and $f(0, 0)$; and correspondingly for higher functions $f(x, y, z)$, $f(x, y, z, w)$, etc.

Any equation of the logical algebra can be converted into another whose right member is '0'; for '$z = w$' is equivalent to '$z\bar{w} + \bar{z}w = 0$'. Having thus converted any equation, we may pro-

[4] This version of the sum goes back to Leibniz, 94f. In Boole's own books (1847, 1854) the sum was construed in a slightly different and less convenient way; but Leibniz's version was revived by W. S. Jevons (1864), and became usual.

[5] Whitehead gives the credit rather to C. S. Peirce. For a clarification of the point see Alonzo Church's review of E. T. Bell.

ceed to develop its left member after the manner exemplified in (1). Any logical equation thus admits of a standard form wherein a sort of polynomial is equated to 0. Since there are such striking analogies between equations of logic and those of ordinary algebra, the problem of solving logical equations for unknowns was among the first to command interest in connection with Boole's algebra.

The general equation in one unknown, '$ax + b\bar{x} = 0$', can be satisfied just in case $ab = 0$; and, where this condition is fulfilled, the equation proves to be satisfied by $\bar{a}c + b\bar{c}$ for every choice of c, and by nothing else. The nearest thing to a solution of '$ax + b\bar{x} = 0$', in short, is '$x = \bar{a}c + b\bar{c}$'. This was known to Boole. The "solution" —in the same sense—of the general equation in two unknowns was given by Schröder in 1890.

Whitehead sets all these matters forth systematically in Chapters I and II of his Book II, and derives new results of his own. Among these is the solution of the general equation in three or more unknowns; also the general solution of n simultaneous equations in one unknown. A principle which he establishes in the course of these developments is that a function $f(x, y, z, \ldots)$, in any number of unknowns, is capable of assuming all and only those values which can be assumed by this function in one unknown:

$$abc \ldots k + u(a + b + c + \ldots + k),$$

where $a, b, c, \ldots, k$ are the successive coefficients of f according to the law of development. These findings are accompanied by numerous others in the same vein.

In his "Memoir on the algebra of symbolic logic" of three years later, Whitehead delves further into the theory of equations and theory of functions of Boolean algebra. He investigates the problem of factoring any function into a product of so-called *linear primes*. By a linear prime he means any function $f(x, y, z, \ldots)$ that is expressible in the fashion:

$$\bar{a}x + a\bar{x} + \bar{b}y + b\bar{y} + \bar{c}z + c\bar{z} + \ldots.$$

The importance of this notion is reflected in these principles: (i) a function capable of the value 0 is a linear prime if and only if no factor of it (other than itself) is capable of the value 0; (ii) no sum of distinct linear primes, with the same variables, is capable of the value 0. In arriving at various laws of factoring, Whitehead makes extensive use of *invariants*—in striking analogy to the procedure of ordinary theory of equations. His invariants are symmetric functions of the coefficients a, b, etc., obtained under the principle of development. He shows on the basis of the principle of duality that another theory, closely parallel to all this, subsists for what he calls *separable primes*—complements of linear primes. This parallel theory is concerned not with factoring but with resolving into summands.

The second part of the article deals with transformations of functions. Any transformation of x and y into u and v is represented by a pair of equations:

$$x = f_1(u, v), \qquad y = f_2(u, v). \tag{2}$$

In case the equations (2) happen to be equivalent to another pair of the form:

$$u = F_1(x, y), \qquad v = F_2(x, y),$$

he calls the transformation a *substitution*. He shows that the substitutions, unlike the transformations generally, constitute a group; and that, given any function f, the substitutions that leave f unchanged constitute a group by themselves—the *identical group* of f, as he calls it. Among the results that he establishes with regard to substitution groups, perhaps the most notable is this: if the identical groups of two functions f_1 and f_2 have nothing in common (except the *vacuous* substitution), then (2) above is itself a substitution.

It was while this paper was at press that Whitehead came upon Giuseppe Peano's powerful mathematical logic; and forthwith he embarked with Bertrand Russell on *Principia Mathematica.* But he did not turn his back on Boolean algebra without according it one more paper, by way of extending his old theory of equations with the help of the new Peano devices. In this paper, "The logic of relations, logical substitution groups, and cardinal numbers," Whitehead formulated the general notion of a Boolean equation rigorously within Peano's formal notation. The following verbal sketch, though diverging somewhat from Whitehead's meaning, depicts the general type of approach. Given an expression of equational form, in n variables, we may think of each of its *solutions* as an n-place sequence of classes which, as values of the respective variables, make the expression true. Such a sequence may be explained in turn as a class of n pairs, wherein the first of the classes is paired with the number 1, the second with 2, etc. Finally an *equation* (as distinct from the equational expression) may be conceived as the class of the solutions. Equations become identified thus with certain classes of classes of class-number pairs; and the exact definition can be couched in Peano's symbols.

An interesting effect of defining equation along such lines was that the idea of an equation in infinitely many variables came to have meaning. Whitehead then extended various of his earlier results to apply to equations in this widened sense. He formulated a solution of the general equation, and he determined the number of possible solutions. As an instrument in these investigations he used Georg Cantor's theory of infinite numbers—a theory that had itself been the object meanwhile of investigations on Whitehead's part (cf. §9).

3

Such, in outline, were Whitehead's mathematically oriented studies of Boolean algebra. But he also directed his attention, even in *Universal Algebra*, to the more strictly logical type of problem: that which concerns analysis and systematization of the basic forms of discourse. The equations of Boolean algebra provide directly for universal statements, to the effect that *everything* or that *nothing* belongs to a class x (viz., '$x = 1$' and '$x = 0$'); but they do not provide thus directly for existential statements, to the effect that *something* does or does not belong to x. Accordingly Whitehead[6] introduced a curious quasi-term 'j', which he thought of as a modification of '1' to the following effect: xj, like $x1$, is x; but the use of the notation 'xj' is understood as implying incidentally the further information that something belongs to x. Analogously he introduced another quasi-term 'ω', thought of as a modification of '0' to the following effect: $x + \omega$, like $x + 0$, is x, but the use of the notation '$x + \omega$' implies incidentally that something does *not* belong to x. When used in isolation, rather than written in an equation, 'xj' drops its status of term altogether and comes to function simply as a statement to the effect that something belongs to x; and correspondingly for '$x + \omega$'. The expression 'xj' or '$x + \omega$' may also function simply as a statement when it stands as a member of an equation, provided the adjacent equality sign is modified in the fashion '$\equiv$' and read 'if and only if'.

Certain of the laws of Boolean algebra remain valid when 'j' and

[6] *Universal Algebra*, Bk. II, Chap. 3.

'ω' occur among the terms, but the analogy is not thoroughgoing. Additional rules are formulated to guide the manipulation of 'j' and 'ω', and even some additional auxiliary notations are adopted. Seeing how this engine grates and creaks, we may wonder with Vacca why Whitehead did not favor the simple expedient of expressing existence statements by means of inequalities: '$x \neq 0$' for 'Something belongs to x', and '$x \neq 1$' for 'Something does not belong to x'. Perhaps the answer is that Whitehead was viewing algebras strictly as systems of equations, as opposed to inequalities.

The traditional formal logic falls neatly into two parts, which may for brevity be called the *categorical* and the *hypothetical*. The categorical logic embraces the theory of immediate inference and the categorical syllogism. The hypothetical logic received only fragmentary treatment in the Aristotelian tradition, under the head of hypothetical and disjunctive syllogisms; its fuller development took place rather at the hands of the Stoic logicians and their followers—notably Chrysippus in ancient times and Petrus Hispanus in the Middle Ages.[7] Now the algebra of classes deals, in a simple and systematic way, with the matters that were dealt with more haltingly and inelegantly in the old categorical logic. Whitehead accordingly devotes a chapter[8] to deriving the various moods of categorical syllogisms. But, as Boole was aware, the algebra can be made also to provide for hypothetical logic, simply by dropping the *classial* interpretation of the algebra in favor of a *propositional* interpretation. To this course Whitehead devotes a chapter in turn.[9]

Under the propositional interpretation of the algebra, $\bar{x}$ is construed as the *denial* of the proposition x; and xy is construed as the *conjunction* and $x + y$ as the *alternation* of the propositions x and y. Thus $\bar{x}$ is true just in case x is false, xy is true just in case x and y are both true, and $x + y$ is true just in case one or both of x and y are true. In construing '$=$' propositionally, there was some divergence among Boole and his followers. The simplest choice is to construe '$x = y$' as true whenever x and y are both true or both false. So construed, '$x = y$' reduces to '$xy + \bar{x}\bar{y}$'. The sign '$=$' becomes dispensable, and so do '1' and '0'; in fact '$x = 1$' and '$x = 0$' reduce to 'x' and '$\bar{x}$'. But Whitehead chose rather to construe '$x = y$' as true only in case "any motives . . . to assent, which on presenta-

[7] See Łukasiewicz, 1935–1936.

[8] *Universal Algebra*, Bk. II, Chap. 4.

[9] *Ibid.*, Chap. 5.

tion to the mind induce assent to x, also necessarily induce assent to y and conversely."[10] For him, '$x = 1$' does not reduce to 'x'; it affirms rather that x is not merely true, but self-evident. Correspondingly '$x = 0$' affirms that x is "self-condemned." Again 'xj' and '$x + \omega$' (which might have been '$x \neq 0$' and '$x \neq 1$') deny respectively that x is self-condemned and that x is self-evident. Substantially a logic of modalities—necessity, impossibility, possibility, contingency, equivalence—is thus forthcoming.

Let us take stock again of the subject matter of the algebra. Originally, under the classial interpretation, the elements x, y, etc., of the algebra were said to be classes; i.e., the *letters* 'x', 'y', etc., were thought of as replaceable by any actual names of specific classes. Now, under the propositional interpretation, the elements x, y, etc., are said to be propositions; and this means, correspondingly, that 'x', 'y', etc., are to be replaceable by *names of* propositions. Actually, in getting specific instances of the algebraic laws under the so-called propositional interpretation, the letters are ordinarily replaced by *statements;* so we seem called upon to understand "propositions" no longer as statements, as was traditionally done, but rather as certain other entities—abstract and non-linguistic, presumably—whereof statements as wholes are names. A compound of the form '$x = y$', then, is to be true when the statements joined by '=' are names of the same proposition; and perhaps Whitehead's vague criterion in terms of "motives to assent" is as reasonable a criterion as any for deciding whether two statements are names of the same proposition. It does seem more natural than the simpler alternative previously considered, whereby '$x = y$' holds whenever both components are true or both false.

By rephrasing the so-called propositional interpretation of the algebra, though, we can easily dispense with obscure entities and reinstate the common-sense view, according to which statements are not names at all. We may stipulate simply that the constant expressions substitutable for 'x', 'y', etc., are to be statements; we need not countenance any *entities* x, y, etc., whereof the substituted statements are names. Whereas '=' in its ordinary sense of 'is' or 'is equivalent to' is a verb, a connective of names, we must now reconstrue it in a fashion appropriate for connecting statements; and the obvious reading is 'if and only if'. Just as 'xy' and '$x + y$'

[10] *Ibid.*, 108.

are read 'x and y' and 'x or y', so '$x = y$' is read 'x if and only if y'; verbs appear only inside the component statements that are thought of as supplanting 'x' and 'y'. And now it *is* quite natural to explain a compound of the form '$x = y$' as true whenever both its components are true or both false.

Modalities, e.g., logical necessity, logical impossibility, logical equivalence, are most clearly construed as properties and relations of statements, and treated in a theory that discourses *about* statements. In such a theory, known nowadays as *metalogic*, variables 'x', 'y', etc., occur which refer to statements and thus admit not statements but *names of* statements as substituends. Thus the modalities are lifted out of logic proper, and reserved to a discipline that *treats of* the expressions *used in* that logic. Whitehead's own subsequent work conformed to this trend; the modalities do not recur in his definitive formalization of logic.[11]

In *Universal Algebra*, however, Whitehead had a special use for his modal version of the algebra of logic; viz., in dealing with categorical statements by MacColl's method. The method consists in rendering 'Every *A* is a *B*', 'No *A* is a *B*', etc., in the respective forms '$x\bar{y} = 0$', '$xy = 0$', etc., where 'x' and 'y' stand for 'It is an *A*' and 'It is a *B*'. The apparent advantage of this method is that it renders the propositional interpretation of the algebra adequate not only to the hypothetical logic but to the categorical logic as well; the shift to the classial interpretation for purposes of categorical logic becomes unnecessary. Thus it was that Whitehead conceived of the propositional interpretation as having "perhaps the best right to be called a system of Symbolic Logic."[12]

But the method has shortcomings. First, it requires us to extend the notion of statement or proposition to include such expressions as 'It is mortal', where 'it' is thought of as having no grammatical antecedent, expressed or implied. This extension is drastic, for clearly such expressions admit neither of truth nor of falsehood. Second, the method is not very clearly suited to Whitehead's versions of '$=0$' and '$=1$'. There is an excess of rationalism in the view that 'Every vertebrate has a heart' expresses impossibility or "self-condemnedness" of 'It is a vertebrate and it has no heart'. Third, the method cannot be extended to more complex cases. If, e.g., we construe:

[11] For further discussion of these matters see §4 below; also §§4–5 of my *Mathematical Logic*.

[12] *Universal Algebra*, 111.

(3) Whatever interests every man interests Socrates

as:

(4) (it interests every man and it does not interest Socrates) = 0,

and then we construe the fragment 'it interests every man' in (4) correspondingly as:

(5) (it is a man and it does not interest it) = 0,

we find ourselves involved in ambiguity; for the final result is indistinguishable from the result obtained by starting not with (3) but with:

(6) Whatever every man interests interests Socrates.

Inadequacy to the analysis of complex cases like (3) is a limitation that is shared by the classial interpretation of the Boolean algebra, and by the traditional formal logic as well; and that it obtrudes itself particularly as a shortcoming of MacColl's device is perhaps a virtue of the latter. Actually Frege had overcome this limitation during the very period of MacColl's papers, and nineteen years before the appearance of *Universal Algebra;* for it was in 1879 that Frege created quantification theory and thereby founded modern mathematical logic.[13] But Frege's books remained long unnoticed. Only during the five years preceding *Universal Algebra* had Peano come to make extensive use of techniques similar to Frege's; and not until two years after *Universal Algebra* did Whitehead come to know Peano's work. Frege remained unknown to Whitehead for yet another two years.

4

Peano's logic, together with certain emendations by Russell, came to Whitehead's enthusiastic attention in 1900. "I believe," Whitehead wrote, "that the invention of the Peano and Russell symbolism . . . forms an epoch in mathematical reasoning."[14] In particular, he deemed it virtually indispensable as a tool for exploring Cantor's new theory of infinite cardinal numbers.

The abstract nature of the [latter] subject makes ordinary language totally ineffective, only gaining precision by verbosity, and imagination

[13] Quantification theory will be taken up in §5.
[14] 1902, 367.

is very misleading, since it presents to us special aggregates which are denumerable or of the power of the continuum. Thus we are thrown back onto a strict logical deduction by the symbolic method.[14]

Russell, in 1900, was working on the first volume of his *Principles of Mathematics.* Here he undertook to analyze the logical foundations of arithmetic and other parts of mathematics within the medium of ordinary language, without explicit recourse to Peano's symbolism. This volume, "which may be regarded either as a commentary upon, or as an introduction to, the second volume, is addressed in equal measure to the philosopher and to the mathematician."[15] The projected second volume, on the other hand, was to spare no rigor and no detail. Here the reader was to be exposed to the full blast of Peano's symbols. To quote Russell:

The second volume, in which I have had the great good fortune to secure the collaboration of Mr. A. N. Whitehead, will be addressed to mathematicians; it will contain chains of deductions, from the premises of symbolic logic through Arithmetic, finite and infinite, to Geometry, in an order similar to that adopted in the present volume; it will also contain various original developments, in which the method of Professor Peano, as supplemented by the Logic of Relations, has shown itself a powerful instrument of mathematical investigation.[15]

Such was the collaboration on which Whitehead and Russell embarked in 1900, with little thought that they were to be engaged in it for eleven years. But, they recounted afterward,

as we advanced it became increasingly evident that the subject is a very much larger one than we had supposed; moreover, on many fundamental questions which had been left obscure and doubtful in the former work, we have now arrived at what we believe to be satisfactory solutions. It therefore became necessary to make our book independent of *The Principles of Mathematics.*[16]

So Volume I of the *Principles* remained, like that of *Universal Algebra,* without a mate. Instead of Volume II there appeared, in 1910–1913, one of the great intellectual monuments of all time: the three volumes of *Principia Mathematica.* Even this vast work stops short of the geometry that had been slated as part of Volume II of *Principles;* this material was deferred still to a projected fourth volume of *Principia.*[17]

[15] *Principles of Mathematics,* Preface.
[16] *Principia Mathematica,* Vol. 1, v.
[17] *Ibid.,* Vol. 3, v–vi.

Part I of *Principia*, occupying the first half of the first volume, is entitled "Mathematical Logic."[18] It begins with what is substantially Boolean algebra in its simplest propositional interpretation; but without '=', '0', and '1', for we have seen (§3) that these are superfluous under this interpretation. The letters 'p', 'q', and others are used as propositional variables; and the Boolean operations of negation, addition, and multiplication—i.e., in the present interpretation, denial, alternation, and conjunction—are expressed in the fashion '$\sim p$', '$p \vee q$', '$p \, . \, q$'. Only the first two of these are taken as *primitive*, or undefined; the third is defined in terms of the other two as '$\sim(\sim p \vee \sim q)$'. Further defined compounds are '$p \supset q$' and '$p \equiv q$'; these are defined respectively as '$\sim p \vee q$' and '$(p \supset q) \, . \, (q \supset p)$', and are read '$p$ implies q' and 'p is equivalent to q'.

The laws:

$$(p \vee p) \supset p, \qquad q \supset (p \vee q), \qquad (p \vee q) \supset (q \vee p),$$
$$(q \supset r) \supset [(p \vee q) \supset (p \vee r)]$$

are adopted as formal axioms, together with a fifth that has since been proved redundant;[19] and a couple of hundred further laws, hitherto recorded for the most part by Boole's early followers C. S. Peirce and Ernst Schröder, are deduced from these axioms as theorems. The deductive procedures used are two: *substitution* of appropriate expressions for variables, and *modus ponens* (i.e., cancellation of the first part of a theorem or axiom of the form '$p \supset q$' when that first part is itself a theorem or axiom). Such rules of deductive procedure call for metalogical formulation (cf. §3), as rules *about* expressions of the sort that occur as axioms and theorems; however, the rule of *modus ponens* shows its metalogical status less clearly in *Principia* than it had in Frege's work, and the rule of substitution is left tacit altogether.[20]

Whitehead and Russell view definitions as conventions of abbreviation; thus '$p \, . \, q$', '$p \supset q$', and '$p \equiv q$' are mere shorthand for the more official renderings '$\sim(\sim p \vee \sim q)$', '$\sim p \vee q$', and '$(\sim p \vee q) \, . \, (\sim q \vee p)$'. Now over the legitimacy of such conventions there can be no dispute; but dispute may still arise over the

[18] My discussion of *Principia* will relate solely to the first edition; for Whitehead had no hand in the Introduction and Appendices that were added to Vol. 1 in the second edition. Cf. *Mind* 35 (1926), 130.

[19] Cf. Bernays, 1926.

[20] See Frege, 1893, 25; Russell, 1919, 151.

attempt to paraphrase such a defined sign in words—e.g., '.' as 'and', '⊃' as 'implies', '≡' as 'is equivalent to'. Against reading '⊃' as 'implies', objections have indeed been raised.[21] It is objected that every false proposition then comes to imply every proposition, and that every true proposition comes to be implied by every proposition, in glaring violation of any ordinary idea of implication. Exception has been taken similarly to the proposed reading of '≡'.

This controversy would not have arisen if the notion of statements as naming had been carefully avoided, and the variables '*p*', '*q*', etc., had been treated explicitly as standing in positions appropriate to statements rather than names (cf. §3). The contested readings of '≡' and '⊃' would then never have suggested themselves. The natural readings are 'if and only if' and 'only if', which, like 'and' and 'or', are the sort of expressions that appropriately join statements to form statements. '≡' is the *biconditional* sign, and '⊃' the *conditional* sign. Implication and equivalence, on the other hand, are relations between statements, and hence are properly attributed by putting a verb 'implies' or 'is equivalent to' between *names of* the statements related. Such discourse belongs to metalogic.

In *Principia*, as in Frege's logic, one statement is capable of containing other statements *truth-functionally* only; i.e., in such a way that the truth value (truth or falsehood) of the whole remains unchanged when a true part is replaced by any other truth, or a false part by any other falsehood. Preservation of this principle of truth-functionality is essential to the simplicity and convenience of logical theory. In all departures from this norm that have to my knowledge ever been propounded, moreover, a sacrifice is made not only with regard to simplicity and convenience, but with regard even to the admissibility of a certain common-sense mode of inference: inference by interchanging terms that designate the same object.[22] On grounds of technical expediency and on common-sense grounds as well, thus, there is a strong case for the principle of truth-func-

[21] Notably by Lewis, Chaps. 4–5.

[22] Lewis and Langford, e.g., use a non-truth-functional operator '$\Diamond$' to express logical possibility. Thus the statements:

$$\Diamond \text{ (number of planets in solar system} < 7),$$
$$\Diamond\ (9 < 7)$$

would be judged as true and false respectively, despite the fact that they are interconvertible by interchanging the terms '9' and 'number of planets in solar system', both of which designate the same object. Similar examples are readily devised for the early Whitehead system discussed in §3.

tionality. But it is a mistake to suppose that in order to preserve this principle we must construe the relations of implication and equivalence truth-functionally. It would be as reasonable to suppose that we must so construe the relation of rhyming as to make it depend on the truth values of the rhyming statements. The principle of truth-functionality concerns only the constructing of statements from statements; whereas relationships such as implication or equivalence or rhyming are properly ascribed rather by attaching verbs to *names of* statements. It is regrettable that Frege's own scrupulous observance of this distinction between an expression and its name, between use and mention, was so little heeded by Whitehead, Russell, and their critics.

5

The theory of *quantification* occupies the next portion of Part I of *Principia. Universal* quantification consists in attaching the so-called *universal quantifier* '(x)' [or '(y)', etc.], which may be read 'whatever object x [or y, etc.] may be', to an expression that has the form of a statement but exhibits recurrences of the variable 'x' [or 'y', etc.]. Thus (3), above, can be rendered as:

(7) $(x)(x \text{ interests every man} \supset x \text{ interests Socrates})$.

The part 'x interests every man' here can be rendered in turn as:

$$(y)(y \text{ is a man} \supset x \text{ interests } y),$$

so the whole becomes:

(8) $(x)((y)(y \text{ is a man} \supset x \text{ interests } y) \supset x \text{ interests Socrates})$,

whereas (6) becomes rather:

(9) $(x)((y)(y \text{ is a man} \supset y \text{ interests } x) \supset x \text{ interests Socrates})$.

Thus it is that quantification theory solves the problem of distinguishing between (3) and (6).

Existential quantification consists in applying rather the prefix '$(\exists x)$' [or '$(\exists y)$', etc.], which may be read 'there is an object x [or y, etc.] such that'. Thus 'Some primes are even' would be rendered:

(10) $(\exists x)(x \text{ is a prime} \,.\, x \text{ is even})$.

Whitehead and Russell define this sort of quantification in terms of the other, by explaining '$(\exists x)$' as short for '$\sim(x)\sim$'.[23]

Just as in the simpler part of logic Whitehead and Russell used 'p', 'q', etc., to stand in place of statements, so in quantification theory they use 'ϕx', 'ψy', '$\chi(x, y)$', etc., to stand in place of expressions of the kind that I call *matrices*[24]—such expressions as 'x interests Socrates', 'y is a man', 'x interests y'. To the axioms hitherto noted, two more are now added:

$$(x)\phi x \supset \phi y, \qquad (x)(p \vee \phi x) \supset (p \vee (x)\phi x).$$

A hundred theorems are derived, by use of the two deductive procedures hitherto noted and three more: substitution for complexes such as 'ϕx', relettering of variables used in connection with quantifiers, and introduction of new initial quantifiers. The new rule of substitution, like the old one, is left tacit; and so is the rule of relettering. Correct formulation of these rules, particularly that of substitution, is not easy.[25]

In its main lines this theory of quantification follows Frege's. Peano's methods, though adequate to the same purposes, differed in essential respects and were not as elegant. Whitehead and Russell's notation, set forth above, is more expedient typographically than Frege's, but Frege's exposition was more precise.

Embedded within the midst of quantification theory, as rendered by Whitehead and Russell, there is an inconspicuous detail that embodies the germ of a Platonic ontology of universals. This detail is properly inessential to quantification theory itself, but in some form it is essential to any foundation of classical mathematics. It is just this: 'ϕ', 'ψ', etc., are allowed to occur in quantifiers. The significance of this detail will be clarified.

Let us consider again the letters 'p', 'q', etc. These belong to a schematism for diagrammatically depicting the patterns of compound statements. The letters enter the diagrams '$p \supset q$', '$\sim(p\,.\sim p)$', etc., as dummies for statements; they occupy positions that would be occupied by actual statements within any actual compound statement of the depicted pattern. Analogously, the

[23] I am passing over the alternative development proposed in *9 of *Principia*. The main point of this alternative is in relation to the ramified theory of types, discussed in §7 below.

[24] *Mathematical Logic*, 71ff.

[25] For a formulation of the rule of substitution see Hilbert and Ackermann, 2d ed., 56f. The attempted formulation in the 1st ed., 53, was wrong. For the rule of relettering, see my *Mathematical Logic*, §21.

complex variables 'ϕx', 'ϕy', 'ψx', '$\chi(x, y)$', etc., enter the diagrams as dummies for matrices; they are written in complex form only to remind us, e.g., that 'ϕx' and 'ϕy' supplant matrices that are alike except for their component variables 'x' and 'y'. Expressions involving dummies 'p', 'q', 'ϕx', etc., are from this point of view not statements, nor matrices, but diagrams or schemata; such in particular are the six axioms noted above. Moreover the variables 'p', 'q', etc., used thus in schemata, need not refer to objects of any sort as their *values;* nor do 'ϕx', 'ψy', etc. The statements and matrices that these variables supplant need not be viewed as *names of* anything at all (cf. §3).

The letters 'x', 'y,' etc., themselves, fundamentally different in status from 'p', 'q', 'ϕx', etc., turn up not merely in schemata but also in the matrices themselves and even in actual statements—e.g. (7)–(10). These letters, adjuncts to the quantification notation, must be recognized as ordinary variables referring to objects. The context (10), e.g., is read 'There is *something* x such that *it* is prime and even'; and (7) is read '*Whatever entity* x may be, if *it* interests every man then *it* interests Socrates.' The letter 'x' does *refer*, in its pronominal fashion, to each of the entities of our universe—whatever those may be.[26]

The effect of letting 'ϕ', 'ψ', etc., occur in quantifiers, now, is that these letters cease to be fragments merely of dummy matrices[27] 'ϕx', 'ψy', etc., and come to share the genuinely referential power of 'x', 'y', etc. They must now be regarded as variables in their own right, referring to some sort of abstract entities, perhaps *attributes*, as their values; and they are eligible now to occur in genuine matrices and statements.[28] One such statement is '$(\exists\phi)(x)\phi x$', which may be read 'There is an attribute ϕ such that, no matter what x may be, x has the attribute ϕ.' The juxtapositive notation 'ϕx', no longer an indissoluble dummy matrix, comes to express the *attribution* of an attribute ϕ on the one hand to an object x on the other. '$\phi(x, y)$', similarly, comes to express attribution of a *dyadic* or *relative* attribute ϕ to the respective objects x and y.

[26] Cf. my "Designation and existence."

[27] My technical term for these is 'atomic matrix frames'. In general, diagrams or schemata for statements and matrices are in my terminology *frames.* The 'ϕ' occurring as a fragment of 'ϕx', 'ϕy', etc., I call a *predicate variable;* and 'p', 'q', etc., I call *statement variables.* Variables such as 'x', 'y', etc., that can occur in quantifiers and hence in actual matrices and statements, I call *pronominal variables.* See my *Elementary Logic* (1941), §§14, 33, 42.

[28] I.e., the letters 'ϕ', 'ψ', etc., cease to be predicate variables and become pronominal variables whose values are attributes; cf. preceding footnote.

In putting 'ϕ', 'ψ', etc., in quantifiers Whitehead and Russell leap from quantification theory to a theory of attributes—a theory involving over and above quantification the notion of attribution. But this new notion is never explicitly recognized. The relevant distinctions are blurred by use of the phrase 'propositional function' to refer indiscriminately both to expressions of the kind that I have called matrices and to objects of the kind that I have called attributes.

It is properly on the theory of attributes, rather than that of quantification, that Whitehead and Russell's definition of *identity* is rested; for '$x = y$' is defined with help of quantified 'ϕ' as '$(\phi)(\phi x \supset \phi y)$',[29] i.e., 'Every attribute of x is an attribute of y'. The theory of identity is one of the many branches of logic and mathematics that are successively developed from the foregoing logical basis, in the course of *Principia*, by adoption of appropriate definitions. The logical basis itself remains as above; further primitive equipment is never added.

The next branch of logical theory developed in *Principia* is that of *descriptions*. The notation of description consists in applying the prefix '$(\imath x)$' [or '$(\imath y)$', etc.] to a matrix in order to designate the one and only object x [or y, etc.] that satisfies the matrix; e.g., $(\imath x)(x^3 = 8)$ is the one and only number whose cube is 8, viz., 2. Notations to this effect were used by both Frege and Peano, but Russell was the first (1905, 1908) to define the device in terms of more basic notions. His definition, used in *Principia*, is contextual: a description is explained not in isolation but as part of a broader context, which is defined as a whole. A whole context '$\psi(\imath x)\phi x$'—to use the schematic notation—is explained as an abbreviation for:

$$(\exists y)(x)((x = y \equiv \phi x) \,.\, \psi y).$$

If there is one and only one object x such that ϕx—symbolically, if $(\exists y)(x)(x = y \equiv \phi x)$, or briefly $\text{E}!(\imath x)\phi x$—then the description '$(\imath x)\phi x$' as contextually defined comes to behave as if it designated that one object; and in other cases the context of the description simply becomes false. To speak of "the context" here is really ambiguous, since a single occurrence of a description commonly has many contexts of varying lengths; conventions are added, however, to resolve the ambiguity.

29 I omit a complication involving the notion, discussed in §7 below, of "predicative function."

6

In *Principia* the prefix '$\hat{x}$' (or '$\hat{y}$', etc.) is applied to a matrix to designate the class of all objects x (or y, etc.) satisfying that matrix. The class of all sons of lawyers, e.g., is

$$\hat{x}(\exists y)(y \text{ is a lawyer} \, . \, x \text{ is son of } y).$$

This device of *abstraction of classes* had been used, under different notations, by Frege and Peano. A companion notation, due to Peano, is that of *membership:* '$x \in \alpha$', meaning that x is a member of the class α. Thus the combination:

$$z \in \hat{x}(\exists y)(y \text{ is a lawyer} \, . \, x \text{ is son of } y)$$

amounts merely to:

$$(\exists y)(y \text{ is a lawyer} \, . \, z \text{ is son of } y).$$

Any instance of the schema:

(11) $$(z \in \hat{x}\phi x) \equiv \phi z$$

evidently holds in similar fashion.

But what sort of things are these classes? Not mere collections, or aggregates, in any concrete sense. A class α of concrete things is by no means identifiable with the concrete total object t made up of those things. On the contrary, α is not even determined by t; for α might have as members either many small parts of t or a few large ones. A class is an abstract entity, a universal, even if it happens to be a class of concrete things.

To the nominalist temper, accordingly, the elimination of classes in favor of expressions is a congenial objective; and this is what Russell is sometimes believed[30] to have done in 1908 when he showed how contexts ostensibly treating of classes could be construed as abbreviations of other expressions wherein reference is made only to "propositional functions." These constructions reappear in *Principia;* membership, abstraction, even quantification with respect to class variables 'α', 'β', etc., are introduced by contextual definition as notational abbreviations. The principle (11) is deduced, in view of these definitions, from the antecedent logical basis.

[30] See, e.g., Hahn, 22.

So long as 'propositional function' is thought of in the sense of 'matrix', such a construction would seem to serve its nominalistic objective; but actually Russell's construction involves use of 'ϕ', 'ψ', etc., in quantifiers, and hence calls for propositional functions in the sense rather of attributes. To have reduced classes to attributes is of little philosophical consequence, for attributes are no less universal, abstract, intangible, than classes themselves.

Indeed, there is no call even to distinguish attributes from classes, unless on this one technical score: classes are identified when they coincide in point of members, whereas it may be held that attributes sometimes differ though they are attributes of just the same things. It is precisely this difference, in fact, and nothing more, that Russell's contextual definition of classes accommodates; his is a technical construction enabling us to speak ostensibly of identical classes by way of shorthand for discourse about coincident but perhaps non-identical attributes.

Such definition rests the clearer on the obscurer, and the more economical on the less. Classes are more economical than attributes because they are scarcer: they coalesce when their members are the same. Classes are clearer than attributes because they have a relatively definite principle of individuation: they differ from one another just in case their members differ, whereas attributes (if they diverge from classes at all) differ from one another also under additional circumstances whose nature is left, in *Principia*, quite unspecified. Furthermore any attempt to specify those additional circumstances may be expected eventually to run afoul of the rule of "putting equals for equals," analogously to what was observed earlier (§4) in the case of non-truth-functional statement composition.

In any case there are no specific attributes that can be proved in *Principia* to be true of just the same things and yet to differ from one another. The theory of attributes receives no application, therefore, for which the theory of classes would not have served. Once classes have been introduced, attributes are scarcely mentioned again in the course of the three volumes.

The clear course would have been to introduce the membership notation '$x \epsilon \alpha$' at an earlier point, as a primitive notation taking the place of the juxtapositive notation 'ϕx' insofar as the latter is used in its ill-recognized *attributional* sense. Thus, e.g., '$(\exists\alpha)(x)(x \epsilon \alpha)$' would supplant '$(\exists\phi)(x)\phi x$'. The notation of class abstraction would still admit of definition, viz., by explaining '$\hat{x}\phi x$' as short for '$(\imath\alpha)(x)(x \epsilon \alpha \equiv \phi x)$'.[31] Just one axiom schema would have to be added, viz., '$\text{E}!\hat{x}\phi x$';[32] whereupon (11) and all other principles of the *Principia* theory of classes would be forthcoming. The notation 'ϕx' might survive in the status of dummy matrix for expository convenience (as here), but 'ϕ' would never be isolated in quantifiers nor used in actual statements and matrices. The notion of attribute, insofar as it diverges from that of class, would not occur.

The course proposed would have been a little closer to Peano and Frege, and its adoption would have obviated some of the vaguest stretches of *Principia*. Perhaps it would have been adopted if the use of the phrase 'propositional function' indiscriminately for matrices and for attributes had not obscured essential cleavages.

The contextual definition of classes is repeated in *Principia* for the dyadic case. Here, instead of classes properly so called, we have "relations in extension"—classes, substantially, of ordered pairs. Parallel to the notation '$x \epsilon \alpha$' of class membership, there is in the case of relations the notation 'xRy' to the effect that x bears the relation R to y. Abstraction, in the case of relations, is expressed by double prefixes such as '$\hat{x}\hat{y}$'.

The reform proposed above for the theory of classes carries over to the theory of relations in strict analogy. '$\hat{x}\hat{y}\phi(x, y)$' comes to be explained as short for:

$$(\imath R)(x)(y)[xRy \equiv \phi(x, y)],$$

while 'xRy' comes to figure as a primitive notation supplanting the attributional version of '$\phi(x, y)$'. An axiom schema analogous to '$\text{E}!\hat{x}\phi x$' has to be added, viz., '$\text{E}!\hat{x}\hat{y}\phi(x, y)$'.

This reform of the foundations does not affect the ensuing constructions. In the course of these constructions Boolean algebra is reconstructed in its classial interpretation, by defining the complement $-\alpha$ of a class α as $\hat{x} \sim (x \epsilon \alpha)$, the product of classes α and β as $\hat{x}(x \epsilon \alpha \,.\, x \epsilon \beta)$, and the sum as $\hat{x}(x \epsilon \alpha \vee x \epsilon \beta)$. The universal class, designated by 'V', is defined as $\hat{x}(x = x)$; and the null class Λ is defined in turn as $-\text{V}$. An exactly parallel algebra of relations is also developed, wherein the complement $\dot{-}R$ of a relation R is defined as $\hat{x}\hat{y} \sim (xRy)$, the product of relations Q and R as $\hat{x}\hat{y}(xQy \,.\, xRy)$, and so on. Theorems are deduced at considerable

[31] Substantially this definition was used by Whitehead on a later occasion (1934).

[32] Cf. §5, above. This schema combines P1 and R3 of my "New foundations."

length in the class algebra, and then parallels are listed for relations.

This wasteful duality would have been avoided if, like Peano, the authors had treated relations quite literally as classes of ordered pairs. The notion of an ordered pair $x;y$ could be adopted as primitive, as in Peano, whereupon 'xRy' could be explained as short for '$x;y \in R$'. Relational abstraction, correspondingly, could be reduced to class abstraction by explaining $\hat{x}\hat{y}\phi(x, y)$ as

$$\hat{z}(\exists x)(\exists y)(z = x;y \,.\, \phi(x, y)).$$

Such of relation theory as parallels general class theory then comes, in large part, simply to be absorbed into the latter. Incidentally the axiom schema '$\text{E}!\hat{x}\hat{y}\phi(x, y)$', noted above, becomes dispensable in favor of:

$$(x;y = z;w) \supset (x = z \,.\, y = w).$$

And one of the advances in logic since *Principia* is the discovery by Wiener that this latter axiom and the primitive notion of ordered pair that it governs can be eliminated in turn. The ordered pair is satisfactorily definable on the basis of class theory alone.

7

Russell was the first to discover that the principle (11), if admitted without special restrictions of one sort or another, leads to contradiction. If in particular we put 'α' for 'x', '$\sim(\alpha \in \alpha)$' for 'ϕx', and '$\hat{\alpha} \sim (\alpha \in \alpha)$' for '$z$', we get as an instance of (11) the self-contradictory statement:

$$(12) \qquad [\hat{\alpha} \sim (\alpha \in \alpha) \in \hat{\alpha} \sim (\hat{\alpha} \in \alpha)] \equiv \sim[\hat{\alpha} \sim (\alpha \in \alpha) \in \hat{\alpha} \sim (\alpha \in \alpha)].$$

Both Frege's logic and Peano's turn out, in this way, to be involved in contradiction.

Russell's remedy is his *theory of types*. Every class is conceived as belonging to one and only one of a hierarchy of so-called types; and any formula that represents membership as holding otherwise than between members of consecutive ascending types is rejected as meaningless, along with all its contexts. In particular, thus, '$\alpha \in \alpha$' and all its contexts are meaningless. Such is the status of (12), which thus ceases to count as an instance of (11). (12) is only one of infinitely many contradictions derivable from (11); but all these, so far as is known, are banished like (12) by the theory of types.

Relation theory, though, involves analogous contradictions, so Russell has to extend the theory of types to cover relations as well as classes. The theory here is more complicated; the two degrees of freedom implicit in the ordered pair call for more than a simple hierarchy of types. The theory of "propositional functions," insofar as it makes use of 'ϕ', 'ψ', etc., in quantifiers, is of course no less liable to the contradictions than are class theory and relation theory; and from the point of view of *Principia* it is actually not to classes and relations but to "propositional functions" that the basic version of type theory applies. From this equivocal realm the theory is transmitted to classes and relations through the contextual definitions of these latter.

As applied to propositional functions the theory undergoes a special complication: a hierarchy of *orders* is superimposed, such that propositional functions may differ as to order even though they be of the same type. This ramification of type theory proves to subject logic and mathematics to certain intolerable restrictions, for the removal of which an *axiom of reducibility* is adopted. According to this axiom, every propositional function is satisfied by exactly the same arguments as some propositional function which is *predicative*, i.e., which has the lowest order compatible with its type.

This ramification of type theory is designed for the avoidance of certain contradictions of a quite different sort from (12). But the treatment is vague, on account of failure to distinguish between expressions and their names. On restoring this distinction one finds that the contradictions against which this part of type theory was directed are no business of logic anyway; they can arise only in discourse that goes beyond pure logic and imports semantic terms such as 'true' or 'designates'. The whole ramification, with the axiom of reducibility, calls simply for amputation.[33]

It is readily seen also on other grounds that this part of type theory was bound to be wholly idle. The axiom of reducibility assures us that from the beginning we could have construed the notations of *Principia* as referring exclusively to so-called predicative "propositional functions" (predicative *attributes*); but when this is done, the resulting logic is the same as if neither "orders" nor "predicativity" nor "reducibility" had been thought of in the first place.[34] That this simple situation escaped the atten-

[33] Cf. Ramsey, 20–29.
[34] Cf. my paper "On the axiom of reducibility."

tion of the authors is attributable, again, to the ambiguity of 'propositional function' and the underlying difficulty over use and mention.

The residual unramified type theory, as applied to classes and relations, is actually the only form of type theory that figures even in *Principia* after the first couple of hundred pages; for, as remarked, "propositional functions" are soon submerged. But even this simpler version of type theory is a source of much complexity of technical detail.

Because the theory allows a class to have members only of uniform type, the universal class V gives way to an infinite series of quasi-universal classes, one for each type. The negation $-\alpha$ ceases to comprise all non-members of α, and comes to comprise only those non-members of α which are next lower in type than α. Even the null class Λ gives way to an infinite series of null classes. The Boolean class algebra no longer applies to classes in general, but is reproduced rather within each type. The same is true of the calculus of relations. Even arithmetic, when introduced by definitions on the basis of logic, proves to be subject to the same reduplications. Thus the numbers cease to be unique; a new 0 appears for each type, likewise a new 1, and so on, just as in the case of V and Λ. Not only are all these cleavages and reduplications intuitively repugnant, but they call continually for more or less elaborate technical manoeuvres by way of restoring severed connections.[35]

In particular, an awkward effect is obstruction of the proof that $n \neq n + 1$ for all finite n; this principle comes rather to be cited as hypothesis where needed (cf. §9), and Whitehead and Russell avoid it whenever they can at the cost of more circuitous proofs. In one way and another the theory of types accounts for perhaps a fifth of the page-count of the three volumes.

In 1934 Whitehead presented an alternative foundation for arithmetic, designed both to obviate the reduplication of numbers and to render '$n \neq n + 1$' demonstrable in straightforward logical fashion. His method, though, is costly; for it turns essentially on the use of statements in non-truth-functional contexts (cf. §4). For all its cost, moreover, the method continues to presuppose the theory of attributes (using 'ϕ', 'ψ', etc., in quantifiers); and in that domain the theory of types remains intact.

Whatever the inconveniences of type theory, contradictions such as (12) show clearly enough that the previous naïve logic needed reforming. The theory of types (as applied to classes

[35] From my "New foundations."

and relations, hence without the *ramus amputandus*) remains one of the important proposals for a reformed logic. There have been other proposals to the same end—one of them even coeval with the theory of types.[36] None of these other proposals involves that reduplicative situation whose irksomeness, for Whitehead among others, has been noted; and not all of these proposals obstruct the proof that $n \neq n + 1$.[37]

But a striking circumstance is that none of these proposals, type theory included, has an intuitive foundation. None has the backing of common sense. Common sense is bankrupt, for it wound up in contradiction. Deprived of his tradition, the logician has had to resort to mythmaking. That myth will be best that engenders a form of logic most convenient for mathematics and the sciences; and perhaps it will become the common sense of another generation.

8

In the remainder of Part I numerous special notions having to do with relations are defined and hundreds of theorems are derived. One important notion is $R``\alpha$, the class of all objects bearing R to any members of α. The definition is obvious: $\hat{x}(\exists y)(y \in \alpha \,.\, xRy)$. Another is the *relative product* $R \mid S$, defined as $\hat{x}\hat{z}(\exists y)(xRy \,.\, ySz)$. Another is $\breve{R}$, the *converse* of R, defined as $\hat{y}\hat{x}(xRy)$. These notions had figured prominently in the early work on relation theory by Augustus De Morgan and C. S. Peirce. But these pioneers did not distinguish explicitly between the first two of the notions; Frege was the first to do so.

Another important notion is $R`x$, defined as $(\iota y)(yRx)$. So long as one and only one thing bears $R$ to $x$, that thing is $R`x$. If in keeping with modern trends we explain a *function* in general as a one-many relation, i.e., a relation that no two things bear to the same thing,[38] then the notation '$R`x$' may be spoken of as that of functional *application;* where $R$ is a function, $R`x$ is the value of R for the argument x.

[36] Zermelo, 1908.

[37] In my *Mathematical Logic*, e.g., this is readily deducible from †677 (p. 252) with help of mathematical induction.

[38] Cf. Peano, 1911.

Special functions D, Ɑ, $\overrightarrow{R}$, and $\overleftarrow{R}$ are then defined, in such a way that D'R, Ɑ'R, $\overrightarrow{R}$'x, and $\overleftarrow{R}$'x turn out to be respectively $\hat{x}(\exists y)(xRy)$, $\hat{y}(\exists x)(xRy)$, $\hat{y}(yRx)$, and $\hat{y}(xRy)$. But this and other portions of *Principia* would have been shorter and better if every new notation had been required to pay its way or suffer deletion. D'R and Ɑ'R, called the *domain* and *converse domain* of R, could have been expressed quite as briefly in terms of previous notions, without further definition; viz., as R"V and R"V. Also, given Peano's notation 'ιx' for the class $\hat{y}(y = x)$ whose sole member is x, the notations '$\overrightarrow{R}$'x' and '$\overleftarrow{R}$'x' could have been dropped in favor of R"ιx and $\breve{R}$"ιx. Use of 'R"V', '$\breve{R}$"V', 'R"ιx', and '$\breve{R}$"ιx' would have called for very few special theorems, over and above the general ones governing 'R"α'. On the other hand the adoption of 'D'R' and the rest calls for chapters of additional theorems by way of relating these new notations to old ones and to one another; and thereupon we find ourselves manipulating 'D'R', 'Ɑ'R', etc., according to the new special laws, neglecting general laws about 'R"α' that would have served as well. It is important to remember that algorithmic power turns not on assorted occurrences of many signs, but on repeated occurrences of a few.

Functional application, under a different notation, played a prominent role in Frege's logic; and so did a companion notion of functional *abstraction*. This latter consists in applying the prefix 'λ_x' (or 'λ_y', etc.)[39] to a term containing 'x' (or 'y', etc.), in order to designate the function whose value, for any argument x, is the object referred to by the original term; thus $\lambda_x(x^3)$ is the function "cube of," i.e., the function whose value for any argument x is x^3. Functional abstraction is related to functional application precisely as class abstraction is related to membership. Just as membership cancels class abstraction (cf. (11)), so application cancels functional abstraction; $\lambda_x(x^3)$ ' y, e.g., is y^3. Functional abstraction is readily introduced on the basis of relational abstraction; $\lambda_x(x^3)$, e.g., is simply $\hat{y}\hat{x}(y = x^3)$.

The fact that functional abstraction was not carried over into *Principia* accounts for a good deal of inelegance. A special definition is adopted, e.g., explaining 'R_ϵ' as short for '$\hat{\beta}\hat{\alpha}(\beta = R$"$\alpha)$'; whereas '$\lambda_\alpha(R$"$\alpha)$', if available, would have served instead of that special sign. The devious course of defining 'D' in isolation

[39] I depart from Frege's notation in favor of Church's, which is more familiar nowadays.

as '$\hat{\alpha}\hat{R}[\alpha = \hat{x}(\exists y)(xRy)]$', instead of defining '$\mathrm{D}R$' outright as '$\hat{x}(\exists y)(xRy)$' (or using '$R$"V' instead), is another consequence of the lack of functional abstraction. The course was prompted by the need of D, on rare occasions, as a function in its own right; but if functional abstraction had been at hand, the infrequent need of 'D' in isolation would have been served by '$\lambda_R \mathrm{D}R$' (or '$\lambda_R(R$"V)'). The situation is precisely similar with 'Ꮯ', '$\overrightarrow{R}$', and '$\overleftarrow{R}$'; and the situation is similar also with 'ι', for Whitehead and Russell introduce Peano's 'ιx' as 'ι'x' in parallel fashion to 'D'R' and the rest. Profitable use might have been made of functional abstraction at many other places in *Principia* as well.[40]

9

Classes are said to have the same *cardinal number* just in case they are respectively the domain and the converse domain of a *one–one* relation; i.e., of a function (in the sense lately explained) whose converse is a function. Where α and β are any mutually exclusive classes whose respective cardinal numbers are μ and ν, the arithmetical *sum* of μ and ν is defined as the cardinal number of the logical sum of α and β; the arithmetical *product* of μ and ν is the cardinal number of the class of all pairs $i;j$ such that $i \epsilon \alpha$ and $j \epsilon \beta$; and μ to the *power* ν is the cardinal number of the class of all functions having β as converse domain and part or all of α as domain. A number is *infinite* if it is at once the cardinal number of distinct classes α and β such that $\alpha \subset \beta$, i.e., such that $(x)(x \epsilon \alpha \supset x \epsilon \beta)$; otherwise *finite.* 0 is defined as the cardinal number of the null class; 1 is the cardinal number of classes of the form ιx; and each further finite cardinal is expressible in terms of 1 and arithmetical addition. The first infinite cardinal, $\aleph_0$, is defined as the cardinal number of the class of all finite cardinals. The *ordering* of cardinals is fixed by the stipulation that $\mu \leqq \nu$ wherever μ and ν are the cardinal numbers respectively of classes α and β such that $\alpha \subset \beta$.

Such are the elementary constructions of Cantor's theory of cardinal numbers. This much was set forth explicitly by Peano in his logical notation.[41] But note that the cardinal number of

[40] Notably Vol. 1, *38 *passim;* Vol. 2, *150·01·02.
[41] 1901, 70–72.

α, symbolically Num α, has been defined only in the context 'Num α = Num β'; not in isolation. Actually Num α could very easily be defined in isolation, viz., as the class of all domains of one–one relations having α as converse domain; and such, years earlier, was Frege's course.[42] But Peano rejected this course, asserting groundlessly that Num α and the class in question "ont des propriétés différentes."[43]

In early sections of Whitehead's 1902 paper "On cardinal numbers," Peano's formulation of Cantor's constructions is reproduced with certain emendations attributed to Russell. Here Frege's definition of cardinal number that Peano had rejected is adopted. Here also we find a definition of the class of finite cardinals that goes back to Frege; it turns not on the criterion indicated above, but rather on the idea of accessibility from 0 by successive additions of 1. It goes into the *Principia* notation thus:

$$\hat{\mu}(\kappa)[(\nu)(\nu \in \kappa \supset \nu + 1 \in \kappa) \supset (0 \in \kappa \supset \mu \in \kappa)].$$

Russell had learned it through Dedekind, being ignorant still of Frege when this paper went to press.

In this paper Whitehead redefines the power μ^ν as the number of ways of picking exactly one member from each of ν mutually exclusive classes having μ members apiece; and he derives the old definition as a theorem. Further, he defines the sum and the product of any class of cardinals—covering the case where the cardinals belonging to the class are not merely infinite but infinitely numerous. He proves various familiar arithmetical theorems, in extension to infinite cardinals; the most striking case, perhaps, is the binomial theorem, whose explicit formulation alone is no small undertaking.

The proofs of various of the theorems in this paper and its 1904 sequel depend on two hypotheses: (1) every infinite class is exhaustively resoluble into parts having $\aleph_0$ members apiece, and (2) of any two cardinal numbers one exceeds the other. Both are reducible to a far more basic hypothesis, Zermelo's famous *axiom of choice;* but this was for the future, for the axiom itself dates only from 1904.

The definitions in the two Whitehead papers tend to be less

[42] 1884, 79–85; 1893, 56f.
[43] 1901, 70.

rigorous than in Peano. Many of them omit essential quantifiers.[44] In the definition of the number 1 there is also a further defect, whereby the null class comes inadvertently to be admitted as a member of 1.[45] There is a notation of multiplication that receives no definition, though it appears in two theorems.[46] In general the proofs of theorems are sketchy; and in particular I have been unable to decipher the purported proof that $n \neq n + 1$ for finite n.[47]

Still the two papers were highly significant, affording as they did the first considerable development of infinite arithmetic within mathematical logic. Cantor and others had used no logical formalism; Peano had deduced none but a few trivial theorems in infinite arithmetic; and Frege, though deducing the laws of finite arithmetic in rigorous detail, did little with infinite numbers.

Principia was in progress, and these two papers were early progress reports. Subsequent progress was both qualitative and quantitative. In the finished *Principia*, Parts II–III, the concepts of cardinal arithmetic are constructed more elegantly than before and a good level of rigor is maintained. The axiom of choice is now used explicitly as a hypothesis where needed; and so is another principle, the so-called *axiom of infinity*, which for *Principia* is equivalent to the troublesome law that $n \neq n + 1$ for finite n (cf. §7). With and without the help of these hypotheses, hundreds of theorems on finite and infinite cardinals and ancillary topics are deduced. In Part V, Cantor's theory of finite and infinite *ordinal* numbers is developed, followed by remnants of cardinal arithmetic that depend on the theory of ordinals. In point both of rigor and of comprehensiveness, these portions of *Principia* remain the authoritative work on cardinals and ordinals.

The theory of ordinals is part of that of *ordered sets;* for, just as a cardinal is a class of classes all having the same number of members, so an ordinal is a class of so-called *well-ordered* sets all having the same number of members arranged in similar orders. To an ordered set, two things matter—the members and their order; so we might think of an ordered set as a complex, somehow, of a class α and a "before–after" relation R among members of α. However, specification of α is superfluous; α is already determined by R, being simply the field of R, i.e., the logical sum C‘R of D‘R and Ɑ‘R. Hence the

[44] I.e., essential subscripts; for Peano's notation is used.
[45] 1902, 378; also 373.
[46] *Ibid.*, 381 (4·21·22).
[47] *Ibid.*, 379 (2·1).

ordered set can be adequately treated simply by identifying it with *R;* and such is the course adopted by Whitehead and Russell. Ordered sets are not identified with relations in general, but with those relations *R* that have the "before–after" kind of structure. This condition on *R* breaks up into three:

Asymmetry: $(x)(y) \sim (xRy \,.\, yRx)$,

Transitivity: $(x)(y)(z)[(xRy \,.\, yRz) \supset xRz]$,

Connexity: $(x)(y)[(x \in \text{C}`R \,.\, y \in \text{C}`R) \supset (xRy \vee yRx \vee x = y)]$.

In *Principia* such a relation *R* is called *serial.* For *well*-ordering, yet a fourth condition is needed:

$$(\beta)[(\beta \subset \breve{R}``\beta) \supset (\beta = \Lambda)].$$

Given all four conditions on *R*, there is still latitude as regards further details of structure; and the class of all well-ordered serial relations that agree with *R* in all such further details is taken as the *ordinal number* of *R*.

It should be noted that Whitehead and Russell's identification of an ordered set with the relation of "before–after" therein is somewhat arbitrary; we could identify it rather with the relation "no later than" in the set (thus choosing the analogue of "$\leqq$" rather than that of "$<$"). This alternative approach, which is gaining in favor, has certain advantages; e.g., it restores the ordinal number 1,[48] anomalously missing under the Whitehead–Russell method.

The theory of ordered sets, or series, is broader than that of well-ordered sets and ordinals. In general, ordered sets or serial relations that coincide in all further details of structure are said to belong to the same *order type.* Ordinal numbers are thus special sorts of order types, viz., those of well-ordered series. In *Principia* order types are spoken of rather as *serial numbers;* but their analogy to numbers is slight, for, unlike the ordinals, they do not all fall into a serial order of "magnitude." In the theory of ordered sets generally, what has interested mathematicians is not a quasi-arithmetic of order types, but rather the notion of the *limit* of a set and derivative notions. This branch of theory, known as analytic set theory, is rigorously developed from logic in the course of Part V of *Principia.*

Order type or serial number is, we saw, the generalization of ordinal number that is reached by waiving the requirement of well-ordering. But a still broader generalization—called *relation number*

[48] This was called to my attention by Dr. Alfred Tarski.

in *Principia*—is reached by waiving the requirement of seriality in turn and considering relations generally. The theory of relation numbers is the general theory of isomorphism, i.e., of structural identity among relations. It embraces the theory of ordering and of well-ordering, inasmuch as serial numbers and ordinal numbers are simply the relation numbers of ordered and well-ordered sets; but it also embraces wider theories, e.g., that of partial order. The theory of relation numbers occupies Part IV of *Principia;* serial and ordinal numbers appear only afterward, as specializations. Emphasis is put on the analogies, insofar as there are such, between relation numbers and cardinals; but these relationships would have come out somewhat more clearly and simply if relations had been treated literally as classes of ordered pairs (cf. §6).

10

Part VI, "Quantity," occupies the last half of the last volume of *Principia.* Attention is here turned to the arithmetic of signed integers, ratios, and real numbers. Following Peano, the authors construe the signed integers $+\mu$ and $-\mu$ in effect as the function $\lambda_\nu(\nu + \mu)$ and its converse, where μ is any finite cardinal. Arithmetical notions such as sum, product, and power, defined hitherto for cardinals, are now defined again appropriately for signed integers; and a train of theorems is deduced.

Peano's way of construing ratios, viz., by identifying μ/ν with $\hat{\mu}'\hat{\nu}'(\mu \times \nu' = \mu' \times \nu)$ for all finite cardinals μ and ν, is abandoned by Whitehead and Russell in favor of a version whereby μ/ν becomes a relation not between cardinal numbers but between relations. Roughly, μ/ν is construed as the relation which Q bears to R just in case there are things x and y such that x bears $Q|Q|$ . . . (ν times) and likewise $R|R|$ . . . (μ times) to y. Think of Q and R as vectors or transformations, applicable over and over; then Q bears μ/ν to R if ν applications of Q do the work of μ applications of R. (In the definition actually adopted a complication is added whose purpose is to minimize the dependence of rational arithmetic on the axiom of infinity; but it is a complication engendered merely by the theory of types.)

This version of ratios is interesting in that it makes ratios immediately applicable to relations generally, arithmetical and otherwise. The grandparent relation, e.g., stands in the ratio 2/5 to the great-great-great-grandparent relation. Such applicability proves useful in a subsequently expounded theory of measurement. A further virtue of this version is the naturalness with which the series of ratios so construed admits of extension to include negatives. The negative of a ratio P is defined in effect as $P \mid \lambda_R \breve{R}$. The negative of the ratio 2/5 obtains, e.g., between the grandparent relation and the great-great-great-grandchild relation.

A real number is explained, substantially, as any class of ratios that (1) does not contain all the ratios, but (2) contains any given ratio if and only if it contains also a higher. (Actually an exception is made, inelegantly and gratuitously, in connection with 0.[49]) That those classes form a model of the traditional real number series was first pointed out by Dedekind. In this version of real numbers, the ratios alluded to are to be understood of course as just positive and zero; and the real numbers thus accounted for are likewise just positive and zero. But one can build the negative reals on the negative ratios in quite analogous fashion; and Whitehead and Russell do so.

They also develop an attractive alternative construction of real numbers, the effect of which is to increase the kinship between real numbers and ratios. Here a real number is identified not with a class α of ratios, as above, but rather with the relation whose ordered pairs are got by pooling all the ratios belonging to such a class α. Real numbers so construed are, like ratios, relations between relations.

For real numbers in both senses, as well as for ratios, Whitehead and Russell set up the full complement of associated arithmetical notions and prove many theorems. Then they turn to the concluding topic of *Principia*, which is *measurement*. In dim outline, the development of this topic proceeds as follows.

Any one–one relation R that is *repeatable* (i.e., such that everything to which R is borne bears R to something in turn) is called a *vector*. A class κ ($\neq \Lambda$) of vectors all having the same field α, and such further that the order of applying any two of the vectors is immaterial ($P|Q = Q|P$), is called a *vector family of* α. Now a *magnitude* is thought of as a vector; the gram, e.g., is thought of as the vector "a gram more than." *Kinds* of magnitude, e.g., mass, length, etc., are certain vector families. *Measurement*, finally, consists in determining ratios between members of some vector family κ; and here we see the special utility of the adopted version of ratios as

[49] *Principia*, Vol. 3, 316f.

relations of relations. In cases where irrational measures are called for, use is made not of ratios but of real numbers—which still are relations of relations, under the second version. A general theory of so-called *nets* is begun, with a view to the introduction of geometrical co-ordinates in the projected fourth volume.

Measurement is ordinarily thought of as a concern of natural science; and we should scarcely venture to derive the concepts of natural science from pure logic. But we may still venture to formulate the conceptual *structure* of natural science in purely logical terms. Insofar as certain terms, say of physics, are constructible from other more basic ones by logical devices, we may reproduce the constructions using variables in place of those basic physical terms. Along these lines we arrive at purely logical functions that make up—more and more exhaustively as we proceed—the logical component of natural science. "Application" of these logical constructs to the world consists merely in assigning values, of the appropriate extra-logical sort, to the variables.

Such is the intended status of the theory of measurement developed in *Principia*. When we take κ as a certain physically specified class of vectors, we have a rudimentary theory of mass; when we take κ as another class, we have a rudimentary theory of length; and so on. Physical laws, insofar as they imply relevant differences between these various choices of κ, will supply differences in detail between the theory of mass, the theory of length, etc.

Application of the general theory in this wise encounters some difficulty on the score of the repeatability clause in the definition of vector. If we construe the gram, e.g., as the relation "heavier by a gram than" as between physical objects, then after a certain point the finitude of mass of the universe will obstruct repeatability. If we are to take the gram as a vector, it seems we must take it not as the described relation between bodies but rather as the relation "a gram more than" as between entities that are in turn abstract quantities in some sense or other. Such, indeed, is the intention of Whitehead and Russell;[50] but then we are left farther from the physical application than might have been desired.

Analysis of the logical structure of natural science had been occupying Whitehead as early as 1906, when he published a paper "to initiate the mathematical investigation of various possible ways of conceiving the nature of the material world." The constructions in that paper are couched in the regular *Principia* nota-

[50] Cf. *Principia*, Vol. 3, 339.

tion, and foreshadow to some degree the projected volume on geometry; and a continuation is outlined in Whitehead's later writings[51] under the head of "extensive abstraction." Other constructions in the 1906 paper go far outside geometry; this was the beginning of a quest for the broadest, most basic concepts and principles of nature, and in the decades since *Principia* the quest has issued in a metaphysics.

[51] 1916; 1919; 1920; 1929.

II

Logic, Symbolic

Notations reminiscent of algebra were used sporadically in deductive or formal logic from Gottfried von Leibniz onward, and increasingly in the 19th century (George Boole, Augustus DeMorgan, William Stanley Jevons, Charles Sanders Peirce). Gottlob Frege, in 1879, supplanted the algebraic notation by another which better accentuated the structural traits most germane to deduction. Flourishing like other happily formulated branches of mathematics, deductive logic soon so exceeded its earlier powers as to invite rechristening: whence "symbolic" or "mathematical" logic.

If in a sentence we put dummy letters for all portions other than the *logical particles* 'or', 'and', 'not', 'if', 'every', 'some', and the like, we get roughly what may be called a *logical form.* A form is called *valid* if all sentences having that form are true. The *logical truths*, finally, are the sentences valid in form; and the concern of deductive logic, or symbolic logic, is systematic recognition of logical truths.

When a logical truth has the form of a conditional ('If . . . then . . .'), the one clause is said to *imply* the other logically. Implication underlies the practical use of deductive logic, namely, *deduction:* the inferring of sentences, on any subject, from any supposed truths which logically imply them.

The above description is inexact, mainly because of the imperfect inventory of the logical particles. A more adequate accounting of these particles will emerge as we get on with the substantive theory of symbolic logic in the following pages.

This article was written in 1954 and is reprinted from *Encyclopedia Americana*, 1957 and later editions, by permission.

1. Truth-Function Logic, or Propositional Calculus. The *conjunction* of any sentences is a sentence compounded of them by juxtaposition, let us say, and construed as true if and only if the component sentences are all true. The *alternation* of any sentences, formed by a connective '$\vee$', is false if and only if the components are all false. The *negation* of a sentence, formed by writing '–' before or above, is true if and only if the sentence itself is false. Thus juxtaposition, '$\vee$', and '–' may be read 'and', 'or', and 'not', though in abstraction from such verbal usage as may diverge from the rigid truth conditions just now stated.

Thus, let 'p', 'q', and 'r' be dummy sentences. Then '$pq \vee \bar{p}\bar{q} \vee p\bar{r}$' will be true if and only if at least one of these three combinations is realized: 'p' and 'q' both true, or both false, or 'p' true and 'r' false.

A compound sentence is said to be a *truth function* of its component sentences if the *truth value* (truth or falsity) of the compound is determined by the truth values of the components; that is, if no substitution of truths for the component true sentences and falsehoods for the false ones will alter the truth value of the compound. Obviously any compound is a truth function of its components if built up of them by conjunction, alternation, and negation. It is easily shown also, conversely, that conjunction, alternation, and negation provide a complete notation for the truth functions.

Alternation can even be dropped, since '$p \vee q$' can be rendered '$-(\bar{p}\bar{q})$'. But the threefold notation is convenient. It enables us to render any truth function of given components 'p', 'q', etc., in the perspicuous *alternational normal form;* that is, as an alternation of conjunctions of elements from among 'p', '$\bar{p}$', 'q', '$\bar{q}$', etc. Transformation into that form is accomplished by distribution according to three laws: '$-(s \vee t \vee \ldots)$' becomes '$\bar{s}\bar{t} \ldots$'; '$-(st \ldots)$' becomes '$\bar{s} \vee \bar{t} \vee \ldots$'; and '$r(s \vee t \vee \ldots)$' becomes '$rs \vee rt \vee \ldots$'. (Terminological note: we speak of conjunction not only of many components but also of one, thus counting anything a conjunction of itself, and similarly for alternation; so 'p', '$p\bar{q}$', '$\bar{p} \vee q$', etc., count as in alternational normal form.)

Everything said in the foregoing paragraph remains true when we systematically switch the roles of alternation and conjunction. Thus any truth function can be put also into a *conjunctional* normal form. This so-called *duality* between alternation and conjunction rests on the fact that their truth conditions are alike except for a systematic interchange of 'true' and 'false'.

The compounds '$\bar{p} \vee q$' (or equivalently '$-(p\bar{q})$') and '$pq \vee \bar{p}\bar{q}$' are commonly rewritten '$p \supset q$' and '$p \equiv q$' respectively, and called the (material) *conditional* and *biconditional*, and read 'if p then q' and 'p if and only if q'. Though they mirror only imperfectly the vague idioms 'if–then' and 'if and only if', they suffice for much of the business of those idioms. Eked out by "quantification" (see below), they suffice for more of it still—indeed for all of it but the questionable business of the subjunctive or contrary-to-fact conditional. The importance of truth-function theory is due largely to the connective '$\supset$' and its intimate connection with logical implication, namely this: one sentence implies another if and only if the material conditional formed from the two sentences is logically true. The connective '$\equiv$' is similarly related to logical equivalence, or mutual implication.

In order to avoid excessive parentheses, dots are used to mark major breaks in formulas. A dot, when used instead of mere juxtaposition to express conjunction, marks a greater break than '$\vee$', '$\supset$', or '$\equiv$'; any of these connectives with a dot added marks a greater break still; a double dot marks a greater break still; and so on. Thus '$p \vee . p \vee q . pq \vee r :\supset p$' stands for '$\{p \vee [(p \vee q)(pq \vee r)]\} \supset p$'.

We can *evaluate* (that is, determine the truth value of) any truth function of 'p', 'q', etc., for any given assignment of truth values to 'p', 'q', etc., by applying the truth conditions for conjunction, alternation, and negation step by step. *Validity* of a formula of the logic of truth functions (for example, '$pq \vee p\bar{r} \vee \bar{p}r \vee \bar{p}s \vee \bar{q}r \vee \bar{r}\bar{s}$') is therefore decidable by tabulating all possible assignments of truth values to letters of the formula and evaluating the formula for each. Such is the method of *truth tables* (which in practice admits of certain shortcuts).

Implication between formulas of truth-function logic is likewise decidable by truth tables; for one formula implies another if the corresponding conditional is valid. Equivalence is then decidable in turn by two implication tests. Or, more simply, we may test two formulas for equivalence by constructing a truth table for each and then comparing the truth tables to see if they are the same.

Simple examples of implication in the logic of truth functions are these: 'pq' implies 'p'; 'p' implies '$p \vee q$'; '$p . p \supset q$' implies 'q'. Each, characteristically, repeats 'p' and so could quickly engender fallacy if a sentence substituted for 'p' were capable of being true at some points and false at others within the same train of logical argument. To avoid this *fallacy of equivocation* we do not need to fix all ambiguities in the sentences to which logic is applied, nor all references of pronouns and demonstratives; but we do need to fix such of them as might otherwise vary by force of context within the space of the argument.

Truth-function logic was pursued by the Stoics and by Petrus Hispanus and William of Ockham. Reappearing as a variant of the algebra of classes (next topic), it was perfected by Peirce, Frege, Ernst Schröder, and Emil L. Post.

2. Algebra of Monadic Predicates or Classes. General terms or predicates are roughly nouns, adjectives, and verbs. This grammatical trichotomy is indifferent to logic; a more germane distinction is that between absolute general terms or monadic predicates (for example, 'man', 'red', 'thinks') and relative general terms or polyadic predicates (for example, 'uncle of', 'greater than', 'takes'). Sentences are true or false; monadic predicates are true or false *of* objects; dyadic predicates are true or false of pairs of objects; and so on. Accordingly the truth functions, which apply to sentences, have analogues—called *Boolean functions*—applicable to predicates: a conjunction ("logical product") of predicates is true of whatever the predicates are jointly true of; an alternation ("logical sum") is true of what at least one of the predicates is true of; and a negation is true of what the predicate is false of.

In the algebra of monadic predicates, also called class algebra, we build Boolean functions of dummy predicates 'F', 'G', etc. Also two special predicates emerge, 'V' and 'Λ', true of everything and nothing. Joining any such expressions by '$=$', we get *Boolean equations*. An appropriate reading of '$F = G$' in general is 'All F are G and vice versa'; hence in particular '$FG = \Lambda$' amounts to 'No F are G', and '$F\overline{G} = \Lambda$' to 'All F are G'. '$F\overline{F} = \Lambda$' and '$F \vee \overline{F} = \mathrm{V}$' are valid, or true for all interpretations of 'F'. Any Boolean equation has an equivalent with 'V' as one side, and another with 'Λ' as one side; for '$F = \Lambda$' is equivalent to '$\overline{F} = \mathrm{V}$', '$F = \mathrm{V}$' to '$\overline{F} = \Lambda$', and, in general, '$F = G$' to '$FG \vee \overline{F}\overline{G} = \mathrm{V}$' and to '$F\overline{G} \vee \overline{F}G = \Lambda$'.

This algebra was developed mainly by Boole, Jevons, and Schröder. Its formulas (valid and otherwise) comprise the Boolean equations and all truth functions of them. Valid examples include:

$$(1) \qquad FG \neq \Lambda \,.\, G\overline{H} = \Lambda \,.\supset.\, FH \neq \Lambda$$

and the like, answering to syllogisms in traditional logic.

What things 'V' is to be true of, and what things '$\bar{F}$' is to be true of, given an interpretation of 'F', depend on our choice of "universe of discourse" (DeMorgan). This choice may conveniently be varied from application to application; so formulas are counted valid only if true under all interpretations of 'F', 'G', etc., in *all* non-empty universes. The empty universe is profitably excepted because some formulas, for example '$V \neq \Lambda$', fail for it which hold generally elsewhere. The question whether a formula also holds for the empty universe is easily settled, when desired, by a separate test; for *all* Boolean equations hold true for the empty universe, and accordingly any truth function of them can be tested by "evaluation" (see above).

Validity is of interest mainly as a key to implication, which is validity of the conditional. Now in simple cases implications are easily checked directly, by diagramming classes as overlapping circles (John Venn). To explore the consequences of given Boolean equations and inequalities we shade regions of the diagram which the equations declare empty, and flag regions which the inequalities declare occupied, and observe the effects.

But the prime desideratum is a general *decision procedure* for this part of logic, such as the truth table provides for truth-function logic; i.e., a mechanical method of testing *any* truth function of Boolean equations for validity. The earliest such procedure was established by Leopold Löwenheim; others, easier, have appeared since. One is as follows.

Let us suppose all equations (and inequalities) standardized so as to have 'Λ' as right-hand member, and no 'Λ' nor 'V' in the left member. (Occurrences of 'Λ' and 'V' on the left can be got rid of by substituting '$F\bar{F}$' and '$F \vee \bar{F}$', or by a more efficient method which need not detain us.) Now any alternation of (one or more) such inequalities, e.g.:

$$(2) \qquad -(FG) \neq \Lambda \,.\vee.\, G\bar{H} \neq \Lambda \,.\vee.\, FH \neq \Lambda,$$

can be tested for validity as follows: delete '$\neq \Lambda$' everywhere, and test the result ('$-(FG) \vee G\bar{H} \vee FH$', in the case of (2)) for validity by truth table (as if 'F', 'G', etc., were sentence letters).

The procedure can be extended to any alternation of formulas whereof one is an equation and the rest (if any) are inequalities, as follows: weaken the alternation by changing its one equation to an inequality and negating the left member thereof; then test the thus weakened alternation as in the preceding paragraph. For example,

'$FG = \Lambda . \vee . G\bar{H} \neq \Lambda . \vee . FH \neq \Lambda$' (which is the syllogism (1), converted to normal form) weakens to (2). Such weakening is by no means an equivalence transformation; yet it does leave non-valid formulas non-valid and valid ones valid, as long as we adhere to alternations with only one affirmative equation. (This is not evident, but can be proved.)

The procedure can be extended in turn to *any* alternation of equations and/or inequalities; for an alternation which includes several affirmative equations is valid if and only if, by dropping all but a certain one of its affirmative equations, it can be got down to an alternation valid according to the preceding paragraph. (This again is not evident, but can be proved.)

Finally we can test any truth function whatever of Boolean equations, as follows. We put the whole into conjunctional normal form, handling its equations as one would sentence letters. The result is a conjunction of alternations as of the preceding paragraph; and the whole is valid if and only if each of those alternations is valid.

3. Quantification. Conjunction, alternation, and negation have their analogues for polyadic predicates, as for monadic predicates. But there are also further operations, applicable to polyadic predicates, which have no analogues for sentences or monadic predicates. One is *converse*, which, applied to 'greater than' or 'parent', gives 'less than' or 'offspring'. Another is *relative product*, illustrated by 'friend of father of'. Another is *image*, which combines dyadic and monadic predicates as in 'friends of musicians'. The algebra of dyadic predicates or relations (DeMorgan, Peirce, Schröder), which treats of these matters, is far more complex and less intuitive than the algebra of monadic predicates or classes. On the other hand the logical inferences for which this extended algebra provides, and further ones for which it does not, prove easily manageable under a more analytical approach which departs from the pattern of an algebra of predicates; namely, the *logic of quantification*, founded by Frege.

The *universal quantifier* '(x)' may be read 'Each object x is such that', and the *existential quantifier* '$(\exists x)$' may be read 'At least one object x is such that'. These are prefixed to *open* sentences such as 'x is red' which, of themselves, are neither true nor false because of the *free* 'x'. The resulting *quantifications* in this instance, '$(x)(x$ is red)' and '$(\exists x)(x$ is red)', are *closed* sentences and are respectively false and true.

Writing 'Fx' to indicate application of the predicate 'F' to 'x', we can express 'All F are G' and 'Some F are G' as '$(x)(Fx \supset Gx)$' and '$(\exists x)(Fx \,.\, Gx)$', and 'No F are G' indifferently as '$(x)(Fx \supset -Gx)$' or '$-(\exists x)(Fx \,.\, Gx)$'. Typical purposes of Boolean equations can thus be served alternatively by quantification and truth functions. Indeed any Boolean equation can be translated into these terms; first we rephrase it with 'V' as its right side, and then we translate it as '$(x)(\ \ldots\ )$' where '. . .' is got from the left side by inserting 'x' after each predicate letter.

But the great value of quantification theory resides in the fact that it is adequate equally to polyadic matters. Here we write predicate letters followed by multiple variables: 'Fxy', '$Gxyz$'. The effects of the above notions of converse, relative product, and image are then got by 'Fyx', '$(\exists y)(Fxy \,.\, Gyz)$', and '$(\exists y)(Fxy \,.\, Gy)$'.

The use of variables other than 'x' in quantifiers changes the sense of the quantifiers in no way, but serves merely to preserve cross-references, as in '$(\exists x)(y)Fxy$'; this is the quantification by '$(\exists x)$' of the open sentence '$(y)Fxy$'.

The valid formula '$(\exists x)(y)Fxy \supset (y)(\exists x)Fxy$' illustrates the extended coverage which quantification theory affords as contrasted with the algebra of monadic predicates or, *a fortiori*, the traditional theory of the syllogism.

The formulas of quantification theory are built up from *atomic* formulas 'p', 'q', 'Fx', 'Fy', 'Gxy', 'Hyx', '$Jxyz$', etc., by truth functions and quantification. The convention is that the atomic formulas represent any sentences, subject to these conditions: (1) If the atomic formula occurs under a quantifier whose variable it lacks, then the sentence which it represents must lack free occurrences of that variable. (2) If two atomic formulas are alike except for variables (e.g., 'Fx' and 'Fy'), then the represented sentences must be similarly related.

Interpretation of a formula consists in choosing a universe as range of values of 'x', 'y', etc., choosing truth values for 'p', 'q', etc., choosing specific objects of the universe for any free variables, and deciding what objects (or pairs, etc.) the predicates 'F', 'G', etc., are to be true of. A formula is *valid* if true under all interpretations with non-empty universes. As before, the case of the empty universe is easily handled by a separate test; for all universal quantifications are there true, and all existential ones false.

Implication, as usual, is validity of the conditional. In particular 'Fyy' implies '$(\exists x)Fxy$'. This example of implication, and closely similar ones, will now be given a special name. The existential quantification of any formula ξ, with respect to a variable α, will be called an *existential consequence* of any formula which is like ξ except for having free occurrences of some variable β wherever ξ has free occurrences of α.

By a *surface occurrence* of a formula ϕ in a formula ψ let us understand an occurrence which is overlaid by no quantifier or negation or '$\supset$' or '$\equiv$'; nothing but conjunction and alternation. Now it is readily seen that the following rule of inference leads from formulas always to formulas which they imply.

RULE I: *Supplant a surface occurrence of ϕ in ψ by an existential consequence of ϕ.*

Example: two steps by Rule I lead from '$-Fwz \lor Fwz$' to '$(\exists y) -Fwy \lor (\exists x)Fxz$'.

The next rule of inference does not lead always to implied formulas, but it does lead from valid formulas to none but valid formulas.

RULE II: *If α is a variable whose free occurrences in ψ lie wholly within a surface occurrence of ϕ, then insert a universal quantifier so as to quantify ϕ with respect to α. In so doing you may also change α to a new letter β, provided that β is foreign to ϕ.*

Example: two steps by Rule II lead from the result of the preceding example to '$(x)(\exists y)-Fxy \lor (y)(\exists x)Fxy$'.

The next two rules obviously lead from formulas to equivalent formulas.

RULE III: *Supplant any clause at will by any which is equivalent to it by truth tables.*

RULE IV: *Change '$(\exists x)-$', '$(x)-$', '$(\exists y)-$', etc., at will to '$-(x)$', '$-(\exists x)$', '$-(y)$', etc., respectively.*

Example: two steps by Rule IV lead from the result of the preceding example to '$-(\exists x)(y)Fxy \lor (y)(\exists x)Fxy$', or '$(\exists x)(y)Fxy \supset (y)(\exists x)Fxy$'.

As the above chain of examples illustrates, Rules I–IV enable us, starting with a formula which is valid by truth table ('$-Fwz \lor Fwz$' in the example), to generate further valid formulas of quantification theory. This technique is in fact *complete* (Kurt Gödel, Jacques Herbrand), that is, capable of yielding *any* valid formula.

It is convenient in practice, though strictly unnecessary, to invoke supplementary rules, based, for example, on the implication of 'Fy' by '$(x)Fx$', or the equivalence of '$(x)(Fx \,.\, Gx)$' to '$(x)Fx \,.\, (x)Gx$' or of '$(\exists x)(Fx \vee Gx)$' to '$(\exists x)Fx \vee (\exists x)Gx$'.

Despite its completeness, the described proof procedure is not a *decision procedure* (see above). For, even if we fail to find the proof of a formula, we may not know whether the formula is nevertheless valid, its proof having merely eluded us. In truth-function logic and again in the algebra of monadic predicates we saw decision procedures; for quantification theory, however, none is possible (Alonzo Church).

4. Identity. The sign '$=$' was used in earlier pages to form true sentences from coextensive predicates. But it has its primary use rather between variables 'x', 'y', etc., as a dyadic predicate in its own right, expressing identity. The theory of identity can be summed up in the axiom '$(x)(x = x)$' and the axiom schema '$(x)(y)(x = y \,.\, Fx \,.\!\supset\!.\, Fy)$', wherein '$Fx$' and '$Fy$' represent any sentences which are alike except that the one has free 'x' at some points where the other has free 'y'.

Gödel showed that every truth in the notation of identity theory is obtainable from this basis by quantification theory. For example, one case of the axiom schema is '$(x)(y)(x = y \,.\, x = x \,.\!\supset\!.\, y = x)$', which, with '$(x)(x = x)$', yields '$(x)(y)(x = y \,.\!\supset\!.\, y = x)$'.

Identity, added to the truth functions and quantifiers, enables us to deal with the idioms 'only x', 'everything else', and the like. From 'Someone on the team admires everyone else on the team' and 'Some fielder on the team is admired by no one' we can argue by means of quantification theory plus identity and its axioms, but not by means of quantification theory alone, that some fielder on the team admires everyone else on the team.

The adding of identity provides also for a rudimentary treatment of number: we can express 'There are exactly n objects x such that Fx', symbolically '$(\exists_n x)Fx$', for each fixed n. For, '$(\exists_0 x)Fx$' can be rendered '$-(\exists x)Fx$', and '$(\exists_n x)Fx$' for each succeeding n can be rendered '$(\exists x)[Fx \,.\, (\exists_{n-1} y)(Fy \,.\, x \neq y)]$' (Frege).

The adding of identity enables us also to introduce an operator of *singular description* '(ιx)' (Frege, Giuseppe Peano) in such a way as to serve the useful purposes of the words 'the object x such that'. The trick (essentially Bertrand Russell's) is to explain '$(\iota x)Fx$' not outright, but in any atomic context. Thinking of '$G(\iota x)Fx$' as any such context of '$(\imath x)Fx$', we explain '$G(\imath x)Fx$' as short for '$(\exists y)[Fy \,.\, Gy \,.\, (x)(Fx \supset . \, x = y)]$'; that is, some F is G and nothing but it is F. This device enables us to handle singular terms within the framework of pure quantification theory with identity. Consider, for example, the function sign or operator '+', which produces compound singular terms of the form '$y + z$'. Its purposes can be served by an ordinary triadic predicate 'Σ', where 'Σxyz' means that x is the sum of y and z; for, '$y + z$' can then be taken as '$(\imath x)\Sigma xyz$', subject to the general contextual definition of '$(\imath x)Fx$'.

5. Set Theory. In '=' we have a logical predicate. There is another, the predicate 'ϵ' of class membership, which is more powerful: so much so that it may with some justice be viewed rather as mathematical, in a sense exclusive of logic. Once 'ϵ' is assumed, '=' is dispensable; for '$x = y$' can be paraphrased as '$(z)(x \epsilon z \,. \supset .\, y \epsilon z)$'. Much else also becomes expressible, for which '=', quantifiers, and truth functions were inadequate. For example, we can now express 'ancestor' in terms of 'parent'. For, one's ancestors (if for simplicity we reckon oneself among them) comprise the common members of all classes which contain oneself and all parents of members (Frege); and 'x is ancestor of y' can accordingly be rendered '$(z)[y \epsilon z \,.\, (u)(w)(u$ is parent of $w \,.\, w \epsilon z \,. \supset .\, u \epsilon z) \,. \supset .\, x \epsilon z]$'.

The logic of 'ϵ' is set theory, or class theory, in a more genuine sense than was the algebra of monadic predicates. In the latter there is no call to posit a realm of classes. 'F', 'G', etc., stand in place of predicates, but a predicate, like an open sentence, is simply an expression which is *true of* many or one or no objects. With the advent of 'ϵ', on the other hand, classes are demanded as actual members of the universe of quantification; compare the 'z' of the last example.

At this stage therefore there is a place for class names, as against mere predicates. Such names are formed by the notation of *class abstraction:* $\hat{x}Fx$ is the class of those objects x such that Fx. Actually this notation can be introduced in terms of prior notations, as short for '$(\imath y)(x)(x \epsilon y \,. \equiv Fx)$'. In particular '$\hat{x}(x = x)$' and '$\hat{x}(x \neq x)$' are abbreviated 'V' and 'Λ'; but this use of these signs as names of classes is not to be confused with our earlier use of them as predicates. Similarly the Boolean functions can be explained now for classes: xy as $\hat{z}(z \epsilon x \,.\, z \epsilon y)$, $x \vee y$ as $\hat{z}(z \epsilon x \,. \vee .\, z \epsilon y)$, and $\bar{x}$ as $\hat{z}\text{–}(z \epsilon x)$. The algebra of monadic predicates *can* of course be read from the start with 'F', 'G', etc., as class variables and '$F = G$' as ordinary class identity; but to do so is a gratuitous positing of entities before necessity.

Relations are understood as classes of ordered pairs (or triples, etc.). Now the one thing demanded of a concept of ordered pair, $x;y$, is that $x;y = z;w \,.\!\supset\!.\, x = z \,.\, y = w$. This is demonstrably fulfilled by any of the various artificial definitions of '$x;y$' within the theory of classes (Norbert Wiener). For example, having defined $\{x\}$ as $\hat{z}(z = x)$ and $\{x, y\}$ as $\{x\} \vee \{y\}$, we can take $x;y$ as $\{\{x\}, \{x, y\}\}$. Thereupon relational abstraction, '$\hat{x}\hat{y}Fxy$', becomes definable as '$\hat{z}(\exists x)(\exists y)(z = x;y \,.\, Fxy)$'. The theory of relations is thus obtained within set theory. Analogues, in particular, of the notions of the algebra of dyadic predicates are forthcoming: the converse of a relation z is $\hat{x}\hat{y}(y;x \in z)$, the relative product of u into w is $\hat{x}\hat{y}(\exists z)(x;z \in u \,.\, z;y \in w)$, and the image of w by z is $\hat{x}(\exists y)(x;y \in z \,.\, y \in w)$.

Since the algebras of predicates cover less than quantification theory itself, their reproducibility in set theory is no motive for set theory. The gain in power afforded by 'ϵ' and classes is seen rather in the ancestral construction (above), and again in connection with *number*, to which we now turn.

In defining '$(\exists_n x)Fx$' for each fixed n we made no provision for numbers as values of variables of quantification. In set theory, however, we can so provide, construing each number as the class of those classes having that number of members (Frege). Thus 0 is definable as $\{\Lambda\}$, and in general $w + 1$, or Sw, is definable as $\hat{y}(\exists x)(x \in y \,.\, y - \{x\} \in w)$. Thereupon, following the plan of the definition of ancestor, we can explain 'Num x' ('x is a number') as short for '$(z)[0 \in z \,.\, (w)(w \in z \,.\!\supset\!.\, \mathrm{S}w \in z) \,.\!\supset\!.\, x \in z]$' (Frege).

Now we have the means of saying, for example, not only that a class x has five members, $(\exists_5 z)(z \in x)$ or $x \in 5$, but also that x has just as many members as y; viz., $(\exists z)(\mathrm{Num}\ z \,.\, x \in z \,.\, y \in z)$. We can go farther: we can express the whole of number theory. For example, $x + y$ is definable as comprising those classes z such that part of z belongs to x (i.e., has x members) and the rest to y; symbolically, $\hat{z}(\exists w)(zw \in x \,.\, z\bar{w} \in y)$. The product $x \cdot y$ is definable, more complexly, by exploiting the fact that if a class z has x mutually exclusive classes as members, and each of these has y members, then there are $x \cdot y$ members of members of z.

Numbers, as thus far considered, are the sizes of finite classes, that is, the positive integers and 0. But Georg Cantor's theory of infinite class sizes, or infinite numbers, can likewise be expressed within our present terms; a main step towards it is the easily defined notion of a one–one relation.

Finite numbers of other sorts than 0, 1, 2, . . . are manageable as well. Somewhat artificially we can identify ratios $\frac{1}{2}$, $\frac{2}{3}$, etc., with the pairs 1;2, 2;3, etc., and then redefine sum, product, and other relevant notions appropriately for application to ratios so construed. Irrational numbers prove to be satisfactorily identifiable with certain infinite classes of ratios (Richard Dedekind), and finally negative and imaginary numbers can be accommodated by further recourse to the device of ordered pair. Mathematical *functions* can be identified with certain relations, namely, the relations of values to arguments of the functions ordinarily so-called; for example, the function "square of," symbolically $\lambda_x(x^2)$, is definable as $\hat{y}\hat{x}(y = x^2)$. By such methods, set forth in detail by Frege, Peano, Alfred North Whitehead, Bertrand Russell, and others, set theory is shown to embrace classical mathematics in a very general sense of the term. The truth functions and quantifiers and 'ϵ' thus emerge as, in theory, a comprehensive notation for mathematics.

The question of suitable axioms for 'ϵ' is, in effect, therefore, a question of suitable axioms for mathematics. To begin with there is the axiom of *extensionality:* $(w)(w \epsilon x \mathbin{.\equiv.} w \epsilon y) \mathbin{.} x \epsilon z \mathbin{.\supset.} y \epsilon z$. This is clearly wanted where x and y are classes; and it can be adopted without restriction if we identify each non-class x, artificially but conveniently, with $\{x\}$. Now what are wanted by way of further axioms are those of class existence: axioms of the form '$\hat{x}Fx$ exists', that is, '$(\exists y)(x)(x \epsilon y \mathbin{.\equiv} Fx)$'. But actually we can *disprove* one such sentence, thus: '$-[y \epsilon y \mathbin{.\equiv} -(y \epsilon y)]$' is valid by truth table, and from it by Rule I and Rule II we get '$(y)(\exists x)$ $-[x \epsilon y \mathbin{.\equiv} -(x \epsilon x)]$', and so, by Rule IV, '$-(\exists y)(x)[x \epsilon y \mathbin{.\equiv} -(x \epsilon x)]$' (Russell's paradox). Infinitely many such counter-examples are known. Nor can we somehow banish just such refutable cases and keep '$(\exists y)(x)(x \epsilon y \mathbin{.\equiv} Fx)$' for the rest; for various of the remaining cases, not refutable individually, are mutually inconsistent.

Varied systematic proposals have been made, since 1903 (Frege), in an effort to encompass an in some sense optimum set of consistent cases of '$(\exists y)(x)(x \epsilon y \mathbin{.\equiv} Fx)$'. One system, Russell's *theory of types*, stratifies the universe into individuals, classes of individuals, classes of such classes, and so on, and then, appropriating a distinctive style of variable to each such type, rejects as meaningless any formula containing 'ϵ' otherwise than between variables appropriate to consecutive ascending types. The cases of '$(\exists y)(x)$

'$(x \in y \,.\equiv Fx)$' which survive as meaningful are consistent. But the resulting theory is unwieldy in certain respects; moreover it proves to require supplementation with an axiom of the infinitude of individuals, if we are to preserve the law '$x + 1 = y + 1 \,.\supset.\, x = y$' of number theory.

Ernst Zermelo's method was to assume all cases of the form '$(\exists y)(x)(x \in y \,.\equiv.\, x \in z \,.\, Fx)$' (*Aussonderungsaxiom*) plus a certain assortment of further cases by way of providing classes z for the *Aussonderungsaxiom* to operate on. This method has equally serious drawbacks.

John von Neumann's method was to declare some classes incapable of being members. Thereupon '$(\exists y)(x)(x \in y \,.\equiv Fx)$' can be assumed in general with 'x' restricted to *elements,* i.e., classes of the kind capable of membership. (He did not assume this much, but we may.) It remains, in such a theory, to institute conditions of elementhood. Von Neumann modeled his conditions of elementhood on Zermelo's conditions of class existence; Willard V. Quine and Hao Wang modeled theirs rather on certain traits of the theory of types.

Choice among such alternative foundations of set theory hinges on relative naturalness, elegance, convenience, power, and likelihood of consistency. Consistency proofs are not absolute, since they assume the consistency of the theory in which they are conducted; but a theory is occasionally bolstered by a consistency proof relative to a less suspect theory.

The clear optimum in set theory is not at hand, and, in one sense, never can be: for Kurt Gödel has proved that no theory adequate to expressing so much as the elements of number theory can have a complete and consistent proof procedure. The completeness noted in quantification theory, though attainable also in the elementary algebra of real numbers (Alfred Tarski), is possible neither in the elementary theory of whole numbers nor in various other parts of mathematics; nor, *a fortiori,* in the fountainhead which is set theory.

6. Further Aspects. The lack of a unique clear line in set theory has encouraged some (e.g., Hermann Weyl and at one point Russell) to espouse *constructionalism.* The constructionalist in set theory stratifies the universe of classes into so-called *orders,* and assumes '$(\exists y)(x)(x \in y \,.\equiv Fx)$' only when all quantified variables other than 'y' are limited to orders lower than that assigned to 'y'.

(Henri Poincaré: "predicative definition.") This course is safer, more intuitive, and epistemologically more scrupulous than others, but it is inadequate to certain classical theorems in the theory of functions of real numbers—theorems which constructionalists are accordingly prepared to abandon. An extreme variant of constructionalism is *intuitionism* (Liutzen E. J. Brouwer, Arend Heyting), which even revises elementary logic, abandoning the law '$p \vee \bar{p}$' of excluded middle.

A different departure from truth-function logic is seen in *modal logic* (Clarence I. Lewis, Rudolf Carnap, Frederic B. Fitch), which admits, on a par with 'and', 'or', and 'not', the operator 'necessarily'. Against the need for this departure it has been argued that the purposes thus served are better served by talking *about* formulas, attributing validity and tracing implications as heretofore in this article.

The standard elementary logic is also frequently departed from in the purely exploratory spirit of abstract algebra—notably in many-valued logic (Jan Łukasiewicz, J. Barkley Rosser, Atwell R. Turquette), where the number of truth values is generalized from two to *n*.

Apart from such substantive deviations, we can radically vary the mode of development of the standard sort of theory. For example, instead of taking membership and quantification as fundamental, we may begin with identity, functional abstraction 'λ_x' (see above), and functional application. If by a harmless artifice we look upon sentences as names of their truth values, then identity and functional abstraction and application become a sufficient basis for defining membership and quantification (Frege, Church) and even the truth functions (Tarski). This alternative train of construction is less practical in some ways than that which starts with truth functions, quantification, and membership, but it brings added illumination. For functional abstraction can be shown eliminable, in turn, in favor of a few specific functions, called *combinators* (Moses Schönfinkel, Haskell B. Curry). We thus come out with a foundation for logic, including quantification, set theory, and their entire mathematical suite, which is devoid of variables.

Proof theory is a domain drawn on but not described in the above survey. It includes the proofs of the completeness and undecidability of quantification theory (Gödel, Church), the incompletability of elementary number theory (Gödel), the completeness of elementary algebra (Tarski); also the Löwenheim-Skolem theorem that any consistent set of formulas of quantification theory is interpretable in the universe of whole numbers.

A powerful device in proof theory is that of numbering all the marks and strings of marks available in the notation of a theory, so as to obtain numerical relations parallel to the inferential relations between sentences of the theory concerned. It was by thus applying number theory to the sentences of number theory, in particular, that Gödel contrived to prove incompletability. Such numbering also underlay the discovery of the number-theoretic concept of *recursiveness*, which makes precise sense of the idea of mechanical computability (Herbrand, Gödel, Church, Alan M. Turing, Post, Stephen C. Kleene). The exact definition of "decision procedure" turns on recursiveness, as do the exact statement and proof of Church's theorem and Gödel's incompletability theorem. Relevant also to the theory of machine computation, recursiveness is the worthy focus of a new branch of number theory.

III

A Method of Generating Part of Arithmetic Without Use of Intuitive Logic[1]

1. Introduction. By an *identity* I mean an equation which is a theorem of ordinary arithmetic (and hence true for all values of its variables). What is meant here by "ordinary arithmetic" may be left to the reader, granted the following three reservations:

(a) The equations

$$\text{(A)} \qquad x = x - (y - y),$$

$$\text{(B)} \qquad x - (y - z) = z - (y - x)$$

are identities, that is, theorems of ordinary arithmetic.

(b) Inference according to either of the following rules is valid in ordinary arithmetic:

(R) *Substitute any one expression for all occurrences of any variable.*

(R′) *Given* $\alpha = \beta$, *put* α *for* β *anywhere.*

(c) An equation whose members open with the same variable and contain only variables connected by subtraction, without parentheses, is not an identity unless each variable occurs exactly as many times in one member as in the other.

[1] For suggestions in the preparation of this paper I am indebted to E. V. Huntington and T. P. Palmer.

A *homogeneous linear identity with rational coefficients* is an identity whose members contain only plus and minus signs, parentheses, '0', variables, and rational numerical coefficients. Aside from the prefixture of such coefficients, no multiplicative juxtaposition is admissible. The expressions thus admitted can all be defined in terms of variables, parentheses, and the signs of subtraction and equality. These definitions, which have the status of mere conventions of notational abbreviation, will be set forth in §3.

It is the business of this paper to show that all homogeneous linear identities with rational coefficients, when thus analyzed into subtraction, equality, and variables, can be generated from (A) *and* (B) *by means solely of mechanical substitution according to* (R) *and* (R′).

2. Generation of Theorems. (A) and (B) comprise the postulates, and (R) and (R′) the rules of inference, of a calculus whose primitive language contains only variables, the functor of subtraction, and the equality sign.[2] The parentheses represent nothing in the way of an additional primitive idea, but merely constitute a part of the notation of the functor of subtraction. This functor is the notational scheme of writing expressions in the respective blanks of the matrix '   − (   )'. No parentheses are needed enclosing the blank to the left of '−' in this matrix, for, as is easily verified relatively to subtraction or any other binary operation, the condition that all right-hand operands and only right-hands operands are to be parenthesized suffices in any context for the unique determination of the grouping of left-hand operands as well.

Strictly, (A) and (B) should appear as

$$x = x - (y - (y)), \qquad x - (y - (z)) = z - (y - (x)).$$

The suppression of parentheses enclosing single letters is an ellipsis; in using (R) and (R′), we are to imagine that single letters immedi-

[2] The primitive dyadic relation of equality might be suppressed in favor of a primitive predicate; if namely '$\mathfrak{V}$' denote the predicate of equality with 0, so that '$\mathfrak{V}\zeta$' is read 'ζ vanishes', we can render any equation $\alpha = \beta$ as $\mathfrak{V}\,\alpha - \beta$. (A) and (B) become

$$\mathfrak{V}\ \ x - (x - (y - y)) \qquad \text{and} \qquad \mathfrak{V}\ \ (x - (y - z)) - (z - (y - x)).$$

(R) remains unchanged, but (R′) refers now to $\mathfrak{V}\,\alpha - \beta$ instead of $\alpha = \beta$.

Indeed, since in the thus modified calculus all theorems and postulates begin uniformly with '$\mathfrak{V}$', that letter might be dropped entirely; the list of theorems and postulates would then appear as a list of alternative expressions of 0. A system is thus arrived at whose theorems and postulates are expressive of elements of the system itself, as is the case in the logical calculus of propositions.

ately to the right of minus signs are enclosed in parentheses, and we are to make such parentheses explicit when a complex is substituted for such a letter.

Let us proceed to the generation of theorems from (A) and (B) by (R) and (R′). The manner of generation is indicated, to the right of each theorem, by literal or numerical reference to the postulates or intermediate theorems from which the theorem in question is derived. A single reference '*t*' means that the generation proceeds by substitution in the theorem or postulate (*t*) according to (R). A double reference '(*s*), (*t*)' means that the generation proceeds by replacement of an occurrence of the right member of (*s*), within (*t*), by the left member of (*s*), on the authority of (R′).

(1) $$x = x,$$ (A), (A)

(2) $$x = x - (z - z),$$ (A)

(3) $$y - (x - z) = z - (x - y),$$ (B)

(4) $$y - (x - (z - z)) = z - z - (x - y),$$ (B)

(5) $$z - (z - z - (x - y)) = x - y - (z - z - z),$$ (B)

(6) $$y - y - (x - x - x) = y - y - (x - x - x),$$ (1)

(7) $$y - x = z - z - (x - y),$$ (2), (4)

(8) $$x - z - y = w - w - (y - (x - z)),$$ (7)

(9) $$x - y - z = w - w - (z - (x - y)),$$ (7)

(10) $$z - (y - x) = x - y - (z - z - z),$$ (7), (5)

(11) $$x - (y - y) = y - y - (x - x - x),$$ (10)

(12) $$x - y - z = w - w - (y - (x - z)),$$ (3), (9)

(13) $$x - (y - z) = x - y - (z - z - z),$$ (B), (10)

(14) $$x - (y - y) = x - y - (y - y - y),$$ (13)

(15) $$x - y - z = x - z - y,$$ (8), (12)

(16) $$z - z - (x - y) = z - (x - y) - z,$$ (15)

(17) $$y - x = z - (x - y) - z,$$ (7), (16)

(18) $$y - x = y - (x - z) - z,$$ (3), (17)

(19) $$x = x - y - (y - y - y),$$ (A), (14)

(20) $x = y - y - (x - x - x)$, (A), (11)

(21) $y - y - (x - x - x) = x.$ (20), (6)

3. Phrases. By a *phrase* I shall mean any expression built up of variables and the functor of subtraction. A more rigorous description is the following: Letters, also the expression '$x - y$', are phrases, and if a letter in a phrase be replaced by a phrase (with restoration of requisite parentheses, in conformity with §2) the result is a phrase. A *phrase equation* is an equation whose members are phrases; a *phrase identity* is a phrase equation which is an identity.

A homogeneous linear identity with rational coefficients is not necessarily a phrase identity, for, over and above expressions of subtraction, its members may involve expressions of algebraic negation or addition, the sign '0', and rational numerical coefficients. These further devices are all definable, however, as means of abbreviating phrases or phrase equations. '0' can be explained as an abbreviation for the specific expression '$x - x$'. Negation can be accounted for by defining $-z$ in general as $0 - z$, that is, by construing '$-($ $)$' as an abbreviation for '$0 - ($ $)$'. Addition can be introduced similarly by defining $x + y$ as $x - (-y)$, and the integral numerical coefficients are provided for by defining $2x$ as $x + x$, $3x$ as $2x + x$, and so on.[3] The symbols '$0x$' and '$1x$' may be taken as notational variants of '0' and 'x'.

Fractional numerical coefficients, finally, can be defined contextually by the following abbreviative conventions. An equation

$$\alpha - \beta - \ . \ . \ . \ - \frac{m}{n}\zeta - \ . \ . \ . \ - \theta = \omega,$$

with any disposition of parentheses, is an abbreviation for

$$n\alpha - n\beta - \ . \ . \ . \ - m\zeta - \ . \ . \ . \ - n\theta = n\omega,$$

with the corresponding disposition of parentheses, where m is any numeral and n any numeral other than '0'. The corresponding convention is adopted where the fraction occurs to the right of the equality sign. If several fractional coefficients occur in an equation, their explanation by the above conventions is to proceed in a left-to-right order. This set of conventions provides for the occurrence of fractional coefficients not only in subtraction but in the other

[3] After Huntington, 15.

contexts as well, when the definitions of the preceding paragraph are brought into play.[4]

Every homogeneous linear identity with rational coefficients is either a phrase identity or an abbreviation of a phrase identity by the above abbreviative conventions. The proof that every homogeneous linear identity with rational coefficients is, upon elimination of the above abbreviations, generable by (R) and (R′) from (A) and (B), will therefore consist in showing that every phrase identity is generable by (R) and (R′) from (A) and (B).

4. Canonical Form of an Equation. An equation will be said to be of *canonical form* if each of its members is a phrase in which no parentheses occur and in which like letters appear consecutively, and if the initial letters of the two members are alike and the order of succession of unlike letters is, barring omissions, the same in both members. The canonical form is thus

$$\text{(i)}\quad v_1 - v_1 - v_1 - \ldots - v_2 - v_2 - \ldots - v_n - v_n$$
$$= v_1 - v_1 - v_1 - \ldots - v_2 - v_2 - \ldots - v_n - v_n$$

where v_i and v_j are unlike letters unless $i = j$, and where, for any m, the number of occurrences of '$-v_m$' in either member may be 0.

In saying that an equation E is *derivable* from an equation F, I shall mean that E is generable by (R) and (R′) from (A), (B), and F. In saying that E is *interderivable* with F, I shall mean that E is derivable from F and F from E. In saying that an equation is *reducible to canonical form*, I shall mean that it is interderivable with an equation of canonical form.

Since the initial letters of the members of an equation of canonical form are alike, §1(c) tells us that an equation (i) of canonical form is not an identity unless each variable v_i occurs the same number of times in one member as in the other. But under such circumstances the members of (i) are exact duplicates of each other, so that the equation is generable by (R) from the principle (1) of self-equality. Since (1) is one of the theorems already generated by (R) and (R′) from (A) and (B), it follows that every identity of canonical form is generable by (R) and (R′) from (A) and (B).

[4] It is seen from (A) and (B) that the structure of the calculus developed in §2 admits of another application, where the elements are non-vanishing numbers and '$x - y$' is reinterpreted as meaning 'x divided by y'. Under this reinterpretation, 0 as above defined gives way to 1, the negative gives way to the reciprocal, the sum to the product, and the numerical coefficients to the corresponding numerical exponents.

By §1(b), any equation generable by (R) and (R′) from theorems of ordinary arithmetic is a theorem of ordinary arithmetic, and hence an identity. In view of §1(a), therefore, any equation generable by (R) and (R′) from (A), (B), and E is an identity if E is an identity. Now let E be an identity reducible to canonical form, that is, interderivable with some equation F of canonical form. Equation F is then an identity, since it is generable by (R) and (R′) from (A), (B), and E. But, being an identity of canonical form, F is generable by (R) and (R′) from (A) and (B) alone. Hence E, derivable as it is from F, is likewise generable by (R) and (R′) from (A) and (B). It is thus established that every identity E which is reducible to canonical form is generable by (R) and (R′) from (A) and (B).

In order to show then that every phrase identity is generable by (R) and (R′) from (A) and (B), it will be sufficient to prove that all phrase equations (and hence in particular all phrase identities) are reducible to canonical form. This proof occupies the remaining section.

5. *Proof of Reducibility.* Given any equation

(ii) $$\alpha = \beta,$$

the reverse equation (iv) is derivable as follows:

(iii) $$\beta = \beta, \qquad (1)$$

(iv) $$\beta = \alpha. \qquad \text{(ii), (iii)}$$

Hence the following principle is established.

I. *Any equation* $\alpha = \beta$ *is interderivable with its reverse* $\beta = \alpha$.

By the *terms* of a phrase α I mean all letters of α not lying within parentheses in α, and all parenthesized phrases in α not lying within any broader parenthesis in α. Since parentheses can open only to the right of a minus sign [see §2], the initial term of a phrase is necessarily a letter.

From any phrase equation

(v) $$x - \alpha_1 - \alpha_2 - \ . \ . \ . - \alpha_i - \alpha_{i+1} - \ . \ . \ . - \alpha_n = \omega,$$

we can derive an equation (vii) as follows:

(vi) $$x - \alpha_1 - \ . \ . \ . - \alpha_{i-1} - \alpha_{i+1} - \alpha_i = x - \alpha_1 - \ . \ . \ . - \alpha_{i-1} - \alpha_i - \alpha_{i+1}, \qquad (15)$$

(vii) $x - \alpha_1 - \ldots - \alpha_{i-1} - \alpha_{i+1}$
$- \alpha_i - \alpha_{i+2} - \ldots - \alpha_n = \omega.$ (vi), (v)

By the same process, with α_i and α_{i+1} interchanged, we can derive (v) from (vii). Thus any phrase equation (v) is interderivable with an equation (vii) resulting from the permutation of any non-initial term of the left member of (v) with its successor. Serial application of this principle establishes the interderivability of (v) with the equation resulting from *any* permutation of non-initial terms in the left member of (v). In view of I, furthermore, the same will be true relatively to the right member. Hence the following principle is inferred.

II. *Any phrase equation E is interderivable with any equation resulting from permutation of non-initial terms within either member of E.*

From any phrase equation

(viii) $y - \alpha_1 - \alpha_2 - \ldots - \alpha_m = x - \beta_1 - \beta_2 - \ldots - \beta_n,$

we can derive an equation (ix) as follows:

(ix) $y - \alpha_1 - \ldots - \alpha_m$
$= y - y - (x - x - x) - \beta_1 - \ldots - \beta_n.$ (21), (viii)

Conversely, (viii) is derivable from (ix) as follows:

[viii] $y - \alpha_1 - \ldots - \alpha_m = x - \beta_1 - \ldots - \beta_n.$ (20), (ix)

Therefore (viii) is interderivable with (ix). Hence the following principle is established.

III. *Any phrase equation is interderivable with a phrase equation the initial letters of whose members are alike.*

Since parentheses can occur in a phrase only by way of enclosing a non-initial term thereof, it follows from II that if any parenthesized expression in a phrase equation be transported to the end of the member in which it occurs, the resulting equation will be interderivable with the original one. Thus, in particular, any phrase equation

(x) $x - \alpha_1 - \alpha_2 - \ldots - \alpha_m$
$= x - \beta_1 - \beta_2 - \ldots - \beta_{i-1} - (\zeta - \theta) - \beta_{i+1} - \ldots - \beta_n,$

whose members have like initial letters and whose right member contains parentheses as indicated, is interderivable with

(xi) $x - \alpha_1 - \ldots - \alpha_m$
$= x - \beta_1 - \ldots - \beta_{i-1} - \beta_{i+1} - \ldots - \beta_n - (\zeta - \theta).$

Now from (xi) we can derive an equation (xiii) as follows:

(xii) $x - \beta_1 - \ldots - \beta_{i-1} - \beta_{i+1} - \ldots - \beta_n - \zeta$
$= x - \beta_1 - \ldots - \beta_{i-1} - \beta_{i+1} - \ldots - \beta_n$
$- (\zeta - \theta) - \theta,$ (18)

(xiii) $x - \beta_1 - \ldots - \beta_{i-1} - \beta_{i+1} - \ldots - \beta_n - \zeta$
$= x - \alpha_1 - \ldots - \alpha_m - \theta.$ (xi), (xii)

Conversely, (xi) is derivable from (xiii) as follows:

(xiv) $x - \alpha_1 - \ldots - \alpha_m = x - \alpha_1 - \ldots - \alpha_m$
$- \theta - (\theta - \theta - \theta),$ (19)

(xv) $x - \alpha_1 - \ldots - \alpha_m = x - \beta_1 - \ldots - \beta_{i-1} - \beta_{i+1}$
$- \ldots - \beta_n - \zeta - (\theta - \theta - \theta),$ (xiii), (xiv)

(xvi) $x - \beta_1 - \ldots - \beta_{i-1} - \beta_{i+1} - \ldots - \beta_n - (\zeta - \theta)$
$= x - \beta_1 - \ldots - \beta_{i-1} - \beta_{i+1} - \ldots - \beta_n$
$- \zeta - (\theta - \theta - \theta),$ (13)

[xi] $x - \alpha_1 - \ldots - \alpha_m = x - \beta_1 - \ldots - \beta_{i-1}$
$- \beta_{i+1} - \ldots - \beta_n - (\zeta - \theta).$ (xvi), (xv)

Thus (xi), and hence also (x), is interderivable with (xiii). By I, then, the reverse of (x) is likewise interderivable with (xiii). But in the reverse of (x), $(\zeta - \theta)$ occurs in the left member rather than the right. Hence, in conclusion, a phrase equation whose members have initial letters and either of whose members contains a parenthesized expression is interderivable with a phrase equation (xiii) in which the members still have like initial letters but in which the parenthesized expression is broken up. Serial application of this principle establishes the following one.

IV. *Any phrase equation whose members have like initial letters is interderivable with a phrase equation whose members are free of parentheses and have like initial letters.*

From the definition of the "terms" of a phrase, it is clear that if a phrase is free of parentheses all its terms are letters. Hence, by II, any phrase equation E whose members are free of parentheses is interderivable with any phrase equation resulting from permutation of non-initial letters within members of E. Therefore any phrase equation whose members are free of parentheses and have like initial letters is interderivable with an equation of canonical form. It then follows, by III and IV, that every phrase equation is reducible to canonical form.

In view of §§3–4, this concludes the proof that upon elimination of abbreviations all homogeneous linear identities with rational coefficients are generable by (R) and (R′) from (A) and (B).

IV

Definition of Substitution

1. Basis. The *elements* of this study, denoted by italic capitals, comprise *atoms*, at least two and perhaps infinite in number, and all finite *sequences* of such atoms. (The atoms are interpretable as signs, for example, and the sequences as rows of signs.) Thus each element E is composed successively of possibly duplicative atoms A_1, A_2, . . . , and A_m, for some positive integer m, called the *length* of E; and an element F composed successively of atoms B_1 to B_n will be identical with E if and only if $m = n$ and $A_i = B_i$ for each i to m.

Further terminology is self-explanatory. Thus we may speak of the kth *place* of an element; this, in the case of E above, is occupied by the atom A_k. We may speak of one element as *occurring in* another (as a connected segment thereof), and more particularly as occurring *initially*, *internally*, or *terminally* therein; of two elements as occurring *overlapped* in a third; of the number of occurrences of one element in another; and so on.

Juxtaposition will be used to express that binary operation of *concatenation* whereby any elements E and F, composed as above, are put end to end to form that element EF which is composed successively of the atoms A_1, A_2, . . . , A_m, B_1, B_2, . . . , and B_n. The element E is itself describable, in terms of concatenation of its atoms, as $A_1A_2 \ldots A_m$; parentheses are suppressed, as here, in view of the obvious associativity of concatenation.

It is clear that the length of EF, for any E and F, exceeds the lengths of E and F and equals their sum; also that E occurs initially and F terminally in EF, while EF occurs neither in E

nor in F; also that atoms are length 1, and that an element G is an atom if and only if there are no elements E and F such that $G = EF$.

2. Substitution. The purpose of this paper is a formal definition of *substitution* in terms exclusively of concatenation and the following elementary logical devices: identity, applied to elements; the truth functions; and quantification with respect to elements.[1] The notation will be as in *Principia Mathematica:* the sign '$=$' for identity, the signs '$\sim$', '$\supset$', . . . , for the truth functions, and prefixes of the forms '(X)' and '$(\exists X)$' for quantification.

The proposition to be formulated is expressible verbally thus: W is the result of substituting X for Y throughout Z; briefly, $sub(W, X, Y, Z)$. When the elements are interpreted as signs and rows of signs, the notion under consideration is the notational substitution which figures so prominently in metamathematics.

In the general form in which substitution is here conceived, its formulation is complicated by the fact that the element Y for which substitution is made need not be an atom and hence may have overlapping occurrences in Z. Obviously we cannot in general replace each of two overlapping occurrences of Y by X, since replacement of one occurrence will mutilate the other occurrence. To this extent the notion of substitution is ambiguous. The ambiguity is resolved by stipulating that in case of overlapping occurrences left is to prevail over right; thus the result of substituting X for TT in TTT is to be XT rather than TX. The result of substituting X for Y throughout Z is then describable, in general, as the result Z' of putting X for each of these occurrences of Y in Z: the first (leftmost); the first which begins after the end of that first; the first which begins after the end of this second; and so on. In the trivial case where Y does not occur in Z, Z' is of course Z.

3. Formal Definitions. The following abbreviations are adopted:

D1. $$U \mathit{\ init\ } V \ .=_{\mathrm{df}}\colon U = V \ .\vee : (\exists T) \ . \ UT = V.$$

[1] Gödel showed (1931, 184, 192) that substitution was definable in elementary number theory; and we shall see in the next paper, below, that concatenation theory eked out with names of the atoms amounts to elementary number theory. Still the present construction retains some distinctive traits: (1) It uses an apparatus presumably weaker than elementary number theory, namely, concatenation without names of atoms. (2) The elements substituted for are of any length; Gödel's are atoms. (3) The presentation is more direct, not being involved with other developments.

D2. $U \textit{ in } V .=_{\mathrm{df}}: U \textit{ init } V .\vee: (\exists T) . TU \textit{ init } V.$

D3. $U \sim \textit{in } V .=_{\mathrm{df}}. \sim . U \textit{ in } V.$

D4. $\Theta(U, V, M, N) .=_{\mathrm{df}}. MUMVM \textit{ in } N . M \sim \textit{in } UV.$

D5. $sub1(U, X, Y, V) .=_{\mathrm{df}}:$

$$U = X . V = Y .\vee: (\exists T) . U = TX . V = TY : \sim(\exists S) . YS \textit{ in } V.$$

Obviously 'U *init* V' may be read 'U occurs initially in V', and 'U *in* V' may be read 'U occurs in V'. Again, '$sub1(U, X, Y, V)$' tells us that Y occurs in V terminally and only so and that U is the result of putting X for Y in V; this is seen as follows. For Y to occur terminally in V it is necessary and sufficient that either $V = Y$ or $(\exists T) . V = TY$. Where $V = Y$ it is clear further that Y does not occur in V otherwise than terminally; where $(\exists T) . V = TY$, on the other hand, in order that Y not occur in V otherwise than terminally it is obviously necessary and sufficient to add that $\sim(\exists S) . YS \textit{ in } V$. In general, therefore, for Y to occur in V terminally and only so it is necessary and sufficient that

$$V = Y .\vee: (\exists T) . V = TY : \sim (\exists S). YS \textit{ in } V.$$

Now if U is the result of putting X for Y in V, U will be X or TX according as V is Y or TY. D5 thus yields the described meaning.

The definition of substitution follows:

D6. $sub(W, X, Y, Z) .=_{\mathrm{df}}:::. Y \sim \textit{in } Z . W = Z .\vee :::.$

$(\exists G)(\exists H) ::: (M)(N) ::. (U)(V) :: sub1(U, X, Y, V) .\supset$

$:. V \textit{ init } Z .\supset. \Theta(U, V, M, N) :. (S)(T) : \Theta(S, T, M, N)$

$. TV \textit{ init } Z .\supset. \Theta(SU, TV, M, N) ::\supset. \Theta(G, H, M, N)$

$::: W = G . Z = H .\vee: (\exists K) . Y \sim \textit{in } K . W = GK$

$. Z = HK.$

When abbreviations introduced by D1–D5 are eliminated in favor of their definientia, the definiens in D6 is seen to involve only concatenation and the elementary logical devices mentioned in §2.

4. Demonstrandum. It remains to show that D6 yields substitution in the sense of §2; that is, that $sub(W, X, Y, Z)$, in the sense of D6, if and only if W is Z' as of §2.

Supposing X, Y, and Z given as constants, we define as follows:

Dt1. $\Phi(M, N) \mathrel{.{=}_{\mathrm{df}}{::}} (U)(V) :: sub1(U, X, Y, V) \mathrel{.{\supset}{:.}}$

$V \; init \; Z \mathrel{.{\supset}.} \Theta(U, V, M, N) :. (S)(T) : \Theta(S, T, M, N)$

$. \, TV \; init \; Z \mathrel{.{\supset}.} \Theta(SU, TV, M, N).$

Dt2. $\Psi(F, G, H) \mathrel{.{=}_{\mathrm{df}}{:.}} (M)(N) : \Phi(M, N) \mathrel{.{\supset}.} \Theta(G, H, M, N)$

$:. \, F = G \, . \, Z = H \, . \vee : (\exists K) \, . \, Y \sim in \; K \, . \, F = GK$

$. \, Z = HK.$

By §1, $(U)(V) \, . \, XUXVX \sim in \; X$; by D4, then, $(U)(V). \sim\Theta (U, V, X, X)$, so that

(1) $(U)(V) :. V \; init \; Z \mathrel{.{\supset}.} \Theta(U, V, X, X) :\equiv. \sim. V \; init \; Z,$

(2) $(G)(H) :. \Phi(X, X) \mathrel{.{\supset}.} \Theta(G, H, X, X) :\equiv. \sim\Phi(X, X),$

and, trivially,

(3) $(U)(V)(S)(T) : \Theta(S, T, X, X) \, . \, TV \; init \; Z \mathrel{.{\supset}.} \Theta(SU, TV, X, X).$

By Dt1, (1), and (3),

$$\Phi(X, X) \mathrel{.{\equiv}:} (U)(V) : sub1(U, X, Y, V) \mathrel{.{\supset}.} \sim. V \; init \; Z,$$

whence $\sim\Phi(X, X) \mathrel{.{\supset}.} (\exists U)(\exists V) \, . \, sub1(U, X, Y, V) \, . \, V \; init \; Z$, and therefore, by D5,

$$\sim\Phi(X, X) \mathrel{.{\supset}{:.}} (\exists V) :. V = Y \, . \vee : (\exists T) \, . \, V = TY :. V \; init \; Z,$$

that is, $\sim\Phi(X, X) \mathrel{.{\supset}:} Y \; init \; Z \, . \vee : (\exists T) \, . \, TY \; init \; Z$, which is to say, by D2,

(4) $\sim\Phi(X, X) \mathrel{.{\supset}.} Y \; in \; Z.$

By Dt2, $(G)(H) :. \Psi(W, G, H) \mathrel{.{\supset}:} \Phi(X, X) \mathrel{.{\supset}.} \Theta(G, H, X, X)$, whence, by (2) and (4),

$$(G)(H) : \Psi(W, G, H) \mathrel{.{\supset}.} Y \; in \; Z,$$

that is, $(\exists G)(\exists H) \, . \, \Psi(W, G, H) \mathrel{.{\supset}.} Y \; in \; Z$, or, equivalently,

(5) $(\exists G)(\exists H) \, . \, \Psi(W, G, H) \mathrel{.{\equiv}:} Y \; in \; Z : (\exists G)(\exists H) \, . \, \Psi(W, G, H).$

If Y does not occur in Z, then, by §2, Z' is Z. Hence

(6) $Y \sim in \; Z \, . \, W = Z \mathrel{.{\equiv}.} Y \sim in \; Z \, . \, W = Z'.$

By D6, Dt1, and Dt2,

$$sub(W, X, Y, Z) \,.{\equiv}:\, Y \sim in\ Z \,.\, W = Z \,.{\vee}:\, (\exists G)(\exists H) \,.\, \Psi(W, G, H).$$

Hence, by (5) and (6),

(7) $$sub(W, X, Y, Z) \,.{\equiv}:\, Y \sim in\ Z \,.\, W = Z' \,.{\vee}:\, Y\ in\ Z \,:\, (\exists G)(\exists H) \,.\, \Psi(W, G, H).$$

Now if we can prove that

(I) $$Y\ in\ Z \,.{\supset}:\, (\exists G)(\exists H) \,.\, \Psi(W, G, H) \,.{\equiv}.\, W = Z',$$

so that $Y\ in\ Z : (\exists G)(\exists H) \,.\, \Psi(W, G, H) :\equiv.\, Y\ in\ Z \,.\, W = Z'$, then from (7) we shall have

$$sub(W, X, Y, Z) \,.{\equiv}.\, Y \sim in\ Z \,.\, W = Z' \,.{\vee}.\, Y\ in\ Z \,.\, W = Z',$$

that is, $sub(W, X, Y, Z) \,.{\equiv}.\, W = Z'$ which was to be proved. It thus remains only to establish (I).

5. *Proof of* (I). Given that Y occurs in Z, it is to be proved that

$$(\exists G)(\exists H) \,.\, \Psi(W, G, H) \,.{\equiv}.\, W = Z'.$$

Consider the following segments Z_i of Z. Z_1 extends from the beginning of Z to the end of the first occurrence of Y in Z; Z_2 extends from the beginning of Z^1 to the end of the first occurrence of Y in Z^1, where Z^1 is Z deprived of its initial segment Z_1; and, in general, Z_{i+1} extends from the beginning of Z^i to the end of the first occurrence of Y in Z^i, where Z^i is Z deprived of its initial segment $Z_1Z_2 \ldots Z_i$. By construction, Y occurs in each Z_i terminally and only so; in view of §3, then, where the Z'_i are the results of putting X for Y in the respective Z_i,

(8) $$(i) \,.\, sub1(Z'_i, X, Y, Z_i).$$

Let '$Z_1Z_2 \ldots Z_i$' and '$Z'_1Z'_2 \ldots Z'_i$' be written '$Z_i!$' and '$Z'_i!$'. Thus

(9) $$Z_1! = Z_1 \,.\, Z'_1! = Z'_1,$$

(10) $$(i) \,.\, Z_{i+1}! = Z_i!Z_{i+1} \,.\, Z'_{i+1}! = Z'_i!Z'_{i+1},$$

and, by construction,

(11) $$(i) \,.\, Z_i!\ init\ Z.$$

We exhaust the segments Z_i only when we reach a point in Z

beyond which Y occurs no more. Thus, where Z_n is the last of the Z_i,

(12) $$(K) : Z = Z_n!K \,.\!\supset\!.\, Y \sim in\ K.$$

Quantification with respect to subscripts, as in (8) – (11), refers of course only to the n or fewer significant values; for example, '$(i) . \phi(Z_i, Z'_i)$', '$(\exists i) . \phi(Z_i, Z'_i)$', and '$(i) . \phi(Z_i, Z_{i+1})$' are short for

$$\text{`}\phi(Z_1, Z'_1) . \phi(Z_2, Z'_2) . \;\ldots\; \phi(Z_n, Z'_n)\text{'},$$

$$\text{`}\phi(Z_1, Z'_1) \vee \phi(Z_2, Z'_2) \vee \;\ldots\; \phi(Z_n, Z'_n)\text{'},$$

and

$$\text{`}\phi(Z_1, Z_2) . \phi(Z_2, Z_3) . \;\ldots\; \phi(Z_{n-1}, Z_n)\text{'}.$$

By §1, there are distinct atoms; let A and B be any two such, and, where k is the length of $Z'_n!Z_n!$, let $C = ABB \ldots B$ to k occurrences of B. Clearly

(13) $$(i) . C \sim in\ Z'_i!Z_i!,$$

since the length of C is greater by one even than that of $Z'_n!Z_n!$. Now it will be shown that, for any elements G and H such that $C \sim in\ GH$, there are no occurrences of C in $CGCHC$ except the three indicated ones. First, no two occurrences of C can overlap; for, if they are distinct, one must start later than the other and hence must start at a non-initial place of the other; but all these non-initial places are occupied by B, whereas C starts with A. Hence if there is an occurrence of C in $CGCHC$ other than the three indicated ones, it overlaps none of the latter; it therefore lies wholly within G or H. But it cannot, since, by hypothesis, $C \sim in\ GH$. Consequently there are none but the three occurrences of C in $CGCHC$. In particular, then, it follows from (13) that there are none but the three occurrences of C in $CZ'_i!CZ_i!C$.

Since, where

(14) $$D = CZ'_1!CZ_1!CCZ'_2!CZ_2!C \;\ldots\; CZ'_n!CZ_n!C,$$

D is made up wholly of segments of the form $CZ'_i!CZ_i!C$, any occurrence of C in D must lie either wholly within or partly within and partly beyond such a segment. But in the latter case the occurrence of C in question would overlap the terminal occurrence of C in $CZ'_i!CZ_i!C$, whereas we saw that no two occurrences of C could overlap. Hence every occurrence of C in D lies wholly within $CZ'_i!CZ_i!C$ for some i. But $CZ'_i!CZ_i!C$ was seen to contain only the three indicated occurrences of C. Therefore D contains only the $3n$ occurrences of C indicated in (14).

Where $C \sim$ *in* GH, $CGCHC$ contains, as was seen, only the three indicated occurrences of C, and is hence describable as beginning and ending with C and containing just three occurrences of C and no two adjacent. But, since D contains none but its $3n$ indicated occurrences of C, inspection of (14) shows that the only segments of D fulfilling this description of $CGCHC$ are the segments $CZ'_i!$ $CZ_i!C$ for the various i; any other segment of D beginning and ending with C and containing three occurrences of C would contain two adjacent. Hence, if $C \sim$ *in* GH and $CGCHC$ *in* D, $CGCHC$ must be $CZ'_i!CZ_i!C$ for some i; then G and H must be $Z'_i!$ and $Z_i!$. Thus, in view of D4,

(15) $$(G)(H) : \Theta(G, H, C, D) \,.\supset.\, (\exists i) \,.\, G = Z'_i! \,.\, H = Z_i!.$$

Conversely, by (14), (13), and D4,

(16) $$(i) \,.\, \Theta(Z'_i!, Z_i!, C, D).$$

By (15) and (16),

(17)[2] $$(G)(H) : \Theta(G, H, C, D) \,.\equiv.\, (\exists i) \,.\, G = Z'_i! \,.\, H = Z_i!.$$

If *sub*1(U, X, Y, V), then, by §3, Y occurs in V terminally and only so and U is the result of putting X for Y in V. But, if V contains Y just thus and if further $Z_i!V$ *init* Z, then V must be Z_{i+1}, so that U becomes Z'_{i+1}; and where U and V are Z'_{i+1} and Z_{i+1} it follows from (10) and (16) that $\Theta(Z'_i!U, Z_i!V, C, D)$. Thus

[2] This exemplifies a general technique, within a concatenation system, for eliminating reference to a finite class or relation of elements in favor of reference to two properly selected elements C and D. Where α is the m-adic relation (or class, if $m = 1$) exhibited by just the elements Q_{i1}, Q_{i2}, . . . , and Q_{im} in that order, for the various i from 1 to n, and k is the length of the element

$$Q_{11}Q_{12} \ldots Q_{1m}Q_{21}Q_{22} \ldots Q_{2m} \ldots Q_{n1}Q_{n2} \ldots Q_{nm},$$

and C is $ABB \ldots B$ to k occurrences of B, and D is

$$CQ_{11}CQ_{12} \ldots CQ_{1m}CCQ_{21}CQ_{22} \ldots CQ_{2m}C \ldots CQ_{n1}CQ_{n2} \ldots CQ_{nm}C,$$

it can be shown that

$$CG_1CG_2 \ldots CG_mC \textit{ in } D \,.\, C \sim \textit{in } G_1G_2 \ldots G_m$$

if and only if G_1, G_2, . . . , and G_m exhibit in that order the relation α. In (17) this equivalence is proved for the special case where $m = 2$; G, H, Z'_i !, and Z_i! answer to G_1, G_2, Q_{i1}, and Q_{i2}.

$(U)(V)(i) : sub1(U, X, Y, V) . Z_i!V \; init \; Z . \supset . \Theta(Z'_i!U, Z_i!V, C, D),$

and hence

$$(U)(V) :. sub1(U, X, Y, V) . \supset : (S)(T) : (\exists i) . \\ S = Z'_i! . T = Z_i! . TV \; init \; Z . \supset . \Theta(SU, TV, C, D);$$

that is, by (17),

$$(18) \quad (U)(V) :. sub1(U, X, Y, V) . \supset : (S)(T) : \\ \Theta(S, T, C, D) . TV \; init \; Z . \supset . \Theta(SU, TV, C, D).$$

Again, if Y occurs in V terminally and only so, and V *init* Z, then V must be Z_1; thus, where $sub1(U, X, Y, V)$ and V *init* Z, U and V will be Z'_1 and Z_1. But, by (9) and (16), $\Theta(Z'_1, Z_1, C, D)$. Thus

$$(U)(V) : sub1(U, X, Y, V) . V \; init \; Z . \supset . \Theta(U, V, C, D).$$

From this and (18) it follows, by Dt1, that $\Phi(C, D)$. By Dt2, then,

$$(G)(H) :: \Psi(W, G, H) . \supset :. \Theta(G, H, C, D) :. W = G . Z = H . \vee : \\ (\exists K) . Y \sim in \; K . W = GK . Z = HK,$$

that is, by (17),

$$(G)(H) :: \Psi(W, G, H) . \supset :. (\exists i) . G = Z'_i! . H = Z_i! :. \\ W = G . Z = H . \vee : (\exists K) . Y \sim in \; K . W = GK . Z = HK,$$

and hence

$$(\exists G)(\exists H) . \Psi(W, G, H) . \supset : (\exists i) : W = Z'_i! . Z = Z_i! . \vee : \\ (\exists K) . Y \sim in \; K . W = Z'_i!K . Z = Z_i!K.$$

But, whether $Z = Z_i!$ or $(\exists K) . Y \sim in \; K . Z = Z_i!K$, i must be n: for in neither case does Z contain any occurrence of Y after $Z_i!$. Thus

$$(19) \quad (\exists G)(\exists H) . \Psi(W, G, H) . \supset . W = Z'_n! . Z = Z_n! . \vee : \\ (\exists K) . W = Z'_n!K . Z = Z_n!K.$$

Of the occurrences of Y in Z, the one in Z_1 is, by construction, the first, the one in Z_2 is the first which begins after the end of that first, and so on. Therefore if each Z_i is supplanted in Z by Z'_i, so that $Z_n!$ is supplanted by $Z'_n!$, the result will be Z' as described in §2. Z' is thus $Z'_n!$ or $Z'_n!K$ according as Z is $Z_n!$ or $Z_n!K$. By (19), then,

$$(20) \quad (\exists G)(\exists H) . \Psi(W, G, H) . \supset . W = Z'.$$

If $\Phi(M, N)$, then, by Dt1,

$$sub1(Z'_1, X, Y, Z_1) .\supset: Z_1 \; init \; Z .\supset. \Theta(Z'_1, Z_1, M, N)$$

and

$$(i) :. sub1(Z'_{i+1}, X, Y, Z_{i+1}) .\supset: \Theta(Z'_i!, Z_i!, M, N). \\ Z_i!Z_{i+1} \; init \; Z .\supset. \Theta(Z'_i!Z'_{i+1}, Z_i!Z_{i+1}, M, N).$$

But these two results reduce, in view of (8)–(11), to

$$\Theta(Z'_1!, Z_1!, M, N)$$

and

$$(i) : \Theta(Z'_i!, Z_i!, M, N) .\supset. \Theta(Z'_{i+1}!, Z_{i+1}!, M, N),$$

and from these it follows that $\Theta(Z'_n!, Z_n!, M, N)$. Thus

(21) $$(M)(N) : \Phi(M, N) .\supset. \Theta(Z'_n!, Z_n!, M, N).$$

By (11) and D1, Z is $Z_n!$ or else $Z_n!K$ for some K; and, as seen above, Z' is in these respective cases $Z'_n!$ and $Z'_n!K$. Moreover, in view of (12), $Y \sim in \; K$. Thus

$$Z' = Z'_n! \,.\, Z = Z_n! \,.\vee: (\exists K) \,.\, Y \sim in \; K \,. \\ Z' = Z'_n!K \,.\, Z = Z_n!K.$$

From this and (21) it follows, by Dt2, that $\Psi(Z', Z'_n!, Z_n!)$. Hence

$$W = Z' .\supset. (\exists G)(\exists H) \,.\, \Psi(W, G, H),$$

and consequently, by (20),

$$(\exists G)(\exists H) \,.\, \Psi(W, G, H) .\equiv. W = Z',$$

which was to be proved.

V

Concatenation as a Basis for Arithmetic

1. Introduction. General syntax, the formal part of the general theory of signs, has as its basic operation the operation of *concatenation*, expressed by the connective '$\frown$' and understood as follows: where x and y are any expressions, $x \frown y$ is the expression formed by writing the expression x immediately followed by the expression y. E.g., where 'alpha' and 'beta' are understood as names of the respective signs 'α' and 'β', the syntactical expression 'alpha$\frown$beta' is a name of the expression '$\alpha\beta$'.

Tarski[1] and Hermes have presented axioms for concatenation, and definitions of derivative syntactical concepts. Hermes has also related concatenation theory to the arithmetic of natural numbers, constructing a model of the latter within the former. Conversely, Gödel's proof of the impossibility of a complete consistent systematization of arithmetic depended on constructing a model of concatenation theory within arithmetic.

Like Tarski and Hermes, I also have used concatenation as a basis for various constructions;[2] but my constructions differ essentially from theirs in presupposing no auxiliary logical machinery beyond the *elementary* level: truth functions, quantification, and identity. It can be easily shown to follow from my constructions that the elementary arithmetic of natural numbers (elementary in the sense of using none but the aforementioned logical auxiliaries)

Reprinted from the *Journal of Symbolic Logic*, Volume 11, 1946.

[1] 1935, 287ff.

[2] Preceding paper; "On derivability"; *Mathematical Logic*, Chap. 7.

can be embedded in the elementary theory of concatenation. The only proviso is that the atomic components from which concatenations can be formed must be at least two in number, and distinguishable by name; e.g., alpha and beta.

The present paper, undertaken at Professor Tarski's suggestion, will establish the above more explicitly and in a strengthened form: it will be shown not only that the elementary arithmetic of natural numbers can be embedded in the elementary theory of concatenation, but that it can be so embedded as to exhaust the latter, rendering the elementary theory of concatenation and the elementary arithmetic of natural numbers identical.

Actually it will be more convenient to consider, in place of the arithmetic of natural numbers, that of positive integers. The conclusions reached can afterward be transferred to the arithmetic of natural numbers, as will be seen.

The paper will presuppose no acquaintance with previous work on concatenation.

Let us now turn to a more exact statement of what is meant by the elementary theory of concatenation and the elementary arithmetic of positive integers, and a more exact statement of what is to be proved about them.

The theory of concatenation need not be thought of as syntactical in subject matter; it may be regarded as having to do with finite sequences of any manner of objects. The objects, called *atoms*, are themselves considered sequences, viz., sequences of length one; and concatenation is the operation of laying sequences end to end to form new sequences. Thus, where x is the sequence consisting successively of the atoms a, b, b, a, and c, and where y is the sequence consisting successively of b and a, the sequence $x \frown y$ will consist successively of a, b, b, a, c, b, a. Parentheses will be suppressed by construing '$x \frown y \frown z$' as '$(x \frown y) \frown z$'; clearly the grouping is in fact indifferent.

The *elementary theory of concatenation* comprises that body of theory which can be expressed in terms of concatenation, identity, names of the several atoms, truth functions, and quantification with respect to variables 'x', 'y', 'z', . . . whose values are sequences. The theory varies in detail according to the number of atoms assumed. Thus, if we suppose the atoms to be just two in number and designated by 'a' and 'b', the formulas of the elementary theory of concatenation are the following:

(i) identities, consisting of '$=$' flanked by terms each of which is either a simple constant 'a', or 'b', or a variable 'x', 'y', 'z', . . . , or an expression compounded of such simple signs by one or more applications of the concatenation sign;

(ii) all compounds formed from such identities by means of truth-functional connectives and quantification with respect to variables 'x', 'y', etc.

The *elementary arithmetic of positive integers* comprises that body of theory which can be expressed in terms of sum, product, power, identity, names of the several positive integers, truth functions, and quantification with respect to variables 'x', 'y', 'z', . . . whose values are positive integers. Thus the formulas of the elementary arithmetic of positive integers are the following:

(i) identities, consisting of '=' flanked by terms each of which is either a simple constant '1', '2', . . . , or a variable 'x', 'y', 'z', . . . , or an expression compounded of such simple signs by one or more applications of the notational forms '$x + y$', '$x \times y$', 'x^y' of sum, product, and power;

(ii) all compounds formed from such identities by means of the truth-functional connectives and quantification with respect to variables 'x', 'y', etc.

It will be proved that a model of arithmetic can be constructed, in terms of finite sequences, in such a way that all the notations of the elementary arithmetic of positive integers become definable in the notation of the elementary theory of concatenation of two or more atoms.

Identification of the positive integers with sequences may be either *unilateral*, in the sense that the integers are exhaustively identified with an inexhaustive subclass of sequences, or *bilateral*, in the sense that the integers and sequences are so identified as to exhaust both the integers and the sequences. The construction of arithmetic within the theory of concatenation will be carried through first in unilateral fashion (§3), since this is easier. But the bilateral construction (§4) is of especial interest in that it makes the elementary theory of concatenation and the elementary arithmetic of positive integers completely intertranslatable. And it shows that concatenation can be interpreted as a purely arithmetical operation, in terms of which the other operations of arithmetic are definable.

After proving these things with regard to the arithmetic of positive integers, we can infer the same with regard to the arithmetic of natural numbers; for it is known (and will be re-established briefly in §5) that the arithmetic of natural numbers is bilaterally constructible within that of positive integers.

The definitions comprised in all these constructions will commonly be, in a certain sense, indirect; that is, free use will be made of the descriptive notation '$(\imath x)(\ldots)$', which is not eliminable by any direct substitution of expressions built up of primitive terms. This notation has not been cited in the above inventory of the notations of the theories under consideration, because it is well known that the presence of the notational machinery of quantification, truth functions, and identity renders the descriptive notation eliminable from any theorem or other formula in which it occurs.

2. Finite Relations. The chief circumstance which makes possible the construction of arithmetic from concatenation theory is that single sequences can be made to do the work of all finite relations of sequences, by a method which will now be set forth. I shall assume here that our theory of concatenation involves at least two atoms, *a* and *b;* there may be more.

A finite relation may be thought of first as a finite collection of ordered pairs, and represented graphically as a two-column list. Consider now any such relation; let it pair u_1 with v_1, and u_2 with v_2, and so on to u_n and v_n. (The elements u_1, v_1, u_2, etc., are themselves any sequences.) Let z be a certain *tally,* i.e., a certain sequence consisting wholly of occurrences of *a*. (The reason for calling such a sequence a tally will become evident in §4.) Further, let this tally z be longer than any tally appearing within any of the sequences u_1, v_1, u_2, etc. Now form n sequences, one corresponding to each of the n pairs of the original relation, as follows:

$$w_1 = b^\frown z^\frown b^\frown u_1{}^\frown b^\frown z^\frown b^\frown v_1{}^\frown b^\frown z,$$
$$w_2 = b^\frown z^\frown b^\frown u_2{}^\frown b^\frown z^\frown b^\frown v_2{}^\frown b^\frown z,$$
$$\vdots$$
$$w_n = b^\frown z^\frown b^\frown u_n{}^\frown b^\frown z^\frown b^\frown v_n{}^\frown b^\frown z,$$

and lay all these end to end in turn to form a single sequence:

$$w = w_1{}^\frown w_2{}^\frown \ldots {}^\frown w_n.$$

Next let us observe certain peculiarities of w. (i) *The only occurrences of z in w are the 3n occurrences of z which are shown explicitly in the above expansions of $w_1, w_2, \ldots, w_n$;* there are no additional hidden occurrences of z. This is seen as follows: There can be no additional occurrence of z hidden within any of the occurrences of u_1, v_1, u_2, etc., because z exceeds any tally therein; nor can there be any additional occurrence of the tally z partially overlapping upon one of the explicitly shown occurrences of z or of u_1, v_1, u_2, etc., because each of those explicitly shown occurrences is insulated in front and back by the atom b, which cannot occur in a tally. The possibilities are thus exhausted.

(ii) *The only segments of w which have $z^\frown b$ just before them and $b^\frown z$ just after, and do not themselves contain any occurrence of z, are the occurrences of u_1, v_1, u_2, etc., which are shown explicitly in the above expansions of $w_1, w_2, \ldots, w_n$.* This follows from (i) on inspection of the expansions of $w_1, w_2, \ldots, w_n$.

(iii) *If x and y are sequences neither of which contains any occurrence of z, and if*

(1) $$z^\frown b^\frown x^\frown b^\frown z^\frown b^\frown y^\frown b^\frown z$$

occurs as part of w, then x and y must be respectively u_i and v_i for some i. For, by (ii), x must be one of u_1, v_1, u_2, etc., and y must be a later one of them. Yet the occurrences of x and y in question cannot be within different ones of the segments $w_1, w_2, \ldots, w_n$ of w, because if they were they would be separated by at least $b^\frown z^\frown b^\frown z^\frown b$ instead of just $b^\frown z^\frown b$. So x and y must be respectively u_i and v_i for some one i.

In view of (iii) we have the following result: *instead of saying that x stands to y in our original finite relation, we can omit mention of that relation and speak instead of the sequence w*, saying that (1) is part of w and that x and y contain no occurrences of z (z being explained in turn as the longest tally in w).

Let us write '$w(x, y)$' to mean that (1) is part of w and that x and y contain no occurrences of z (where z is explained as the longest tally in w); then what we have found is that we can construct a sequence w such that $(x)(y)[w(x, y) \equiv .\ x$ stands to y in our original finite relation].

Preparatory to setting up the formal definition of '$w(x, y)$' we shall need to introduce the notation '$\dot{\subset}$', meaning 'occurs in', 'is part of'. It is definable within concatenation theory as follows:

D1. $x \mathrel{\dot{\subset}} y =_{\mathrm{df}} (\exists z)(\exists w)(x = y \,.\!\vee\!.\, z^\frown x = y \,.\!\vee\!.\, x^\frown w = y \,.\!\vee\!.\, z^\frown x^\frown w = y).$

Thus '$x \mathrel{\dot{\subset}} y$' means that the sequence x is a continuous part (or all) of the sequence y.[3]

Next the notation '$\mathrm{T}z$', meaning that z is a tally, i.e., contains only a's, is readily defined:

D2. $$\mathrm{T}z =_{\mathrm{df}} (x)(x \mathrel{\dot{\subset}} z \mathbin{.\supset.} a \mathrel{\dot{\subset}} x).$$

To say that z is the longest tally in w is to say that z is a tally and is part of w and that every tally occurring anywhere in w reappears as part of z. In symbols this becomes:

$$\mathrm{T}z \,.\, z \mathrel{\dot{\subset}} w \,.\, (v)(\mathrm{T}v \,.\, v \mathrel{\dot{\subset}} w \mathbin{.\supset.} v \mathrel{\dot{\subset}} z),$$

which is equivalent to:

(2) $$(v)(\mathrm{T}v \,.\, v \mathrel{\dot{\subset}} w \mathbin{.\equiv.} v \mathrel{\dot{\subset}} z).$$

So now we are ready to define '$w(x, y)$' as meaning that there is a sequence z which satisfies (2), and is not part of x or y, and is such further that the sequence expressed in (1) is part of w.

D3. $$w(x, y) =_{\mathrm{df}} (\exists z)[(v)(\mathrm{T}v \,.\, v \mathrel{\dot{\subset}} w \mathbin{.\equiv.} v \mathrel{\dot{\subset}} z) \,.\, \sim(z \mathrel{\dot{\subset}} x) \,.\, \sim(z \mathrel{\dot{\subset}} y) \,.\, z^\frown b^\frown x^\frown b^\frown z^\frown b^\frown y^\frown b^\frown z \mathrel{\dot{\subset}} w].$$

The reasoning of the present section has shown that, for *every* finite relation of sequences, *there is* a sequence w such that

$$(x)(y)[w(x, y) \mathbin{\equiv.} x \text{ bears the relation to } y].$$

We have seen how, given a list of the pairs comprising the relation, such a sequence w can actually be constructed.

3. Unilateral Construction. A convenient way of getting a model of the realm of positive integers within the realm of sequences based on two or more atoms a, b, . . . is by identifying each integer n with the tally which comprises n occurrences of a. Thus 1, 2, 3, . . . become definable respectively as a, $a^\frown a$, $a^\frown a^\frown a$, . . . ; and to say that x is a positive integer is to say simply that $\mathrm{T}x$.

Where x and y are positive integers, clearly '$x \mathrel{\dot{\subset}} y$' amounts to '$x \leqq y$'; and $x^\frown y$ is the *sum* of x and y.

[3] The definiens in D1 could be simplified to '$(\exists z)(\exists w)(z^\frown x^\frown w = y)$' if we were to assume a null sequence among the values of our variables. However, I have chosen rather to repudiate the null sequence throughout the present paper, lest it be thought to be an essential assumption.

The *product* $x \times y$ is the sequence which we would get by laying down the sequence x over and over, end to end, y times—i.e., as many times as a occurs in y. (This explanation makes good sense even where x is not an integer; but this is an incidental extension that need not interest us.) Let us now turn to the problem of constructing an actual definition to this effect.

It will first be shown that, for any sequence z, the following condition implies that z is the product $x \times y$ in the desired sense:

$$(3)\quad (\exists w)\{w(y, z) \,.\, (s)(t)[w(s, t) \supset : s = a \,.\, t = x \,.\vee\, (\exists u)(\exists v)(w(u, v) \,.\, s = a^\frown u \,.\, t = x^\frown v)]\}.$$

This is seen as follows. (3) says there is a sequence w such that

$$(4)\quad w(y, z),$$

$$(5)\quad (s)(t)\{w(s, t) \supset : s = a \,.\, t = x \,.\vee\, (\exists u)(\exists v)[w(u, v) \,.\, s = a^\frown u \,.\, t = x^\frown v]\}.$$

By (4) and (5),

$$(6)\quad y = a \,.\, z = x \,.\vee\, (\exists u)(\exists v)[w(u, v) \,.\, y = a^\frown u \,.\, z = x^\frown v].$$

Now if the sequence y is an atom, and hence no concatenation, the second alternative in the alternation (6) must fail; and then the first alternative in (6) tells us that y is a and z is x. If on the other hand y is longer than an atom, then the second alternative in (6) tells us that y and z begin respectively with a and x, and also that the remainders y' and z' of y and z are such that

$$(7)\quad w(y', z').$$

By (7) and (5),

$$(8)\quad y' = a \,.\, z' = x \,.\vee\, (\exists u)(\exists v)[w(u, v) \,.\, y' = a^\frown u \,.\, z' = x^\frown v].$$

Continuing thus, for as many steps as there are places in the original sequence y, we see finally that y must consist wholly of a's and that z must consist of a concatenation of a like number of x's; in brief, y is a positive integer and

$$(9)\quad z = x \times y.$$

It will now be shown conversely that, for all integers x and y, (9) implies (3). Consider the following list of pairs:

$$\begin{array}{ll} a & x \\ a^\frown a & x^\frown x \\ a^\frown a^\frown a & x^\frown x^\frown x \\ \cdot & \cdot \\ \cdot & \cdot \\ \cdot & \cdot \\ y & x \times y \end{array}$$

(We know, from the intended sense of '$x \times y$', that the sequence reached in the right-hand column opposite y will in fact be $x \times y$.) Now the principle stated at the end of §2 assures us that there is a sequence w such that, for any sequences s and t, '$w(s, t)$' holds if and only if s and t are paired in the above list. From inspection of the list, then, it is evident that (5) holds, and also that

(10) $$w(y, x \times y).$$

From (10) and (9) we get (4), and from (5) and (4) we get (3).

The product $x \times y$, therefore, is definable as the one and only sequence z fulfilling (3).

D4. $$x \times y =_{\text{df}} (\iota z)(\exists w)\{w(y, z) \,.\, (s)(t)[w(s, t) \supset : s = a \,.\, t = x \,. \vee\, (\exists u)(\exists v)(w(u, v) \,.\, s = a^\frown u \,.\, t = x^\frown v)]\}.$$

The *power* x^y can be defined quite analogously. The only difference is that whereas the product $x \times y$ was a continued concatenation $x^\frown x^\frown \ldots ^\frown x$ to y occurrences of x, the power x^y is a continued *product* $x \times x \times \ldots \times x$ to y occurrences of x. So the definition of x^y differs from D4 only in using '$x \times v$' instead of '$x^\frown v$' at the end.

D5. $$x^y =_{\text{df}} (\iota z)(\exists w)\{w(y, z) \,.\, (s)(t)[w(s, t) \supset : s = a \,.\, t = x \,. \vee\, (\exists u)(\exists v)(w(u, v) \,.\, s = a^\frown u \,.\, t = x \times v)]\}.$$

The definitions D4 and D5 are of course of interest only where the sequences x and y are positive integers; what they generate in other cases need not concern us. It may, however, be remarked in passing that, where x is not an integer but y is, $x \times y$ continues to be the sequence $x^\frown x^\frown \ldots ^\frown x$ to y occurrences of x.

4. Bilateral Construction. We now turn to an alternative method of identifying the positive integers with sequences; this time a bilateral method, i.e., one which uses up all the sequences.

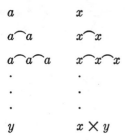

Up to now we have been able to leave the number of atoms unspecified, requiring only that there be at least two. For the bilateral construction, however, we need to know how many there are. Any specified finite number of them would serve, provided there are at least two. The construction will first be set forth for the case where there are exactly two atoms, a and b. Afterward we shall see how to adapt the method to any larger finite number of atoms.

Bilateral identification of the positive integers with the finite sequences of atoms a and b can be accomplished by arranging the sequences *lexicographically;* i.e., in order of length and alphabetically within each length:

$$(11)\quad \begin{array}{cccccccc} 1 & 2 & 3 & 4 & 5 & 6 & 7 & 8 \\ a & b & a\frown a & a\frown b & b\frown a & b\frown b & a\frown a\frown a & a\frown a\frown b \\ & & & & & 9 & 10 & 11 \quad \ldots \\ & & & & & a\frown b\frown a & a\frown b\frown b & b\frown a\frown a \ \ldots \end{array}$$

In this way not only do the integers receive an interpretation as sequences, but also conversely, the finite sequences of a and b all receive an interpretation as positive integers, and concatenation thus itself becomes an arithmetical operation on positive integers. In fact, concatenation becomes expressible within elementary arithmetic, as follows:

$$x\frown y = y + [x \times (\imath z)(\exists w)(z = 2^w \,.\, z \leqq y + 1 < z + z)].$$

This identity will be left unsubstantiated;[4] our avowed business lies in the opposite direction, viz., to find ways of defining $x + y$, $x \times y$, and x^y, conformable to (11), within the theory of concatenation. Our business is to show that the new arithmetical operation of concatenation is an arithmetical operation in terms of which the more familiar operations of sum, product, and power can be defined.

Though the sequences composed purely of occurrences of a no longer exhaust the positive integers as they did in §3, they will continue to play an important role under the earlier name of *tallies.* Definitions D1–3 will be retained. D4 and D5, no longer available as definitions of products and powers of positive integers, will still be useful in an auxiliary status as defining what may be called the tally products and tally powers of tallies; they are accordingly reproduced here with accented designations and modified notations:

D4′. $x \times_\tau y =_{\text{df}} (\imath z)(\exists w)\{w(y, z) \,.\, (s)(t)[w(s, t) \supset: s = a \,.\, t = x$
$\quad .\vee\ (\exists u)(\exists v)(w(u, v) \,.\, s = a\frown u \,.\, t = x\frown v)]\}.$

[4] The reasoning behind it is evident from "On derivability," 115, where the present identification of integers with sequences is so rephrased as to exhibit its relation to the dual system of numeration.

D5′. $x \wedge_{\tau} y =_{\mathrm{df}} (\imath z)(\exists w)\{w(y, z) \,.\, (s)(t)[w(s, t) \supset: s = a \,.\, t = x \,.\!\vee\, (\exists u)(\exists v)(w(u, v) \,.\, s = a\frown u \,.\, t = x \times_{\tau} v)]\}.$

A tally consisting of n occurrences of a will be called the *tally of* n. Where x is any positive integer (hence any sequence whatever, under the method of the present section), the tally of x will be referred to as τx. It is definable in concatenation theory in the light of the following considerations.

Hereunder are listed the successive positive integers from 1 to x, paired off with their tallies.

a	a
b	$a\frown a$
$a\frown a$	$a\frown a\frown a$
$a\frown b$	$a\frown a\frown a\frown a$
$b\frown a$	$a\frown a\frown a\frown a\frown a$
$b\frown b$	$a\frown a\frown a\frown a\frown a\frown a$
$a\frown a\frown a$	$a\frown a\frown a\frown a\frown a\frown a\frown a$
$a\frown a\frown b$	$a\frown a\frown a\frown a\frown a\frown a\frown a\frown a$
.	.
.	.
.	.
x	τx

A method of generating the column on the left, comprising the integers in the normal order 1, 2, 3, . . . , is described by the following rules:

(i) Start with a and b.

(ii) If u appears in the column, put $u\frown a$ one place more than twice as far down the column, and put $u\frown b$ next after (i.e., $u\frown a = 2u + 1$ and $u\frown b = 2u + 2$).

From (ii), together with the nature of the right-hand column (the tallies), it is evident that, where v appears opposite u (so that $v = \tau u$), what will appear opposite $u\frown a$ is $v\frown v\frown a$; and what will appear opposite $u\frown b$ is $v\frown v\frown a\frown a$.

In view of these considerations, it can be shown that the definition:

D6. $\tau x =_{\mathrm{df}} (\imath y)(\exists w)\{w(x, y) \,.\, (s)(t)[w(s, t) \supset: s = a \,.\, t = a \,.\!\vee.\, s = b \,.\, t = a\frown a \,.\!\vee\, (\exists u)(\exists v)(w(u, v): s = u\frown a \,.\, t = v\frown v\frown a \,.\!\vee.\, s = u\frown b \,.\, t = v\frown v\frown a\frown a)]\}$

defines the tally of x in the intended sense. The reasoning which shows that the condition following '$(\imath y)$' in D6 implies that y is τx in the intended sense, and vice versa, is parallel to the reasoning which showed in §3 that (3) implied (9) and vice versa.

Now the definitions of $x + y$, $x \times y$, and x^y are immediate. We can define $x + y$ as the integer whose tally is the concatenate of the tallies of x and y; we can define $x \times y$ as the integer whose tally is the tally product (as defined in D4′) of the tallies of x and y; and we can define x^y analogously.

D7. $$x + y =_{\mathrm{df}} (\imath z)(\tau z = \tau x \frown \tau y).$$

D8. $$x \times y =_{\mathrm{df}} (\imath z)(\tau z = \tau x \times_\tau \tau y).$$

D9. $$x^y =_{\mathrm{df}} (\imath z)(\tau z = \tau x \wedge_\tau \tau y).$$

The methods of construction which have just now been explained for the case of two atoms a and b will now be adapted to the general case of k atoms $a_1, a_2, \ldots, a_k$. We are to think of k as some specified number, finite and greater than 1.

Bilateral identification of the positive integers with the finite sequences of atoms $a_1, a_2, \ldots, a_k$ can still be accomplished by the old expedient of arranging the sequences in order of length and alphabetically within each length:

$$\begin{array}{llllllll} 1 & 2 \ldots & k & k+1 & k+2 \ldots & 2k & 2k+1 \ldots & \\ a_1 & a_2 \ldots & a_k & a_1 \frown a_1 & a_1 \frown a_2 \ldots & a_1 \frown a_k & a_2 \frown a_1 \ldots & \\ & & & & & & k^2 + k & k^2 + k + 1 \ldots \\ & & & & & & a_k \frown a_k & a_1 \frown a_1 \frown a_1 \ldots \end{array}$$

This generalization requires us to generalize the instructions (i) and (ii) above to read as follows:

(i) Start with $a_1, a_2, \ldots$, and a_k.

(ii) If u appears in the column, put $u \frown a_1$ one place more than k times as far down the column, then put $u \frown a_2$ next, and so on to $u \frown a_k$.

Thereupon D6 has to be generalized correspondingly. The following auxiliary notation will be used:

$$(x)_2 =_{\mathrm{df}} x \frown x, \qquad (x)_3 =_{\mathrm{df}} x \frown x \frown x, \qquad \text{etc.}$$

The generalized version of D6 then appears as follows:

$$\tau x =_{\mathrm{df}} (\imath y)(\exists w)\{w(x, y) \,.\, (s)(t)[w(s, t) \supset : s = a_1 \,.\, t = a_1 \,.\vee.\, s = a_2 \,.\, t = (a_1)_2 \,.\vee.\, \ldots \,.\vee.\, s = a_k \,.\, t = (a_1)_k \,.\vee\, (\exists u)(\exists v)(w(u, v) : s = u \frown a_1 \,.\, t = (v)_k \frown a_1 \,.\vee.\, s = u \frown a_2 \,.\, t = (v)_k \frown (a_1)_2 \,.\vee.\, \ldots \,.\vee.\, s = u \frown a_k \,.\, t = (v)_k \frown (a_1)_k)]\}.$$

The definitions D7–9 now carry over to the general case without modification.

5. *Natural numbers.* We saw in §3 how the elementary arithmetic of positive integers can be constructed unilaterally within any elementary theory of concatenation which provides at least two atoms. We then saw in §4 how that same arithmetic can be constructed bilaterally within any elementary theory of concatenation which provides an explicit finite number of atoms, at least two.

What has thus been shown for the elementary arithmetic of positive integers could be shown equally for the elementary arithmetic of *natural numbers* (i.e., positive integers and 0). This follows from the fact that the elementary arithmetic of natural numbers can be constructed in turn, and indeed in bilateral fashion, within the elementary arithmetic of positive integers. A method of carrying out the last-mentioned construction will now be presented.

The natural numbers, which I shall call 0_n, 1_n, 2_n, etc., may be arbitrarily identified with the positive integers (which I shall continue to call 1, 2, 3, etc.) thus:

$$\begin{array}{cccc} 0_n & 1_n & 2_n & \ldots \\ 1 & 2 & 3 & \ldots \end{array}$$

I shall call 1_n the *nominal* correspondent of 1, and 2_n of 2, and so on, alluding thus to the resemblance in names; but nominal correspondence is not to be confused with the *real* correspondence (*identity*) which, under our construction, holds rather between 0_n and 1, between 1_n and 2, and so on. In general, the nominal correspondent of any integer k is $k + 1$; 2_n, for example, is 3.

Now let us consider how to define the addition '$+_n$' of the arithmetic of natural numbers, in terms of the addition '$+$' of the arithmetic of positive integers. Where x' and y' are the nominal correspondents of x and y, we shall want $x' +_n y'$ to turn out as the nominal correspondent of $x + y$. (E.g., we want $5_n +_n 6_n$ to be 11_n.) Therefore, since the nominal correspondent of any integer k is $k + 1$, we want to realize the identity:

$$(12) \qquad (x + 1) +_n (y + 1) = x + y + 1.$$

Similarly, where '$x \times_n y$' represents the product of natural arithmetic and '$x \wedge_n y$' the power, we want to realize the identities:

$$(13) \qquad (x + 1) \times_n (y + 1) = (x \times y) + 1,$$

$$(14) \qquad (x + 1) \wedge_n (y + 1) = x^y + 1,$$

where '$x \times y$' and 'x^y' represent the product and power as of positive arithmetic.

The desiderata (12)–(14) are not quite enough to determine our choice of the general definitions of '$+_n$', '$\times_n$' and '$\wedge_n$', because they describe these operations only in application to numbers of the form '$x + 1$' and '$y + 1$'; and there is one number, namely, 1 ($= 0_n$), which cannot be rendered in that form. So we must supplement (12)–(14) with stipulations of what we want when one or both operands are 0_n:

$$0_n +_n z = z, \tag{15}$$

$$z +_n 0_n = z, \tag{16}$$

$$0_n \times_n z = 0_n = 1, \tag{17}$$

$$z \times_n 0_n = 0_n = 1, \tag{18}$$

$$0_n \wedge_n (y + 1) = 0_n = 1, \tag{19}$$

$$z \wedge_n 0_n = 1_n = 2. \tag{20}$$

Verification that the following definitions meet the requirements is left to the reader.

$$x +_n y =_{df} (\iota z)(x + y = z + 1),$$

$$x \times_n y =_{df} (\iota z)[x + y + z = (x \times y) + 2],$$

$$x \wedge_n y =_{df} (\iota z)[y = 1 \,.\, z = 2 \,.\vee.\, y \neq 1 \,.\, x = z = 1 \,.\vee\, (\exists w)(x = w + 1 \,.\, z \times w = w^y + w)].$$

VI

Set-theoretic Foundations for Logic

1. Introduction. In his set theory, 1908, Zermelo uses the variables 'x', 'y', etc., for the representation of "things" generally. Among these things he includes *sets*, or, as I shall say henceforth, *classes*. He adopts the connective 'ϵ' of membership as his sole special primitive; thus the *elementary formulae* of his system are describable simply as expressions of the form '$x \epsilon y$', with any thing-variables 'x', 'y', 'z', etc., supplanting 'x' and 'y'. The postulates of his system are so fashioned as to avoid the logical paradoxes without use of the theory of types. One of the postulates, the so-called *Aussonderungsaxiom*, may be stated in familiar logical notation as:

$$(\exists x)(y)((y \epsilon x) \equiv ((y \epsilon z) \,.\, \mathfrak{E}(y)))$$

where '$\mathfrak{E}(y)$' is understood as any statement about y which is *definite* in a certain sense which Zermelo introduces informally for the purpose. Skolem in 1930 pointed out that it is adequate here to construe "definite" statements as embracing just the elementary formulae and all formulae thence constructible by the truth functions and by quantification with respect to thing-variables. A second of Zermelo's postulates is the principle of extensionality; this asserts that mutually inclusive classes are identical, i.e., are members of just the same classes. There are further postulates which provide for the existence of the null class, the class of all subclasses of any

Reprinted from the *Journal of Symbolic Logic,* Volume 1, 1936.

given class, the class of all members of members of any given class, the unit class of any given thing, and the class whose sole members are any two given things. Finally the multiplicative axiom (*Auswahlprinzip*) and the axiom of infinity are adopted.

In the expression of Zermelo's postulates and the proof of his theorems the notions and technique of elementary logic are presupposed as an implicit substructure. The only logical notions which are here required are the truth functions and quantification with respect to thing-variables, and the only logical technique required is that governing the truth functions and quantification. To frame the Zermelo system as a deductive system in its own right, then, we must extend its foundations to include this part of logic, in application to the elementary formulae. This can be done by adopting quantification and the truth functions (or an adequate selection of these) as further primitives, and providing the system with rules of inference of such kind as to provide all the deductive technique of truth functions and quantification.

It is usual, in the full presentation of a deductive system, to begin metamathematically by specifying what expressions are to be formulae of the system; then to use this notion of formula in a metamathematical account of the rules of inference of the system. In the present case, since the primitives are just membership, quantification, and the truth functions, clearly the formulae of the system will embrace just the "definite" statements as construed by Skolem. As to the rules of inference, one will be the familiar logical rule which allows the inference of a formula $\mathfrak{f}$ as a theorem whenever the result of substituting $\mathfrak{f}$ for 'Q' and some theorem for 'P' in '$P \supset Q$' is a theorem; and there will be other such rules, of familiar kind, providing in the aggregate for the whole technique of truth functions and quantification. Moreover, since a "definite" statement is now simply any formula of the system, we can express the *Aussonderungsaxiom* itself as another ordinary rule of inference, which we may call the *Aussonderungsregel: Each result of putting a formula for 'P' in*

$$\text{`}(\exists x)(y)((y \in x) \equiv ((y \in z) \,.\, P))\text{'}$$

is a theorem. (Strictly, we should add explicitly that 'x' must not be a free variable of the substituted formula.) The *Aussonderungsaxiom* thus ceases to depend on the notion of "definiteness" and acquires the same formal status as the logical rules of inference. Finally the rest of Zermelo's postulates can be translated into the primitive notation and retained as formal postulates. Zermelo's system is thus transformed into a formal deductive system containing rules of inference and postulates.

The purpose of this paper is the presentation of a system Γ which resembles the above system but is more economical. Γ has the same rules of inference as the above system, including the *Aussonderungsregel;* the latter, however, is modified to the extent of supplanting '$y \epsilon z$' by the inclusion '$y \subset z$', which we may suppose defined in the familiar fashion. By way of formal postulates, Γ contains only the extensionality principle; the described modification of the *Aussonderungsregel* enables us to abandon all the other postulates and still derive the whole of standard mathematical logic, as measured, e.g., by *P.M.*[1]

This does not mean that Γ, so constituted, is adequate to the derivation of all Zermelo's postulates; it means that Γ is adequate to the derivation of as many consequences of Zermelo's postulates as are needed for standard logic in the adopted sense. In particular the multiplicative axiom and the axiom of infinity are as requisite to Γ as they are to Zermelo's system; I follow *P.M.*,[2] however, in suppressing these as postulates and requiring their statement rather as explicit hypotheses wherever necessary.

There is a further respect in which Γ is to be contrasted with Zermelo's system and others: it contains no null class. The null class presupposes a distinction between classes and individuals (non-classes) which is inexpressible in terms of membership, since the null class is like an individual in lacking members. Repudiation of the null class enables us to explain the variables of Γ as representing objects generally, classes and otherwise, and then to define classes simply as objects y such that $(\exists x)(x \epsilon y)$.

Though Γ lacks two chief features of the standard logic, viz., types and the null class, we shall see that within Γ we can construct definitionally a derivative theory Δ in which both the null class and the familiar stratification into types are ostensibly restored and all theorems of the standard logic are forthcoming.

2. Formal Construction of Γ. The Γ-formulae, or formulae of Γ, are describable recursively thus: expressions of the form '$(x \epsilon y)$', with any Γ-variables 'x', 'y', 'z', etc., supplanting 'x' and 'y', are Γ-formulae; so also are the results of putting any Γ-formulae for

[1] Whitehead and Russell, 2d ed.
[2] Vol. 2, 183; Vol. 1, 481.

'P' and 'Q' and any Γ-variable for 'x' in '$\sim P$', '$(P \supset Q)$', and '$(x)P$'. A Γ-variable $\mathfrak{x}$ is said to be *bound* at a given point (say at the kth sign) of a Γ-formula $\mathfrak{p}$ if that point lies with a Γ-formula $\mathfrak{q}$ which forms part of $\mathfrak{p}$ and begins with a parenthesized occurrence of $\mathfrak{x}$ (as universal quantifier). An occurrence of $\mathfrak{x}$ is *free* in $\mathfrak{p}$ if $\mathfrak{x}$ is not bound at that occurrence in $\mathfrak{p}$. $\mathfrak{x}$ is said to be free in $\mathfrak{p}$, or to be a free Γ-variable of $\mathfrak{p}$, if $\mathfrak{x}$ has a free occurrence in $\mathfrak{p}$.

Γ-formulae are abbreviated through the following familiar definitions.

D1. $$(P \,.\, Q) =_{\mathrm{df}} \sim(P \supset \sim Q).$$

D2. $$(P \equiv Q) =_{\mathrm{df}} ((P \supset Q) \,.\, (Q \supset P)).$$

D3. $$(\exists x)\, P =_{\mathrm{df}} \sim(x) \sim P.$$

D4. $$(x \subset y) =_{\mathrm{df}} (z)((z \in x) \supset (z \in y)).$$

Definitions are viewed as conventions extraneous to the formal system. For formal purposes we may think of definitional abbreviations as expanded always into full primitive expression.

Among various ways of compressing the familiar technique of the propositional calculus and theory of quantifiers into a few rules for the generation of theorems in Γ, one way is to declare that a Γ-formula $\mathfrak{f}$ is a Γ-theorem under any of the following conditions:

Γ1. $\mathfrak{f}$ is formed by putting Γ-formulae for the capitals in one of the schemata:

(a) $$((P \supset Q) \supset ((Q \supset R) \supset (P \supset R))),$$

(b) $$(P \supset (\sim P \supset Q)),$$

(c) $$((\sim P \supset P) \supset P).$$

Γ2. The result of putting $\mathfrak{f}$ for 'Q' and some Γ-theorem for 'P' in '$(P \supset Q)$' is a Γ-theorem.

Γ3. There are Γ-formulae $\mathfrak{p}$ and $\mathfrak{q}$ and a Γ-theorem $\mathfrak{r}$ such that $\mathfrak{f}$ and $\mathfrak{r}$ are formed respectively from '$(P \supset (x)Q)$' and '$(P \supset Q)$' by replacing 'P' by $\mathfrak{p}$, 'Q' by $\mathfrak{q}$, and 'x' by a Γ-variable which is not free in $\mathfrak{p}$.

Γ4. There are Γ-formulae $\mathfrak{p}$ and $\mathfrak{q}$ and a Γ-theorem $\mathfrak{r}$ such that $\mathfrak{f}$ and $\mathfrak{r}$ are formed respectively from '$(P \supset Q)$' and '$(P \supset (x)Q)$' by replacing 'P' by $\mathfrak{p}$, 'Q' by $\mathfrak{q}$, and 'x' by a Γ-variable.

Γ5. $\mathfrak{f}$ is formed from a Γ-theorem by replacing all free occurrences of a Γ-variable $\mathfrak{x}$ therein by a Γ-variable $\mathfrak{y}$ which is not bound at any of those occurrences of $\mathfrak{x}$.

Γ1–2 are an adaptation of one of Łukasiewicz's systematizations of the propositional calculus.[3] They provide as Γ-theorems all Γ-formulae which are instances of valid forms of the propositional calculus.[4] Γ2–5 answer to Tarski's definition of logical consequence.[5] Given the machinery of the propositional calculus as provided by Γ1–2, Γ3–5 provide all the familiar technique of quantification.

As intimated in §1, the general theory of deduction as embodied in Γ1–5 is supplemented in Γ by one special postulate and one special rule as follows:

Γ6. '$((x \subset y) \supset ((y \subset x) \supset ((z \in x) \supset ((x \in w) \supset (y \in w)))))$'

is [a transcription, under D4, of] a Γ-theorem.

Γ7. If 'P' is supplanted in '$(\exists x)(y)((y \in x) \equiv ((y \subset z) \,.\, P))$' by a Γ-formula in which 'x' is not free, the result is [a transcription, under D1–3, of] a Γ-theorem.

The clause '$(z \in x)$' in the extensionality principle Γ6 is inserted to restrict the principle to classes and thus leave room for the existence of more than one individual.

As framed above, Γ involves denial, material implication, universal quantification, and membership as primitive. Actually denial is superfluous; we could define it thus:

$$\sim P =_{\mathrm{df}} (P \supset (x)(y)(x \in y)).$$

(a)–(c) could then be supplanted in Γ1 by:

$$(((P \supset Q) \supset ((R \supset S) \supset T)) \supset \\ ((U \supset ((R \supset S) \supset T)) \supset ((P \supset U) \supset (S \supset T)))),$$

which answers to Wajsberg's postulate for the calculus of material implication.[6] The resulting system is demonstrably equivalent to Γ. If on the other hand it is thought desirable to provide for the properties of the truth functions independently of those of membership, as is done in Γ, there remains an alternative reduction of primitives, namely the adoption of Sheffer's stroke function instead of implication and denial.[7] Γ2 would then be refashioned to match

[3] See Łukasiewicz and Tarski, Satz 6.
[4] See my "Truth by convention," note 18 [17 in one edition].
[5] Tarski, 1933, Def.9. Note that "$Fr(\theta)$" here is a misprint for "$Fr(\eta)$".
[6] See Łukasiewicz and Tarski, Satz 30.
[7] See *P.M.*, Vol. 1, xiii, xvi.

Nicod's rule of inference,[8] and (a)–(c) would be supplanted in Γ1 by:

$$((P \mid (Q \mid R)) \mid ((S \mid (S \mid S)) \mid ((S \mid Q) \mid ((P \mid S) \mid (P \mid S))))),$$

which answers to Łukasiewicz's reduced form[9] of Nicod's postulate. Throughout this paper, however, it will be convenient to retain Γ in its original redundant form.

3. The System Δ. A system Δ due to Tarski[10] will be identified with "standard logic" and shown to be derivable from Γ. Δ, unlike Γ, countenances nullity of classes and imports the simple theory of types. A distinctive kind of variables is appropriated to each type. All the Δ-variables are Γ-variables with positive integral indices attached: those with the index '1' take individuals as values, those with '2' take classes of individuals, those with '3' take classes of such classes, and so on. The Γ-variable to which the index is attached will be called the *base* of the Δ-variable.

The elementary Δ-formulae are formed by replacing '*x*' and '*y*' in '$(x \epsilon y)$' by Δ-variables whose indices are consecutive and ascending. These formulae are elaborated into further ones, as in Γ, by the truth functions and quantification. For simplification of later matters it will be demanded that no Δ-formula contain Δ-variables with like bases and unlike indices; this restriction does no violence to Tarski's scheme, since it touches only the arbitrary choice of letters. A Δ-formula is describable in general, then, in terms of the Γ-formulae, as any expression $\mathfrak{f}$ such that every Γ-variable in $\mathfrak{f}$ bears a numeral (positive and integral, as will always be understood hereafter) as index, all like Γ-variables in $\mathfrak{f}$ bear like indices, 'ϵ' occurs only between Γ-variables bearing consecutive ascending indices, and the result of deleting all indices from $\mathfrak{f}$ is a Γ-formula. Δ-formulae are then abbreviated as in D1–2.

Despite its simplicity, the language of Δ is adequate "*zum Ausdrucke jedes in* Principia Mathematica *formulierbaren Gedankens.*"[11] Relations, e.g., can be introduced in terms of classes by the method of Wiener or Kuratowski.

A Δ-formula $\mathfrak{f}$ is declared to be a Δ-theorem under any of the following conditions:

Δ1–4. (Same as Γ1–4, but with 'Δ' put for 'Γ' throughout.)

[8] *Ibid.*, xvi.

[9] See Łukasiewicz, "Uwagi o aksyomacie Nicod'a".

[10] 1933. My formulation departs from Tarski in inessential respects, largely notational.

[11] Tarski, 1933, 97.

Δ5. [A transcription, under D1–2, of] $\mathfrak{f}$ is formed by putting Δ-variables for the letters in '$((z)((z \epsilon x) \equiv (z \epsilon y)) \supset ((x \epsilon w) \supset (y \epsilon w)))$'.

Δ6. [A transcription of] $\mathfrak{f}$ is formed by putting Δ-variables $\mathfrak{x}$ and $\mathfrak{y}$ for 'x' and 'y' in '$\sim(x)\sim(y)((y \epsilon x) \equiv P)$' and supplanting '$P$' by a Δ-formula in which $\mathfrak{x}$ is not free.

For purposes of Δ1–6 the words "bound" and "free" are of course explained just as in §2, but with 'Δ' supplanting 'Γ'.

In Tarski's formulation there is a further Δ-rule, paralleling Γ5. He needs this because in his formulation of Δ5–6 he specifies the bases of the Δ-variables involved. It has been convenient here, on the other hand, to phrase Δ5–6 without reference to specific sets of variables. Since there is consequently no such reference anywhere in Δ1–6, the substitution of one free variable for another in a theorem can be accomplished by repeating the whole derivation of that theorem under a different initial choice of variables. A rule of substitution parallel to Γ5 therefore becomes superfluous. Note that Γ5 could similarly be eliminated from Γ, by so rephrasing Γ6–7 as to avoid reference to specific variables. Conversely, also, the system Δ admits of reduction in ways parallel to those sketched for Γ in §2.

4. Construction of Δ *Within* Γ. Δ differs from Γ not only in depending upon the theory of types but also in involving some extra elements, viz., the null class in each type. The problem of deriving Δ from Γ thus resembles the problem of deriving the system of rational numbers from that of integers, or the system of integers from that of natural numbers. In the latter derivation the natural numbers are not directly supplemented by the negative integers; rather the whole series of integers is developed anew, in such fashion that the non-negative integers do not coincide with the natural numbers with which they are intuitively associated. A similar course is adopted in deriving Δ from Γ; rather than directly supplementing Γ somehow with null classes, the procedure is to present a general reconstruction of the elements of Δ in terms of Γ.

For each element of Δ let us define a *correspondent* recursively thus: the correspondent of an individual is its unit class, and the correspondent of a class x is the class whose members comprise all individuals and in addition the correspondents of the members (if any) of x. Now I incorporate Δ into Γ by reinterpreting Δ to the extent of supposing all its elements replaced by their correspondents. Thus a Δ-element of first type, represented in Δ by a variable with '1' as index, and formerly construed as an individual, is reconstrued as a class (a unit class, as it happens) of individuals. A Δ-element of $n + 1$st type, formerly construed as a class of Δ-elements of nth type, is reconstrued in two respects: its members are reconstrued in the manner appropriate to the nth type, and it is then assigned all individuals as additional members. In particular, thus, the null class of each type is reconstrued simply as the class of all individuals. All Δ-elements are thus reconstrued as classes; and this in the strict sense of Γ, viz., classes with members.

Now '$1!x$', read 'x is of first Γ-type', is defined in Γ thus:

D5. $$1!x =_{df} ((\exists y)(y \epsilon x) \,.\, (y)((y \epsilon x) \supset (w) \sim (w \epsilon y))).$$

Thus $1!x$ if and only if x has members but none of them have members in turn; i.e., the first Γ-type comprises all and only the classes of individuals. Hence the "individuals" or first-type elements of Δ, reconstrued as they are as certain classes of individuals, become classes of first Γ-type.

Next, given the nth Γ-type, the $n + 1$st is defined thus:

D6. $$n + 1!x =_{df} (y)(((y \epsilon x) \equiv (\exists w)(w \epsilon y)) \supset n!y).$$

Where $n + 1!x$, D6 obviously provides that if $y \epsilon x$ and y has members then $n!y$; further D6 can be shown to provide that $y \epsilon x$ if y has no members.[12] In effect, then, the $n + 1$st Γ-type is defined as comprising just those classes x which have all individuals and in addition none but classes of nth Γ-type as members. From the described reinterpretation of Δ it thus follows that if all Δ-elements of nth type are reconstrued as classes of nth Γ-type then all Δ-elements of $n + 1$st type are reconstrued as classes of $n + 1$st Γ-type. Since all Δ-individuals are reconstrued as of first Γ-type, it follows by induction that the Δ-elements of every type n are reconstrued as of nth Γ-type. In particular the null class of any type n, reconstrued as it is as the class of all individuals, turns out to belong at once to all Γ-types.[13]

Formally the incorporation of Δ into Γ will consist in regarding each Δ-variable, having say the nth numeral as index, as restricted in range to the nth Γ-type. Thus *indexed* quantifiers are introduced into Γ through this definition:

D7. $$(x^n)P =_{df} (x)(n!x \supset P).$$

[12] See the next-to-the-last formula in the proof of Lemma 3, below.
[13] This is the basis of the proof of Lemma 5, below.

This convention is added:

C1. An index which is attached to a Γ-variable within an indexed quantifier may be attached also at will to any recurrence of that variable within the scope of that quantifier.

Strictly, D5–6 should be regarded not as a definition of the general case '$n!x$' but as a convention for the adoption of an infinite series of specific abbreviations '$1!x$', '$2!x$', etc. D7 then introduces a further series of abbreviations.

A Δ-formula will be called *closed* if it contains no free Δ-variables. Now let $\mathfrak{p}$ be a Δ-formula with just $k(\geqq 0)$ free Δ-variables. Any result of putting $\mathfrak{p}$ for 'P' in '$(x_1{}^{(1)})\ \ldots\ (x_k{}^{(k)})P$', and putting the free Δ-variables of $\mathfrak{p}$ in any order for '$x_1{}^{(1)}$' to '$x_k{}^{(k)}$', will be called a c.g. (closed generalization) of $\mathfrak{p}$. Now D1–7 and C1 explain every closed Δ-formula as a conventional transcription of a Γ-formula. In particular, all closed Δ-theorems are thus translated into Γ. The Δ-theorems in general may then be translated into Γ by interpreting each as a closed theorem in the familiar fashion, viz., by supposing each supplanted by one of its c.g.'s.[14] (If a Δ-theorem is closed to begin with, it is of course its own c.g.) To show that the system Δ proceeds from Γ, then, we need only show that every c.g. of a Δ-theorem is [a transcription, under D1–7 and C1, of] a Γ-theorem.

5. Proof That Every c.g. of a Δ-theorem Is a Γ-theorem. The proof will only be sketched here; in rigorous form it would involve elaborate metamathematical developments and run to greater length. All the familiar technique of the propositional calculus and theory of quantifiers will be taken for granted, since there is no essential difficulty in showing that the technique accrues to Γ through Γ1–5. Such clauses as the bracketed ones in Γ6–7 and Δ5–6 and at the end of §4 will be suppressed entirely, as in the title of §5; in effect, thus, definitional transcriptions of Γ-formulae or of Δ-formulae will be treated as Γ-formulae or Δ-formulae in their own right.

LEMMA 1. *If Γ-formulae are put for the capitals in the following schemata, the results are Γ-theorems:*

(a) $((P \supset Q) \supset (((R \equiv {\sim}P) \supset Q) \supset (R \supset Q)))$

(b) $((Q \supset {\sim}P) \supset (((R \equiv {\sim}P) \supset Q) \supset (P \supset R)))$

(c) $(((P \,.\, Q) \supset (R \supset S)) \supset ((P \supset R) \supset ((P \,.\, Q) \supset S)))$

[14] See *P.M.*, Vol. 1, xiii. Indeed, Tarski has revised Δ in just this fashion (1935, 365–366, 291–299).

(d) $((((P \equiv Q) \supset R) \,.\, ((S \equiv Q) \supset R)) \supset$
$((R \supset (P \equiv S)) \supset ((P \supset S) \,.\, (S \supset P))))$

(e) $((P \supset Q) \supset ((R \supset \sim P) \supset ((R \supset Q) \supset ((S \equiv (Q \,.\, (\sim P \supset$
$(R \,.\, T)))) \supset (((S \equiv \sim P) \supset R) \,.\, (R \supset (S \equiv T)))))))$

Proof. All these are valid forms of the propositional calculus, as can be checked by the truth-table method or otherwise.

LEMMA 2. *The following are Γ-theorems:*

(a) $((w) \sim (w \in y) \supset (y \subset z))$

(b) $(\exists x)(y)((y \in x) \equiv (y \subset z))$

(c) $(\exists y)(w) \sim (w \in y)$

(d) $(\exists x)(y)((y \in x) \equiv (w) \sim (w \in y))$

(e) $(\exists x) 1 ! x$

(f) $(\exists x)(z^1)(z \subset x)$

Proof. The case of (a) is clear from D4. (b)–(d) are derivable as follows. By Γ7,

$$(\exists x)(y)((y \in x) \equiv ((y \subset z) \,.\, (y \subset z))), \tag{1}$$

$$(\exists x)(y)((y \in x) \equiv ((y \subset z) \,.\, (w) \sim (w \in y))), \tag{2}$$

and $$(\exists y)(w)((w \in y) \equiv ((w \subset z) \,.\, \sim(w \subset z))). \tag{3}$$

(b) proceeds from (1), (c) from (3), and (d) from (2) and (a). (e) and (f), finally, are derivable as follows. By (d),

$$(\exists x)((y)((w) \sim (w \in y) \supset (y \in x)) \,.\, (y)((y \in x) \supset (w) \sim (w \in y))).$$

Hence, by (c), $(\exists x)((\exists y)(y \in x) \,.\, (y)((y \in x) \supset (w) \sim (w \in y)))$. (4)

Again, by (d), $(\exists x)(z)((y)((y \in z) \supset (w) \sim (w \in y)) \supset$
$(y)((y \in z) \supset (y \in x)))$.

Hence, by D5, $(\exists x)(z)(1 ! z \supset (y)((y \in z) \supset (y \in x)))$. (5)

In view of D5, D4, and D7, (4) and (5) are (e) and (f).

LEMMA 3. *A Γ-theorem results from putting any numeral for 'n' in:*

(a) $$(n ! y \supset (\exists w)(w \in y)).$$

Proof. Let the nth and $n + 1$st numerals be represented as 'n' and '$n + 1$', and suppose (a) to be a Γ-theorem. Then we can derive another Γ-theorem as follows. By Lemma 1(b) and D3,

$$((n!y \supset (\exists w)(w \in y)) \supset ((((y \in x) \equiv (\exists w)(w \in y)) \supset n!y) \supset ((w) \sim (w \in y) \supset (y \in x)))).$$

Hence, by (a), $$((((y \in x) \equiv (\exists w)(w \in y)) \supset n!y) \supset ((w) \sim (w \in y) \supset (y \in x))).$$

Hence, by D6, $(n + 1!x \supset (y)((w) \sim (w \in y) \supset (y \in x)))$.

Hence, by Lemma 2(c), $(n + 1!x \supset (\exists y)(y \in x))$.

In this way, if the result of putting the nth numeral for 'n' in (a) is a Γ-theorem, the result of putting the $n + 1$st numeral for 'n' in (a) is derivable as a Γ-theorem. But the result of putting '1' for 'n' in (a) is a Γ-theorem, as is seen immediately from D5. Lemma 3 then follows by induction.

LEMMA 4. *A Γ-theorem results from putting any numeral for 'n' in*

(a) $$(\exists z)(y^n)(y \subset z).$$

Proof. Let the nth and $n + 1$st numerals be represented as 'n' and '$n + 1$' and suppose (a) to be a Γ-theorem. Then we can derive another Γ-theorem as follows. By D6–7,

$$((y^n)(y \subset z) \supset (x)(n + 1!x \supset (y)(((y \in x) \equiv (\exists w)(w \in y)) \supset (y \subset z)))).$$

Hence, by (a),

$$(\exists z)(x)(n + 1!x \supset (y)(((y \in x) \equiv (\exists w)(w \in y)) \supset (y \subset z))). \quad (1)$$

By Lemma 1(a) and D3,

$$(((w) \sim (w \in y) \supset (y \subset z)) \supset ((((y \in x) \equiv (\exists w)(w \in y)) \supset (y \subset z)) \supset ((y \in x) \supset (y \subset z)))).$$

Hence, by Lemma 2(a),

$$((((y \in x) \equiv (\exists w)(w \in y)) \supset (y \subset z)) \supset ((y \in x) \supset (y \subset z))).$$

Hence, by (1), $(\exists z)(x)(n + 1!x \supset (y)((y \in x) \supset (y \subset z)))$.

Hence, by Lemma 2(b), $(\exists t)(x)(n + 1!x \supset (y)((y \in x) \supset (y \in t)))$.

I.e., by D7 and D4, $(\exists t)(x^{n+1})(x \subset t)$.

In this way, if the result of putting the nth numeral for 'n' in (a) is a Γ-theorem, the result of putting the $n + 1$st numeral for 'n' in (a) is derivable as a Γ-theorem. From Lemma 2(f), then, Lemma 4 follows by induction.

LEMMA 5. *A Γ-theorem results from putting any numeral* $\mathfrak{n}$ *for 'n' in* '$(\exists x)n!x$'.

Proof. Lemma 2(e) covers the case where $\mathfrak{n}$ is '1'. If $\mathfrak{n}$ is not '1', then, representing $\mathfrak{n}$ as '$m + 1$', we can derive the Γ-theorem thus. By Γ1(b),

$$(((y \in x) \equiv (w) \sim (w \in y)) \supset (\sim((y \in x) \equiv (w) \sim (w \in y)) \supset m!y)).$$

Hence, by Lemma 2(d),

$$(\exists x)(y)(\sim((y \in x) \equiv (w) \sim (w \in y)) \supset m!y).$$

I.e., $$(\exists x)(y)(((y \in x) \equiv \sim(w) \sim (w \in y)) \supset m!y).$$

I.e., by D3 and D6, $(\exists x)m + 1!x$.

Definition. If $\mathfrak{p}$ is a Δ-formula, that Γ-formula which is obtained by dropping the indices from the free Δ-variables of $\mathfrak{p}$ will be called $|\mathfrak{p}|$.

Lemma 6. *If $\mathfrak{x}_1$ to $\mathfrak{x}_k$ $(0 \leqq k)$ are the bases of the free Δ-variables of a Δ-formula $\mathfrak{p}$, $\mathfrak{n}_1$ to $\mathfrak{n}_k$ are the respective indices attached, and $\mathfrak{q}$ is the result of putting $|\mathfrak{p}|$ for 'Q', $\mathfrak{x}_1$ to $\mathfrak{x}_k$ for 'x_1' to 'x_k', and $\mathfrak{n}_1$ to $\mathfrak{n}_k$ for '(1)' to '(k)' in:*

$$(((1)!x_1 \; . \; . \; . \; . \; (k)!x_k) \supset Q),$$

then $\mathfrak{q}$ is a Γ-theorem if and only if every c.g. of $\mathfrak{p}$ is a Γ-theorem.

Proof. Every c.g. $\mathfrak{r}$ of $\mathfrak{p}$ has the form '$(y_1{}^{[1]}) \ldots (y_k{}^{[k]})P$', with '$P$' replaced by $\mathfrak{p}$, and 'y_1' to 'y_k' replaced by the $\mathfrak{x}_i$ in some permutation, and '[1]' to '$[k]$' replaced by the $\mathfrak{n}_i$ in the corresponding permutation. By D7 and C1, $\mathfrak{r}$ will be a Γ-theorem if and only if $\mathfrak{s}$ is a Γ-theorem, where $\mathfrak{s}$ is formed from '$(y_1)([1]!y_1 \supset \ldots (y_k)([k]!y_k \supset Q) \ldots)$' by putting $|\mathfrak{p}|$ for 'Q' and replacing 'y_1' to 'y_k' and '[1]' to '$[k]$' as before. But, by the propositional calculus and theory of quantifiers, $\mathfrak{s}$ will be a Γ-theorem if and only if the result $\mathfrak{t}$ of the same replacements in '$(([1]!y_1 \; . \; . \; . \; . \; [k]!y_k) \supset Q)$' is a Γ-theorem. But $\mathfrak{t}$ is carried into $\mathfrak{q}$ and vice versa by permutations which are allowed by the propositional calculus. Hence $\mathfrak{t}$, and therefore $\mathfrak{r}$, will be a Γ-theorem if and only if $\mathfrak{q}$ is a Γ-theorem. But $\mathfrak{r}$ was any c.g. of $\mathfrak{p}$. Hence $\mathfrak{q}$ is a Γ-theorem if and only if every c.g. of $\mathfrak{p}$ is a Γ-theorem, q.e.d.

Lemma 7. *If $\mathfrak{p}$ is a Δ-formula and $|\mathfrak{p}|$ is a Γ-theorem, every c.g. of $\mathfrak{p}$ is a Γ-theorem.*

Proof. If $|\mathfrak{p}|$ is a Γ-theorem, the $\mathfrak{q}$ of Lemma 6 follows immediately as a Γ-theorem. By Lemma 6, then, every c.g. of $\mathfrak{p}$ is a Γ-theorem, q.e.d.

LEMMA 8. *If* $\mathfrak{p}$, $\mathfrak{q}$, $\mathfrak{r}$, *and* $\mathfrak{s}$ *are* Δ-*formulae,* $\mathfrak{x}$ *is a* Δ-*variable, and* $\mathfrak{r}$ *and* $\mathfrak{s}$ *are formed respectively from* '$(P \supset Q)$' *and* '$(P \supset (x)Q)$' *by putting* $\mathfrak{p}$ *for* 'P', $\mathfrak{q}$ *for* 'Q', *and* $\mathfrak{x}$ *for* 'x', *then* (i) *if all c.g.'s of* $\mathfrak{p}$ *and of* $\mathfrak{r}$ *are* Γ-*theorems, so are all c.g.'s of* $\mathfrak{q}$; (ii) *if* $\mathfrak{x}$ *is not free in* $\mathfrak{p}$, *and all c.g.'s of* $\mathfrak{r}$ *are* Γ-*theorems, then so are all c.g.'s of* $\mathfrak{s}$; (iii) *if all c.g.'s of* $\mathfrak{s}$ *are* Γ-*theorems, then so are all c.g.'s of* $\mathfrak{r}$.

Representations. Let those Δ-variables which are free in $\mathfrak{p}$ but not in $\mathfrak{q}$ be represented as '$x_1{}^{(1)}$' to '$x_{h-1}^{(h-1)}$' ($1 \leqq h$), let those which are free in both $\mathfrak{p}$ and $\mathfrak{q}$ be represented as '$x_h{}^{(h)}$' to '$x_k{}^{(k)}$' ($h \leqq k+1$), and let those which are free in $\mathfrak{q}$ but not in $\mathfrak{p}$ be represented as '$x_{k+1}^{(k+1)}$' to '$x_m{}^{(m)}$' ($k \leqq m$). Let $\mathfrak{p}$ and $\mathfrak{q}$ be represented accordingly as '$\phi(x_1{}^{(1)}, \ldots x_k{}^{(k)})$' and '$\psi(x_h{}^{(h)}, \ldots x_m{}^{(m)})$'. Let $\mathfrak{x}$ be represented as '$x_n{}^{(n)}$', where n is 0, m, 1, or h according as $\mathfrak{x}$ is free in neither $\mathfrak{p}$ nor $\mathfrak{q}$ (Case 1), in $\mathfrak{q}$ but not in $\mathfrak{p}$ (Case 2), in $\mathfrak{p}$ but not in $\mathfrak{q}$ (Case 3), or in both $\mathfrak{p}$ and $\mathfrak{q}$ (Case 4). Consequently

$$\text{`}\phi(x_1, \ldots x_k)\text{'}, \qquad \text{`}\psi(x_h, \ldots x_m)\text{'},$$
$$\text{`}(\phi(x_1, \ldots x_k) \supset \psi(x_h, \ldots x_m))\text{'}$$

answer respectively to $|\mathfrak{p}|$, $|\mathfrak{q}|$, and $|\mathfrak{r}|$, and $|\mathfrak{s}|$ is represented as

$$\text{`}(\phi(x_1, \ldots x_k) \supset (x_n{}^{(n)})\psi(x_h, \ldots x_m))\text{'} \qquad (n < h;\ \text{Cases 1 and 3})$$

or

$$\text{`}(\phi(x_1, \ldots x_k) \supset (x_m{}^{(m)})\psi(x_h, \ldots x_{m-1}, x_m{}^{(m)}))\text{'} \qquad \text{(Case 2)}$$

or

$$\text{`}(\phi(x_1, \ldots x_k) \supset (x_h{}^{(h)})\psi(x_h{}^{(h)}, x_{h+1}, \ldots x_m))\text{'} \qquad \text{(Case 4).}$$

Proof of (i). A Γ-theorem is derivable as follows. By the hypothesis of (i), together with Lemma 6,

$$(((1)\,!x_1 \,.\, \ldots \,.\, (k)\,!x_k) \supset \phi(x_1, \ldots x_k)) \tag{1}$$

and

$$(((1)\,!x_1 \,.\, \ldots \,.\, (m)\,!x_m) \supset (\phi(x_1, \ldots x_k) \supset \psi(x_h, \ldots x_m))). \tag{2}$$

By Lemma 1(c),

$$((((1)\,!x_1 \,.\, \ldots \,.\, (m)\,!x_m) \supset (\phi(x_1, \ldots x_k) \supset \psi(x_h, \ldots x_m))) \supset$$
$$((((1)\,!x_1 \,.\, \ldots \,.\, (k)\,!x_k) \supset \phi(x_1, \ldots x_k)) \supset (((1)\,!x_1 \,.\, \ldots \,.\, (m)\,!x_m) \supset \psi(x_h, \ldots x_m)))).$$

Hence, by (2) and (1),

$$(((1)\,!x_1 \,.\, \ldots \,.\, (m)\,!x_m) \supset \psi(x_h, \ldots x_m)).$$

I.e.,

$$((\exists x_1)(1)!x_1 \supset \ldots ((\exists x_{h-1})(h-1)!x_{h-1} \supset (((h)!x_h \ldots . (m)!x_m) \supset \psi(x_h, \ldots x_m))) \ldots).$$

Hence, by Lemma 5, $(((h)!x_h \ldots . (m)!x_m) \supset \psi(x_h, \ldots x_m))$.

By Lemma 6, then, every c.g. of $\mathfrak{q}$ is a Γ-theorem, q.e.d.

Proof of (ii). By the hypothesis of (ii), together with Lemma 6, (2) above is a Γ-theorem. By hypothesis, also, Cases 3 and 4 are excluded. In Cases 1 and 2, Γ-theorems are derivable as follows.

Case 1. By (2),

$$(((1)!x_1 \ldots . (m)!x_m) \supset (\phi(x_1, \ldots x_k) \supset (x_n)((n)!x_n \supset \psi(x_h, \ldots x_m)))). \quad (3)$$

I.e., by D7, $(((1)!x_1 \ldots . (m)!x_m) \supset (\phi(x_1, \ldots x_k) \supset (x_n{}^{(n)})\psi(x_h, \ldots x_m))). \quad (4)$

By Lemma 6, then, every c.g. of $\mathfrak{s}$ is a Γ-theorem, q.e.d.

Case 2. By (2),

$$(((1)!x_1 \ldots . (m-1)!x_{m-1}) \supset (\phi(x_1, \ldots x_k) \supset (x_m)((m)!x_m \supset \psi(x_h, \ldots x_m)))). \quad (5)$$

I.e., by D7 and C1,

$$(((1)!x_1 \ldots . (m-1)!x_{m-1}) \supset (\phi(x_1, \ldots x_k) \supset (x_m{}^{(m)})\psi(x_h, \ldots x_{m-1}, x_m{}^{(m)}))). \quad (6)$$

By Lemma 6, then, every c.g. of $\mathfrak{s}$ is a Γ-theorem, q.e.d.

Proof of (iii). Cases 1 and 3. By the hypothesis of (iii), together with Lemma 6, (4) is a Γ-theorem. By D7, then, so is (3). Hence so is:

$$(((1)!x_1 \ldots . (m)!x_m) \supset (\phi(x_1, \ldots x_k) \supset ((\exists x_n)(n)!x_n \supset \psi(x_h, \ldots x_m)))),$$

and consequently, by Lemma 5, so is (2).

Case 2. By hypothesis and Lemma 6, (6) is a Γ-theorem. By D7 and C1, then, (5) is a Γ-theorem. Hence so is (2).

Case 4. (2) is derivable as follows. By hypothesis and Lemma 6,

$$(((1)!x_1 \ldots . (m)!x_m) \supset (\phi(x_1, \ldots x_k) \supset (x_h{}^{(h)})\psi(x_h{}^{(h)}, x_{h+1}, \ldots x_m))).$$

I.e., by D7 and C1,

$$(((1)!x_1 \ldots . (m)!x_m) \supset (\phi(x_1, \ldots x_k) \supset (x_h)((h)!x_h \supset \psi(x_h, \ldots x_m)))).$$

Hence $(((1)!x_1 \ldots . (m)!x_m) \supset (\phi(x_1, \ldots x_k) \supset ((h)!x_h \supset \psi(x_h, \ldots x_m)))).$

Deletion of the repeated premise reduces this to (2).

(2) is thus a Γ-theorem in all four cases. By Lemma 6, then, all c.g.'s of 𝔯 are Γ-theorems, q.e.d.

Lemma 9. *If the Δ-formula* 𝔣 *is formed by putting Δ-formulae for the capitals in* (a), (b), *or* (c) *of* Γ1, *then every c.g. of* 𝔣 *is a* Γ-*theorem.*

Proof. If 𝔣 results from putting 𝔭, 𝔮, and 𝔯 for the capitals in (a), then |𝔣| results from putting the Γ-formulae |𝔭|, |𝔮|, and |𝔯| for the capitals in (a). Then, by Γ1, |𝔣| is a Γ-theorem. Consequently, by Lemma 7, every c.g. of 𝔣 is a Γ-theorem. The cases of (b) and (c) are analogous.

Lemma 10. *If a Δ-formula* 𝔣 *is formed by putting Δ-variables* 𝔵, 𝔶, 𝔷, *and* 𝔴 *for* 'x', 'y', 'z', *and* 'w' *in* '$((z)((z \in x) \equiv (z \in y)) \supset ((x \in w) \supset (y \in w)))$', *every c.g. of* 𝔣 *is a* Γ-*theorem.*

Proof. Let us represent 𝔵, 𝔶, 𝔷, and 𝔴 as 'x^{n+1}', 'y^{n+1}', 'z^n', and 'w^{n+2}'. (The indices must be consecutive as indicated, since 𝔣 is a Δ-formula.) We can derive a Γ-theorem as follows. By Lemma 1(d),

$$(((((z \in x) \equiv (\exists w)(w \in z)) \supset n!z) . (((z \in y) \equiv (\exists w)(w \in z)) \supset n!z)) \supset ((n!z \supset ((z \in x) \equiv (z \in y))) \supset (((z \in x) \supset (z \in y)) . ((z \in y) \supset (z \in x))))).$$

Hence, by D6–7, C1, and D4,

$$((n + 1!x . n + 1!y) \supset ((z^n)((z^n \in x) \equiv (z^n \in y)) \supset ((x \subset y) . (y \subset x)))).$$

Hence, by Lemma 3,

$$((n + 1!x . n + 1!y) \supset ((z^n)((z^n \in x) \equiv (z^n \in y)) \supset ((x \subset y) . (y \subset x) . (\exists z)(z \in x)))).$$

Hence, by Γ6,

$$((n + 1!x . n + 1!y) \supset ((z^n)((z^n \in x) \equiv (z^n \in y)) \supset ((x \in w) \supset (y \in w)))).$$

Hence

$$((n + 2!w . n + 1!x . n + 1!y) \supset ((z^n)((z^n \in x) \equiv (z^n \in y)) \supset ((x \in w) \supset (y \in w)))).$$

Then, since '$((z^n)((z^n \epsilon x) \equiv (z^n \epsilon y)) \supset ((x \epsilon w) \supset (y \epsilon w)))$' is $|\mathfrak{f}|$, it follows from Lemma 6 that every c.g. of $\mathfrak{f}$ is a Γ-theorem, q.e.d.

LEMMA 11. *If a Δ-formula $\mathfrak{f}$ is formed by putting Δ-variables $\mathfrak{x}$ and $\mathfrak{y}$ for 'x' and 'y' in '$\sim(x)\sim(y)((y \epsilon x) \equiv P)$' and supplanting '$P$' by a Δ-formula $\mathfrak{p}$ in which $\mathfrak{x}$ is not free, then every c.g. of $\mathfrak{f}$ is a Γ-theorem.*

Proof. Let $\mathfrak{y}$ and $\mathfrak{x}$ be represented as '$y_k^{(k)}$' and '$x^{(k)+1}$', and let the free Δ-variables of $\mathfrak{p}$ be represented as '$y_1^{(1)}$' to '$y_h^{(h)}$' ($0 \leqq h \leqq k \leqq h + 1$). If $\mathfrak{y}$ is free in $\mathfrak{p}$, $h = k$; otherwise $h = k - 1$. Finally, let us represent $\mathfrak{p}$ as '$\phi(y_1^{(1)}, \ldots y_h^{(h)})$'. Now a Γ-theorem is derivable as follows. Let

$$\text{`}((y_k \epsilon x) \equiv ((y_k \subset z) \,.\, ((\exists w)(w \epsilon y_k) \supset ((k)!y_k \,.\, \phi(y_1, \ldots y_h)))))\text{'}$$

be abbreviated as 'Φ'. By Lemma 1(e) and D3,

$$(((w) \sim (w \epsilon y_k) \supset (y_k \subset z)) \supset (((k)!y_k \supset (\exists w)(w \epsilon y_k)) \supset (((k)!y_k \supset (y_k \subset z)) \supset (\Phi \supset ((((y_k \epsilon x) \equiv (\exists w)(w \epsilon y_k)) \supset (k)!y_k) \,.\, ((k)!y_k \supset ((y_k \epsilon x) \equiv \phi(y_1, \ldots y_h)))))))).$$

Hence, by Lemmas 2(a) and 3,

$$(((k)!y_k \supset (y_k \subset z)) \supset (\Phi \supset ((((y_k \epsilon x) \equiv (\exists w)(w \epsilon y_k)) \supset (k)!y_k) \,.\, ((k)!y_k \supset ((y_k \epsilon x) \equiv \phi(y_1, \ldots y_h)))))).$$

Hence, by D6–7,

$$((y_k^{(k)})(y_k \subset z) \supset ((y_k)\, \Phi \supset ((k) + 1!x \,.\, (y_k^{(k)})((y_k \epsilon x) \equiv \phi(y_1, \ldots y_h))))).$$

But, by Γ7, $(\exists x)(y_k)\, \Phi$. Hence

$$((y_k^{(k)})(y_k \subset z) \supset (\exists x)((k) + 1!x \,.\, (y_k^{(k)})((y_k \epsilon x) \equiv \phi(y_1, \ldots y_h)))).$$

Hence, by Lemma 4,

$$(\exists x)((k) + 1!x \,.\, (y_k^{(k)})((y_k \epsilon x) \equiv \phi(y_1, \ldots y_h))).$$

I.e.,

$$\sim(x)((k) + 1!x \supset \sim(y_k^{(k)})((y_k \epsilon x) \equiv \phi(y_1, \ldots y_h))).$$

I.e., by D7 and C1,

$$\sim(x^{(k)+1}) \sim (y_k^{(k)})((y_k^{(k)} \epsilon x^{(k)+1}) \equiv \phi(y_1, \ldots y_h)).$$

The Γ-theorem thus derived is $|\mathfrak{f}|$ if $h = k - 1$. If $h = k$, it becomes $|\mathfrak{f}|$ when 'y_h' is rewritten according to C1 as '$y_k^{(k)}$'. In either case, then, it follows from Lemma 7 that every c.g. of $\mathfrak{f}$ is a Γ-theorem, q.e.d.

THEOREM. *Every c.g. of a Δ-theorem is a Γ-theorem.*

Proof. A Δ-theorem $\mathfrak{f}$ will be said to be of *rank* 0 if it satisfies Δ1, Δ5, or Δ6. A Δ-theorem $\mathfrak{f}$ will be said to be of *rank* $n + 1$ if there are Δ-theorems $\mathfrak{p}$ and $\mathfrak{r}$, one of rank n and the other of rank n or less, such that $\mathfrak{r}$ is the result of putting $\mathfrak{p}$ for 'P' and $\mathfrak{f}$ for 'Q' in '$(P \supset Q)$'; or if there are Δ-formulae $\mathfrak{p}$ and $\mathfrak{q}$ and a Δ-theorem $\mathfrak{r}$ of rank n such that $\mathfrak{f}$ and $\mathfrak{r}$ are formed respectively from '$(P \supset (x)Q)$' and '$(P \supset Q)$' by replacing 'P' by $\mathfrak{p}$, 'Q' by $\mathfrak{q}$, and 'x' by a Δ-variable which is not free in $\mathfrak{p}$; or if there are Δ-formulae $\mathfrak{p}$ and $\mathfrak{q}$ and a Δ-theorem $\mathfrak{s}$ of rank n such that $\mathfrak{f}$ and $\mathfrak{s}$ are formed respectively from '$(P \supset Q)$' and '$(P \supset (x)Q)$' by replacing 'P' by $\mathfrak{p}$, 'Q' by $\mathfrak{q}$, and 'x' by a Δ-variable.

If we assume that every c.g. of any Δ-theorem of rank n or less is a Γ-theorem, and take $\mathfrak{f}$ as a Δ-theorem of rank $n + 1$, then Lemma 8 shows that every c.g. of $\mathfrak{f}$ is a Γ-theorem. Then, since by Lemmas 9–11 every c.g. of any Δ-theorem of rank 0 is a Γ-theorem, it follows by induction that every c.g. of any Δ-theorem of rank m is a Γ-theorem, for every natural number m. But it is clear from the above definition of rank, together with Δ1–6, that every Δ-theorem has at least one natural number as its rank. Therefore every c.g. of any Δ-theorem is a Γ-theorem, q.e.d.

VII

Logic Based on Inclusion and Abstraction

All notions of mathematical logic, as measured, e.g., by *Principia Mathematica*, can be constructed from a basis which embraces variables and just two further primitives: the familiar notions of inclusion and abstraction. Inclusion will be expressed by the usual form of notation '$(x \subset y)$', which may be read 'x is included in y.' Abstraction will be expressed by the form of notation '$x \ni$ . . .' as with Peano,[1] the blank being filled by any formula (statement or statement form); the whole may be read 'the class of all objects x such that . . .'.

A system of logic based on these primitives will be presented in this paper. The system involves the familiar theory of class types, which, for metamathematical convenience, will be recorded in the system by use of distinctive styles of variables; thus the variables 'x', 'y', and 'z', also with subscripts when further variety is needed, will take individuals as values; the variables 'x''', 'y''', and 'z''', also with subscripts, will take classes of individuals as values; the variables 'x'''', 'y'''', and 'z'''', also with subscripts, will take classes of classes of individuals as values; and so on. The metamathematical notion of *term*, covering all variables and also all expressions of

Reprinted from the *Journal of Symbolic Logic*, Volume 2, 1937. An improvement which was described in a last-minute footnote of the original paper has here been worked into the text.

[1] In the notation of *Principia Mathematica* the sign '$\ni$' is dropped, and instead a circumflex accent is placed over the initial variable; but this presents typographical difficulties.

abstraction, is now describable recursively thus: a variable is a term, and the number of accents which it bears is called its rank; and if terms of equal rank are put for 'ζ' and 'η' and a variable of rank n is put for 'α' in '$\alpha \ni (\zeta \subset \eta)$', the result is a term of rank $n + 1$. A *formula*, finally, is any result of putting terms of equal rank for 'ζ' and 'η' in '$(\zeta \subset \eta)$'.

Customarily, in logic, inclusion is thought of as applying only to classes, and as meaning that every member of the one class is a member of the other. But the above definition of formula countenances the notation of inclusion in application also to variables of rank 0, and hence calls for an interpretation of inclusion as applied to individuals. Various interpretations of this limiting case are compatible with the system which is to follow; we might interpret '$(x \subset y)$' as meaning that the individual x is spatially or temporally included in the individual y, or as meaning simply that x and y are the same individual. The latter course has the advantage of avoiding any assumption as to the nature of our individuals.[2] So far as the system is concerned, indeed, there is no need to posit individuals at all; the lowest type might be empty, so that the lowest occupied type would have the null class of individuals as sole occupant, and the variables of rank 0 might then be appropriated to this lowest occupied type. Again, the hierarchy of types might run downward infinitely, and the variables of rank 0 might be regarded as corresponding merely to the lowest logical type concerned in the context at hand. On either of these latter views, the values of variables of rank 0 would enter the inclusion relation simply as classes. These two views and the more usual one, which countenances individuals, are all suited equally to the system which is to follow.

To facilitate metamathematical discourse about the system, the letters 'α', 'β', 'γ', and 'δ' will be used to denote any variables of the system; 'ζ', 'η', and 'θ' will denote any terms; and 'τ', 'υ', 'ϕ', 'ψ', 'χ', and 'ω' will denote any formulae. When expressions denoted by these Greek letters are thought of as combined into a complex expression by '$\subset$', '$\ni$', or other signs, the whole complex expression will be referred to metamathematically by combining the Greek letters themselves in corresponding fashion and enclosing the whole in corners, '$\ulcorner$', '$\urcorner$'. Thus $\ulcorner(\zeta \subset \eta)\urcorner$ is the expression which is formed by combining the terms ζ and η, whatever they may be, by an inclusion sign and parentheses in the indicated fashion. If ζ and η are the respective terms 'x'''' and '$y'' \ni (y'' \subset z'')$', then $\ulcorner(\zeta \subset \eta)\urcorner$

[2] However, see Leonard and Goodman, 63f.

is the formula '$(x''' \subset y''\ni(y'' \subset z''))$'. In general, an expression beginning and ending in corners is to denote the expression which we obtain, from the expression between the corners, by replacing all Greek letters by the expressions which those Greek letters are intended to denote. The corners may thus be viewed as "quasi-quotes"; but they must not be confused with ordinary quotation marks. For example, $\ulcorner(\zeta \subset \eta)\urcorner$ is a certain unknown expression; it is not wholly specified until the terms ζ and η are specified, and it becomes a formula if these are specified as of equal rank; whereas '$(\zeta \subset \eta)$' is the specific non-formula depicted between the quotes, and containing the sixth and seventh letters of the Greek alphabet.

α will be said to *cover* a given occurrence of β in ϕ (or in ζ) if that occurrence lies within a context of the form $\ulcorner\alpha\ni\psi\urcorner$ within ϕ (or ζ). An occurrence of α in ϕ (or in ζ) is *bound* in ϕ (or in ζ) if it is covered by α in ϕ (or in ζ); otherwise *free*. A variable is said to be free in ϕ (or in ζ) if it has a free occurrence in ϕ (or in ζ). Replacement of every free occurrence of α in ϕ by ζ is called *substitution* of ζ for α in ϕ, provided that no variable which is free in ζ covers a free occurrence of α in ϕ.

We turn now to nine definitions, building up from the primitive notions of inclusion and abstraction. The definitions are to be regarded as conventions of notational abbreviation extraneous to the formal system. The first introduces the material conditional:

D1. $\ulcorner(\phi \supset \psi)\urcorner$ *for* $\ulcorner(\alpha\ni\phi \subset \beta\ni\psi)\urcorner$, *where* α *is alphabetically the first variable of rank* 0 *which is not free in* ϕ, *and* β *is similarly related to* ψ.

The conformity of this definition to the usual sense of the sign '$\supset$' rests on the fact that, where α is not free in ϕ nor β in ψ, the respective classes denoted by $\ulcorner\alpha\ni\phi\urcorner$ and $\ulcorner\beta\ni\psi\urcorner$ are universal or null according as ϕ and ψ are true or false.[3] So far as the meaning is concerned, α and β might be chosen as any variables of equal rank not free respectively in ϕ or ψ; to make the definitional abbreviation unambiguous notationally as well as interpretationally, however, the choice of α and β is specified uniquely in D1. For purposes of D1 we may fix the alphabetical order of variables of rank 0 arbitrarily as 'x', 'y', 'z', 'x_1', 'y_1', 'z_1', 'x_2', . . . ; and for purposes of the subsequent definition D8 we may order the variables of each higher rank correspondingly.

The next definition introduces universal quantification:

[3] See my *System of Logistic*, 37–38, 45.

D2. $\ulcorner(\alpha)\phi\urcorner$ *for* $\ulcorner(\alpha \ni (\phi \supset \phi) \subset \alpha \ni \phi)\urcorner$.

The next introduces denial, utilizing the falsity of '$(x')(y')(x' \subset y')$':

D3. $\ulcorner{\sim}\phi\urcorner$ *for* $\ulcorner(\phi \supset (x')(y')(x' \subset y'))\urcorner$.

The next three definitions are familiar:

D4. $\ulcorner(\phi \,.\, \psi)\urcorner$ *for* $\ulcorner{\sim}(\phi \supset {\sim}\psi)\urcorner$.

D5. $\ulcorner(\phi \equiv \psi)\urcorner$ *for* $\ulcorner((\phi \supset \psi) \,.\, (\psi \supset \phi))\urcorner$.

D6. $\ulcorner(\exists\alpha)\phi\urcorner$ *for* $\ulcorner{\sim}(\alpha){\sim}\phi\urcorner$.

The remaining definitions introduce identity, unit classes, and membership:

D7. $\ulcorner(\zeta = \eta)\urcorner$ *for* $\ulcorner((\zeta \subset \eta) \,.\, (\eta \subset \zeta))\urcorner$.

D8. $\ulcorner\iota\zeta\urcorner$ *for* $\ulcorner\alpha \ni (\alpha = \zeta)\urcorner$, *where* α *is alphabetically the first variable of the rank of* ζ *which is not free in* ζ.

D9. $\ulcorner(\zeta \in \eta)\urcorner$ *for* $\ulcorner(\iota\zeta \subset \eta)\urcorner$.

The definitions D1, D4, and D5 are of course adopted for all formulae ϕ and ψ; D3 for every formula ϕ; D2 and D6 for every formula ϕ and every variable α; D8 for every term ζ; and D7 and D9 for all terms ζ and η. Similar generality is intended for the rules and "metatheorems" which will follow. However, D7 is useful only where η is of the same rank as ζ, and D9 only where η is of next higher rank than ζ, since otherwise the expressions abbreviated are not formulae.

Definition of all further notions of mathematical logic can now proceed along familiar lines. Relations, for example, can be introduced in terms of classes by Wiener's method or Kuratowski's.[4]

Rules R1–5 will next be presented which generate the formal theorems of the system. In stating these rules the sign '$\vdash$' will be used to express the metamathematical property of being a theorem of the system—a property which the rules R1–5 themselves recursively define. Statement of the rules will be facilitated further by sometimes attaching exponents to first occurrences of Greek letters to indicate the relative ranks of the terms denoted. Thus R1, '$\vdash\ulcorner((\alpha^n \subset \beta^n) \supset ((\beta \subset \gamma^n) \supset (\alpha \subset \gamma)))\urcorner$,' tells us that, where α, β, and γ are any variables of equal rank (say n), $\ulcorner((\alpha \subset \beta) \supset ((\beta \subset \gamma) \supset (\alpha \subset \gamma)))\urcorner$ is a theorem (better, an abbreviation under D1 of a theorem) of the system. Finally, for perspicuity most

[4] See next paper.

parentheses will be suppressed hereafter and dots will be used for punctuation in familiar fashion.

R1. $\vdash \ulcorner \alpha^n \subset \beta^n . \supset : \beta \subset \gamma^n . \supset . \alpha \subset \gamma \urcorner$.

R2. $\vdash \ulcorner \hat{\alpha}^n (\alpha \in \gamma^{n+1} . \supset \phi) \subset \hat{\alpha} (\alpha \in \beta^{n+1} . \supset . \alpha \in \gamma) . \supset . \beta \subset \gamma \urcorner$.

R3. *If* $\vdash \phi$ *then* $\vdash \ulcorner \zeta^{n+1} \subset \hat{\alpha}^n \phi \urcorner$.

R4. *If* $\vdash \phi$ *and* $\vdash \ulcorner \phi \supset \psi \urcorner$ *then* $\vdash \psi$.

R5.[5] *If* $\vdash \phi$, *and* ψ *is formed from* ϕ *by replacing an occurrence of* $\ulcorner \zeta \in \hat{\alpha} \chi \urcorner$ *by the result (if any) of substituting* ζ *for* α *in* χ, *then* $\vdash \psi$.

By way of establishing the adequacy of these rules, it will be proved that they provide all the theorems of Tarski's system.[6] Tarski's primitives are the four notions defined in D1–3 and D9 above, together with variables like those of the present system. His rules are as follows (supposing D4–6 carried over):

T1. $\vdash \ulcorner \phi \supset \psi . \supset : \psi \supset \chi . \supset . \phi \supset \chi \urcorner$.

T2. $\vdash \ulcorner \sim \phi \supset \phi . \supset \phi \urcorner$.

T3. $\vdash \ulcorner \phi \supset . \sim \phi \supset \psi \urcorner$.

T4. $\vdash \ulcorner (\gamma^n)(\gamma \in \alpha^{n+1} . \equiv . \gamma \in \beta^{n+1}) . \supset . (\delta^{n+2})(\alpha \in \delta . \supset . \beta \in \delta) \urcorner$.

T5. *If* α^{n+1} *is not free in* ϕ, $\vdash \ulcorner (\exists \alpha)(\beta^n)(\beta \in \alpha . \equiv \phi) \urcorner$.

T6. *If* $\vdash \ulcorner \phi \supset (\alpha)\psi \urcorner$ *then* $\vdash \ulcorner \phi \supset \psi \urcorner$.

T7. *If* $\vdash \ulcorner \phi \supset \psi \urcorner$, *and* α *is not free in* ϕ, *then* $\vdash \ulcorner \phi \supset (\alpha)\psi \urcorner$.

T8. *If* $\vdash \phi$, *and* ψ *results from substituting* β^n *for* α^n *in* ϕ, *then* $\vdash \psi$.

T9. *If* $\vdash \phi$ *and* $\vdash \ulcorner \phi \supset \psi \urcorner$ *then* $\vdash \psi$.

A series of *metatheorems* M1–29, metamathematical theorems about the theorems provided by R1–5, will now be proved. This will establish the adequacy of the present system to Tarski's; for T1–8 will all reappear among M1–29, and T9 is already at hand as R4.

M1 (cf. T8). *If* $\vdash \phi$, *and* ψ *results from substituting* ζ^n *for* α^n *in* ϕ, *then* $\vdash \psi$.

[5] R3 and R5 answer to the rules of *subsumption* and *concretion* used in my *System of Logistic* (43, 48). The rule of concretion was used by Whitehead and Russell (*20.3) and by Frege, 1893, 52.

[6] See Tarski, 1933, 97–103, especially Definitions 7 and 9.

Proof. By 1st hp and R3 (and D9), $\vdash\ulcorner\zeta \in \alpha \ni \phi\urcorner$; ∴, by 2d hp and R5, $\vdash\psi$.

M2. $\vdash\ulcorner\zeta^n \subset \eta^n .\supset: \eta \subset \theta^n .\supset. \zeta \subset \theta\urcorner$.

Proof from R1 by repeated use of M1.

M3. *If* α^n *is free in neither* ζ^{n+1} *nor* η^{n+1},
$\vdash\ulcorner\alpha \ni(\alpha \in \eta .\supset \phi) \subset \alpha \ni(\alpha \in \zeta .\supset. \alpha \in \eta).\supset. \zeta \subset \eta\urcorner$.

Proof similar from R2.

M4 (=T1). $\vdash\ulcorner\phi \supset \psi .\supset: \psi \supset \chi .\supset. \phi \supset \chi\urcorner$.

Proof: M2 (and D1).

M5. $\vdash\ulcorner\phi \supset: \phi \supset \psi .\supset \psi\urcorner$.

Proof. Let α and β be as in D1. By M2 (and D1, D9),

$$\vdash\ulcorner\alpha \in \alpha \ni \phi .\supset: \phi \supset \psi .\supset. \alpha \in \beta \ni \psi\urcorner.$$

M5 then follows, by R5.

M6. $\vdash\ulcorner\phi \supset: \phi \supset \phi .\supset \phi\urcorner$. *Proof:* M5.

M7. $\vdash\ulcorner\phi \supset. \psi \supset \chi :\supset: \psi \supset. \phi \supset \chi\urcorner$.

M8. $\vdash\ulcorner\phi \supset. \psi \supset \chi :\supset:. \chi \supset \omega .\supset: \phi \supset. \psi \supset \omega\urcorner$.

M9. $\vdash\ulcorner\phi \supset \psi .\supset:. \psi \supset \chi .\supset: \chi \supset \omega .\supset. \phi \supset \omega\urcorner$.

Proofs of M7–9, from M4–5 (and R4), are analogous to the proofs of 2·7, 2·87, and 2·94 from 2·1 and 2·6 in my *System of Logistic* (72–74).

M10. $\vdash\ulcorner\phi \supset \phi\urcorner$.

Proof. By M7, $\vdash\ulcorner[\text{M6}] \supset$
$\vdash\ulcorner\phi \supset \phi .\supset. \phi \supset \phi\urcorner$. (1)

Let α be as in D1. By M3 (and D1),

$$\vdash\ulcorner\alpha \ni(\alpha \in \alpha \ni \phi .\supset \phi) \subset \alpha \ni(\alpha \in \alpha \ni \phi .\supset. \alpha \in \alpha \ni \phi) .\supset. \phi \supset \phi\urcorner;$$

∴, by R5 (and D1), $\vdash\ulcorner[(1)] \supset [\text{M10}]\urcorner$.

The above proof is abbreviated in ways which will be usual hereafter. '[M6]' is short for the whole expression '$\phi \supset: \phi \supset \phi .\supset \phi$' which stands between corners in the metatheorem M6. '[M10]' and '[(1)]' are analogous. The end of the proof involves tacit use of R4 in obvious fashion; similarly the ends of the proofs of M14 and

M18, below, involve two and three applications of R4. When R4 is used in a non-terminal step of a proof, it is indicated by renewal of the signs '$\vdash\ulcorner$' without closure of the preceding line; thus the step leading to (1) in the above proof amounts to the following:

By M7, $\vdash\ulcorner[\text{M6}] \supset : \phi \supset \phi . \supset . \phi \supset \phi\urcorner$;

$\therefore$, by M6 and R4, $\vdash\ulcorner\phi \supset \phi . \supset . \phi \supset \phi\urcorner$. (1)

Similarly the step leading to (3) in the proof of M18 amounts to the following:

By M8, $\vdash\ulcorner[\text{M6}] \supset ::. [\text{M6}] \supset :: \phi \supset :. \phi \supset \phi . \supset : \phi \supset \phi . \supset \phi\urcorner$;

$\therefore$, by M6 and R4, $\vdash\ulcorner[\text{M6}] \supset :: \phi \supset :. \phi \supset \phi . \supset : \phi \supset \phi . \supset \phi\urcorner$;

$\therefore$, by M6 and R4, $\vdash\ulcorner\phi \supset :. \phi \supset \phi . \supset : \phi \supset \phi . \supset \phi\urcorner$. (3)

M11. $\vdash\ulcorner\eta^n \subset \theta^n . \supset : \zeta^n \subset \eta . \supset . \zeta \subset \theta\urcorner$.

Proof: By M7, $\vdash\ulcorner[\text{M2}] \supset [\text{M11}]\urcorner$.

M12. $\vdash\ulcorner(\alpha^n)\phi . \supset . \zeta^{n+1} \subset \alpha\ni\phi\urcorner$.

Proof. By M10 and R3, $\vdash\ulcorner\zeta \subset \alpha\ni(\phi \supset \phi)\urcorner$. (1)

By M2 (and D2), $\vdash\ulcorner[(1)] \supset [\text{M12}]\urcorner$.

M13. $\vdash\ulcorner(\alpha^n)\phi . \supset . \zeta^n \epsilon\, \alpha\ni\phi\urcorner$. *Proof:* M12 (and D9).

M14. *If* α^n *is free in neither* ζ^{n+1} *nor* η^{n+1},
$\vdash\ulcorner(\alpha)(\alpha \epsilon \zeta . \supset . \alpha \epsilon \eta) . \supset . \zeta \subset \eta\urcorner$.

Proof. By M12, $\vdash\ulcorner(\alpha)(\alpha \epsilon \zeta . \supset . \alpha \epsilon \eta) . \supset . \alpha\ni(\alpha \epsilon \eta . \supset \phi) \subset \alpha\ni(\alpha \epsilon \zeta . \supset . \alpha \epsilon \eta)\urcorner$. (1)

By M4, $\vdash\ulcorner[(1)] \supset . [\text{M3}] \supset [\text{M14}]\urcorner$.

M15. *If* $\vdash\phi$ *then* $\vdash\ulcorner(\alpha)\phi\urcorner$. *Proof:* R3 (and D2).

M16. *If* $\vdash\ulcorner\phi \supset \psi\urcorner$ *then* $\vdash\ulcorner(\alpha)\phi . \supset . (\alpha)\psi\urcorner$.

Proof. By hp and M15, $\vdash\ulcorner(\alpha)(\phi \supset \psi)\urcorner$. (1)

By M14, $\vdash\ulcorner(\alpha)(\alpha \epsilon \alpha\ni\phi . \supset . \alpha \epsilon \alpha\ni\psi) . \supset . \alpha\ni\phi \subset \alpha\ni\psi\urcorner$;

$\therefore$, by R5, $\vdash\ulcorner[(1)] \supset$
$\vdash\ulcorner\alpha\ni\phi \subset \alpha\ni\psi\urcorner$. (2)

By M12, $\vdash\ulcorner(\alpha)\phi . \supset . \alpha\ni(\psi \supset \psi) \subset \alpha\ni\phi\urcorner$. (3)

By M11 (and D2), $\vdash\ulcorner[(2)] \supset$
$\vdash\ulcorner\alpha\ni(\psi \supset \psi) \subset \alpha\ni\phi . \supset . (\alpha)\psi\urcorner$. (4)

By M4, $\vdash\ulcorner[(3)] \supset. [(4)] \supset [\text{ths}]\urcorner$.

Here 'hp' and 'ths' refer respectively to the hypothesis '$\vdash\ulcorner\phi \supset \psi\urcorner$' and the thesis '$\vdash\ulcorner(\alpha)\phi .\supset. (\alpha)\psi\urcorner$' of the metatheorem which is being proved. Thus '[ths]' here is short for '$(\alpha)\phi .\supset. (\alpha)\psi$'.

M17 (=T6). *If* $\vdash\ulcorner\phi \supset (\alpha)\psi\urcorner$ *then* $\vdash\ulcorner\phi \supset \psi\urcorner$.

Proof. By M13, $\vdash\ulcorner(\alpha)\psi .\supset. \alpha \in \alpha з\psi\urcorner$;

∴, by R5, $\vdash\ulcorner(\alpha)\psi .\supset \psi\urcorner$. (1)

By M4, $\vdash\ulcorner[\text{hp}] \supset. [(1)] \supset [\text{ths}]\urcorner$.

M18 (=T7). *If* $\vdash\ulcorner\phi \supset \psi\urcorner$, *and* α *is not free in* ϕ, *then* $\vdash\ulcorner\phi \supset (\alpha)\psi\urcorner$.

Proof. Let β be alphabetically the first variable of rank 0 which is not free in ϕ. By M3 (and D2),

$$\vdash\ulcorner\beta з(\beta \in \alpha з\phi .\supset \phi) \subset \beta з(\beta \in \alpha з(\phi \supset \phi) .\supset. \beta \in \alpha з\phi) .\supset. (\alpha)\phi\urcorner;$$

∴, by 2d hp and R5, $\vdash\ulcorner\beta з(\phi \supset \phi) \subset \beta з(\phi \supset \phi .\supset \phi) .\supset. (\alpha)\phi\urcorner$;

i.e. (by D1), $\vdash\ulcorner\phi \supset \phi .\supset: \phi \supset \phi .\supset \phi .:\supset. (\alpha)\phi\urcorner$. (1)

By 1st hp and M16, $\vdash\ulcorner(\alpha)\phi .\supset. (\alpha)\psi\urcorner$. (2)

By M8, $\vdash\ulcorner[\text{M6}] \supset. [\text{M6}] \supset \vdash\ulcorner\phi \supset:. \phi \supset \phi .\supset: \phi \supset \phi .\supset \phi\urcorner$. (3)

By M9, $\vdash\ulcorner[(3)] \supset: [(1)] \supset. [(2)] \supset [\text{ths}]\urcorner$.

M19 (=T2). $\vdash\ulcorner\sim\phi \supset \phi .\supset \phi\urcorner$.

Proof. Let α be as in D1. By M3 (and D2–3),

$$\vdash\ulcorner\alpha з\sim(\alpha \in \alpha з\phi) \subset \alpha з(\alpha \in \alpha з(\phi \supset \phi) .\supset. \alpha \in \alpha з\phi) .\supset. (\alpha)\phi\urcorner;$$

∴, by R5 (and D1), $\vdash\ulcorner\sim\phi .\supset: \phi \supset \phi .\supset \phi .:\supset. (\alpha)\phi\urcorner$;

∴, by M17, $\vdash\ulcorner\sim\phi .\supset: \phi \supset \phi .\supset \phi .:\supset \phi\urcorner$. (1)

By M11 (and D1), $\vdash\ulcorner[\text{M6}] \supset \vdash\ulcorner\sim\phi \supset \phi .\supset:. \sim\phi \supset: \phi \supset \phi .\supset \phi\urcorner$. (2)

By M4, $\vdash\ulcorner[(2)] \supset. [(1)] \supset [\text{M19}]\urcorner$.

M20 (=T3). $\vdash\ulcorner\phi \supset. \sim\phi \supset \psi\urcorner$.

Proof. By M5 (and D3), $\vdash \ulcorner \phi \supset . \sim\phi \supset (x')(y')(x' \subset y')\urcorner$. (1)

By M13, $\vdash$ '$(x')(y')(x' \subset y') . \supset . \iota z \epsilon x' \ni (y')(x' \subset y')$';

∴, by R5 (and D9), $\vdash$ '$(x')(y')(x' \subset y') . \supset . (y')(z \epsilon y')$'. (2)

By M13, $\vdash \ulcorner (y')(z \epsilon y') . \supset . z \ni \psi \epsilon y' \ni (z \epsilon y')\urcorner$;

∴, by R5, $\vdash \ulcorner (y')(z \epsilon y') . \supset . z \epsilon z \ni \psi \urcorner$;

∴, by R5, $\vdash \ulcorner (y')(z \epsilon y') . \supset \psi \urcorner$. (3)

By M4, $\vdash \ulcorner [(2)] \supset . [(3)] \supset$
$\vdash \ulcorner (x')(y')(x' \supset y') . \supset \psi \urcorner$. (4)

By M8, $\vdash \ulcorner [(1)] \supset . [(4)] \supset [\text{M20}]\urcorner$.

M21. $\vdash \ulcorner \phi \supset \sim\psi . \supset . \psi \supset \sim\phi \urcorner$.

M22. $\vdash \ulcorner \phi \equiv \phi \urcorner$.

M23. $\vdash \ulcorner \phi \equiv \psi . \supset . \phi \supset \psi \urcorner$.

M24. $\vdash \ulcorner \phi \equiv \psi . \supset . \psi \supset \phi \urcorner$.

M25. $\vdash \ulcorner \phi \supset \psi . \supset :. \phi \supset \chi . \supset : \phi \supset . \psi . \chi \urcorner$.

M26. $\vdash \ulcorner \tau \supset . \upsilon \supset \phi : \supset :: \psi \supset . \chi \supset \omega : \supset :. \tau . \psi . \supset : \chi . \upsilon . \supset . \omega . \phi \urcorner$.

Proofs of M21–26 may be omitted, for it is known that all formulae which are tautological, or valid by virtue solely of their structure in terms of the truth functions, are provided as theorems by R4, M4, M19, and M20.[7]

M27 (=T5). *If* α^{n+1} *is not free in* ϕ, $\vdash \ulcorner (\exists\alpha)(\beta^n)(\beta \epsilon \alpha . \equiv \phi)\urcorner$.

Proof. By M13,
$\vdash \ulcorner (\alpha) \sim (\beta)(\beta \epsilon \alpha . \equiv \phi) . \supset . \beta \ni \phi \epsilon \alpha \ni \sim (\beta)(\beta \epsilon \alpha . \equiv \phi)\urcorner$;

∴, by hp and R5,
$\vdash \ulcorner (\alpha) \sim (\beta)(\beta \epsilon \alpha . \equiv \phi) . \supset . \sim (\beta)(\beta \epsilon \beta \ni \phi . \equiv \phi)\urcorner$;

∴, by R5, $\vdash \ulcorner (\alpha) \sim (\beta)(\beta \epsilon \alpha . \equiv \phi) . \supset . \sim(\beta)(\phi \equiv \phi)\urcorner$. (1)

By M22 and M15, $\vdash \ulcorner (\beta)(\phi \equiv \phi)\urcorner$. (2)

By M21 (and D6), $\vdash \ulcorner [(1)] \supset . [(2)] \supset [\text{M27}]\urcorner$.

[7] See §2 of preceding paper.

M28. $\vdash \ulcorner \zeta^n = \eta^n \,.\supset: \zeta \in \theta^{n+1} \,.\supset.\, \eta \in \theta \urcorner$.

Proof. Let α^n be free in neither ζ nor η. By M2,

$$\vdash \ulcorner \zeta \subset \eta \,.\supset: \eta \subset \alpha \,.\supset.\, \zeta \subset \alpha \urcorner. \quad (1)$$

By M11, $\vdash \ulcorner \eta \subset \zeta \,.\supset: \alpha \subset \eta \,.\supset.\, \alpha \subset \zeta \urcorner$. (2)

By M26 (and D7), $\vdash \ulcorner [(1)] \supset. [(2)] \supset$
$\vdash \ulcorner \zeta = \eta \,.\supset: \alpha = \eta \,.\supset.\, \alpha = \zeta \urcorner$;

∴, by M18, $\vdash \ulcorner \zeta = \eta \,.\supset.\, (\alpha)(\alpha = \eta \,.\supset.\, \alpha = \zeta) \urcorner$. (3)

By M14, $\vdash \ulcorner (\alpha)(\alpha \in \iota\eta \,.\supset.\, \alpha \in \iota\zeta) \,.\supset.\, \iota\eta \subset \iota\zeta \urcorner$;

∴, by R5 (and D8), $\vdash \ulcorner (\alpha)(\alpha = \eta \,.\supset.\, \alpha = \zeta) \,.\supset.\, \iota\eta \subset \iota\zeta \urcorner$. (4)

By M2 (and D9), $\vdash \ulcorner \iota\eta \subset \iota\zeta .\supset: \zeta \in \theta \,.\supset.\, \eta \in \theta \urcorner$. (5)

By M9, $\vdash \ulcorner [(3)] \supset: [(4)] \supset. [(5)] \supset [\text{M28}] \urcorner$.

M29 (=T4). $\vdash \ulcorner (\gamma^n)(\gamma \in \alpha^{n+1} \,.\equiv.\, \gamma \in \beta^{n+1}) \,.\supset.$
$(\delta^{n+2})(\alpha \in \delta \,.\supset.\, \beta \in \delta) \urcorner$.

Proof. By M23, $\vdash \ulcorner \gamma \in \alpha \,.\equiv.\, \gamma \in \beta :\supset: \gamma \in \alpha \,.\supset.\, \gamma \in \beta \urcorner$;

∴, by M16, $\vdash \ulcorner (\gamma)(\gamma \in \alpha \,.\equiv.\, \gamma \in \beta) \,.\supset.\, (\gamma)(\gamma \in \alpha \,.\supset.\, \gamma \in \beta) \urcorner$. (1)

By M14, $\vdash \ulcorner (\gamma)(\gamma \in \alpha \,.\supset.\, \gamma \in \beta) \,.\supset.\, \alpha \subset \beta \urcorner$. (2)

By M4, $\vdash \ulcorner [(1)] \supset. [(2)] \supset$
$\vdash \ulcorner (\gamma)(\gamma \in \alpha \,.\equiv.\, \gamma \in \beta) \,.\supset.\, \alpha \subset \beta \urcorner$. (3)

Similarly, using M24 instead of M23,

$$\vdash \ulcorner (\gamma)(\gamma \in \alpha \,.\equiv.\, \gamma \in \beta) \,.\supset.\, \beta \subset \alpha \urcorner. \quad (4)$$

By M25 (and D7), $\vdash \ulcorner [(3)] \supset. [(4)] \supset$
$\vdash \ulcorner (\gamma)(\gamma \in \alpha \,.\equiv.\, \gamma \in \beta) \,.\supset.\, \alpha = \beta \urcorner$. (5)

By M28, $\vdash \ulcorner \alpha = \beta \,.\supset: \alpha \in \delta \,.\supset.\, \beta \in \delta \urcorner$;

∴, by M18, $\vdash \ulcorner \alpha = \beta \,.\supset.\, (\delta)(\alpha \in \delta \,.\supset.\, \beta \in \delta) \urcorner$. (6)

By M4, $\vdash \ulcorner [(5)] \supset. [(6)] \supset [\text{M29}] \urcorner$.

VIII

On Ordered Pairs and Relations

Wiener, in 1914, reduced the theory of relations to that of classes by construing relations as classes of ordered pairs and defining the ordered pair in turn on the basis of class theory alone. The definition, as improved by Kuratowski, identifies the ordered pair $x;y$ with $\iota x \cup \iota(\iota x \cup \iota y)$.

In terms of Russell's theory of types, $x;y$ in the above sense is two types higher than x and y. Even when we abandon Russell's theory of fixed types of objects in favor of a theory of stratified formulae,[1] there is still significance in saying that '$x;y$' is of type 2 relative to 'x' and 'y'—meaning that a test of the stratification of any context involves assigning a higher number by 2 to '$x;y$' than to 'x' and 'y'.

In 1941, I proposed a definition of the ordered pair which reduced the type difference to 1, construing $x;y$ as the class of unit subclasses of x and complements of units subclasses of y.[2] Goodman then presented a more complicated definition in which my reduction of type was coupled with another advantage, that of im-

---

This paper has been formed by telescoping two notes, "On ordered pairs" and "On relations as coextensive with classes," which appeared in the *Journal of Symbolic Logic,* Volumes 10 and 11, 1945 and 1946.

[1] This is done in my "New foundations" (see next paper) and "On the theory of types," in Hailperin's "A set of axioms for logic," and, with ill consequences, in my *Mathematical Logic* (1940; see paper after next).

[2] See Goodman's footnote 5. Note that thc concluding twelve words of that footnote are in error.

mediate extensibility beyond ordered pairs to the general case of a sequence of any finite length.

The purpose of the present note is to show that the type difference can be reduced to 0; i.e., that '$x;y$' can be so defined that it turns out to be of the *same* type as 'x' and 'y'. Thereupon sequences of any finite length $x;y;z;w; \ldots$ can be obtained by iteration as $x;(y;(z;(w; \ldots)))$ without increase of type. Relations of all degrees thus come to be of the same type, relatively to the objects which they relate, as classes of those objects. But the definition will be of narrowly theoretical interest only, being too inelegant to aspire to adoption as a standard version of the ordered pair.

For general applicability, this new definition will depend on the assumption that all entities are classes—an assumption upon which my previous definition and Goodman's likewise depended. This assumption is fulfilled if individuals are identified with their unit classes; i.e., if membership in individuals is explained as identity.[3] This is compatible with Russell's theory of types, modified to the extent of accrediting all individuals to all types.[4]

The rationale of the new definition is as follows. I define a certain notion 'θz' in such a way as to provide that

(i) 'θz' is like 'z' in type,
(ii) there is no object z for which $0 \in \theta z$,
(iii) given θz we can determine z uniquely.

This done, I take $x;y$ as the class whose members comprise the correspondents θz of the several members z of x, together with the "tagged" correspondents $\theta z \cup \iota 0$ of the several members z of y. I.e.,

$$x;y = \hat{w}(\exists z)(z \in x \,.\, w = \theta z \,.\!\vee\!.\, z \in y \,.\, w = \theta z \cup \iota 0).$$

This will meet the formal requirement which any satisfactory definition of the ordered pair must meet, namely that x and y each be uniquely determined by $x;y$. For, given $x;y$, in view of (ii) we can spot the correspondents of members of x as those members w of $x;y$ such that $\sim 0 \in w$; and given these we can in turn get x, in view of (iii). Similarly we can get y from the other members of $x;y$, after dropping 0 from each. In brief,

$$x = \hat{z}(\theta z \in x;y), \qquad y = \hat{z}(\theta z \cup \iota 0 \in x;y).$$

So it remains only to define 'θz'. We can realize (i)–(iii) by con-

[3] This is done in "New foundations," 71, and *Mathematical Logic*, 122, 135.
[4] See Goodman, 151.

struing θz as formed from z by adding 1 to all natural numbers belonging to z, leaving other members of z unchanged. I.e.,

$$\theta z = \hat{u}(\exists v)(v \in z : \sim v \in \mathrm{Nn} \,.\, u = v \,.\vee.\, v \in \mathrm{Nn} \,.\, u = \mathrm{S}v)$$

where Nn is the class of natural numbers and Sv is the successor of v. Clearly this version of 'θz' fulfills (i). Also it fulfills (ii), since $0 \in \mathrm{Nn}$ and $(v)(0 \neq \mathrm{S}v)$. Also it fulfills (iii); for,

$$z = \hat{v}(\sim v \in \mathrm{Nn} \,.\, v \in \theta z \,.\vee.\, v \in \mathrm{Nn} \,.\, \mathrm{S}v \in \theta z).$$

The arithmetical notations used above must of course be defined without presupposing the theory of relations, and thereby the notion of ordered pair, if we are to avoid circularity. But this can be done in familiar fashion:

$$0 = \iota\Lambda,$$

$$\mathrm{S}v = \hat{x}(\exists y)(y \in x \,.\, x \cap \overline{\iota y} \in v),$$

$$\mathrm{Nn} = \hat{x}(y)(0 \in y \,.\, (z)(z \in y \,.\supset.\, \mathrm{S}z \in y) \,.\supset.\, x \in y).$$

The special advantage claimed for this definition of the ordered pair, over the simpler alternatives due to Wiener and others, was that it causes $x;y$ to be of the same logical type as x and y. The definition has also the following further advantage: *it makes everything an ordered pair.* Any object a whatever becomes identical with the ordered pair

$$\hat{z}(\theta z \in a);\ \hat{z}(\theta z \cup \iota 0 \in a).$$

Every class accordingly comes to be a class of ordered pairs, i.e., a relation. Indeed, everything comes to be at once an ordered pair, a class, and a relation. The terms 'ordered pair', 'class', and 'relation' fuse and become valueless as designations of categories, because all-embracing; but they retain importance still as relative terms—thus an object a is in general an ordered pair *of* certain objects b and c, a class *of* different objects d, e, f, . . . , and a relation *of* different objects still.

There results a notable simplification in the relationship between the calculus of relations and the calculus of classes. So long as there were objects which were not ordered pairs, the universal relation (class of all ordered pairs) had to be distinguished from the universal class V. Likewise the relational complement of a relation x (viz. the class of all ordered pairs foreign to x) had to be distinguished from the classial complement $\bar{x}$. These distinctions were made in *Principia Mathematica* (Vol. 1, 213–215), and in my *Mathematical Logic* (205–209), by applying a dot to the relational analogue. But when everything becomes an ordered pair, these distinctions drop out. What had been a relational counterpart of the calculus of classes becomes identical with the calculus of classes; for relations and classes come to be one and the same thing.

Simplification results also in connection with such further relational concepts as converse, relative product, and ancestral. So long as there were objects which were not ordered pairs, the principles

$$x = \breve{\breve{x}}, \qquad x \subset y \,.\!\equiv.\, \breve{x} \subset \breve{y}, \qquad x = x \mid \mathrm{I}, \qquad x \subset {}^{*}x$$

(for example) held only under the hypothesis that x is a relation. Or, what comes to the same thing, they held only when modified by restricting the class x, at its first mention in each of the four principles, to its *relational part*.[5] But when everything comes to be an ordered pair, these four principles and all others like them become valid without restriction. The notion of relational part drops out altogether, for the relational part of a class comes to be the class itself.

[5] I.e., the class of all ordered pairs belonging to x. It is expressed in *Mathematical Logic* by applying a dot.

IX

On ω-Inconsistency and a So-called Axiom of Infinity

The purpose of the present paper[1] is to dispel such mystery as may be traceable to use of the ill-chosen term 'ω-inconsistency' and to a certain application of the term 'axiom of infinity'. The application of 'axiom of infinity' which I have in mind is made by Rosser in his penetrating studies of the system of my "New foundations." Let me begin with a synopsis of that system, which I shall call NF.

NF assumes as primitive just the membership connective 'ϵ', the truth functions, and quantification over a single style of variables 'x', 'y', etc., without type distinctions. The axioms, superimposed on standard quantification theory, comprise the axiom of extensionality '$(x)(x \epsilon y . \equiv . x \epsilon z) . y \epsilon w . \supset . z \epsilon w$' and the axioms of abstraction, these latter being all sentences of the form '$(\exists y)(x)(x \epsilon y . \equiv Fx)$' in which the sentence supplanting 'Fx' is stratified (i.e., adaptable to type theory by some assignment of types to variables).

Identity is defined in NF in a familiar way, and then singular description is defined contextually by essentially Russell's method. Class abstraction, next, is defined by the schema:

$$\hat{x}Fx =_{\text{df}} (\imath y)(x)(x \epsilon y . \equiv Fx),$$

and ιx, V, and Λ are then of course defined as $\hat{y}(y = x)$, $\hat{x}(x = x)$,

This paper, first drafted in May 1951, went, in January 1952, to the *Journal of Symbolic Logic*, from which it is here reprinted (Volume 18, 1953).

[1] I gratefully acknowledge Rosser's helpful criticism of earlier drafts.

and $\hat{x}(x \neq x)$. 0 and successor (Sx) are defined in Frege's way, as $\iota\Lambda$ and $\hat{y}(\exists z)(z \in y \,.\, \hat{w}(w \in y \,.\, w \neq z) \in x)$.

Existence of each of the classes Λ, $\iota\Lambda$, $\iota\iota\Lambda$, etc., is provided by the axioms of abstraction, and the distinctness of each from each is also readily proved; so we are assured that any model of NF must be infinite. Moreover some of the classes provided in NF must individually be infinite; notably V, which contains everything.

But how is the existence of infinite classes, or say the infinity of V, to be expressed within NF? A natural suggestion is '$(x)(x \in \text{Nn} \,.\supset.\, \text{V} \,\bar{\in}\, x)$', where Nn is the class of all natural numbers. Nn itself can be defined, it would seem, by Frege's method as

(1) $$\hat{x}(y)(0 \in y \,.\, (z)(z \in y \,.\supset.\, \text{S}z \in y) \,.\supset.\, x \in y),$$

and its existence is assured by the axioms of abstraction. A shorter formula which is easily proved equivalent to '$(x)(x \in \text{Nn} \,.\supset.\, \text{V} \,\bar{\in}\, x)$' is '$\Lambda \,\bar{\in}\, \text{Nn}$',[2] so Rosser has called '$\Lambda \,\bar{\in}\, \text{Nn}$' the *axiom of infinity* for NF. It seems odd that no way of proving it in NF has been found,[3] despite the apparent fact, argued above, of its intuitive truth for NF. Is it possible that a finitude axiom '$\Lambda \in \text{Nn}$' is compatible with NF despite the obvious inadequacy of a finite model?

This seeming paradox may, before we resolve it, be pressed further. It is easy in NF to prove each of the theorems '$\Lambda \neq 0$', '$\Lambda \neq 1$', '$\Lambda \neq 2$', etc., individually. Yet, no way having been found of proving '$\Lambda \,\bar{\in}\, \text{Nn}$', it is conceivable that '$\Lambda \in \text{Nn}$' can be added without formal contradiction. The resulting system exhibits what, following Gödel (1931), has come to be called *ω-inconsistency;* that is to say, each of 0, 1, 2, . . . can be proved to fulfill a certain condition (in this case non-nullity), and yet it can be proved (in '$\Lambda \in \text{Nn}$') that some natural number violates the condition. Such ω-inconsistency does not imply real inconsistency (i.e., occurrence of theorems of the form '$p\bar{p}$'), but it seems equally intolerable.

However, the whole situation comes to appear much less queer if we critically re-examine the Fregean version (1) of Nn. Its rationale is that 0, 1, 2, . . . comprise all and only the common members of all classes which contain 0 and are closed with respect to successor. Now obviously 0, 1, 2, . . . are indeed common members of all classes which contain 0 and are closed with respect to successor. The question is whether 0, 1, 2, . . . exhaust those

[2] Cf. T10 in Rosser, 1939.

[3] *Note added 1965:* Specker subsequently found a proof and published it in 1953.

common members. The answer to this question depends on what classes there are, in NF (or in a given model of NF), for us to take common members of. There is no assurance, in the axioms of abstraction of NF, that every intuitively conceivable class of entities of NF must exist as an entity of NF.

Case 1: A class containing just 0, 1, 2, . . . does exist. Then, since this is one of the classes which contain 0 and are closed with respect to successor, we are assured that 0, 1, 2, . . . do exhaust the common members of such classes. Accordingly (1) expresses the genuine Nn.

Case 2: No class containing just 0, 1, 2, . . . exists; all classes big enough to contain all of 0, 1, 2, . . . are too big to contain just these. Then (1), which expresses a class for NF in any case (by the axioms of abstraction), does not express the genuine Nn; it merely expresses a certain class to which all of 0, 1, 2, . . . belong *among other things.* One of those other things may well be Λ, despite infinity of V. Infinity of V precludes nullity of any of 0, 1, 2, . . . , but it need not prevent Λ from belonging to the class expressed in (1) in case that class includes other things besides 0, 1, 2, ...

It is therefore misleading to define 'Nn' as (1) and then speak of '$\Lambda \bar{\epsilon}$ Nn' as the axiom of infinity. This course is appropriate only in Case 1. If '$\Lambda \epsilon$ Nn' is in fact demonstrable in NF, or better if '$\Lambda \epsilon$ K' is demonstrable where 'K' is defined as (1), then we can make sense of the situation only by acquiescing in Case 2 and concluding that neither K nor any class, for NF, contains all and *only* 0, 1, 2, . . . ; Λ is none of 0, 1, 2, . . . , and '$\Lambda \epsilon$ K' means simply that every class which contains all of 0, 1, 2, . . . contains Λ as additional member.[4]

There is evidence that NF must in fact be allocated to Case 2, unless we are prepared to settle for some heterodox results in the theory of ordinal numbers or elsewhere. Rosser and Wang have shown in effect that any model of NF which interprets the '=' of NF as genuine identity, and interprets the '0', '1', etc., of NF as the natural numbers, and interprets K (defined by (1)) as containing only the natural numbers, must fail to preserve well-ordering in the modeling of a theory of ordinal numbers constructed in NF. They sum up this situation in Henkin's terminology by saying that NF

[4] Incidentally it can be shown that if every such class contains Λ as additional member then every such class contains also other additional members; viz., ιV, also the class of complements of unit classes, also the class of complements of two-member classes, and so on.

admits of no standard model. They show also that the other familiar logics are in a somewhat related predicament—viz., that none of them can be proved, even by means of certain stronger logics, to admit of a standard model. But in the case of NF the impossibility of a standard model is proved outright.

We saw earlier that NF, with '$\Lambda \epsilon$ Nn' proved or added, would be ω-inconsistent, and this eventuality seemed as intolerable as real inconsistency; but the matter took on a very different complexion when we took 'K' rather than 'Nn' as our abbreviation of (1). Now a similar reflection dispels the queerness of ω-inconsistency in general, also apart from NF. Where ω-inconsistency co-exists with simple consistency, there is nothing outlandish afoot; there is merely a predicate, misinterpreted as "is a natural number", which has proved to be true of some other things besides the natural numbers.

Moving to a closer examination of the general notion of ω-inconsistency, let us consider an at least partially interpreted formal deductive system $\mathfrak{S}$ which contains, among other notations, the familiar notations of the truth functions and quantification subject to the usual interpretations. Suppose that $\mathfrak{S}$ is consistent (in the ordinary sense of the word) and that its theorems proceed from axioms by the usual logic of truth functions and quantification. The universe appropriated to the variables of quantification is to be interpreted as including, among other things, all of 0, 1, 2, etc., ad infinitum.

Suppose further that each of 0, 1, 2, etc., is expressible in $\mathfrak{S}$ at least indirectly, in the following sense: there is a standard method whereby, for each natural number i and each sentence ϕ of $\mathfrak{S}$ in 'x' (i.e., having 'x' as sole free variable), a statement (or closed sentence) ϕ_i of $\mathfrak{S}$ can be formed which is true (under adopted interpretations of the notations of $\mathfrak{S}$) if and only if ϕ is satisfied by i as value of 'x'. (If $\mathfrak{S}$ contains explicit names of numbers, ϕ_i might be formed from ϕ by substituting the name of i for 'x'. Otherwise ϕ_i might be taken as $\ulcorner(x)(\psi \supset \phi)\urcorner$ where ψ is some standard equivalent of '$x = i$'.) Let us then speak of ϕ as *numerically general* if ϕ_i is a theorem of $\mathfrak{S}$ for each i.

Now we can say what it would mean for $\mathfrak{S}$ to be ω-inconsistent. It would mean that there is a sentence ϕ in 'x' which, through interpretations supplementary to those exploited above, is interpreted as 'x is a natural number', and that there is a numerically general ψ such that $\ulcorner(\exists x)(\phi\bar{\psi})\urcorner$ is a theorem of $\mathfrak{S}$.

It may be presumed that the choice in $\mathfrak{S}$ of a translation ϕ of 'x is a natural number' was not wholly capricious, and in particular we may reasonably require that the chosen ϕ be numerically general. (Under ω-inconsistency, certainly, we can find numerically general sentences without resorting to sentences which are true of everything; witness ψ above.) Suppose then that $\mathfrak{S}$ is ω-inconsistent, i.e., that there are ϕ and ψ as described in the preceding paragraph, and that ϕ is numerically general. Then $\ulcorner\phi\psi\urcorner$ is also numerically general, and hence not too restrictive to serve as a translation of 'x is a natural number'. Moreover, $\ulcorner\phi\psi\urcorner$ is more accurate than ϕ as a translation of 'x is a natural number'; for ϕ is true not only of everything that $\ulcorner\phi\psi\urcorner$ is true of, but also of some things that $\ulcorner\phi\psi\urcorner$ is not true of (since $\ulcorner(\exists x)(\phi\bar{\psi})\urcorner$ is a theorem). It behooves us therefore to correct the translation in $\mathfrak{S}$ of 'x is a natural number', to read $\ulcorner\phi\psi\urcorner$; and then to re-examine $\mathfrak{S}$ for ω-inconsistency.

Under the corrected choice of translation $\mathfrak{S}$ may still be ω-inconsistent; for there may be a numerically general χ such that $\ulcorner(\exists x)(\phi\psi\bar{\chi})\urcorner$ is a theorem. If so, then we can further improve the translation of 'x is a natural number' by taking it as $\ulcorner\phi\psi\chi\urcorner$, and try again.

This series of corrections may or may not terminate. If it terminates, it terminates in a numerically general conjunction ϕ' which, if taken as the translation in $\mathfrak{S}$ of 'x is a natural number', leaves the system ω-consistent. In case the series terminates, therefore, the ω-inconsistency originally supposed is seen to be of no logical interest; it consisted merely in wanton choice of the broader ϕ instead of the narrower ϕ' for the reading 'x is a natural number'.

Surely then the only case of ω-inconsistency worth studying is the case of non-termination. In this case let us call $\mathfrak{S}$ *numerically insegregative*. The situation here is simply that for *every* numerically general ϕ there is a numerically general ψ such that $\ulcorner(\exists x)(\phi\bar{\psi})\urcorner$ is a theorem of $\mathfrak{S}$. Here the so-called ω-inconsistency of $\mathfrak{S}$ cannot be blamed on the wanton choice of a worse candidate ϕ, instead of a better candidate ϕ', for the interpretation 'x is a natural number'. It can still be blamed on a wantonness of interpretation, since if $\mathfrak{S}$ is numerically insegregative we would do better to face the fact that 'x is a natural number' has no translation into $\mathfrak{S}$ at all. The term 'ω-inconsistent' is thus misleading also here, but at least there is in this case a logically significant situation which deserves notice under some better terminology. I have now proposed such a terminology: numerical insegregativity.

The property of numerical insegregativity may be restated intuitively thus: *every sentence* ϕ *which is demonstrably true of all natural numbers* (i.e., numerically general) *is also demonstrably true of something else* (i.e., $\ulcorner(\exists x)(\phi\bar{\psi})\urcorner$ is demonstrable for some numerically general ψ). In such a system there is no proper translation of 'x is a natural number', but only an infinite series of better and better approximations (see next to last paragraph above).

Note that a system $\mathfrak{S}$ is numerically insegregative relatively only to an at least partial interpretation of its signs: normal interpretation of the notations of truth functions and quantifiers, interpretation of the universe of quantification to include all of 0, 1, 2, etc., and a determination in effect of the several numerals (sufficient to determine ϕ_i for every ϕ and i). On the other hand the notion of numerical insegregativity does not, like that of ω-inconsistency, depend on any preassigned translation of 'x is a natural number'.

The primary interest of the notion of numerical insegregativity consists in this: as has been seen, so-called ω-inconsistency reduces to numerical insegregativity the moment we repudiate those captious cases which depend merely on neglecting the best available translation of 'x is a natural number'. Insofar as the notion of ω-inconsistency is found to be applicable beyond the bounds of numerical insegregativity, it can be made inapplicable by a better choice of translation of 'x is a natural number' in the system under investigation. Insofar as the notion of ω-inconsistency is interesting, the notion of numerical insegregativity is interesting—and less misleading. A numerically insegregative system is not absurd, or incapable of coherent interpretation, as the phrase 'ω-inconsistent' suggests. It is merely uneven in its power of expression. It is too weak to express a necessary and sufficient condition for membership in the series 0, 1, 2, . . . , but it is strong enough to be able to better each of its own approximations.

The term 'ω-inconsistent' has also another misleading connotation. On the analogy of genuine inconsistency, any system containing an ω-inconsistent system as a part would be expected to be ω-inconsistent. Actually, as Rosser remarks (1952), NF might be ω-inconsistent and yet a stronger system containing NF as a part might be ω-consistent. He concludes that "such questions as whether a logic is ω-consistent . . . are rather more subjective than objective," but he might better have concluded that the terminology is misleading. It is obvious that a contained system might be numerically insegregative and a containing system numerically segregative, since in the containing system there is more machinery for numerical segregation.

At this writing some doubt remains as to the exact relationship between numerical insegregativity and the impossibility of an admissible translation of 'x is a natural number'. Consider a system $\mathfrak{S}$ and a sentence ϕ therein, with free 'x'. Relatively again to an assumed partial interpretation as of three paragraphs back, we might speak of ϕ as an *admissible translation* of 'x is a natural number' if there is at least *some* way of so finishing out that partial interpretation as to cause ϕ to be true of all of 0, 1, 2, . . . and false of everything else. Now I know of no proof that if $\mathfrak{S}$ is numerically segregative (i.e., not insegregative) it is bound to contain an admissible translation of 'x is a natural number'. What is obvious is only the converse.

Whether in particular NF is numerically segregative is an open question; and whether it contains an admissible translation of 'x is a natural number' is an open question. If '$\Lambda \in \mathrm{K}$' can be proved in NF, then certainly the defining condition of K, viz.:

$$(2) \qquad (y)(0 \in y \,.\, (z)(z \in y \,.\!\supset\!.\, \mathrm{S}z \in y) \,.\!\supset\!.\, x \in y),$$

is not an admissible translation of 'x is a natural number'; but NF might, even under these circumstances, contain a formula other than (2) which is an admissible translation of 'x is a natural number'. Some unstratified formula might serve as a translation of 'x is a natural number' without even guaranteeing existence of the class Nn of natural numbers. Two unstratified formulas which suggests themselves as possibilities are:

$$x \in \mathrm{K} \,.\, \hat{y}(y \in \mathrm{K} \,.\, x \neq y \,.\, (\exists z)(\exists w)(z \in x \,.\, z \cap w \in y)) \in x,$$

$$(\exists y)(x \in y \,.\, y \in \mathrm{S}x \,.\, (z)(z \in y \,.\!\supset\!: z = 0 \,.\!\vee\, (\exists w)(z = \mathrm{S}w \,.\, w \in y))).$$

X

Element and Number

*1. Inconsistency of *200.* Rosser pointed out (1941) that the system of my *Mathematical Logic*, when curtailed by leaving out the elementhood principle *200, would hold true even of a universe wherein the only entity is the null class. In other words, all theorems of the curtailed system remain true when all atomic formulae $\ulcorner \alpha \epsilon \beta \urcorner$ are construed as false for all values of their variables. This observation constitutes a consistency proof of that curtailed system, in an extraordinarily strict sense; for it shows that every theorem of that curtailed system is of a very special kind such that if all its quantifiers be simply rubbed out and all its atomic formulae be marked 'F' then the whole will receive a 'T' under the ordinary truth-table computation.

Thus, as I remarked in my review of Rosser's paper, "the system exclusive of *200 is a completely safe basal logic, to which more

---

This paper was called forth in 1941 by Rosser's discovery that the system of set theory in the first edition of my *Mathematical Logic* was inconsistent. A makeshift repair was made in the remainder of that edition by means of a corrigendum slip, and incorporated also into the 1947 printing; but the demands of brevity precluded, there, any such broad revision as was set out in this paper. In 1950 Wang hit upon a different repair, nearer in spirit to the book; and it, rather than the present paper, set the form of the revised edition of *Mathematical Logic* in 1951 and later printings.—At points the present paper calls for consultation of *Mathematical Logic*, even invoking theorems of that book by numerical reference in proofs. These numbers refer to the first edition, but readers using the revised edition will have little trouble tracing the few discrepancies. Such dependence on outside material is not usual in the present volume, but it seemed allowable here partly because of the easy accessibility of *Mathematical Logic* and partly because of what can be gleaned from the paper without bothering with that book. The paper is reprinted from the *Journal of Symbolic Logic*, Volume 6, 1941. A pair of definitions in §6 has been corrected in a small way.

daring structures such as *200 may be added at the constructor's peril." The review was written months ago, on the basis of galley proofs of Rosser's paper. But the remark now takes on a prophetic ring, for news is forthcoming that the system including *200 is *inconsistent.*

The contradiction is the Burali-Forti paradox, wherein it is argued that there can be no greatest ordinal number, and yet that the ordinal number of the series of ordinal numbers must be the greatest. The discovery that this paradox is implicit in *Mathematical Logic* is due, again, to Rosser. He has carried through the formal derivation of the contradiction, a long and complicated matter, in clear and incontrovertible detail.

The system that has thus been proved inconsistent embodied a synthesis of two features, whereof one came from von Neumann's set theory and the other from my "New foundations." The one feature is the recognition of non-elements; the other is the appeal to stratification. The synthesis was effected by taking stratification as a sufficient condition of elementhood; *200 says, roughly, that stratified functions of elements are elements.

It is by no means clear that the contradiction infects either of the two antecedent systems. Von Neumann's system is saved, presumably, by the circumstance that many classes that come to be elements under the stratification principle *200 cannot be shown to be elements under von Neumann's own elementhood axioms. For purposes of the present paradox, one crucial class of this sort would appear to be the class of all ordinal numbers; another, the relation of greater and less among ordinals.

"New foundations," on the other hand, is presumably saved by a different circumstance: the circumstance that stratification figures there as a condition of existence rather than merely of elementhood. Derivation of the paradox involves use of a certain class, called Q by Rosser,[1] whose defining condition is unstratified. Since the use made of Q happens to be independent of any considerations of elementhood, the want of stratification is no protection for *Mathematical Logic;* whereas for "New foundations" this want of stratification effectively obstructs the proof that the required class Q exists at all.

The particular obstacle that seems to bar the paradox from von

[1] 1942, second proof of †841. Note that the A of Rosser's first proof of †841 likewise has an unstratified defining condition.

Neumann's system is absent from "New foundations," and vice versa. But *Mathematical Logic* lacks both obstacles, and the paradox comes to be derivable. The same would seem to be the case, moreover, in the system of *Principia Mathematica,* so long as we take typical ambiguity seriously; i.e., so long as we leave the variables without type indices and construe the theory of types merely as prescribing a stratification test for meaningfulness of formulae.[2] The system of *Principia* so conceived is not protected from the paradox in the way that von Neumann's system seemed to be; in this regard the system of *Principia* behaves exactly like that of "New foundations." But neither is the system of *Principia* protected from the paradox as was the system of "New foundations"; for it happens that the class Q alluded to earlier becomes for purposes of *Principia* a "heterogeneous relation" (relating consecutive types) whose defining condition *is* stratified. Whereas in "New foundations" the expressions corresponding to heterogeneous relations are short for unstratified class expressions, in *Principia* relations have an irreducible status and may be heterogeneous without any hindrance from the stratification requirement. Thus it is that in order to avert Burali-Forti's paradox the authors of *Principia* felt called upon to suspend typical ambiguity and introduce explicit type indices at the crucial point.[3] The mere requirement of stratification does not suffice to bar Burali-Forti's paradox from the system of *Principia,* though sufficing to bar Russell's paradox and the infinite bundle of related paradoxes.[4]

Note that these remarks relate to *Principia* with its unreduced theory of relations, and not to that simplified variant of *Principia* wherein the theory of relations is reduced to that of classes.[5] That simplified variant enjoys the same protection as does "New foundations." It is only in the ground-floor admittance of heterogeneous relations that *Principia* gains an added freedom demanding type indices for its control.

Burali-Forti's paradox has an analogue in Cantor's paradox,

[2] The sense of stratification concerned here is more elaborate than in "New foundations" or *Mathematical Logic,* since in *Principia* relations are not reduced to classes.

[3] Vol. 3, 75, 80.

[4] For an account of this bundle of paradoxes see §2 of my paper "On the theory of types."

[5] It is of the latter system that "On the theory of types" treats. Thus the view, accepted in that paper, that the mere requirement of stratification suffices for the avoidance of paradoxes, is not controverted by the present remarks.

which says of cardinal numbers what the other says of ordinals. In Cantor's paradox it is argued that there can be no greatest cardinal number, and yet that the cardinal number of the class of cardinal numbers (or, indeed, of the class V) must be the greatest. The obstacle to deriving this paradox, in von Neumann's system, is like the obstacle to deriving Burali-Forti's. In the system of "New foundations" and in the simplified variant of *Principia* noted above, the obstacle to Cantor's paradox is again like the obstacle to Burali-Forti's.[6] In *Principia* proper, with its unreduced theory of relations, the two paradoxes again behave alike: Cantor's, like Burali-Forti's, is dodged only by recourse to explicit type indices.[7]

The parallelism between the two paradoxes breaks down, for the first time, in the system of *Mathematical Logic*. The argument that leads to Cantor's paradox *is* obstructed in that system; for the argument depends on showing that $\hat{y}(y \subset x)$ always has more members than x, and it is obstructed by the fact that $\hat{y}(y \subset x)$ comprises in general only certain of the subclasses of x, viz., those that are elements. My own inattention to Burali-Forti's paradox came, indeed, of confidence in the parallelism between that paradox and Cantor's.

2. Elementhood in Driblets. The system of *Mathematical Logic* without *200 is, as observed, consistent. It is adequate, moreover, to a substantial portion of the material covered in the book. Most of the theorems and metatheorems survive, with proofs unchanged, right up to the end of Chapter IV—hence to the beginning of relation theory. Chapters I–III, of course, survive intact.

Let us keep to solid rock while we can. Accordingly, before we consider bringing in any new axioms of elementhood to supplant *200, let us suppose Chapter IV carried over with mere omission of such few theorems and metatheorems as depended directly or indirectly on *200. These turn out to be nineteen in number: †210–†212, †241, *253, *254, *256–*259, †261, *263, †272–†274, †359–†361, and †363. Nearly all of these are concerned explicitly with elementhood.

The proof given in the book for Case 2 of *221 makes use unnecessarily of *200 (via †212), and should be supplanted by the following new proof: Let χ be the formula just after the occurrence

[6] Concerning the solution of Cantor's paradox for the system of "New foundations" see my paper "On Cantor's theorem."

[7] See *Principia*, Vol. 2, 31.

of $\ulcorner(\zeta)\urcorner$ in question, let $\beta_1, \ldots, \beta_m$ be the variables of χ, and let γ be new. Form χ_i from χ by putting γ for the first i free occurrences of ζ. Suppose ζ' is not ζ (for otherwise $\vdash\ulcorner 221\urcorner$ by *100). Since ζ is one of $\alpha_1, \ldots, \alpha_n$ (cf. old proof), and similarly for ζ',

*116, *117	$\vdash\ulcorner \text{L}221 \supset (\zeta')(\zeta)(\zeta = \zeta')\urcorner$	
*104	$\supset (\zeta)(\zeta = \gamma)\urcorner$	
*221, Case 1	$\supset . (\zeta)\chi_{i-1} \equiv (\zeta)\chi_i\urcorner$	(i)

for each i from 1 to the number k of free occurrences of ζ in χ. Thus

*100	$\vdash\ulcorner[1 . 2 . \ldots . k .]\ \text{L}221 . \supset . (\zeta)\chi \equiv (\zeta)\chi_k\urcorner$	
*118, *123	$\supset . (\zeta)\chi \equiv \chi_k\urcorner$.	$(k + 1)$
*104	$\vdash\ulcorner[(\gamma)\ k + 1 \supset :]\ \text{L}221 \supset . (\zeta)\chi \equiv \chi\urcorner$.	$(k + 2)$
Similarly	$\vdash\ulcorner \text{L}221 \supset . (\zeta')\chi \equiv \chi\urcorner$.	$(k + 3)$
*100, *117	$\vdash\ulcorner \text{L}221 \supset (\beta_1) \ldots (\beta_m)([k + 2 . k + 3 . \supset .]\ (\zeta)\chi \equiv (\zeta')\chi)\urcorner$	
*121	$\supset . \phi \equiv \phi'\urcorner$.	

Then we may proceed, in an addendum to Chapter IV, to "more daring structures . . . at the constructor's peril." We may add axioms of elementhood adequate to those nineteen postponed theorems and metatheorems and adequate also to the succeeding chapter on relations. Actually the only ones needed are these two:

†400.[8]	(x)	$\iota x \in \text{V}$
†401.	$(x)(y)$	$x, y \in \text{V} . \supset . \bar{x} \cap \bar{y} \in \text{V}$

From these the five theorems hitherto known as †211, †274, †210, †272, and †273 are respectively derivable as follows:

†410a.[9] $\Lambda \in \text{V}$

Proof.	*†400*	$\iota\hat{x}(x \mathrel{\bar{\in}} x) \in \text{V}$	(1)
	†343	$[260 \equiv .]\ \iota\hat{x}(x \mathrel{\bar{\in}} x) = \Lambda$	(2)
	*223	$[2 \supset . 1 \equiv]$ *410a*	

†410b. (x) $\quad x \in \text{V} . \equiv . \bar{x} \in \text{V}$

Proof.	*†401*	$x, x \in \text{V} . \supset . \bar{x} \cap \bar{x} \in \text{V}$	
	†276, *224	$\supset . \bar{x} \in \text{V}$	(1)
	*231	$[(x)1 \supset :]\bar{x}, \bar{x} \in \text{V} . \supset . \bar{\bar{x}} \in \text{V}$	

[8] I shall use italics to distinguish newly applied reference numbers from reference numbers whose application remains as in the book.

[9] This and its sequel are called †*410a*ff. rather than †*402*ff. in view of *Mathematical Logic,* 90n. But note still that †410 is to be understood as coming *after* all these.

†275, *224 $\supset . x \in V$ (2)

*100 [1 . 2 .⊃] *410b*

†*410c*. $V \in V$

Proof. †293, *224 $\overline{V} \in V$ [.≡ *410*a] (1)

†*410b* *410c* [≡ 1]

†*410d*. $(x)(y)$ $x, y \in V . \supset . x \cap y \in V$

Proof. †*410b*, *123 $x, y \in V . \supset . \bar{x}, \bar{y} \in V$

†*401* $\supset . \bar{\bar{x}} \cap \bar{\bar{y}} \in V$

†275, *224 $\supset . x \cap y \in V$

†*410e*. $(x)(y)$ $x, y \in V . \supset . x \cup y \in V$

Proof. †281, *224 $x, y \in V . \supset . \overline{x \cup y} \in V$ [:≡ *401*]

†*410b* $\supset . x \cup y \in V$

*259, moreover, is derivable from †*410b* in obvious fashion:

**410f*. $\vdash \ulcorner \hat{\alpha}\phi \in V . \equiv . \hat{\alpha} \sim \phi \in V \urcorner$.

Proof. †*410b* (& D20) $\vdash \ulcorner \hat{\alpha}\phi \in V . \equiv . \hat{\alpha}(\alpha \mathrel{\bar{\in}} \hat{\alpha}\phi) \in V \urcorner$

*245, *224 $\equiv . \hat{\alpha} \sim \phi \in V \urcorner$.

From among the nineteen theorems and metatheorems enumerated earlier, seven have now been covered: †210, †211, *259, †272–†274, and †359, which last is †*400* itself. The other twelve were proved in the book mediately on the basis of these seven; they may be renumbered as †*410g*–†*410r*, and their old proofs may now simply be reproduced in the new setting. Moreover, the succeeding Chapter V, on relations, remains intact (except insofar as occasional references in proofs have to be renumbered in the light of the foregoing rearrangement); for it happens that *200 is nowhere directly cited in Chapter V, all use of *200 being mediated rather by three (†211, †359, †360) of the derivative theorems that have already been provided for.

The whole of the book, therefore, up to the beginning of arithmetic, remains essentially unchanged when *200 is supplanted by its two meager instances †*400*–†*401*. The only effect is to shift and renumber nineteen theorems and metatheorems and to re-prove a few as above. Yet †*400*–†*401* say no more than that unit classes (genuine and vacuous) are elements and that Boolean functions of elements are elements.

When we push on to the matter of natural numbers, in Chapter VI, we do need a third axiom of elementhood, viz., the instance of

*200 designated in the book as †610; but no more than this, for it is only here that *200 is cited in the course of Chapter VI. Reconstrued as an axiom, †610 might be called *†600*.

It seems advantageous to adhere thus to a minimum of elementhood axioms adequate to purposes at hand, rather than running the risk of something like *200. Then as we proceed to higher branches of theory we can set down supplementary axioms of elementhood explicitly as needed. We can do this with the realization that the ensuing theory is tenuous to the extent that those special axioms of elementhood are tenuous. Economy in the elementhood axioms governing a given portion of theory becomes a virtue to be striven for, providing as it does a measure of the soundness of the theory. The most solid part of class logic, thus, comprises everything up through the newly expurgated Chapter IV. The next most solid part comprises the addendum to Chapter IV, together with Chapter V; this theory, which is primarily the theory of relations, is tenuous only to the mild degree measured by the special elementhood axioms *†400*–*†401* (or by still weaker axioms, if such prove adequate; see below). The next degree of tenuousness is exhibited by natural arithmetic (unless the special elementhood axiom *†600* for this domain proves dispensable after all; see below). As we proceed into more and more remote and speculative branches of mathematics, we have before us always a growing record of our sins; and if our sins catch up with us we can repent them by degrees, prudently withholding any penitence in excess of what the occasion demands.

Such wary postulation of elementhood piecemeal would seem indeed to be the procedure dictated by the scientific temper, once we have cast loose from patently consistent domains. And this procedure fits with the familiar old postulational attitude toward mathematics, as opposed to the idea that the whole of mathematics is theoretically reducible to a bedrock of logical truisms. Reducibility to logical notation remains a fact; but, at the latest, the truism idea received its deathblow from Gödel's incompleteness theorem.

Gödel's incompleteness theorem can be made to show that we can never approach *completeness* of elementhood axioms without approaching contradiction. For if every statement of elementhood were demonstrable or refutable then *every* logical statement would be demonstrable or refutable, since

$$\vdash \ulcorner \phi \equiv . \hat{\alpha}(\alpha \in \alpha . \supset \phi) \in \mathrm{V} \urcorner \text{ where } \alpha \text{ is not free in } \phi.$$

Proof. †260	$\vdash \ulcorner \hat{\alpha}(\alpha \,\tilde{\epsilon}\, \alpha) \,\tilde{\epsilon}\, \mathrm{V} \urcorner.$	(1)
*100, *117 (& hp)	$\vdash \ulcorner {\sim}\phi \supset (\alpha)(\alpha \,\tilde{\epsilon}\, \alpha \,.\!\equiv\!:\, \alpha \,\epsilon\, \alpha \,.\!\supset \phi) \urcorner$	
*121	$\supset: [1 \equiv.]\; \hat{\alpha}(\alpha \,\epsilon\, \alpha \,.\!\supset \phi) \,\tilde{\epsilon}\, \mathrm{V} \urcorner.$	(2)
*100, *117 (& hp)	$\vdash \ulcorner \phi \supset (\alpha)(\alpha \,\epsilon\, \alpha \,.\!\supset \phi) \urcorner$	
*193	$\supset.\; \hat{\alpha}(\alpha \,\epsilon\, \alpha \,.\!\supset \phi) = \mathrm{V} \urcorner$	
*223	$\supset: \hat{\alpha}(\alpha \,\epsilon\, \alpha \,.\!\supset \phi) \,\epsilon\, \mathrm{V}$ [.≡ *410c*]$\urcorner$.	(3)
*100	$\vdash \ulcorner [3\,.\,2\,.\!\supset:]\phi \equiv.\; \hat{\alpha}(\alpha \,\epsilon\, \alpha \,.\!\supset \phi) \,\epsilon\, \mathrm{V} \urcorner.$	

The growing list of elementhood axioms traverses the interval between the patent consistency of *Mathematical Logic* without *200 and the inconsistency of *Mathematical Logic* including *200; and as it grows it provides for progressively more tenuous branches of mathematics, from natural and rational arithmetic through real arithmetic, theory of functions, infinite cardinal arithmetic, infinite ordinal arithmetic, and worse.

3. Elementhood by Enumeration. Further investigation reveals that even the axioms †*400*–†*401* are more powerful than need be for purposes of the topics covered in the book. We could supplant †*401* by the weaker statement †*410e* without any real detriment to the sequel. Of the nineteen theorems and metatheorems in Chapter IV that depended originally on *200, ten do indeed drop when †*401* is weakened to †*410e;* but these ten are pretty readily dispensable. They are †210, †272, and †274 (i.e., †*410b–d* above), together with †241, *256, *258, *259, †261, *263, and †363.

Under this improved theory, accordingly, the addendum to Chapter IV would consist of the axioms:

†*400.*	(x)	$\iota x \,\epsilon\, \mathrm{V}$
†*401′.*	$(x)(y)$	$x, y \,\epsilon\, \mathrm{V} \,.\!\supset.\; x \cup y \,\epsilon\, \mathrm{V}$

and a sequence of theorems and metatheorems answering to such others of the old nineteen as survive when the ten last enumerated are deleted. †*400*–†*401′* answer to the old †359 and †273, and the following answer respectively to the old †211, †360, †361, *257, *253, *254, and †212.

†*410a.*		$\Lambda \,\epsilon\, \mathrm{V}$	*Proof* given above.
†*410b′.*	$(x)(y)$	$\iota x \cup \iota y \,\epsilon\, \mathrm{V}$	
†*410c′.*	$(x)(y)$	$\iota x \cap y \,\epsilon\, \mathrm{V}$	
**410d′.*	$\vdash \ulcorner (\alpha){\sim}\phi \supset.\; \hat{\alpha}\phi \,\epsilon\, \mathrm{V} \urcorner.$		

Proofs of †*410b′*–**410d′* like those given in the book under †360,

†361, and *257 (but with '359', '273', and '211' changed of course to '*400*', '*401*″', '*410a*').

**410e′*. *If* α *is not free in* ϕ, $\vdash \ulcorner \hat{\alpha}\phi = \mathrm{V} \,.\!\equiv \phi \urcorner$.

Proof. *231 (& hp) $\vdash \ulcorner (\alpha)(\alpha \in \mathrm{V} \,.\!\supset \phi) \supset . \, [410a \supset] \, \phi \urcorner$. (1)
*100, *117 (& hp) $\vdash \ulcorner \phi \supset (\alpha)(\alpha \in \mathrm{V} \,.\!\supset \phi) \urcorner$. (2)
*100 $\vdash \ulcorner [249 \,.\, 1 \,.\, 2 \,.\!\supset] \, 410e' \urcorner$.

**410f′*. *If* α *is not free in* ϕ, $\vdash \ulcorner \hat{\alpha}\phi = \Lambda \,.\!\equiv \sim\!\phi \urcorner$.

Proof similar, using *250 instead of *249.

†410g′. (y) $(\exists x)(x \neq y)$

Proof. *231 $(x)(x = y) \supset . \, \hat{x}(x \bar{\in} x) = y$
*223 $\supset : [260 \equiv .] \, y \bar{\in} \mathrm{V}$ (1)
*231 $(x)(x = y) \supset . \, \Lambda = y$
*223 $\supset : [410a \equiv .] \, y \in \mathrm{V}$ (2)
*100 $[1 \,.\, 2 \,.\!\supset] \sim\!(x)(x = y)$ (3)
*130 $[3 \equiv] \, 410g'$

Though †*401′* asserts far less than †*401*, the theory founded on †*400*–†*401′* is quite adequate to relation theory. Chapter V remains intact, except of course for change of the few occurrences of '211', '359', and '360' in proofs to '*410a*', '*400*', '*410b*″'. For it has already been remarked that the three theorems thus designated constituted the only channel through which Chapter V drew on *200.

And it turns out that the meager basis under consideration will suffice even for the arithmetic of natural numbers, provided that we alter our definitions to suit. This new theory of natural numbers will be set forth in the next section. It is only when we proceed to derive theorems in higher branches, e.g., in the theory of real numbers or in that of infinite numbers, that we have to add another axiom or so of elementhood.

†*400*–†*401′* do not provide infinite elements, but they guarantee that every finite class is an element. Any class of n members, say

(i) $$\iota x_1 \cup \iota x_2 \cup \ldots \cup \iota x_n,$$

is shown to be an element by iteration of the process that leads from †*400*–†*401′* to †*410b′*. Whenever a class is specified by enumeration of its members, it is thereby shown to be an element under †*400*–†*401′*; for to specify a class by enumeration is to specify the class by an expression of the form of (i).

The need of adding an axiom or two providing for infinite elements arises only when we proceed to derive theorems in branches of mathematics beyond the scope of the theorems actually presented in the book; e.g., when we turn to the theory of real numbers or to that of infinite numbers. A boundary thus appears which is suggestive of the old distinction, drawn traditionally in a pretty vague way, between the *actual infinite* and the *potential infinite*. The axioms of elementhood †*400*–†*401′* might be said to posit the potential infinite only, in that they guarantee infinite classes but not infinite elements; whereas an axiom such as '$\omega \in$ V' (see D*39* below) posits an actual infinite, viz., an infinite element.

4. Natural Numbers as Counter Sets. A revised theory of natural numbers that avoids any elementhood assumptions beyond †400 and †401 is obtained by construing the natural numbers as classes of the sort that in the book were called counter sets.[10] Thus, we define the successor relation S in the way that the self-augment relation Sa was defined in the book, viz.:

D*36*. 'S' *for* '$\lambda_x(x \cup \iota x)$'.

The number 0 becomes the null class. We may think of the old definition D16, accordingly, as elaborated thus:

D*16*. 'Λ' *or* '0' *for* '$\hat{x}(x \neq x)$'.

The sign 'Λ' might well be dispensed with in favor of '0' from the start, in reversion to Boole's original notation; but for the present I am keeping both signs so as to avoid needless departure from the style of *Mathematical Logic* and from current practice generally. Let us merely think of 'Λ' and '0' hereafter as if they were one and the same sign. I shall supplant the one by the other at will without even citing D*16*.

The numbers 1, 2, etc., are defined in obvious fashion:

D*37*. '1' *for* '(S'0)',

D*38*. '2' *for* '(S'1)',

etc. The class of natural numbers is defined in terms of '0' and 'S' as before; but I shall use 'ω' now rather than 'Nn' to designate this class, for the class will subsequently turn out to be the same thing

[10] Von Neumann has construed the finite ordinals in this way. See below, §6.

as the ordinal number ω. Thus

D39. 'ω' *for* '$({}_*\text{S}``\iota 0)$'.

The old theory identified each natural number n with the class of all n-membered classes; the new theory, on the other hand, identifies n rather with a certain standard n-membered class. On the score of naturalness, the theories have about equal claims. Insofar as one thinks of a number n as a *property* of aggregates, viz., the property of n-foldness, the old theory is sustained. But the new theory is sustained insofar as one thinks of a number n rather as a certain comparative *standard* of multiplicity used in counting n objects. What we correlate with n objects in counting them, i.e., what we mention as we point to the successive objects, are the first n numbers; and thus there is some appropriateness in construing a number n as the class of the first n numbers themselves. The apparent circularity here is resolved merely by admitting 0 among the first n numbers; thus n ceases to be a class of n numbers *including* itself, and becomes rather the class of the n antecedent numbers. Once we have gone this far in characterizing the natural numbers, the identification of natural numbers with counter sets is inescapable. If 0 is to be the class of all earlier natural numbers, then 0 is clearly Λ; if 1 in turn is to be the class of all earlier natural numbers, then 1 must be $\iota 0$, i.e., $\iota\Lambda$; if 2 is to be the class of all earlier natural numbers, then 2 must be $\iota 0 \cup \iota 1$, i.e., $\iota\Lambda \cup \iota\iota\Lambda$; and so on.

This theory emphasizes the analogy between natural numbers and other standards of measurement. A natural number is a standard of comparison for measuring multiplicity just as the Paris meter stick is a standard of comparison for measuring length. It just happens that measuring sticks for multiplicity are definable within logic whereas measuring sticks for length are not.

Whereas *application* of natural numbers in the old sense proceeded by membership, application of natural numbers in the new sense proceeds rather by correlation. To say that x has n members, under the old theory, we said that $x \in n$. Under the new theory, on the other hand, we say rather that the members of x correspond in one–one fashion to those of n; or, what is equivalent under the new version of natural number, that n is the class of all those natural numbers that have fewer members than has x. This notion of having fewer members will be defined in §6.

But meanwhile, independently of that development, we can

attend to the pure arithmetic of natural numbers. The first two theorems in this direction serve the purpose now of the old †610 and †614, and will be numbered accordingly.

†610. (x) $x \epsilon \mathrm{V} . \supset . x \cup \iota x \epsilon \mathrm{V}$

Proof. *†401′* $x \epsilon \mathrm{V} [.\,\mathit{400}] . \supset . x \cup \iota x \epsilon \mathrm{V}$

†614. (x) $x \epsilon \mathrm{V} . \supset . \mathrm{S}‘x = x \cup \iota x$

Proof from *†610* like that of the old †614 from †610.

Thence we have this corollary:

†615. $1 = \iota 0$

Proof. *†614* (& D*37*) $[\mathit{410a} \supset .]\, 1 = 0 \cup \iota 0$
†297 $= \iota 0$

The following theorem is the analogue of the †624 of the book.

†624. (x) $x \epsilon \mathrm{V} . \equiv . \mathrm{S}‘x \neq 0$

Proof. †317 $\iota x \subset x \cup \iota x$ (1)
*223 $x \cup \iota x = 0 . \supset : [1 \equiv .]\, \iota x \subset 0$
†336 $\supset . \iota x = \Lambda$ (2)
*223 $\mathrm{S}‘x = x \cup \iota x . \supset :. \mathrm{S}‘x = 0 . \supset . \iota x = \Lambda\, [: \equiv 2]$ (3)
†534 $x \,\tilde{\epsilon}\, \mathrm{V} . \supset . \mathrm{S}‘x = 0$ (4)
*100 $[3 . 4 . \mathit{614} . 343 . \supset]\, \mathit{624}$

Nine further theorems and metatheorems are the †617 and †630–*637 of the book, notationally unchanged except of course that 'Nn' becomes 'ω'. The proofs remain as in the book, except for the obvious adjustments of references: †610, †611, D39, †615, †616, and D40 give way respectively to *†610*, *†410a*, D*36–39*.

The remaining crucial theorem to derive, for arithmetical purposes, is the theorem †677 to the effect that no two natural numbers have the same successor. The following three theorems are lemmas for it.

†568. (x) $x \epsilon \mathrm{V} . \supset . x = \mathfrak{E}“\iota x$

Proof. †564 $y \epsilon x . x \epsilon \mathrm{V} . \equiv \mathfrak{E}(y, x)$
†479 $\equiv . y \epsilon \mathfrak{E}“\iota x$ (1)
*100, *117 $x \epsilon \mathrm{V} . \supset (y)([1 \supset :]\, y \epsilon x . \equiv . y \epsilon \mathfrak{E}“\iota x)$,
q.e.d. (cf. D10).

The converse of the above could also be established, but there is no need of that for present purposes.

†675. (x) $x \in \mathrm{V} \,.\!\supset\!.\, \mathfrak{E}``(\mathrm{S}`x) = (\mathfrak{E}``x) \cup x$

Proof. †472 $\mathfrak{E}``(x \cup \iota x) = (\mathfrak{E}``x) \cup (\mathfrak{E}``\iota x)$ (1)
*223 $x = \mathfrak{E}``\iota x \,.\!\supset:\, \mathfrak{E}``(x \cup \iota x) = (\mathfrak{E}``x) \cup x \,[.\equiv 1]$ (2)
*223 $\mathrm{S}`x = x \cup \iota x \,.\!\supset:.\, x = \mathfrak{E}``\iota x \,.\!\supset$ R*675* $[:\equiv 2]$ (3)
*100 [3 . *568* . *614* .$\supset$] *675*

The following theorem plays the role of the old †676, showing as it does how any natural number can be expressed as a function of its successor.

†676. (x) $x \in \omega \,.\!\supset\!.\, x = \mathfrak{E}``(\mathrm{S}`x)$

Proof. †277, *227 $x \cup \iota x = x \cup x \cup \iota x$ (1)
*223 R*676* $\supset: [1 \equiv.]\, x \cup \iota x = (\mathfrak{E}``(\mathrm{S}`x)) \cup x \cup \iota x$ (2)
*223 R*614* $\supset:.$ R*676* $\supset.\, \mathrm{S}`x = (\mathfrak{E}``(\mathrm{S}`x)) \cup (\mathrm{S}`x) [:\equiv 2]$ (3)
†536 $\mathrm{S}`x \in \mathrm{V}$ (4)
†*675* $[4 \supset.]\, \mathfrak{E}``(\mathrm{S}`(\mathrm{S}`x)) = (\mathfrak{E}``(\mathrm{S}`x)) \cup (\mathrm{S}`x)$ (5)
*223 $[5 \supset::]$ R*614* $\supset:$ R*676* $\supset.\, \mathrm{S}`x = \mathfrak{E}``(\mathrm{S}`(\mathrm{S}`x)) [.:\equiv 3]$ (6)
†190 $x \in \omega \,.\!\supset\!.\, x \in \mathrm{V}$ (7)
*100 [6 . 7 . *614* .] $x \in \omega$. R*676* $.\!\supset\!.\, \mathrm{S}`x = \mathfrak{E}``(\mathrm{S}`(\mathrm{S}`x))$ (8)
†*568* [*410a* $\supset$.] $0 = \mathfrak{E}``\iota 0$
†*615*(& D*37*),*227 $= \mathfrak{E}``(\mathrm{S}`0)$ (9)
*637 $[(x)8 \,.\, 9 \,.]\, x \in \omega \,.\!\supset$ R*676*

From †*676*, finally, †677 can be proved precisely as it was proved from †676 in the book. And now all the definitions and theorems and proofs of the succeeding §§47–49 of the book, on powers of relations and the algorithm of arithmetic, can be carried over without any changes whatever except for putting 'ω' for 'Nn' and using †*410a*, D*37*, and †*624* (with its minor complication) instead of †611, †615, and †624.

Note incidentally that the theory of greater and less among numbers is very much simplified by the present approach; for, where x and y are numbers, $x \leqq y$ if and only if $x \subset y$. We can think of '$x \leqq y$' in general as meaning '$x \subset y$', since this reproduces the customary arithmetical sense so long as x and y happen to be numbers.[11] Thus the laws:

[11] The identification of '$\leqq$' with '$\subset$' is suited to the arithmetic not only of natural numbers but of cardinals and ordinals generally (cf. §6 below), and even of real numbers—both when real numbers are taken as Dedekind segment-

$$
\begin{array}{ll}
(x) & 0 \leqq x, \\
(x) & x \leqq x, \\
(x)(y) & x = y \,.\equiv.\, x \leqq y \,.\, y \leqq x, \\
(x)(y)(z) & x \leqq y \,.\, y \leqq z \,.\supset.\, x \leqq z
\end{array}
$$

appear as mere transcriptions of the general laws †334 and †310–†312 of class algebra. Again the law:

$$(x) \qquad x \in \mathrm{V} \,.\supset.\, x \leqq \mathrm{S}\text{‘}x$$

appears as a corollary of †*614* and †317. The idea might be entertained of using '$\leqq$' instead of '$\subset$' in the general class algebra from the start; this would be a reversion to the old notation of the logical algebra, quite like the suggested restoration of '0' in place of 'Λ'. Similarly '$x < y$' could be given the general sense of '$x \subset y \,.\, x \neq y$'.

5. Functional Aspects. As a means to formulating the idea of having n members (see above), and as a means equally to developing a theory of infinite cardinals and ordinal numbers, we need the notion of one–one correspondence between the members of two classes; or, what proves to be just as adequate and more simply manageable, the notion of there being fewer members in one class than another. Treatment of this notion is facilitated by the introduction of a preliminary notion that I call *functional aspect*—a notion that I regard as of some logical interest also apart from its immediate use in this paper.

Membership is, in an obvious sense, inverse to class abstraction. Thus we have:

$$\vdash \ulcorner \alpha \in \mathrm{V} \,.\supset:\, \alpha \in \hat{\alpha}\phi \,.\equiv\, \phi \urcorner. \qquad (*230)$$

Correspondingly relational predication is inverse to relational abstraction:

$$\vdash \ulcorner \alpha, \gamma \in \mathrm{V} \,.\supset.\, \hat{\alpha}\hat{\gamma}\phi(\alpha, \gamma) \equiv \phi \urcorner. \qquad (*433)$$

---

classes of ratios (cf. *Mathematical Logic,* 271f.) and when they are taken rather as relations $\mathfrak{C}$“x such that x is a Dedekind segment-class of ratios (cf. *Principia Mathematica,* Vol. 3, 336). The identification of '$\leqq$' with '$\subset$' is suited also to the arithmetic of ratios, if we merely reconstrue the ratios *cumulatively;* i.e., if in the first definition of §50 of *Mathematical Logic* we change '=' to '<'. This cumulative version of ratios is advantageous also on other grounds; for it causes the ratios to be identical with the rational reals, once the *relational* version of reals mentioned above is adopted. The reals come to constitute a genuine extension of the ratios.

Correspondingly, again, functional application is inverse to functional abstraction:

$$\vdash \ulcorner \alpha, \zeta \in \mathrm{V} .\supset. \lambda_\alpha \zeta ` \alpha = \zeta \urcorner. \qquad (*541)$$

To an important degree, moreover, these relationships of inverseness also hold in the opposite direction. Thus

$$\hat{y}(y \in x) = x \qquad (\dagger 189)$$

whenever x is a *class* (which it necessarily is[12]); again

$$\hat{y}\hat{z}(x(y, z)) = x$$

whenever the x is a *relation;*[13] and finally, as will be proved in †*574* below,

$$\lambda_y(x ` y) = x$$

whenever the x is a *function*— if by a "function" we understand for the present a single-valued function defined for all arguments, or in other words a relation x such that $\mathrm{r}x = \mathrm{V}$.

In view of the second of these last three principles, it was convenient to abbreviate '$\hat{y}\hat{z}(x(y, z))$' as '$\dot{x}$'. In view of the last of the three principles, similarly, it will be convenient to abbreviate '$\lambda_y(x ` y)$' say as '${}_F x$'.

D*33a*. $\ulcorner {}_F\zeta \urcorner$ *for* $\ulcorner \lambda_\alpha(\zeta ` \alpha) \urcorner$.

Just as $\dot{x}$ is a relation in any case, and is the same as x if x is a relation, so ${}_F x$ is a function in any case, and is the same as x if x is a function. Thus, just as '$\dot{x}$' served virtually as a simple relation variable, so '${}_F x$' will serve virtually as a simple function variable.

Whereas $\dot{x}$ is called the relational part of x, we cannot speak of ${}_F x$ as the functional part of x; for ${}_F x$ is not in general included in x. Rather, ${}_F x$ proves to be a relation comprising all those pairs $z;w$ such that $x(z, w)$ and $w \in \mathrm{r}x$, and in addition all those pairs $\Lambda;w$ such that $w \in \overline{\mathrm{r}x}$. Deprived thus of the term 'functional part', I have chosen to call ${}_F x$ the *functional aspect* of x.

Parallel to the theorem:

$$(x)(y)(z) \qquad \dot{x}(y, z) \equiv x(y, z) \qquad (\dagger 436)$$

concerning relational parts, we have this concerning functional aspects:

[12] Cf. *Mathematical Logic,* 135.
[13] *Ibid.*, 204ff.

†*570.* $(x)(y)$ $\digamma x`y = x`y.$

Proof. *541 (& D*33a*) $y \in V\,[.\ 536]\ .\supset.\ x`y = \digamma x`y$ (1)
†534 $y \,\bar{\in}\, V\ .\supset.\ \digamma x`y = \Lambda$
*223 $\supset:.\ y \,\bar{\in}\, V\ .\supset.\ x`y = \digamma x`y\ [:\equiv 534]$ (2)
*100 $[1\ .\ 2\ .\supset.]\ x`y = \digamma x`y$

So we can agree to drop the digamma automatically from contexts of the form $\ulcorner \digamma\zeta`\eta \urcorner$, just as we agreed[14] to drop the dot from $\ulcorner \dot{\zeta}(\eta, \theta) \urcorner$. In particular, '$\digamma\digamma x$' gives way thus to '$\digamma x$', just as '$\dot{\dot{x}}$' gave way to '$\dot{x}$'.

The next two theorems are two ways of saying that $\digamma x$ and x coincide for arguments in $\mathfrak{r}x$.

†*571.* $(x)(y)(z)$ $y \in \mathfrak{r}x\ .\supset.\ \digamma x(z, y) \equiv x(z, y)$

Proof. *540 (& D*33a*) $\digamma x(z, y) \equiv.\ y \in V\,[.\ 536]\ .\ z = x`y$ (1)
*121 $R531 \supset:.\ [1 \equiv:]\ \digamma x(z, y) \equiv.\ y \in V\ .\ x(z, y)$ (2)
*100 (& D24) $[531\ .\ 2\ .\supset]$ *571*

†*572.* $(w)(x)$ $w \subset \mathfrak{r}x\ .\supset.\ \digamma x``w = x``w$

Proof. *100, *117
$y \in w\ .\supset.\ y \in \mathfrak{r}x\ :\supset\ (z)([\mathit{571} \supset:]\ \digamma x(z, y)\ .\ y \in w\ .\equiv.\ x(z, y)\ .\ y \in w)$ (1)

*102 (& D21) $[(y)1 \supset:]\ w \subset \mathfrak{r}x\ .\supset\ (y)R1$
*186 (& D28) $\supset.\ \digamma x``w = x``w$

That $\digamma x$ is a function in any case, and coincides with x whenever x is a function, is recorded in the next two theorems.

†*573.* (x) $\mathfrak{r}\digamma x = V$

Proof. *193 $[(y)536 \supset.]\ V = \hat{y}(x`y \in V)$
*543 (& D*33a*) $= \mathfrak{r}\digamma x$

†*574.*[15] (x) $\digamma x = \dot{x}\ .\equiv.\ \mathfrak{r}x = V$

Proof. *223 $\digamma x = \dot{x}\ .\supset:\ [\mathit{573} \equiv.]\ \mathfrak{r}x = V$ (1)
*223 $\mathfrak{r}x = V\ .\supset.\ [(z)(y)\mathit{571} \equiv](z)(y)(y \in V\ .\supset R\mathit{571})$
*100 (& D24), *123 $\supset (z)(y)R\mathit{571}$ (2)
†447, *123 (& D5) $\mathit{574}\,[\equiv.\ 1\ .\ 2]$

I have set forth the general theory of functional aspects at this length rather out of consideration of the general utility or interest

[14] *Ibid.*, p. 205.
[15] Substantially this principle is mentioned on p. 227n, *ibid.*

of that new notion than by way of groundwork for the brief remainder of the present paper; for the only use that I shall make of that notion here is in giving a somewhat simpler form than otherwise to a couple of definitions.

6. Ordinals and Cardinals. A class x is said to *have no fewer members than* a class y if the members of y can be exhausted by assigning each to one or more members of x without ever assigning two members of y to a single member of x; in other words, if y consists of values of some function for arguments belonging to x; in other words, if $(\exists z)(y \subset {}_F z``x)$. Thus $x$ *has fewer members than* $y$ just in case $(z) \sim(y \subset {}_F z``x)$. The notation '$x \prec y$', read '$x$ has fewer members than y', is accordingly introduced in the following fashion:

$$\ulcorner(\zeta \prec \eta)\urcorner \textit{ for } \ulcorner(\alpha) \sim(\eta \subset {}_F\alpha``\zeta)\urcorner.$$

As remarked in §4, x will have z members, for any natural number z, just in case z is the class of all those natural numbers that have fewer members than x. In other words, where x is any finite class, the number of members in x is $\hat{y}(y \in \omega \,.\, y \prec x)$. But where x is an infinite class, the "number of members in x" in the sense just proposed reduces to ω itself; for where x is infinite the clause '$y \prec x$' is fulfilled by every natural number y. The proposed sense of "number of members in x" thus works properly only for finite x; it ceases to discriminate sizes of classes when the classes are infinite. This is of course to be expected, since we have been dealing so far only with finite numbers. So let us turn our attention now to infinite numbers; for after we have considered these, the above formulation of "number of members in x" will turn out to admit of immediate extension so as to accommodate finite and infinite classes equally well.

The series of ordinal numbers can be taken as the obvious extension of the series of natural numbers. The finite ordinals can be identified with the natural numbers themselves; the first infinite ordinal, next, generally referred to as ω, can be taken as the class ω of all natural numbers; the succeeding ordinals $\omega + 1$, $\omega + 2$, etc., can be explained as $S`\omega$, $S`(S`\omega)$, etc., i.e., as $\omega \cup \iota\omega$, $\omega \cup \iota\omega \cup \iota(\omega \cup \iota\omega)$, etc.; 2ω becomes the class of all these that have gone before, hence $\omega \cup ({}_*S``\iota\omega)$; $2\omega + 1$ is $S`(\omega \cup ({}_*S``\iota\omega))$, and so on.[16] Each ordinal, finite or infinite, is the class of all its predecessors.

[16] Such is von Neumann's way of construing the ordinals in his 1923 paper.

The class of ordinals turns out to be definable in a fairly simple way:

$$\text{'NO' for '}\hat{x}(y)(\text{S``}y \subset y \,.\, (z)(z \subset y \,.\!\supset\!.\, \mathfrak{E}\text{``}z \in y) \,.\!\supset\!.\, x \in y)\text{'}.$$

NO is of course the class only of those ordinals that are elements; and, whereas all the finite ordinals are elements by virtue of being finite classes, the question how far elementhood extends into the infinite ordinals is one that depends on adoption of further elementhood axioms according to taste or to special purposes at hand. Note, though, that at most one ordinal, in the sense informally set forth in the preceding paragraph, can fail of elementhood; for an ordinal is the class of all its predecessors, and hence has only elements as predecessors. So, however far the series of ordinals that are elements is assumed to extend, the very existence of ordinals must be reckoned as leaving off after one more step. The ordinals that are elements are the members of NO; the ordinals in the broader sense are the members of NO and NO itself.

Now we are in position to extend our earlier formulation of 'the number of members in x' so as to allow for infinite x. We have only to use 'NO' where we previously used 'ω', thus: $\hat{y}(y \in \text{NO} \,.\, y \prec x)$. The number of members of x, or, as it will hereafter be called, the *cardinal number* of x, is thus explained as the class of all ordinal numbers that have fewer members than x.

$$\ulcorner \text{nc}\zeta \urcorner \text{ for } \ulcorner \hat{\alpha}(\alpha \in \text{NO} \,.\, \alpha \prec \zeta) \urcorner.$$

The class of all cardinal numbers may thereupon be explained as $\hat{x}(\exists y)(x = \text{nc}y)$; or, what is equivalent,

$$\text{'NC' for '}\hat{x}(x = \text{nc}x)\text{'}.$$

A cardinal number is, according to these constructions, an ordinal number; for a cardinal, like an ordinal, has as members all and only the ordinal numbers up to some point. But still a cardinal is an ordinal only of a special sort. As is evident from the definition of $\ulcorner \text{nc}\zeta \urcorner$, the distinguishing characteristic of cardinals is this: *a cardinal will never have one ordinal z among its members unless it also has among its members all other ordinals that have as few members as z has.* I.e., since the members of an ordinal (and, in particular, of a cardinal) are simply all the preceding ordinals, *a cardinal will never have one ordinal z among its predecessors unless it has also among its predecessors all other ordinals that have as few predecessors as z has.*

In short, *a cardinal is any ordinal that has more predecessors than has any of its predecessors.*

Thus in particular the finite cardinals are the same as the finite ordinals—and hence the same, again, as the natural numbers. The first infinite cardinal, commonly called $\aleph_0$, is the same as the first infinite ordinal ω. But the second infinite cardinal, commonly called $\aleph_1$, is not the same as the second infinite ordinal S'ω; for the predecessors of S'ω are denumerable and hence no more numerous than the predecessors of ω. The first ordinal whose predecessors are more than denumerable is the one commonly known as ω_1; and it is with this that $\aleph_1$ comes to be identified. Similarly $\aleph_2$ is ω_2, $\aleph_\omega$ is ω_ω, and so on. A cardinal number x, in general, is identified with the first ordinal that has x predecessors.

The class of ordinals NO, the class of cardinals NC, and the cardinal number *of* x have all been defined. Let us turn, finally, to the definition of the ordinal number *of* x, where x is thought of now as a well-ordered series. Just as the cardinal number of x is explained as the class of all ordinals y such that y has fewer members than x, so the ordinal number of x may be explained as the class of all ordinals y such that the series of ordinals up to but excluding y is a shorter series than x. I.e.,

$$\text{no}x = \hat{y}(y \in \text{NO} \,.\, \text{sub}y << x),$$

where sub$y$ is yet to be defined as the series of ordinals up to but excluding y, and '$<<$' is to mean 'is shorter than.'

If we identify a series with that relation which (intuitively speaking) each element of the series bears to itself and to each subsequent element of the series, a suitable definition of 'sub$y$' is apparent; for

$$\text{sub}y = \hat{z}\hat{x}(z, x \in \text{NO} \,.\, z \leqq x \,.\, x < y).$$

But, where z, x, and y are ordinals, '$z \leqq x \,.\, x < y$' amounts merely to '$z \subset x \,.\, x \in y$'; and, where y is an ordinal, the clause 'z, $x \in$ NO' amounts to '$z \in y$' alongside '$z \subset x \,.\, x \in y$'. Thus we might explain sub$y$ in very general and elementary terms, for *any* class y, as the relation $\hat{z}\hat{x}(z \subset x \,.\, z, x \in y)$; i.e., simply as the subclass relation among members of y. Then sub$y$, so defined, becomes in particular the series of ordinals up to but excluding y so long as y happens to be an ordinal. As to '$<<$', a definition that proves to give the intended sense so long as x and y happen to be well-ordered series consists in explaining '$x << y$' as short for:

$$(z) \sim (y \subset {}_{F}z \mid x \mid \breve{}_{F}z).$$

Our trio of definitions is accordingly as follows:

$$\ulcorner \text{sub}\zeta \urcorner \textit{ for } \ulcorner \hat{\alpha}\hat{\gamma}(\alpha \subset \gamma \,.\, \alpha, \gamma \in \zeta) \urcorner,$$
$$\ulcorner (\zeta \prec\prec \eta) \urcorner \textit{ for } \ulcorner (\alpha) \sim (\eta \subset {}_{F}\alpha \mid \zeta \mid \breve{}_{F}\alpha) \urcorner,$$
$$\ulcorner \text{no}\zeta \urcorner \textit{ for } \ulcorner \hat{\alpha}(\alpha \in \text{NO} \,.\, \text{sub}\alpha \prec\prec \zeta) \urcorner.$$

Note incidentally that an expression for the *series* of ordinals, as distinct from the class of ordinals, is ready to hand in 'subNO'; and the series of natural numbers is subω, and that of cardinal numbers is subNC.

The revision of *Mathematical Logic* that is called for by the inconsistency of *200 involves nothing of what has been set forth in §§3–6 of the present paper. The essential revision consists rather in merely changing Chapter IV as explained in §2 above, and reconstruing †610 of Chapter VI as an axiom *†600*. Correlative changes elsewhere in the book are slight and obvious: deletion of the Appendix, simplification of §58, and renumbering of any cross-references to the few renumbered theorems. What has been set forth in §§3–6 above is then an alternative development, appropriate perhaps as an appendix.

XI

On an Application of Tarski's Theory of Truth

Consider two interpreted systems of notation, L and L', in which statements can be formed. Let L' contain L together with what I have called the *protosyntax* of L;[1] i.e., the elementary means of talking about the expressions of L. For certain such systems L and L', we know from Tarski's work[2] (familiarity with which will not, however, be presupposed here) how to define truth for L in L'; i.e., how to translate 'y is a true statement of L' (with 'y' as a variable) into a formula of L'.

But if L contains adequate notation for elementary number theory, and L' consists of L and its protosyntax and nothing more, then definability of truth for L in L' leads to paradox. For, Tarski has shown[2] how to derive paradox from definability of truth for L in L; and L' does not essentially exceed L, since protosyntax can be reconstrued as elementary number theory by Gödel's expedient of assigning numbers to expressions.[3]

Hence if in particular the system of *Mathematical Logic* is consistent, Tarski's method of defining truth for L in L' must somehow break down when L is taken as the logical notation of *Mathe-*

The content of this paper had been figuring in my seminar for some years when, early in 1952, I was prompted by outside inquiries to write it up for the *Proceedings of the National Academy of Sciences*. It is reprinted here by permission. This paper, unlike the preceding one, requires no consultation of *Mathematical Logic*.

[1] *Mathematical Logic*, Chap. 7.

[2] "Der Wahrheitsbegriff."

[3] See, e.g., *Mathematical Logic*, 313ff.

matical Logic and L' is taken as just L plus the protosyntax of L. It is the purpose of the present paper to follow out the details of this breakdown. An outcome of the inquiry will be the discovery of a recursive definition which cannot, within the logical resources of *Mathematical Logic*, be turned into a direct definition (if the system is consistent).

So suppose henceforward that L is the logical notation of *Mathematical Logic* and L' is L plus the protosyntax of L. In L there is an infinite alphabet of variables, say 's', 't', . . . , 'z', 's'', etc. Suppose x is a function, or one–many relation, which assigns an entity to each variable. In Tarski's terminology, x is said to *satisfy* a formula y of L if y comes out true for the values of its free variables which are assigned to those variables by x. Vacuously, then, if y is a statement (hence devoid of free variables), y is satisfied by every function x or by none according as y is true or false. So, if we can define satisfaction, we can define 'y is true' as 'Stat y . $(x)(x$ satisfies $y)$' where 'Stat y' means 'y is a statement'. We know how to define 'Stat y' in the protosyntax of L;[4] so the problem of defining truth for L in L' now reduces to the problem of defining satisfaction for L in L'.

The atomic formulas in the notation of L consist of the 'ϵ' of membership flanked by variables; and the other formulas of L are built from atomic ones by joint denial ('$\downarrow$') and universal quantification. Let us refer to the atomic formula whose respective variables are y and z as y e z; let us refer to the joint denial of the respective formulas u and v as u j v; and let us refer to the universal quantification of v with respect to y as y qu v. Thus if y is 'w', z is 'x', u is '$x \epsilon t$', and v is '$(t \epsilon w \downarrow t \epsilon w)$', then y e z is '$w \epsilon x$', u j v is '$(x \epsilon t \downarrow (t \epsilon w \downarrow t \epsilon w))$', and y qu v is '$(w)(t \epsilon w \downarrow t \epsilon w)$'. We know how to define the notations 'y e z', 'u j v', and 'y qu v' in the protosyntax of L.[5]

To say that a function x satisfies an atomic formula of membership is to say that what x assigns to the left-hand variable is a member of what x assigns to the right-hand variable. Thus

(1) $$x \text{ satisfies } y \text{ e } z \,.\!\equiv\!.\, x`y \,\epsilon\, x`z.$$

Next, supposing we already know what it means to say that a function x satisfies a given formula y and that x satisfies a given for-

[4] *Op. cit.*, 298.
[5] *Ibid.*, 295.

mula z, we can easily explain what it means for x to satisfy their joint denial y j z; viz., that x satisfies neither y nor z. So

(2) x satisfies y j z .≡: x satisfies y . ↓ . x satisfies z.

It remains only to explain satisfaction of a quantification y qu z in terms of satisfaction of z; thereupon we shall have determined, recursively, the notion of satisfaction in relation to all formulas of L. Now it would appear that satisfaction of y qu z can be explained as follows: x satisfies y qu z if x not only satisfies z, but continues to satisfy z even when what x assigns to the variable y is changed *ad libitum;* i.e.,

(3) x satisfies y qu z .≡
$$(v)((w)(w \neq y \,.\!\supset\!.\, v`w = x`w) \supset\!.\, v \text{ satisfies } z).$$

In (1)–(3) I have followed Tarski. But Tarski's construction was geared to the Russell–Whitehead logic, in which all entities are *elements*, i.e., they all admit of membership in classes. For L, on the other hand, interpreted conformably to the axioms of *Mathematical Logic*, there are elements and non-elements. The possible relata of relations for L, and hence in particular the possible entities assigned by functions, are exclusively elements; but quantification in L ranges over all entities. Consequently (3) fails for L. For, the right-hand side of (3) says in effect 'x satisfies z and continues to satisfy z when what x assigns to the variable y is changed to any other *element*'. We need 'entity' here rather than 'element' if we are to reproduce the intended force of 'x satisfies y qu z'.

Basically the difficulty is as follows. What are wanted as satisfiers of formulas are, in some sense, systems of values of variables. Functions, taken as assigning values to variables, are what we have been using as systems of values of variables. But functions can assign only elements, whereas both elements and non-elements are wanted as values of variables. Now the difficulty can be overcome by a small adjustment. Intuitively what is wanted of a system of values of variables is a specification of this sort: x_0 as value of 's', x_1 as value of 't', x_2 as value of 'u', and so on. Now instead of representing such a system of values formally as a function, viz., as the relation which relates x_0 to 's', x_1 to 't', x_2 to 'u', and so on, let us represent it rather as the relation which relates each member of x_0 to 's', each member of x_1 to 't', each member of x_2 to 'u', and so on. There then ceases to be any requirement that x_0, x_1, x_2, etc., be elements. They have to be classes, but this is no restriction, since for L everything is a class; individuals are identified with their own unit classes.[6]

Where x was a system of values in the old sense, viz., a function assigning the values to the variables, the value assigned by x to a variable y was $x`y$. Where, on the other hand, x is a system of values in the new sense, viz., the relation of each member of the assigned value to the variable to which it is assigned, the value assigned by x to a variable y comes rather to be describable as the class of all things bearing x to y; briefly, $x``\iota y$. Whereas $x`y$ had to be an element, $x``\iota y$ can be anything.

(1) and (3) can be adjusted to this revision by changing '$x`y$', '$x`z$', '$v`w$', and '$x`w$' to '$x``\iota y$', '$x``\iota z$', '$v``\iota w$', and '$x``\iota w$'. Or, equivalently and more elegantly:

(4) x satisfies $y \text{ e } z \,.\equiv x(x``\iota y, z)$,

(5) x satisfies $y \text{ qu } z \,.\equiv$

$$(v)((w)(y \epsilon w \,.\vee.\, v``w = x``w) \supset.\, v \text{ satisfies } z).$$

(2) remains unchanged.

In (4), (2), and (5) we have a recursive definition which determines satisfaction correctly for all formulas of L. Moreover, all the notations used in (4), (2), and (5), other than the predicate 'satisfies', are notations definable either in the logic L or in the protosyntax of L; all, in short, belong to L'. Satisfaction for L has been recursively defined in L'. Truth for L is then definable, as noted earlier, in one more easy step.

But we are not yet involved in paradox. Paradox would ensue if satisfaction for L were *directly* definable in L'; i.e., if 'x satisfies y' were translatable into L' not merely for each specific formula as value of 'y', but for variable 'y'. Recursive definition does not automatically guarantee such translatability. However, there is a well-known technique due to Frege for turning recursive definitions into direct ones. Applied to (4), (2), and (5), the technique is this: 's satisfies t' is explained as meaning that s bears to t every relation u which obeys the laws which are imposed on the satisfaction relation in (4), (2), and (5). Thus 's satisfies t' would be defined as:

(6) $$(u)\{(x)(y)(z)[u(x, y \text{ e } z) \equiv x(x``\iota y, z) : \\ u(x, y \text{ j } z) \equiv.\, u(x, y) \downarrow u(x, z) : \\ u(x, y \text{ qu } z) \equiv (v)((w)(y \epsilon w \,.\vee.\, v``w = x``w) \supset u(v, z))] \\ \supset u(s, t)\}.$$ [7]

[6] *Ibid.*, 122f., 135.

[7] Strictly, clauses should be inserted stipulating that y and z be variables in certain cases, formulas in others. They are suppressed for perspicuity.

But this maneuver sacrifices an important part of the force of (4), (2), and (5). For (4), (2), and (5) admit, in the roles of v and x, elements and non-elements on an equal footing; whereas (6), by representing v and x as relata of a relation u, renders irrelevant all values of 'v' and 'x' except elements. Because of this divergence, (6) as definiens of 's satisfies t' fails to reproduce the sense of (4), (2), and (5). We may be as confident of this failure on the part of (6), anyway, as we are of the consistency of L. Satisfaction for L has been recursively defined in L', but it is not directly definable in L' unless L is inconsistent.

XII

On Frege's Way Out

In his review of Geach and Black's *Translations from the Philosophical Writings of Gottlob Frege*, Scholz urges that I evaluate the idea which Geach and Black express thus in their Preface:

> Special attention should be paid to Frege's discussion of Russell's paradox in the appendix to vol. ii of the *Grundgesetze*. It is discreditable that logical works should repeat the legend of Frege's abandoning his researches in despair when faced with the paradox; in fact he indicates a line of solution, which others (*e.g.* Quine) have followed out farther.

Geach becomes more explicit in a footnote (p. 243):

> The way out of Russell's Paradox here suggested by Frege has been followed by several later writers—*e.g.* by Quine in *Mathematical Logic*. Quine's particular form of the solution would be stated as follows in Frege's terminology: The concepts *not a member of itself* and *member of some class but not of itself* have the same class as their extension; but the class in question is not a member of *any* class, and thus falls only under the first of these concepts, not under the second. (But the relation of Quine's solution to Frege's is obscured because Quine does not explicitly make Frege's distinction between a concept or property and its extension.)

It is thus that I have been prompted to write the present paper.

Church in his review has described Geach and Black's idea as "far-fetched at best," and a paper on the scale of the present one is not needed to bear him out. It has seemed worth while, however, to

---

First published in *Mind*, 1955. An Italian translation appeared in the *Rivista di Filosofia* the same year. The paper appears here by permission of the editor of *Mind*. I have omitted an appendix because, as Church showed me, it was wrong.

relate Frege's "line of solution" to the history of set theory and also to show how it leads to contradiction.

1. Frege, Whitehead, and Russell on Attributes. Taking our cue from the concluding parenthesis of the note quoted from Geach, we may begin by reflecting briefly on "concepts or properties." Or, since 'concept' hints of mind and 'property' hints of a distinction between essence and accident, let us say *attributes.* An open sentence, e.g., 'x has fins', is supposed to determine both an attribute, that of finnedness, and a class, that of fin bearers (past, present, and future). The class may be called the *extension* of the open sentence; also it may be called the extension of the attribute.

Since Whitehead and Russell's work is nearer home than Frege's, and since occasion will arise anyway for certain comparisons, let us first view the notion of attribute in the context of *Principia Mathematica.* Whitehead and Russell, like Frege, admitted attributes in addition to classes. At the level of primitive notation, indeed, Whitehead and Russell adopted attributes to the exclusion of classes, and then introduced class names and class variables by contextual definition in terms of their theory of attributes; but at any rate their derived body of theory embraces the attributes and classes in effect side by side. The attributes were called *propositional functions* in *Principia,* and there was confusion between propositional functions in this sense and propositional functions in the sense of open sentences or predicates;[1] but this confusion is now inessential, for we know how to rectify it without upsetting the system.[2] To proceed, then: in *Principia* we find variables 'ϕ', 'ψ', etc., for attributes, and 'α', 'β', etc., for classes. Also we find two ways of using circumflex accents in connection with open sentences, one for the abstraction of attributes and the other for the abstraction of classes; thus '$\hat{x}$ has fins' names the attribute and '$\hat{x}(x$ has fins)' the class. Formally the one difference between attributes and classes, for *Principia,* is that the law of extensionality:

$$(1) \qquad (x)(x \in \alpha \,.\!\equiv\!.\, x \in \beta) \supset . \; \alpha = \beta$$

holds for classes whereas the corresponding law.

[1] For a treatment of the relevant notion of predicate see §1 of paper XVII below. Predicates in this sense are, like open sentences, notational forms. They are so devised as to expedite technical discussions of substitution. At those points in *Principia* where the "propositional functions" ambiguously so-called can be construed as notational entities at all (rather than as attributes), they are identifiable more aptly with predicates than with open sentences.

[2] Cf. §5 of I, above.

$$(2) \qquad (x)(\phi x \equiv \psi x) \supset . \phi = \psi$$

is not supposed to hold for attributes. The whole trick of defining class notation contextually in terms of attribute notation, in *Principia*, is indeed a trick of rendering the law of extensionality demonstrable for classes without adopting it for attributes.

The use of distinctive notation for attributes and classes is a feature of Frege's theory as well as of *Principia*. On the other hand there are differences. In *Principia* the realm of attributes can stand intact without benefit of classes—as indeed it explicitly does, from the point of view of primitive notation. For Frege, on the other hand, attributes depended in large part upon classes. Frege treated of attributes of classes without looking upon such discourse as somehow reducible to a more fundamental form treating of attributes of attributes. Thus, whereas he spoke of attributes of attributes as *second-level* attributes, he rated the attributes of classes as of first level; for he took all classes as rock-bottom objects on a par with individuals.[3]

2. In the Jaws of the Press. When most of the second volume (1903) of Frege's *Grundgesetze der Arithmetik* was in type and ready for printing, Russell wrote Frege announcing Russell's paradox and showing that it could be proved in Frege's system. In response Frege wrote an appendix to that second volume. This appendix was a report of the crisis and an essay at surveying the situation after the body of the book was beyond recall. It was to his translation of this appendix that Geach attached the footnote quoted at the beginning of the present paper.

According to Frege's original system, every attribute ϕ had a class $\hat{x}(\phi x)$ as its extension, and

$$(3) \qquad \hat{x}(\phi x) = \hat{x}(\psi x) . \supset (x)(\phi x \equiv \psi x).$$

The line he takes in his appendix is that of revoking (3). In so doing he impoverishes, to some degree, his universe of classes. He now allows attributes to have as their extensions the same class even where the attributes differ to the extent of holding and failing of some object.

Readers of *Principia* know that Russell's paradox of classes has a direct analogue in terms of attributes, and that the authors of *Principia* therefore found need to frame their theory of types for attributes as well as for classes. Indeed, the basic form of the theory

[3] 1893, §§23, 24, 35. See also Carnap, 1937, 138.

of types in *Principia* is the theory of types of attributes, or propositional functions. The type structure is automatically inherited by classes, through the contextual definitions by which the theory of classes is derived in *Principia* from that of attributes. Readers of *Principia* may wonder, therefore, that Frege can leave his own universe of attributes intact, and molest only the classes. Can we not reproduce Russell's paradox in Frege's theory of attributes, without using his classes at all?

We cannot. The reason is that Frege had, even before the discovery of Russell's paradox, the theory of levels of attributes hinted at above; an anticipation, to some degree, of the theory of types.[4] If in response to Russell's paradox Frege had elected to regiment his classes in levels corresponding to those of his attributes, his overall solution would have borne considerable resemblance to that in *Principia.*

Actually it is not to be wondered that Frege did not think of this course, or, thinking of it, adopt it. It was by having all his classes at ground level that he was able to avoid the use of high-level attributes, and this he liked to do. He regularly avoided ascent in his hierarchy of attributes by resorting at appropriate points to classes as zero-level proxies of attributes.[5] Thus, though he gives examples of third-level attributes and alludes to a continuation of the hierarchy,[6] in practice he uses no variables for attributes above the first level, nor constants for attributes above the second.

Russell's *Principles of Mathematics,* like the second volume of *Grundgesetze,* appeared in 1903. Russell had written *Principles* in ignorance of Frege's work; but before *Principles* was off the press he discovered Frege's writings and read various, including the first volume of *Grundgesetze.* There was time for him to add a long and appreciative appendix to *Principles;* time also, we have seen, for him to write Frege and evoke, in turn, an appendix in the second volume of *Grundgesetze;* and time even for him to see that appendix of Frege's and add still a note to his own appendix to *Principles* (p. 522), as follows:

> The second volume of *Gg.,* which appeared too late to be noticed in the Appendix, contains an interesting discussion of the contradiction . . . , suggesting that the solution is to be found by denying that two proposi-

[4] A somewhat clearer anticipation of the theory of types is to be found still earlier, in Schröder, 1890, 245–249. *Cf.* Church, 1939.

[5] Frege, 1893, §35.

[6] *Ibid.,* §24.

tional functions which determine equal classes must be equivalent. As it seems very likely that this is the true solution, the reader is strongly recommended to examine Frege on this point.

3. Frege's Details. Thus far I have described Frege's suggestion only incompletely, viz., as the rejection of (3). Russell in the above note describes it likewise, using different terminology. To be told that (3) is no longer to hold, or is no longer to retain its full generality, is to be told merely in what general quarter the revision is to be sought, and not what the revision is to be. Frege went on, however, in that same appendix to *Grundgesetze*, to make his suggestion more definite. Commenting on a step-by-step recapitulation of the argument of Russell's paradox, he writes:

> In both cases we see that the exceptional case is constituted by the extension itself, in that it falls under only one of two concepts whose extension it is; and we see that the occurrence of this exception can in no way be avoided. Accordingly the following suggests itself as the criterion for equality in extension: The extension of one concept coincides with that of another when every object that falls under the first concept, except the extension of the first concept, falls under the second concept likewise, and when every object that falls under the second concept, except the extension of the second concept, falls under the first concept likewise.[7]

What Frege calls "concepts" (*Begriffe*) in this passage are of course what I have been calling "attributes." Thus Frege is proposing, contrary to (3), that at least for some attributes ϕ and ψ we take $\hat{x}(\phi x)$ and $\hat{x}(\psi x)$ to be one and the same class even though '$\phi x \equiv \psi x$' be false of one special object x, viz., that class itself.[8]

Classically, the members of $\hat{x}(\phi x)$ are such that

(4) $$(y)[y \epsilon \hat{x}(\phi x) . \equiv \phi y].$$

This implies (3). Frege, in departing from (3), is therefore departing from (4), thus allowing the membership of $\hat{x}(\phi x)$ to deviate somewhat from its classical composition. But he keeps the deviation to a minimum, thus providing[9] that

(5) $$(y)[y \neq \hat{x}(\phi x) . \supset : y \epsilon \hat{x}(\phi x) . \equiv \phi y].$$

[7] Geach and Black, 242f., translating Frege, 1903, 262.

[8] I am now abandoning Whitehead and Russell's class variables 'α', 'β', etc. (see §1 above), in favor of the general variables 'x', 'y', etc. This procedure accords with Frege's, and is the appropriate one in the absence of a theory of types.

[9] 1903, 264.

This provision still leaves open the possibility, for any particular ϕ, that $\hat{x}(\phi x)$ either comprise exactly the objects x such that ϕx, or comprise all of them plus $\hat{x}(\phi x)$ itself, or comprise all except $\hat{x}(\phi x)$ itself. Frege implicitly elects this last alternative for all choices of ϕ;[9] thus

(6) $$(y)[y \in \hat{x}(\phi x) \,.\!\equiv\!.\, y \neq \hat{x}(\phi x) \,.\, \phi y].$$

Note that even this stipulation does not quite determine $\hat{x}(\phi x)$; to view (6) as a definition of '$\hat{x}(\phi x)$' would involve circularity, because of the recurrence of '$\hat{x}(\phi x)$' on the right. Frege expresses awareness of this lack of specificity, in a remark immediately following the longer passage which I quoted a page back.

> Obviously this cannot be taken as *defining* the extension of a concept, but only as specifying the distinctive property of this second-level function.

What we have just been examining would seem to be the "way out of Russell's paradox" which, according to Geach, "has been followed by several later writers—*e.g.* by Quine, in *Mathematical Logic.*" But he must have meant to refer only to broader lines of Frege's proposal; for the idea expressed in (5) (let alone (6)) has never been used, so far as I know, by anyone but Frege. This is cause for satisfaction, because the idea leads to contradiction in any universe of more than one member.

4. The New Contradiction. Sobociński reports (220ff.) that Leśniewski proved the inconsistency of Frege's proposal in 1938. Leśniewski's argument, as set forth by Sobociński, is hard to dissociate from special features of Leśniewski's system. But Geach, who lately brought this paper to my attention, has succeeded in reproducing the argument in a Fregean setting, obtaining a contradiction from (6) and:

(7) $$(\exists x)(\exists y)(x \neq y).$$

Before hearing of these developments I had derived a contradiction using, in place of (6), the weaker assumption (5). My derivation is as follows. I define 'V', 'Λ', 'ιz', and 'W' as '$\hat{x}(x = x)$', '$\hat{x}(x \neq x)$', '$\hat{x}(x = z)$', and '$\hat{x}(z)(x \in z \,.\, z \in x \,.\!\supset\!.\, x = z)$', and make use of four cases of (5):

(8) $$(z)(y)(y \neq \iota z \,.\!\supset\!:\, y \in \iota z \,.\!\equiv\!.\, y = z),$$

(9) $$(y)[y \neq \mathrm{W} \,.\!\supset\!:\, y \in \mathrm{W} \,.\!\equiv\, (z)(y \in z \,.\, z \in y \,.\!\supset\!.\, y = z)],$$

and the cases corresponding to 'V' and 'Λ', which reduce quickly to:

(10) $$(y)(y \neq \mathrm{V} \,.\supset.\, y \in \mathrm{V}),$$

(11) $$(y)(y \in \Lambda \,.\supset.\, y = \Lambda).$$

Two corollaries of (8) are:

(12) $$(y)(y \neq \iota y \,.\supset.\, y \in \iota y),$$

(13) $$(x)(z)[(\exists y)(x \in y \,.\, y \in \iota z \,.\, y \neq \iota z) \supset.\, x \in z \,.\, z \neq \iota z].$$

If we change 'ιy' in (12) to 'Λ', then by (11) we can get '$y = \Lambda$'; so

(14) $$(y)(\iota y = \Lambda \,.\supset.\, y = \Lambda).$$

If we change 'ιz' to 'z' in (8) and reduce, we get '$y \in z \,.\supset.\, y = z$'; so

(15) $$(z)(y)(z = \iota z \,.\, y \in z \,.\supset.\, y = z).$$

If we change 'V' to 'Λ' in (10), then by (11) we can get '$(y)(y = \Lambda)$', contrary to (7); so $\mathrm{V} \neq \Lambda$. Hence, by (10) and (14),

(16) $$\Lambda \in \mathrm{V}, \qquad \iota\mathrm{V} \neq \Lambda, \qquad \iota\iota\mathrm{V} \neq \Lambda.$$

By (8), $\Lambda \neq \iota\iota\mathrm{V} \,.\supset:\, \Lambda \in \iota\iota\mathrm{V} \,.\equiv.\, \Lambda = \iota\mathrm{V}$. Hence, by (16), $\sim(\Lambda \in \iota\iota\mathrm{V})$, whereas $\Lambda \in \mathrm{V}$. So

(17) $$\iota\iota\mathrm{V} \neq \mathrm{V}.$$

By (15), $\iota y = \iota\iota y \,.\, y \in \iota y \,.\supset.\, y = \iota y$. Hence, by (12),

(18) $$(y)(\iota y = \iota\iota y \,.\supset.\, y = \iota y = \iota\iota y).$$

From (17), by (18), we have '$\iota\mathrm{V} \neq \iota\iota\mathrm{V}$', and thence, by (18) again,

(19) $$\iota\iota\iota\mathrm{V} \neq \iota\iota\mathrm{V}.$$

If $\iota\iota\mathrm{V} \neq \mathrm{W}$ and $\sim(\iota\iota\mathrm{V} \in \mathrm{W})$, then, by (9),

$$(\exists z)(\iota\iota\mathrm{V} \in z \,.\, z \in \iota\iota\mathrm{V} \,.\, \iota\iota\mathrm{V} \neq z),$$

whence, by (13), $\iota\iota\mathrm{V} \in \iota\mathrm{V}$ and $\iota\iota\mathrm{V} \neq \iota\mathrm{V}$; but then, by (8), $\iota\iota\mathrm{V} = \mathrm{V}$, contrary to (17). So

(20) $$\iota\iota\mathrm{V} = \mathrm{W} \,.\vee.\, \iota\iota\mathrm{V} \in \mathrm{W}.$$

Suppose $\iota\mathrm{W} = \mathrm{W}$. Then, by (15), $\iota\iota\mathrm{V} \in \mathrm{W} \,.\supset.\, \iota\iota\mathrm{V} = \mathrm{W}$, and hence, by (20), $\iota\iota\mathrm{V} = \mathrm{W}$. But then, by (19), $\iota\mathrm{W} \neq \mathrm{W}$. So

(21) $$\iota\mathrm{W} \neq \mathrm{W}.$$

Hence, by (12),

(22) $W \epsilon \iota W.$

By (21) and (9),

(23) $\iota W \epsilon W . \equiv (z)(\iota W \epsilon z . z \epsilon \iota W . \supset . \iota W = z).$

Hence $\iota W \epsilon W . \supset : \iota W \epsilon W . W \epsilon \iota W . \supset . \iota W = W$. So, by (21) and (22),

(24) $\sim(\iota W \epsilon W).$

Then, by (23), $(\exists z)(\iota W \epsilon z . z \epsilon \iota W . \iota W \neq z)$, whence, by (13), $\iota W \epsilon W$, in contradiction to (24).

5. A Kernel of Truth. It is not to Frege's discredit that the explicitly speculative appendix now under discussion, written against time in a crisis, should turn out to possess less scientific value than biographical interest. Over the past half century the piece has perhaps had dozens of sympathetic readers who, after a certain amount of tinkering, have dismissed it as the wrong guess of a man in a hurry. One such reader was probably Frege himself, sometime in the ensuing twenty-two years of his life. Another, presumably, was Russell. We must remember that Russell's initial favorable reaction, quoted at the end of §2, was a hurried conjecture indeed; five years later we have, in significant contrast, his theory of types.

In any event, what Russell actually described in that quoted note was not Frege's full suggestion, but only its broadest feature: restriction, somehow, of (3). This feature, though Russell later turned his back on it, is a good one; and by working out from it we can find what Frege's ill-starred appendix did contain pertinent to the subsequent course of logic. That broad feature, and more, can be said with some plausibility to have "been followed by several later writers—*e.g.* by Quine, in *Mathematical Logic.*"

In order to implement the ensuing comparisons we must eliminate Frege's reference to a realm of attributes. This necessity is remarked, though in an inverted form, in the concluding parenthesis of Geach's well-thumbed footnote. But the required elimination is less difficult than that parenthesis might lead one to expect, thanks to the circumstance that none of Frege's remarks in this connection depend on any principle of individuation of attributes broader than the principle of individuation (viz., sheer sameness of spelling) of the corresponding open sentences themselves. Where Frege speaks of classes as extensions of attributes, we can speak metalogically of classes as determined by open sentences.

This shift requires no rewriting of (3)–(6) and related formulas. These merely change in status from open sentences, with attribute variables 'ϕ' and 'ψ', to schemata with dummy sentences 'ϕx', 'ψx', and 'ϕy'. The difference, conspicuously immaterial here, would become material in cases where 'ϕ' occurs in a quantifier; such cases would cease to be allowable.[10] But we shall not encounter any of them.

To reject (3), as Frege did, was to allow (3) to be false for some attributes ϕ and ψ. Reconstrued now without reference to attributes, his rejection of (3) comes to consist in allowing (3) to be false under some substitutions of open sentences for 'ϕx' and 'ψx'.

Now it is time to point out an important difficulty in connection with rejecting (3). The difficulty lurks equally in Frege's account and in Russell's note. It is this: the prefix '$\hat{x}$' has been understood, to begin with, as 'the class of all and only the objects x such that'. If we presume to declare some case of (3) false, thus taking '$\hat{x}(\phi x) = \hat{x}(\psi x)$' as true and '$(x)(\phi x \equiv \psi x)$' as false (for some particular choice of open sentences in place of 'ϕx' and 'ψx'), then surely we have departed from that original reading of '$\hat{x}$', and left no clue as to what the classes $\hat{x}(\phi x)$ and $\hat{x}(\psi x)$ are supposed to be which are talked of in the allegedly true equation '$\hat{x}(\phi x) = \hat{x}(\psi x)$'. Either we must give some supplementary reading of the notation '$\hat{x}$', or we cannot read the presumed counter-instances of (3). Similar difficulties arise over the word 'extension' in Frege's account, and over the word 'determine' in Russell's note.

Earlier we observed that rejection of (3) involves rejection of (4). Let us accordingly concentrate on (4) instead of (3); for, it happens that the above difficulty as it affects (4) can be coped with. The reasoning is as follows. In case the open sentence represented as 'ϕx' happens to be such that some class z has as members all and only the objects x such that ϕx, certainly $\hat{x}(\phi x)$ is still to be understood as z; it is only in the unfavorable cases that '$\hat{x}$' demands novel interpretation. The question whether to adhere to (4) for all open sentences, or to reject it for some, is thus simply the question whether to adhere to the *abstraction principle:*

$$(\exists z)(x)(x \in z . \equiv \phi x)$$

for all open sentences or to reject it for some. Instead of talking of rejection of (4), therefore, we can talk of rejection of the abstrac-

[10] See §5 of I, above; also *Methods of Logic*, 22, 82, 91f., 129f., 203–208; also *From a Logical Point of View*, 8–11, 102–116.

tion principle. The useful difference between this principle and (4) is that whereas we cannot deny a case of (4) without facing the question what $\hat{x}(\phi x)$ is thenceforward supposed to be, we can deny any case of the abstraction principle without having to recognize the prefix '$\hat{x}$' at all.

All the well-known ways around the paradoxes, except for the theory of types, involve recognizing exceptions to the abstraction principle. This is not to be wondered at, since the abstraction principle yields contradiction by elementary logic as soon as 'ϕx' is taken as the open sentence '$\sim(x \in x)$'. Either you must declare some open sentences to be immune to the abstraction principle or, as is done in the theory of types, you must declare certain harmful forms such as '$\sim(x \in x)$' to be ungrammatical and not sentences at all.

The theories which allow exceptions to the abstraction principle differ from one another, essentially, in where they fix the break between the cases which hold and the cases which fail. Zermelo was perhaps the first to perceive clearly this focal rôle of the abstraction principle; at any rate, his set theory (1908) was the first that proceeded explicitly by postulation of instances and families of instances of that principle.

6. Extension Extended. In turning our attention from (3) and (4) to the abstraction principle as formulated above, we came out where we need no longer worry about novel interpretations of the prefix '$\hat{x}$', and can simply acquiesce in the inappropriateness of that prefix in connection with many open sentences. Some open sentences (those fulfilling the abstraction principle) happen to have extensions; others not. Frege himself touched upon that possibility, in the following words:

> . . . we must take into account the possibility that there are concepts with no extension (at any rate, none in the ordinary sense of the word).[11]

However, he promptly and explicitly discarded that alternative, electing rather to require an extension in every case. He thus presented himself squarely with the problem of reconstruing '$\hat{x}(\phi x)$' compatibly with rejection of (3). Actually he cannot, despite the above passage, have hoped to retain extensions generally "in the ordinary sense of the word," since this would mean retaining (4) and so (3). But he wanted there to be, for every case 'ϕx', an extension $\hat{x}(\phi x)$ under some mildly variant reinterpretation of

[11] Geach and Black, 239, translating Frege, 1903, 257.

'extension' and '$\hat{x}(\phi x)$'. He essayed such a reinterpretation in his final suggestions, as noted above in connection with (6), but recognized that he had not fixed it uniquely.

Since Frege's full suggestion leads to contradiction, there is no point in trying to devise a unique reinterpretation of '$\hat{x}(\phi x)$' suited to exactly his principles. On the other hand, the general question of devising reinterpretations of '$\hat{x}(\phi x)$' for systems which allow exceptions to the abstraction principle is worth considering. Narrowing the field a little, we might require of a satisfactory reinterpretation that $\hat{x}(\phi x)$ continue to contain only objects x such that ϕx, even if it cannot at the same time exhaust them. Now given this condition, a further imperative becomes evident: $\hat{x}(\phi x)$ must not be a subclass of any further class which contains only objects x such that ϕx. For, if $\hat{x}(\phi x)$ is not to exhaust the objects x such that ϕx, at least we want it to come as near as possible to doing so.

How to reconstrue '$\hat{x}(\phi x)$', conformably with the above requirements, will depend on what cases of the abstraction principle hold; and this is the central point on which set theories differ from one another. The particular distribution of cases for which the principle holds, for a given set theory, can be such as to make any general interpretation of '$\hat{x}(\phi x)$' conformable to the foregoing paragraph impossible. This can happen in either of two ways. It may happen, for some open sentences, that every class whose members all fulfill the sentence is a subclass of a further class whose members all fulfill the sentence, so that there is no final class of the kind. Again it may happen, for some open sentences, that each of several classes qualifies under the requirements of the preceding paragraph, and there is no systematic way of choosing one from among them.

Zermelo's system (1908), von Neumann's (1925), and that of my "New foundations" (1937) are three set theories which differ drastically from one another in point of what cases of the abstraction principle are assumed to hold. Each of the three, however, is such as to render impossible any general interpretation of '$\hat{x}(\phi x)$' within the above requirements. In any such system the sensible course is simply not to call for an extension $\hat{x}(\phi x)$, in any sense, for each open sentence 'ϕx'.[12]

A striking feature of von Neumann's theory is that it, unlike its predecessors, provides for there being some classes which are not

[12] But one can still apply '$\hat{x}$', in its full classical import, to the particular open sentences for which the abstraction principle holds, defining this usage via singular description. Such is my procedure in "New foundations."

members of any classes at all. Such classes I called *non-elements* when I gratefully carried his idea over into my *Mathematical Logic*. The set theory of *Mathematical Logic*, though depending heavily on the presence of non-elements, differs from von Neumann's system in consequential ways. The cases of the abstraction principle which hold for my system differ from those which hold for von Neumann's, and can be specified in an unusually simple way, as follows: the principle holds except when there are non-elements fulfilling 'ϕx'.[13] Now for this system, unlike von Neumann's, Zermelo's, and that of "New foundations," a general interpretation of '$\hat{x}(\phi x)$' *is* available which conforms to the requirements lately set forth. It turns out to be this: $\hat{x}(\phi x)$ is the class of all *elements* x such that ϕx. Formally stated, $\hat{x}(\phi x)$ is the y such that $(x)[x \in y \,.\!\equiv\!.\, (\exists z)(x \in z) \,.\, \phi x]$.

The above description of the system of *Mathematical Logic* does not determine it in full, but applies still to a whole genus of systems.[14] The cases of the abstraction principle which hold for my system may seem just now to have been fully specified, leaving no latitude for further variation; but this is not so, for the above specification appeals to the distinction between element and non-element, and we are still free to draw this line very much as we choose.

7. *Frege and the Later Trends.* Let us consider, in summary survey, how the suggestions in Frege's appendix relate to set theory from Zermelo onward. Frege's rejection of (3) implies, we observed, rejecting the universality of the abstraction principle; and this latter departure is a focal point of modern foundations of set theory, from Zermelo onward, aside from the theory of types. But the claim for Frege is weak here. Frege's eyes were on the extension $\hat{x}(\phi x)$, and how to preserve it or a reasonable facsimile in the general case. Zermelo had no such preoccupation, and faced the problem of set-theoretic foundations squarely in terms of the cases of the abstraction principle. Significantly, neither Zermelo's set theory nor von Neumann's nor that of my "New foundations" will accommodate the remotest analogue of an extension operator applicable to open sentences generally. Zermelo, rather than Frege, stands out as the

[13] This can be seen by reflecting that in *202 of *Mathematical Logic* the clause of elementhood is dispensable if and only if it is implied by the formula which stands in conjunction with it.

[14] E.g. my "Element and number," above; Wang, "A new theory of element and number." The earliest instance is perhaps the system of the first edition of *Mathematical Logic*, which, however, proved inconsistent. The emendation of the system, used in the revised edition, is due to Wang (1950).

pioneer in the genre of set theories represented by these three. Not but that von Neumann in turn added a drastic innovation, in his admission of non-elementhood. Moreover "New foundations," though like Zermelo's in that it proceeds by selective adoption of cases of the abstraction principle, is in equal measure indebted to Russell's theory of types. The principle determining what cases of the abstraction principle are to hold for "New foundations" is an adaptation of a formal feature of type theory.

If Frege's preoccupation with a generally applicable analogue of the classical extension operator tends to estrange him from the above company, it should count correspondingly in favor of an affinity between his suggestions and my *Mathematical Logic.* For in the latter system there is, we have seen, a generally applicable adaptation of the extension operator. Moreover, to turn to a prominent individual case, the extension $\hat{x} \sim(x \epsilon x)$ fails to be a member of itself, in *Mathematical Logic* as in Frege's plan; this conformity was remarked in Geach's footnote.

Yet the differences are great. Frege's extension operator resisted actual interpretation, but was supposed, in each application, to approximate to the classical extension to within one possible discrepancy of membership. Mine is defined, and admits of infinite discrepancies. Furthermore von Neumann's non-elementhood concept, utterly un-Fregean, is of the essence of *Mathematical Logic.* Incidentally there is the inconsistency of Frege's specific proposal; this is indeed a point of similarity with the first edition of *Mathematical Logic,* but quite possibly a point of contrast with the current edition, thanks to Wang's brilliant repair.

A passing remark, finally, on genesis. We discerned, in the demand for a generally applicable adaptation of the extension operator, a particular resemblance which Frege's proposal bears to the system of *Mathematical Logic* and not to previous set theories such as Zermelo's, von Neumann's, and that of "New foundations." Now this particular resemblance is due not to heredity but to convergence: response to common demands of algorithmic facility. The ancestry of *Mathematical Logic* is an open book; the parents are von Neumann's system and "New foundations," both of whose genealogies were looked into a page back.

All of modern logic owes an incalculable debt to Frege. If anyone can be singled out as the founder of mathematical logic, it is by all odds he. But I have been concerned in these pages, like Geach and Black in the remarks which I quoted from them, only with the hurried appendix to the second volume of *Grundgesetze.*

XIII

Completeness of the Propositional Calculus

The completeness of the propositional calculus was first proved by Post, 1921. His somewhat condensed proof has been succeeded by more detailed presentations of substantially the same argument,[1] and also by several proofs of radically different forms.[2] The present paper contains still another proof, offered because of its relative simplicity. In part this proof follows a plan which was sketched by Wajsberg[3] for another purpose, viz., for proving the completeness of the sub-calculus involving only the material conditional.

For the present proof a systematization of the propositional calculus will be used which is due to Tarski, Bernays, and Wajsberg.[4] It involves the material conditional '$\supset$' and the falsehood 'F' as primitive; thus the *formulae* are recursively describable as comprising 'F', the variables 'p', 'q', 'r', . . . , and all results of putting formulae for 'p' and 'q' in '$(p \supset q)$'. The denial '$\sim p$' is definable as '$(p \supset \mathrm{F})$', and all other truth functions are then definable in familiar fashion. (Conversely, in a system admitting '$\sim$'

Reprinted from the *Journal of Symbolic Logic,* Volume 3, 1938.

[1] Hilbert and Ackermann, 1928, 9–29, 33; Hilbert and Bernays, Vol. 1, 49–67.

[2] Łukasiewicz, "Ein Vollständigkeitsbeweis"; Kalmár, 1935; Hermes and Scholz.

[3] 154–157.

[4] See Wajsberg, 132, 157–159.

instead of 'F' as primitive, 'F' might be explained as an abbreviation of '$\sim(p \supset p)$'.) The postulates are four:

(1) $((p \supset q) \supset ((q \supset r) \supset (p \supset r)))$
(2) $(((p \supset q) \supset p) \supset p)$
(3) $(p \supset (q \supset p))$
(4) $(\mathrm{F} \supset p)$.

Theorems are derived by substitution and *modus ponens* as usual; among them are the following:

(5) $(s \supset s)$
(6) $((p \supset (t \supset r)) \supset (t \supset (p \supset r)))$
(7) $((s \supset (q \supset r)) \supset ((p \supset q) \supset (s \supset (p \supset r))))$
(8) $((s \supset (p \supset q)) \supset ((q \supset r) \supset (s \supset (p \supset r))))$
(9) $((r \supset s) \supset ((s \supset t) \supset ((t \supset u) \supset (r \supset u))))$
(10) $((r \supset (s \supset t)) \supset ((q \supset r) \supset ((q \supset s) \supset (q \supset t))))$
(11) $((r \supset (s \supset t)) \supset ((p \supset r) \supset ((q \supset s) \supset (p \supset (q \supset t)))))$
(12) $((p \supset (q \supset (s \supset r))) \supset (q \supset (s \supset (p \supset r))))$
(13) $(p \supset (s \supset s))$
(14) $(q \supset (p \supset (s \supset s)))$
(15) $(((p \supset q) \supset r) \supset ((r \supset p) \supset p))$
(16) $(((p \supset q) \supset r) \supset ((p \supset r) \supset r))$
(17) $(((p \supset (s \supset s)) \supset ((q \supset p) \supset r)) \supset (p \supset r))$
(18) $((r \supset s) \supset ((t \supset u) \supset ((s \supset t) \supset (r \supset u))))$
(19) $((q \supset (r \supset s)) \supset$
$((q \supset (t \supset u)) \supset (q \supset ((s \supset t) \supset (r \supset u)))))$
(20) $((p \supset (q \supset (r \supset s))) \supset$
$((p \supset (q \supset (t \supset u))) \supset (p \supset (q \supset ((s \supset t) \supset (r \supset u))))))$
(21) $((s \supset ((p \supset q) \supset r)) \supset ((t \supset (p \supset r)) \supset (s \supset (t \supset r))))$
(22) $(((p \supset q) \supset (s \supset r)) \supset ((p \supset (t \supset r)) \supset (s \supset (t \supset r))))$
(23) $((q \supset ((\mathrm{F} \supset p) \supset r)) \supset (q \supset r))$
(24) $(\mathrm{F} \supset \mathrm{F})$
(25) $(\mathrm{F} \supset (\mathrm{F} \supset \mathrm{F}))$
(26) $((\mathrm{F} \supset \mathrm{F}) \supset (\mathrm{F} \supset \mathrm{F}))$
(27) $(((\mathrm{F} \supset \mathrm{F}) \supset \mathrm{F}) \supset \mathrm{F})$.

The derivation of (5)–(12) from (1)–(3) is recorded elsewhere.[5] (13)–(27) are proved as follows:[6]

[5] In my *System of Logistic*, 68, 72–74: derivation of 2·5, 2·7, 2·86, 2·87, 2·94, 2·96, 2·97, and 2·99 from 2·1, 2·2, and 2·3.
[6] Concerning the notation see *ibid.*, pp. 61–71.

(3)—(5) $\supset$ (13). (3)—(13) $\supset$ (14).
(8)—(1)$(p/(p \supset q);\ q/r;\ r/p) \supset.$ (2) $\supset$ (15).
(1)—(15) $\supset.$ (15)$(p/r;\ q/p;\ r/p) \supset$ (16).
(12)—(7)$(s/(13);\ q/(q \supset p)) \supset:$ (3) $\supset.$ (13) $\supset$ (17).
(1)—(9) $\supset.$ (6)$(p/(s \supset t);\ t/(t \supset u);\ r/(r \supset u)) \supset$ (18).
(10)—(18) $\supset$ (19). (10)—(19) $\supset$ (20). (11)—(16) $\supset$ (21).
(11)—(21) $\supset:$ (6)$(p/(p \supset q);\ t/s) \supset.$ (6) $\supset$ (22).
(6)—(6)$(p/q;\ t/(4)) \supset.$ (4) $\supset$ (23).
(5)—(24). (3)—(25). (5)—(26). (2)—(27).

A formula χ will be called *regular* if, for all ϕ, ψ, and ω such that ω results from putting ψ for $\geqq 0$ occurrences of ϕ in χ,

$$\vdash \ulcorner((\phi \supset \psi) \supset ((\psi \supset \phi) \supset (\chi \supset \omega)))\urcorner \tag{a}$$

and

$$\vdash \ulcorner((\phi \supset \psi) \supset ((\psi \supset \phi) \supset (\omega \supset \chi)))\urcorner. \tag{b}$$

[7]

It will be proved that every formula is regular.

(I) *Every formula with no occurrences of '$\supset$' is regular.*

Proof. Let χ have no occurrences of '$\supset$', and let ω result from putting ψ for $\geqq 0$ occurrences of ϕ in χ. Then χ is a single letter ('F' or a variable); hence either ω is χ, in which case (a) and (b) follow from (14), or else ω is ψ and χ is ϕ, in which case (a) follows from (3) and (b) from (13).

(II) *If every formula with $\leqq m$ occurrences of '$\supset$' is regular, so is every formula with $m + 1$.*

Proof. Let χ have $m + 1$ occurrences of '$\supset$', and let ω result from putting ψ for $\geqq 0$ occurrences of ϕ in χ. In the trivial case where ϕ is χ and ω is ψ, (a) follows directly from (3) and (b) from (13). In all other cases χ is $\ulcorner(\chi_1 \supset \chi_2)\urcorner$ and ω is $\ulcorner(\omega_1 \supset \omega_2)\urcorner$, where ω_1 and ω_2 result from putting ψ for $\geqq 0$ occurrences of ϕ in χ_1 and χ_2. But χ_1 and χ_2 have $\leqq m$ occurrences of '$\supset$'. Hence, by hp,

$$\vdash \ulcorner((\phi \supset \psi) \supset ((\psi \supset \phi) \supset (\chi_1 \supset \omega_1)))\urcorner, \tag{i}$$

$$\vdash \ulcorner((\phi \supset \psi) \supset ((\psi \supset \phi) \supset (\omega_1 \supset \chi_1)))\urcorner, \tag{ii}$$

$$\vdash \ulcorner((\phi \supset \psi) \supset ((\psi \supset \phi) \supset (\chi_2 \supset \omega_2)))\urcorner, \tag{iii}$$

and

$$\vdash \ulcorner((\phi \supset \psi) \supset ((\psi \supset \phi) \supset (\omega_2 \supset \chi_2)))\urcorner. \tag{iv}$$

By (20), $\vdash \ulcorner[\text{(ii)}] \supset. [\text{(iii)}] \supset [\text{(a)}]\urcorner$ and $\vdash \ulcorner[\text{(i)}] \supset. [\text{(iv)}] \supset [\text{(b)}]\urcorner$.

(III) *Every formula is regular. Proof:* (I), (II).

Three corollaries follow:

[7] Concerning the metamathematical notation see VII above.

(IV) *If* ω *is formed from* χ *by putting* '(F ⊃ F)' *for* $\geqq 0$ *occurrences of* ϕ, *then* $\vdash \ulcorner(\phi \supset (\chi \supset \omega))\urcorner$ *and* $\vdash \ulcorner(\phi \supset (\omega \supset \chi))\urcorner$.

Proof. By (III),

$$\vdash \ulcorner((\phi \supset (\mathrm{F} \supset \mathrm{F})) \supset (((\mathrm{F} \supset \mathrm{F}) \supset \phi) \supset (\chi \supset \omega)))\urcorner \quad \text{(i)}$$

and $$\vdash \ulcorner((\phi \supset (\mathrm{F} \supset \mathrm{F})) \supset (((\mathrm{F} \supset \mathrm{F}) \supset \phi) \supset (\omega \supset \chi)))\urcorner. \quad \text{(ii)}$$

By (17), $\vdash \ulcorner[\text{(i)}] \supset (\phi \supset (\chi \supset \omega))\urcorner$ and $\vdash \ulcorner[\text{(ii)}] \supset (\phi \supset (\omega \supset \chi))\urcorner$.

(V) *If* ψ *is formed from* χ *by putting* 'F' *for* $\geqq 0$ *occurrences of* ϕ, *then* $\vdash \ulcorner((\phi \supset \mathrm{F}) \supset (\chi \supset \psi))\urcorner$ *and* $\vdash \ulcorner((\phi \supset \mathrm{F}) \supset (\psi \supset \chi))\urcorner$.

Proof. By (III), $\vdash \ulcorner((\phi \supset \mathrm{F}) \supset ((\mathrm{F} \supset \phi) \supset (\chi \supset \psi)))\urcorner$ (i)

and $\vdash \ulcorner((\phi \supset \mathrm{F}) \supset ((\mathrm{F} \supset \phi) \supset (\psi \supset \chi)))\urcorner$. (ii)

By (23), $\vdash \ulcorner[\text{(i)}] \supset ((\phi \supset \mathrm{F}) \supset (\chi \supset \psi))\urcorner$ and $\vdash \ulcorner[\text{(ii)}] \supset ((\phi \supset \mathrm{F}) \supset (\psi \supset \chi))\urcorner$.

(VI) *If* ψ *and* ω *are formed as in* (V) *and* (IV), *then* $\vdash \ulcorner(\psi \supset (\omega \supset \chi))\urcorner$.

Proof. By (V), $\vdash \ulcorner((\phi \supset \mathrm{F}) \supset (\psi \supset \chi))\urcorner$. (i)

By (IV), $\vdash \ulcorner(\phi \supset (\omega \supset \chi))\urcorner$. (ii)

By (22), $\vdash \ulcorner[\text{(i)}] \supset . [\text{(ii)}] \supset (\psi \supset (\omega \supset \chi))\urcorner$.

Preparatory to showing that every tautology is a theorem, the notion of tautology must be sharply formulated. Roughly, ϕ is a tautology if every result of substituting 'F' for $\geqq 0$ variables of ϕ, and 'T' for the rest, reduces to 'T' by the truth-table process—i.e., by a continued process of putting 'F' for '(T ⊃ F)' and 'T' for '(F ⊃ F)', '(F ⊃ T)', and '(T ⊃ T)'. Hence, if by way of adhering to the notation of the system we use '(F ⊃ F)' instead of the letter 'T', we can formulate the notion of tautology as follows. ϕ is said to *reduce* to ψ if there are $\phi_0, \phi_1, \ldots, \phi_n (n \geqq 0)$ such that ϕ_0 is ϕ, ϕ_n is ψ, and, for each i from 1 to n, ϕ_i is formed from ϕ_{i-1} by putting 'F' for '((F ⊃ F) ⊃ F)' (Case 1) or by putting '(F ⊃ F)' for '(F ⊃ (F ⊃ F))' (Case 2) or for '((F ⊃ F) ⊃ (F ⊃ F))' (Case 3). An *evaluant* of ϕ is any result of substituting 'F' for $\geqq 0$ variables and '(F ⊃ F)' for all other variables in ϕ. ϕ is called a *tautology* if all its evaluants reduce to '(F ⊃ F)'.

(VII) *If* ϕ *reduces to* ψ, $\vdash \ulcorner(\phi \supset \psi)\urcorner$ *and* $\vdash \ulcorner(\psi \supset \phi)\urcorner$.

Proof. In Case 1 (see above), by (V), $\vdash \ulcorner(27) \supset (\phi_{i-1} \supset \phi_i)\urcorner$ and $\vdash \ulcorner(27) \supset (\phi_i \supset \phi_{i-1})\urcorner$; in Case 2, by (IV), $\vdash \ulcorner(25) \supset (\phi_{i-1} \supset \phi_i)\urcorner$ and $\vdash \ulcorner(25) \supset (\phi_i \supset \phi_{i-1})\urcorner$; and in Case 3, by (IV), $\vdash \ulcorner(26) \supset$

$(\phi_{i-1} \supset \phi_i)^\urcorner$ and $\vdash\ulcorner(26) \supset (\phi_i \supset \phi_{i-1})^\urcorner$. Thus $\vdash\ulcorner(\phi \supset \phi_1)^\urcorner$, $\vdash\ulcorner(\phi_1 \supset \phi_2)^\urcorner$, . . . , $\vdash\ulcorner(\phi_{n-1} \supset \psi)^\urcorner$; also $\vdash\ulcorner(\psi \supset \phi_{n-1})^\urcorner$, $\vdash\ulcorner(\phi_{n-1} \supset \phi_{n-2})^\urcorner$, . . . , $\vdash\ulcorner(\phi_1 \supset \phi)^\urcorner$. Hence $\vdash\ulcorner(\phi \supset \psi)^\urcorner$ and $\vdash\ulcorner(\psi \supset \phi)^\urcorner$, by use of (1).

(VIII) *If* ϕ *is a tautology without variables,* $\vdash\phi$.

Proof. Being its own evaluant, and a tautology, ϕ reduces to '(F $\supset$ F)'. Hence, by (VII), $\vdash\ulcorner(24) \supset \phi^\urcorner$.

(IX) *If* $\vdash\tau$ *for all tautologies* τ *with* n *variables, so also for those with* $n + 1$.

Proof. Let χ be a tautology with $n + 1$ variables, one of which is ϕ. Let ψ and ω result respectively from substituting 'F' and '(F $\supset$ F)' for ϕ in χ. Then ψ and ω are tautologies: for all their evaluants are evaluants of the tautology χ and hence reduce to '(F $\supset$ F)'. Also, ψ and ω have just n variables. Hence, by hp, $\vdash\psi$ and $\vdash\omega$. But, by (VI), $\vdash\ulcorner(\psi \supset (\omega \supset \chi))^\urcorner$.

(X) *If* ϕ *is a tautology,* $\vdash\phi$. *Proof:* (VIII), (IX).

The completeness of the system in one sense is thus established. It remains to show that the system is complete also in Post's sense; viz., that from any indemonstrable formula ϕ as premiss every formula χ is derivable. By (X), ϕ is not a tautology; hence ϕ has an evaluant ψ which does not reduce to '(F $\supset$ F)'. But, being a formula without variables, ψ must reduce to '(F $\supset$ F)' or 'F'; hence to 'F'. Therefore, by (VII), $\vdash\ulcorner(\psi \supset \text{F})^\urcorner$. Thus 'F' is derivable from ψ, which is in turn derivable from ϕ by substitution. But from 'F' by (4) we can derive '*p*', and thence, by substitution, χ.

XIV

On Cores and Prime Implicants of Truth Functions

What is called a truth-functional formula in (alternational) *normal form* is built up of sentence letters 'p', 'q', etc., or their negations '$\bar{p}$', '$\bar{q}$', etc., or both, by using only the notations of conjunction and alternation, and in such a way as to subject alternations never to conjunction but only vice versa: thus '$pq \vee \bar{p}r\bar{s} \vee \bar{r}$'. This paper is concerned with the problem of reducing an arbitrary truth-functional formula to a shortest equivalent in normal form. Part of the content of my last previous paper on the subject[1] will be presented anew in an improved way, and a further theorem will be established. I shall not assume familiarity with my previous papers.

Let us sharpen our terminology. Sentence letters and their negations are called *literals*. Literals and conjunctions of them are called *fundamental formulas*, provided that none contains the same letter twice. Fundamental formulas and alternations of them are called *normal*, and are said to have those fundamental formulas as their *clauses*. On these definitions, a formula is convertible to normal form only if it is not self-contradictory; but there is no serious loss in setting aside the self-contradictory cases.

A *prime implicant* of a formula Φ is a fundamental formula that

Reprinted from the *American Mathematical Monthly*, Volume 66, 1959.

[1] "A way to simplify truth functions." Cited hereafter as WSTF.

logically implies Φ but ceases to when deprived of any one literal. A normal formula will be called *uniliterally redundant* if it is equivalent to what remains of itself on dropping some one occurrence of a literal. Obviously then a normal formula is uniliterally redundant if and only if not all its clauses are prime implicants of it. Consequently, in particular,

(I) *Any shortest normal equivalent of a formula Φ will be an alternation of prime implicants of Φ.*

Ignoring tautologies along with self-contradictions, as will be convenient hereafter, one finds that

(II) *The prime implicants of a formula exist and are finite in number.*

To see that they exist, consider a formula Φ and any assignment of truth values to the letters of Φ that verifies Φ—say truth to 'p', 'q', and 's' and falsity to 'r'. The assignment determines a fundamental formula—'$pq\bar{r}s$', in this example—that implies Φ; and it, or part of it, is a prime implicant of Φ. To see further that the prime implicants of Φ are finite in number, we just reflect that they are bound to contain no letters foreign to Φ, since any such letter could be dropped without affecting the implication.

(III) *A formula is equivalent to the alternation of all its prime implicants.*

For a formula Φ is implied by each of its prime implicants and hence by their alternation; and conversely every truth assignment that verifies Φ verifies some Φ-implying fundamental formula (cf. '$pq\bar{r}s$' above) and therewith some prime implicant (viz., that fundamental formula or part of it) and therewith the alternation of the prime implicants.

In view of (I) and (III), a formula can be transformed into a shortest normal equivalent in two stages: (A) transform it into the alternation of all its prime implicants and then (B) delete from that alternation the largest possible combination of jointly superfluous clauses. (A) can be accomplished by a technique due to Samson and Mills, the explanation of which calls for two more definitions. If two fundamental formulas ϕ and ψ are opposed in exactly one letter (so that ϕ contains 'p' affirmatively, say, and ψ contains '$\bar{p}$'), then ϕ and ψ will be said to have as their *consensus* the formula which we get from the conjunction $\phi\psi$ by deleting the two opposed literals and any repetitions.[2] If ϕ and ψ are fundamental formulas opposed in no letter, and all letters (hence all literals) of ψ are in ϕ, then ϕ will be said to (notationally) *subsume* ψ.[3]

Preparatory to the business of (A), we may suppose Φ put into normal form by familiar logical procedures. Now the discovery of Samson and Mills is that Φ, thus prepared, goes over into the alternation of its prime implicants if we persevere in these two equivalence transformations:

(i) If a clause subsumes another, drop the former.

(ii) Adjoin, as an additional clause, the consensus of two clauses (unless it subsumes a clause already present).

That (i)–(ii) are bound eventually to convert Φ into the alternation of just its prime implicants, and all of them (ignoring differences of order in a conjunction), is proved by proving the following four theorems.

(IV) *A normal formula remains susceptible to* (ii) *as long as some prime implicant of it is not a clause of it* (to within a permutation of a conjunction).

(V) *A normal formula remains susceptible to* (i) *or* (ii) *as long as some clause of it is not a prime implicant of it.*

(VI) *Normal formulas go into normal formulas under* (i) *and* (ii).

(VII)[4] *No normal formula is susceptible to* (i)–(ii) *without end.*

Proof of (IV). Let Φ be a normal formula and χ a prime implicant of it that differs (in more than order) from all clauses. Then also, being prime, χ subsumes no clause. So there is at least one fundamental formula, χ anyway, that has the three properties of (a) subsuming χ, (b) subsuming no clause of Φ, and (c) exhibiting no letters foreign to Φ (*cf.* end of proof of (II)). Moreover, there is an obvious limit to how long a fundamental formula having property

[2] This definition of consensus is more liberal than that in WSTF, in that it counts ϕ as consensus of $\alpha\phi$ and $\bar{\alpha}$ (and of $\bar{\alpha}\phi$ and α). (i) below is consequently simpler than its counterpart in WSTF, and correspondingly for the proof of (IV) below. This liberalization of the definition is due essentially to Bing, but note that I avoid his "void formula."

[3] My terminology has proved confusing. When ϕ subsumes ψ in my intended notational sense of having among its literals all those of ψ, then, precisely, ψ subsumes ϕ in a certain logical sense: ψ has among its verifying truth-value assignments all those of ϕ.

[4] This theorem and its proof, which I neglected to include in WSTF, are given here on the appreciated advice of the referee. Note that the parenthetical proviso in (ii), which may look dispensable in view of (i), is needed to assure (VII)—as is indeed remarked in effect in WSTF at the top of p. 628.

(c) can be. So there is at least one fundamental formula, call it ψ, that has the three properties (a)–(c) and is exceeded in length by no fundamental formula having those properties. Yet ψ does not exhibit all letters of Φ; for, if it did, then, having also property (b) as it does, ψ would oppose every clause of Φ in one or another letter, and so not imply Φ; whereas actually ψ must imply Φ, having property (a). So ψ lacks some letter of Φ, say 'p'. Since ψ is a longest fundamental formula with the properties (a)–(c), $p\psi$ must lack one of those properties and so must $\bar{p}\psi$; yet obviously not (a) or (c); so (b). So there are clauses ϕ_1 and ϕ_2 of Φ such that $p\psi$ subsumes ϕ_1 and $\bar{p}\psi$ subsumes ϕ_2. But ψ, having the property (b), subsumes neither; so 'p' and '$\bar{p}$' must occur respectively in ϕ_1 and ϕ_2. Still ϕ_1 and ϕ_2 are not just 'p' and '$\bar{p}$', or Φ would be tautologous; nor are ϕ_1 and ϕ_2 opposed in letters other than 'p', since their further literals are common to ψ. So ϕ_1 and ϕ_2 have a consensus, say ϕ. Moreover ϕ subsumes no clause of Φ; for ψ subsumes ϕ, and ψ has the property (b). So ϕ can be added by (ii).

Proof of (V). Let Φ be a normal formula and ϕ any clause of it that is not a prime implicant. Then ϕ, implying Φ, subsumes some prime implicant ψ. If ψ is a clause of Φ (to within a permutation of a conjunction), we can apply (i) to drop ϕ; and otherwise we can apply (ii) in view of (IV).

Proof of (VI). Obvious.

Proof of (VII). Elimination of a clause ϕ by (i) depends on there surviving some clause ϕ' that ϕ subsumes; elimination of ϕ' in turn depends on there still surviving some clause ϕ'' that ϕ' (and hence ϕ) subsumes; and so on. Therefore, in view of the parenthetical part of (ii), no clause ϕ once dropped by (i) can ever be restored by (ii). But neither, in view of the parenthetical part of (ii), can a clause already present be reintroduced in duplicate by (ii). To sum up, (ii) can never introduce the same clause twice. But there are only finitely many different fundamental formulas for (ii) to introduce, since no letters foreign to Φ are drawn on. So the use of (ii) must terminate. Also the use of (i), being subtractive, obviously must terminate.

So much for task (A), the conversion of a formula into the alternation of all its prime implicants. Toward the continuation task (B), that of determining what largest combination of the resulting clauses can be dropped as jointly superfluous, systematic methods have been developed by Ghazala.

But a shortcoming of the whole (A)–(B) approach is that it depends on exhausting the prime implicants; for, as Rolf K. Müller remarked to me in 1955, their number can even exceed the total number of possible truth-value assignments when there are many letters. According to Fridshal, this can happen after five letters. He cites a formula in nine letters which, by his computations, has 1698 prime implicants—whereas the total number of possible truth-value assignments to nine letters is only 512. So a general technique is needed for finding an adequate minimum alternation of prime implicants without handling all prime implicants on the way.

A normal formula may be called *clausally redundant* if it is equivalent to what remains of itself on dropping one of its clauses of alternation; and *irredundant*, simply, if it is neither clausally nor uniliterally redundant. Obviously any shortest normal equivalent of a formula will be irredundant. Happily we can render a normal formula irredundant without regard to the totality of its prime implicants, simply ridding the formula of superfluous clauses and superfluous literals one by one. To see whether a clause ψ is superfluous in $\Phi \vee \psi$, we just check whether ψ implies Φ. Such implication cannot in general be recognized by mere notational subsumption, as can implication between fundamental formulas, but it can be checked very simply: we have merely to mark the literals of ψ as true and see whether Φ thereupon reduces to a tautology. Again, to see whether a literal ζ is superfluous in $\Phi \vee \zeta\psi$, we just check, in the same swift way, whether ψ implies $\Phi \vee \zeta$. For

(VIII) *ψ implies $\Phi \vee \zeta$ if and only if $\Phi \vee \zeta\psi$ is equivalent to $\Phi \vee \psi$.*

For, the conditional $\psi \supset . \Phi \vee \zeta$ is verifiably equivalent to the biconditional $\Phi \vee \zeta\psi . \equiv . \Phi \vee \psi$, and hence tautologous if and only if the biconditional is tautologous.

Unhappily, however, such reduction of a formula to *an* irredundant equivalent need not deliver a shortest.[5] What it delivers may well lack some of the clauses of every shortest normal equivalent, and contain clauses shared by no shortest normal equivalent.

At the same time there commonly will be, given a formula Φ, certain clauses that are bound to appear in every irredundant equivalent of Φ, and hence in any shortest. The alternation of such clauses I call the *core* of Φ. Commonly also there will be, at the opposite extreme, prime implicants of Φ that are bound never to

[5] E.g., '$p\bar{q} \vee \bar{p}q \vee q\bar{r} \vee \bar{q}r$' is irredundant but equivalent to '$p\bar{q} \vee q\bar{r} \vee \bar{p}r$'.

occur as clauses of irredundant equivalents of Φ. For a prime implicant of Φ to be thus absolutely superfluous, it is obviously sufficient that it imply the core of Φ; but I do not know whether this is necessary.[6]

I shall explain a test whereby, without exhausting the prime implicants of a formula, we can identify its core. This done, we obviously can then quickly decide also, of a prime implicant, whether it implies the core (and is thus absolutely superfluous). Query: Given an irredundant formula, can all its absent prime implicants that are *not* absolutely superfluous be reached by the operation (ii) of iterated consensus-taking without interim retention of any absolutely superfluous ones? This, if true, would allow us to shortcut the (A)–(B) approach to the extent of leaving some of the prime implicants ungenerated in some cases; but I do not know it to be true, and anyway the saving would be limited to formulas with cores.

Guesses aside, there are cases where identifying the core of an irredundant formula settles the question of shortest normal equivalent without further ado. Thus if every clause belongs to the core, the formula is already as short as possible. If every clause but one belongs to the core, then again our simplification is good enough; the only possible improvement would be the negligible one of finding some shorter clause to take the place of the odd one.

But in the general case a technique of core identification has, alas, no evident bearing on our central problem: that of finding shortest normal equivalents without exhausting prime implicants. It seems worth communicating mainly for what it may contribute to one's understanding of the general workings of irredundant formulas.

Criterion, given an irredundant formula Φ, of whether a clause ϕ thereof belongs to the core: From Φ delete ϕ, also each clause that opposes ϕ in more than one letter, and finally all literals whose letters are in ϕ; what remains will be a tautology if and only if ϕ does not belong to the core of Φ. *Examples:* 'pq' does not belong to the core of '$pq \vee qs \vee q\bar{r} \vee \bar{q}r\bar{s}$', for '$s \vee \bar{r} \vee r\bar{s}$' is tautologous; whereas 'qs' belongs to the core, for '$p \vee \bar{r}$' is not tautologous.

That the criterion is geared only to irredundant formulas is no

[6] *Note added 1965:* It is not, as eight readers have proved to me. The first of the counterinstances came from William E. Glass under date of December 15, 1959; namely '$p\bar{r} \vee qr \vee \bar{q}\bar{s} \vee qs$', whose core '$p\bar{r} \vee qs \vee \bar{q}\bar{s}$' is implied by neither of two absolutely dispensable prime implicants, 'pq' and '$p\bar{s}$'.

limitation, for we have seen how to make a formula irredundant. That the criterion enables us to spot as core clauses only clauses already present is again no limitation, for, by definition, in any irredundant formula all the core clauses are present. Actually uniliteral irredundancy would suffice here without clausal; but it is more efficient to start from a fully irredundant formula, since there are then fewer clauses to examine.

It remains to justify the criterion by proving that a clause of an irredundant formula belongs to the core if and only if it meets the stated test. In other words, what is wanted is the theorem:

(IX) *A clause* ϕ *of an irredundant* Φ *belongs to the core of* Φ *if and only if there is an assignment of truth values to letters not in* ϕ *that falsifies all clauses of* Φ, *other than* ϕ, *that oppose* ϕ *in at most one letter*. (I assume as usual that Φ is not simply a tautology $\alpha \vee \bar{\alpha}$.)

Proof.[7] Let Φ be any irredundant formula, ϕ any clause of Φ, and Ψ the alternation of all prime implicants of Φ but ϕ. Then ϕ is in the core of Φ if and only if Ψ is not equivalent to $\phi \vee \Psi$ (and thus to Φ); hence if and only if ϕ does not imply Ψ. So what is to be proved is (a) that if ϕ does not imply Ψ then some assignment to letters not in ϕ falsifies all clauses of Φ, other than ϕ, that oppose ϕ in at most one letter, and (b) that if ϕ implies Ψ then each assignment to letters not in ϕ is compatible with some clause of Φ, besides ϕ, that opposes ϕ in at most one letter.

Proof of (a). Since ϕ does not imply Ψ, some assignment A to the letters of Φ verifies ϕ and falsifies Ψ. Let A' be the part of A that has to do with letters not in ϕ, and let ψ be any clause of Φ other than ϕ that opposes ϕ in at most one letter; to show that A' falsifies ψ. *Case* 1. ψ opposes ϕ in no letter. Then, since A verifies ϕ, A falsifies no literals of ψ whose letters are in ϕ; but A does falsify ψ, for ψ is clearly a clause of Ψ, and A falsifies Ψ; so A' falsifies ψ. *Case* 2. ψ has just one literal, call it $\bar{\zeta}$, opposed to a literal of ϕ. But ψ and ϕ are not simply $\bar{\zeta}$ and ζ, or Φ would be a tautology. So ψ and ϕ have a consensus, and it, since it implies $\psi \vee \phi$ and therefore Φ, subsumes a prime implicant χ of Φ. Since χ lacks ζ, χ is not ϕ; hence χ is a clause of Ψ; and hence A falsifies χ. But all literals of χ whose letters are in ϕ are identical with literals of ϕ, and hence verified by A; so A' falsifies at least one literal of χ. But any such literal of χ is a literal of ψ. So A' falsifies ψ.

[7] Previously proved in one of my lectures on "Simplifying truth functions," College of Engineering, University of Michigan, June 1958.

Proof of (b). Here the assumption is that ϕ implies Ψ; i.e., that Φ and Ψ are equivalent. Let A' be any assignment to the letters not in ϕ. Let Φ' and Ψ' be what Φ and Ψ reduce to under A'; thus Φ' and Ψ' are equivalent. It will be sufficient to show that Φ' has a clause, other than ϕ, that opposes ϕ in at most one letter. Now ϕ, being a clause still of Φ', implies Φ' and therefore Ψ'. Hence ϕ must subsume some clause ψ' of Ψ'; for ϕ subsumes every clause of Ψ' not opposed to ϕ, there being no further letters. This ψ' is the residue in Ψ' of some clause ψ of Ψ. Since ϕ is not a clause of Ψ, ψ is not ϕ; moreover, since any clause of Ψ is a prime implicant of Φ, ψ does not even subsume ϕ. So ψ lacks a literal ζ of ϕ; ϕ subsumes $\zeta\psi'$. Now assign falsity to ζ and truth to the rest of the literals of ϕ. This assignment verifies ψ', and therewith Ψ'; hence also Φ', which is equivalent to Ψ'. Therefore this assignment verifies some clause of Φ'. But a clause of Φ', to be thus verified, must consist solely of literals of ϕ other than ζ, plus perhaps $\bar{\zeta}$; hence it is other than ϕ and opposes ϕ in at most one letter.

XV

Two Theorems about Truth Functions

It will be convenient simply to disregard order in a conjunction, thus treating the fundamental formulas '$p\bar{q}r$', '$pr\bar{q}$', '$r\bar{q}p$', etc., not merely as equivalents but as one and the same formula. From this point of view the fundamental formulas which contain all and only n given statement letters are just 2^n in number. Given any n statement letters, listed in an arbitrary order $\alpha_1, \alpha_2, \ldots, \alpha_n$, the 2^n fundamental formulas containing those letters can be listed exhaustively in a convenient standard order as follows:

$$(1) \quad \ulcorner\alpha_1\alpha_2 \ldots \alpha_n\urcorner, \quad \ulcorner\alpha_1\alpha_2 \ldots \alpha_{n-1}\bar{\alpha}_n\urcorner, \quad \ulcorner\alpha_1\alpha_2 \ldots \alpha_{n-2}\bar{\alpha}_{n-1}\alpha_n\urcorner, \quad \ulcorner\alpha_1\alpha_2 \ldots \alpha_{n-2}\bar{\alpha}_{n-1}\bar{\alpha}_n\urcorner, \quad \ulcorner\alpha_1\alpha_2 \ldots \alpha_{n-3}\bar{\alpha}_{n-2}\alpha_{n-1}\alpha_n\urcorner, \quad \ldots, \quad \ulcorner\bar{\alpha}_1\bar{\alpha}_2 \ldots \bar{\alpha}_n\urcorner.$$

There is a quick *implication criterion* for any two normal formulas Φ and Ψ such that Ψ lacks negation signs; viz., Φ implies Ψ if and only if each clause of Φ subsumes a clause of Ψ. That such subsumption is sufficient in order that Φ imply Ψ is seen as follows. Suppose each clause of Φ subsumes, and therefore implies, a clause of Ψ; then, since each clause of Ψ implies Ψ, each clause of Φ implies Ψ; and accordingly Φ implies Ψ. That the subsumption condition

---

This paper was presented by invitation, but *in absentia*, at the Mexican Scientific Congress, September 1951, and appeared in the *Boletín de la Sociedad Matemática Mexicana* in 1953. I have been able to omit portions explanatory of terms and notation, thanks to foregoing papers. A corollary is inserted from the end of my paper "The problem of simplifying truth functions," *American Mathematical Monthly*, 1952.

is also necessary is seen as follows. Suppose some clause $\ulcorner\alpha_1\alpha_2 \ldots \alpha_m\bar{\beta}_1\bar{\beta}_2 \ldots \bar{\beta}_n\urcorner$ ($m \geqq 0, n \geqq 0$) of Φ subsumes no clause of Ψ. This is the same as supposing (since Ψ lacks negation signs) that every clause ψ_i of Ψ contains a letter γ_i other than $\alpha_1, \ldots, \alpha_m$. If we assign truth to $\alpha_1, \ldots, \alpha_m$ and falsity to all other letters, then $\ulcorner\alpha_1\alpha_2 \ldots \alpha_m\bar{\beta}_1\bar{\beta}_2 \ldots \bar{\beta}_n\urcorner$ comes out true. (Note that the β's repeat no α's, by the definition of "fundamental formula".) Therefore Φ comes out true. On the other hand ψ_i for each i comes out false under the described assignment of truth values, on account of γ_i (for remember that Ψ lacks negation signs); so Ψ comes out false. Therefore Φ does not imply Ψ.

An obvious expedient for shortening normal formulae is that of simply deleting clauses which subsume other clauses (thus exploiting the familiar equivalence of '$pq \vee p$' to 'p'). Now it can be proved that this expedient always eventuates in a *shortest* normal equivalent if the normal formula with which we begin lacks negation. Such is the content of

THEOREM I. *If a formula is normal and lacks negation and none of its clauses subsumes any other of its clauses, then it has no shorter normal equivalent.*

Proof. Suppose (i) that Ψ is a normal formula lacking negation, (ii) that no clause of Ψ subsumes another clause of Ψ, and (iii) that Φ is normal and equivalent to Ψ; to prove that Φ is no shorter than Ψ. By (i) and (iii) and the above implication criterion, each clause of Φ subsumes a clause of Ψ. Let the thus subsumed clauses of Ψ be $\psi_1, \ldots, \psi_n$. Since to subsume is to imply, each clause of Φ implies one of $\psi_1, \ldots, \psi_n$; hence Φ implies $\ulcorner\psi_1 \vee \ldots \vee \psi_n\urcorner$. By (iii), then, Ψ implies $\ulcorner\psi_1 \vee \ldots \vee \psi_n\urcorner$. Then, since $\ulcorner\psi_1 \vee \ldots \vee \psi_n\urcorner$ lacks negation (by (i)), we can conclude from the implication criterion that every clause of Ψ subsumes a clause of $\ulcorner\psi_1 \vee \ldots \vee \psi_n\urcorner$. By (ii), then, Ψ has no clauses but $\psi_1, \ldots, \psi_n$. Now assign truth to all letters of ψ_i, for some i, and falsity to all other letters. By (i), ψ_i lacks negation and hence comes out true. Therefore Ψ comes out true (since truth of ψ_i assures truth of $\ulcorner\psi_1 \vee \ldots \vee \psi_n\urcorner$). Therefore, by (iii), Φ comes out true. Hence some clause ϕ of Φ comes out true. On the other hand each of $\psi_1, \ldots, \psi_n$ other than ψ_i contains a letter other than those of ψ_i, by (ii), and hence comes out false under the given assignment. Therefore ϕ, which comes out true, subsumes none of $\psi_1, \ldots, \psi_n$ other than ψ_i. So, since every clause of Φ subsumes one or another of $\psi_1, \ldots, \psi_n$, we must conclude that ϕ subsumes ψ_i and none of the others. Applying this reasoning to each choice of i, we see that each of $\psi_1, \ldots, \psi_n$ is subsumed by a clause of Φ which subsumes no others of $\psi_1, \ldots, \psi_n$. Therefore Φ is no shorter than $\ulcorner \psi_1 \vee \ldots \vee \psi_n \urcorner$, q.e.d.

COROLLARY. *If a formula is normal and none of its clauses subsumes or conflicts with any other of its clauses, then it has no shorter normal equivalent.*

For, there being no conflict, each letter occurs affirmatively only or negatively only. Read the negative literals as new affirmative letters and apply Theorem I.

Preparatory to the other theorem which it is the business of this paper to prove, viz., Theorem II below, let us look back to the 2^n fundamental formulas listed in (1). The alternation of the first i of those formulas will be called $[i]$. Clearly $[2^n]$ is valid, and hence has '$p \vee \bar{p}$' as shortest normal equivalent. On the other hand

THEOREM II. *If* $m < 2^n$ *then* $[m]$ *has as a shortest normal equivalent a formula which lacks negation.*

Proof. For each h up to n, the first 2^{n-h} formulas of (1) exhaust the ways of distributing negation signs over $\alpha_{h+1}, \ldots, \alpha_n$ while keeping $\alpha_1, \ldots, \alpha_h$ affirmative. Clearly, therefore,

(2) $$[2^{n-h}] \text{ is equivalent to } \ulcorner \alpha_1 \ldots \alpha_h \urcorner.$$

After the 2^{n-h}th formula, the series (1) repeats as from the beginning but with α_h negated. Thus, where $1 \leqq i \leqq 2^{n-h}$,

(3) $$[2^{n-h} + i] \text{ is } [2^{n-h}] \text{ in alternation with } [i] \text{ with } \alpha_h \text{ negated.}$$

Now let $h_1, \ldots, h_k$ be, in ascending order, the integers such that

(4) $$m = 2^{n-h_1} + 2^{n-h_2} + \ldots + 2^{n-h_k}.$$

(They are all positive, since $m < 2^n$; and they are distinct. To find them, write m in binary notation and count the places to the right of each occurrence of '1'. Each of $h_1, \ldots, h_k$ is n minus one of those counts.) By (4) and (3), $[m]$ is $[2^{n-h_1}]$ in alternation with $[2^{n-h_2} + \ldots + 2^{n-h_k}]$ with α_{h_1} negated. But, by (3) again, $[2^{n-h_2} + \ldots + 2^{n-h_k}]$ in turn is $[2^{n-h_2}]$ in alternation with $[2^{n-h_3} + \ldots + 2^{n-h_k}]$ with α_{h_2} negated; so $[m]$ is the alternation of $[2^{n-h_1}]$, $[2^{n-h_2}]$ with α_{h_1} negated, and $[2^{n-h_3} + \ldots + 2^{n-h_k}]$ with α_{h_1} and

α_{h_2} negated. Continuing thus, we finally find that [m] is the alternation of [2^{n-h_1}], [2^{n-h_2}] with α_{h_1} negated, [2^{n-h_3}] with α_{h_1} and α_{h_2} negated, . . . , and [2^{n-h_k}] with α_{h_1}, . . . , $\alpha_{h_{k-1}}$ negated. But, by (2), [2^{n-h_1}] is equivalent to $\ulcorner\alpha_1 \ldots \alpha_{h_1}\urcorner$. Also, by (2), [$2^{n-h_2}$] is equivalent to $\ulcorner\alpha_1 \ldots \alpha_{h_2}\urcorner$, and hence, since substitution for letters preserves equivalence, [2^{n-h_2}] with α_{h_1} negated is equivalent to $\ulcorner\alpha_1 \ldots \alpha_{h_1-1}\bar{\alpha}_{h_1}\alpha_{h_1+1} \ldots \alpha_{h_2}\urcorner$. Continuing thus, we find [m] equivalent to

$$(5)\quad \ulcorner\alpha_1 \ldots \alpha_{h_1} \vee \alpha_1 \ldots \alpha_{h_1-1}\bar{\alpha}_{h_1}\alpha_{h_1+1} \ldots \alpha_{h_2} \vee \alpha_1 \ldots \alpha_{h_1-1}\bar{\alpha}_{h_1}\alpha_{h_1+1} \ldots \alpha_{h_2-1}\bar{\alpha}_{h_2}\alpha_{h_2+1} \ldots \alpha_{h_3} \vee \ldots \vee \alpha_1 \ldots \alpha_{h_1-1}\bar{\alpha}_{h_1}\alpha_{h_1+1} \ldots \alpha_{h_2-1}\bar{\alpha}_{h_2}\alpha_{h_2+1} \ldots \alpha_{h_{k-1}-1}\bar{\alpha}_{h_{k-1}}\alpha_{h_{k-1}+1} \ldots \alpha_{h_k}\urcorner.$$

Now the last two of the k clauses of (5) are related in the manner of 'pq' and '$p\bar{q}r$', with $\alpha_{h_{k-1}}$ in the role of 'q'; and '$pq \vee p\bar{q}r$' is equivalent by truth tables to '$pq \vee pr$'. Hence the occurrence of $\ulcorner\bar{\alpha}_{h_{k-1}}\urcorner$ in (5) can be dropped. Again the last three clauses of the thus amended (5) are related in the manner of 'pq', '$p\bar{q}r$', and '$p\bar{q}s$', with $\alpha_{h_{k-2}}$ in the role of 'q'; and '$pq \vee p\bar{q}r \vee p\bar{q}s$' is equivalent to '$pq \vee pr \vee ps$'. Hence the two occurrences of $\ulcorner\bar{\alpha}_{h_{k-2}}\urcorner$ can be dropped. Continuing thus, we delete all negative literals from (5) and are left with

$$\ulcorner\alpha_1 \ldots \alpha_{h_1} \vee \alpha_1 \ldots \alpha_{h_1-1}\alpha_{h_1+1} \ldots \alpha_{h_2} \vee \alpha_1 \ldots \alpha_{h_1-1}\alpha_{h_1+1} \ldots \alpha_{h_2-1}\alpha_{h_2+1} \ldots \alpha_{h_3} \vee \ldots \vee \alpha_1 \ldots \alpha_{h_1-1}\alpha_{h_1+1} \ldots \alpha_{h_2-1}\alpha_{h_2+1} \ldots \alpha_{h_{k-1}-1}\alpha_{h_{k-1}+1} \ldots \alpha_{h_k}\urcorner.$$

But this lacks negation. Moreover, none of its clauses subsumes any other of its clauses; so, by Theorem I, there is no shorter normal equivalent.

XVI

On Boolean Functions

As auxiliaries to a concurrent study of the utility concept, two theorems of set theory are proving useful. The envisaged application of these theorems concerns only relations, or sets of ordered pairs, whereas the theorems hold for sets generally. Consequently the two theorems are most conveniently set forth separately from the eventual memorandum in which they are to be applied.

Where F and G are sets, their *intersect* or common part will be represented as FG. Where $F_1, \ldots, F_n$ are sets, their *union* will be represented as $\sum_{i=1}^{n} F_i$; this is the set whose members are all and only those objects each of which belongs to at least one of $F_1, \ldots, F_n$. Where F is a set, its *complement* will be represented as $\overline{F}$; this is the set whose members are all and only the objects not belonging to F. Any set which is specifiable in terms of given sets $F_1, \ldots, F_n$ by means exclusively of intersect, union, and complement is called a *Boolean function* of $F_1, \ldots, F_n$.

More particularly, the 2^n intersects:

$$F_1F_2F_3 \ldots F_n, \quad \overline{F}_1F_2F_3 \ldots F_n, \quad F_1\overline{F}_2F_3 \ldots F_n, \quad \overline{F}_1\overline{F}_2F_3 \ldots F_n,$$
$$F_1F_2\overline{F}_3 \ldots F_n, \quad \overline{F}_1F_2\overline{F}_3 \ldots F_n, \quad \ldots, \quad \overline{F}_1\overline{F}_2\overline{F}_3 \ldots \overline{F}_n$$

are called the *constituent functions* of $F_1, F_2, \ldots, F_n$. For brevity they will be designated respectively as $F^1, F^2, \ldots, F^{2^n}$. Clearly

(1) For every object x there is an i such that x is an element of F^i.

This paper is assembled from excerpts from two working memoranda issued under Project RAND in 1949. It is printed by permission of the RAND Corporation, Santa Monica, Calif.

1. Parametric Boolean Functions. Consider now any n-ary function ϕ, Boolean or otherwise, which takes sets as arguments and as values. ϕ will be called a *parametric Boolean function* if there are sets $H_1, \ldots, H_r$ for some r, and an $(n + r)$-ary Boolean function ψ, such that

(2) For all sets $F_1, \ldots, F_n$,
$$\phi(F_1, \ldots, F_n) = \psi(H_1, \ldots, H_r, F_1, \ldots, F_n).$$

Two sets will be said to *agree in* an object x when x belongs to both or to neither. An n-ary function ϕ of sets will be said to *preserve agreement* when this law holds: If $F_1, \ldots, F_n, G_1, \ldots, G_n$ are any sets, and x is any object in which F_i and G_i agree pairwise for each i, then $\phi(F_1, \ldots, F_n)$ and $\phi(G_1, \ldots, G_n)$ will agree in x.

Now the purpose of this section is to establish

THEOREM I. *A function is a parametric Boolean function if and only if it preserves agreement.*

Consider to begin with any parametric Boolean function ϕ. I.e., there are sets $H_1, \ldots, H_r$ and a Boolean function ψ such that (2) holds. Now we want to show that ϕ preserves agreement. I.e., given any object x such that, for each i, F_i agrees with G_i in x, we want to show that $\psi(H_1, \ldots, H_r, F_1, \ldots, F_n)$ agrees with $\psi(H_1, \ldots, H_r, G_1, \ldots, G_n)$ in x. But this is evident by the following consideration. Since Boolean functions are constructed solely by intersect, union, and complement, membership of x in $\psi(H_1, \ldots, H_r, F_1, \ldots, F_n)$ will depend solely on membership or non-membership of x in the successive arguments $H_1, \ldots, H_r, F_1, \ldots, F_n$; so the change of $F_1, \ldots, F_n$ to $G_1, \ldots, G_n$ here will make no difference so far as x is concerned.

It now remains only to prove the converse half of the theorem; viz., that any function which preserves agreement is a parametric Boolean function.

Suppose then that ϕ preserves agreement. Let K_i be the set of all and only those objects x for which there are sets $G_1, \ldots, G_n$ such that x belongs both to the constituent function G^i and to ϕ_G, if we write ϕ_G for $\phi(G_1, \ldots, G_n)$. Note that K_i depends only on i and ϕ. By (1), every element of ϕ_F belongs, for some i, to $F^i\phi_F$ and hence to K_i and hence to K_iF^i. So

(3) $$\phi_F \text{ is a subset of} \sum_{i=1}^{2^n} K_iF^i.$$

Next consider any z and i such that z belongs to K_iF^i. Then, by the definition of K_i, there are $G_1, \ldots, G_n$ such that z belongs to $G^i\phi_G$. Now F^i is the intersect of F_1 or $\overline{F}_1$ with F_2 or $\overline{F}_2$ and so on, and G^i is similarly constituted with 'G' in place of 'F'; hence z, belonging as it does to F^i and G^i, must, for each j, belong to both F_j and G_j or to both $\overline{F}_j$ and $\overline{G}_j$. I.e., F_j and G_j agree in z for each j. Then, since ϕ preserves agreement, ϕ_F and ϕ_G agree in z. But z belongs to ϕ_G. Hence z belongs to ϕ_F. For each i, then, each element z of K_iF^i belongs to ϕ_F. Therefore $\sum_{i=1}^{2^n} K_iF^i$ is a subset of ϕ_F. Hence, by (3),

$$\phi_F = \sum_{i=1}^{2^n} K_iF^i. \tag{4}$$

But this summation is a Boolean function of $K_1, \ldots, K_{2^n}, F_1, \ldots, F_n$. Moreover, (4) has been seen to hold for all choices of $F_1, \ldots, F_n$. So ϕ is a parametric Boolean function.

Corollary: *The number of the parameters of a parametric Boolean function of n variables need never exceed* 2^n. This is evident from the use of $K_1, \ldots, K_{2^n}$ in the above reasoning.

2. Commutativity and Incidence. An n-ary Boolean function ϕ is called *thoroughly commutative* if

(5) For all sets $F_1, \ldots, F_n$, and every permutation $G_1, \ldots, G_n$ of them, $\phi(F_1, \ldots, F_n) = \phi(G_1, \ldots, G_n)$.

Now the theorem which is to be established is one which affirms a correspondence between the thoroughly commutative Boolean n-ary functions and the classes of natural numbers $\leqq n$.

Let us write $\mathrm{I}_x(F_1, \ldots, F_n)$ for the *incidence* of the element x in the sets $F_1, \ldots, F_n$; i.e., for the number of sets from among $F_1, \ldots, F_n$ to which x belongs. Now what is to be proved is

Theorem II. *An n-ary function ϕ, whose arguments and values are sets, is a thoroughly commutative Boolean function if and only if there is a class N of natural numbers $\leqq n$ such that*

(6) For all sets $F_1, \ldots, F_n$, and all objects x, x is an element of $\phi(F_1, \ldots, F_n)$ if and only if $\mathrm{I}_x(F_1, \ldots, F_n)$ belongs to N.

It is well known that every Boolean function is expressible as a union of $\geqq 0$ constituent functions; i.e., for every n-ary Boolean function ϕ there are numbers $p_1, \ldots, p_k \leqq 2^n$ ($k \geqq 0$) such that, for all $F_1, \ldots, F_n$,

$$\phi(F_1, \ldots, F_n) = \sum_{i=1}^{k} F^{p_i}. \tag{7}$$

For each i from 1 to 2^n, let $g_n(i)$ be the number of unbarred components in the constituent function F^i. In other words, $g_n(i)$ is n minus the number of bars (indicating complement) in F^i. Clearly $g_n(i)$ depends only on n and i, and is independent of the choice of sets $F_1, \ldots, F_n$.

Any element x of F^i is an element of all and only those of $F_1, \ldots, F_n$ which appear as unbarred components of F^i. Hence

(8) If x is an element of F^i then $I_x(F_1, \ldots, F_n) = g_n(i)$.

Conversely, suppose $I_x(F_1, \ldots, F_n) = g_n(i)$. Then x is an element of some constituent function F^j which has just $g_n(i)$ unbarred components. But F^j is the same as F^i except for a permutation of $F_1, \ldots, F_n$. So

(9) If $I_x(F_1, \ldots, F_n) = g_n(i)$ then x is an element of G^i for some permutation $G_1, \ldots, G_n$ of $F_1, \ldots, F_n$.

We turn next to the proof of the forward half of Theorem II. Here we assume a Boolean function ϕ for which (5) holds, and seek a class N of natural numbers $\leqq n$ for which (6) holds.

N will be taken as the class of numbers $g_n(p_1), \ldots, g_n(p_k)$, where $p_1, \ldots, p_k$ are as in (7). So what is to be shown is that (6) holds for this choice of N. I.e., what is to be shown, for all sets $F_1, \ldots, F_n$ and all objects x, is that

$$x \text{ is an element of } \phi(F_1, \ldots, F_n) \tag{10}$$

if and only if there is a j such that

$$I_x(F_1, \ldots, F_n) = g_n(p_j). \tag{11}$$

But if (10) holds, then by (7) there is a j such that x is an element of F^{p_j}; and accordingly (11) follows in view of (8). Conversely, if (11) holds, then by (9) there is a permutation $G_1, \ldots, G_n$ of

$F_1, \ldots, F_n$ such that x is an element of G^{p_i} and hence of $\sum_{i=1}^{k} G^{p_i}$, or $\phi(G_1, \ldots, G_n)$; so (10) follows in view of (5).

We turn finally to the proof of the converse half of Theorem II. Here, adopting any class N of natural numbers $\leqq n$ and assuming (6), what we have to show is that ϕ is a Boolean function fulfilling (5).

Let $q_1, \ldots, q_h$ be all the numbers $i \leqq 2^n$ such that $g_n(i)$ belongs to N. Consider any sets $F_1, \ldots, F_n$. By (8), then, any element x of F^{q_i} will be such that $\mathrm{I}_x(F_1, \ldots, F_n)$ belongs to N. By (6), therefore, every element of F^{q_i} belongs to $\phi(F_1, \ldots, F_n)$. So

(12) $$\sum_{i=1}^{h} F^{q_i} \text{ is a subset of } \phi(F_1, \ldots, F_n).$$

Conversely, consider any element x of $\phi(F_1, \ldots, F_n)$. By (6), $\mathrm{I}_x(F_1, \ldots, F_n)$ belongs to N. Also, by (1) and (8), there is a j such that x belongs to F^j and $\mathrm{I}_x(F_1, \ldots, F_n) = g_n(j)$. So j is one of $q_1, \ldots, q_h$, and hence x belongs to $\sum_{i=1}^{h} F^{q_i}$. Therefore $\phi(F_1, \ldots, F_n)$ is a subset of $\sum_{i=1}^{h} F^{q_i}$. Hence, by (12), $\phi(F_1, \ldots, F_n) = \sum_{i=1}^{h} F^{q_i}$ for all $F_1, \ldots, F_n$. But this summation is a Boolean function. Moreover it fulfills (5); this is seen as follows. Where F^r is any result of permutation of $F_1, \ldots, F_n$ in F^{q_j}, the number of bars in F^r is the same as in F^{q_j}; hence $g(r) = g(q_j)$; hence $g(r)$ belongs to N; hence r is one of $q_1, \ldots, q_h$; and hence F^r, like F^{q_j}, figures in $\sum_{i=1}^{h} F^{q_i}$.

XVII

On the Logic of Quantification

1. Predicates, Schemata, Matrices. The notation that I shall use here for the logic of quantification is of the familiar kind wherein the letters '*p*', '*q*', etc., stand in place of unspecified statements and the letters '*f*', '*g*', etc., stand in place of unspecified predicates. The present section will deal with the significance of this notation; the purpose and scope of the paper as a whole can better be indicated afterward, in §2.

By "predicates" I mean, not properties (or classes) and relations, but merely certain notational expressions. As a first approach they may be thought of as expressions like 'walks', 'is red', 'touches', 'gives to'. Where '*f*', '*g*', '*h*', and '*k*' represent these four predicates, we may read '*fx*', '*gy*', '*hxy*', and '*kxyz*' as '*x* walks', '*y* is red', '*x* touches *y*', '*x* gives *y* to *z*'.

Given any statement and any sequence of $n(\geqq 1)$ distinct names which occur in the statement, we want there to be a predicate whose application to the sequence yields the statement. Clearly, then, the above tentative version of predicates as mere verbs is too confining. We can, however, construe predicates satisfactorily as expressions of a somewhat more elaborate sort; namely, as expressions which are like statements except for containing circled numerals (an arbitrary device) in various places appropriate to names. For example, where '*fxy*' represents '*x* paid *y* more than Jones paid *x*', the predicate represented by '*f*' is taken to be '①

Reprinted from the *Journal of Symbolic Logic*, Volume 10, 1945.

paid ② more than Jones paid ①'. Thus '*f*' followed by one or more variables represents the result of putting those successive variables respectively for '①', '②', etc., throughout the predicate represented by '*f*'.[1]

The word 'represent', as used above, is intended in the sense of 'supplant', 'stand in the place of'; not in the sense of 'refer to', 'take as value'. The letters '*p*', '*q*', '*f*', '*g*', etc., are thus not related to statements and predicates in the way in which the variables of ordinary algebra are related to numbers. Whereas the '*x*', '*y*', etc., of algebra behave as *names of* unspecified numbers, on the other hand '*p*', '*q*', '*f*', '*g*', etc., behave as unspecified statements and predicates outright, not as names of them.

The analogy that does hold between '*p*', '*q*', '*f*', '*g*', etc., and the '*x*', '*y*', etc., of algebra is rather this: the former supplant unspecified expressions of certain kinds, namely statements and predicates, while the variables of algebra supplant unspecified expressions of another kind, namely *numerals* such as '5', 'π' etc. But even of this analogy we must beware. It is safe so long as we do not think of the numerals as names of anything; but mathematics cannot be pushed far until we do. Implicit or explicit use of quantification over numbers (e.g., in the fashion 'Whatever positive number *x* may be, there is a number *y* such that . . .') immediately commits us to recognizing a realm of numbers of which the numerals are names.[2] At this point the analogy of '*p*', '*q*', '*f*', '*g*', etc., to the variables of algebra breaks down, unless we care to assume also a realm of entities (truth values, classes, and relations?) of which statements and predicates are names. These entities, if assumed, would be values of the variables '*p*', '*q*', '*f*', '*g*', etc., just as numbers are values of the variables of algebra; but the assumption of such entities exceeds the scope of the logic of quantification, which has no need of them.[3]

[1] Predicates in this sense were introduced in my *Elementary Logic* (1941), 119, as an auxiliary to the theory of substitution. But I called them stencils, not perceiving how aptly the traditional term 'predicate' might be used at this point.

[2] See my "Designation and existence."

[3] In higher logic, where quantification over classes and relations takes place, such entities have indeed to be assumed. Even there, however, I prefer not to admit '*f*', '*g*', etc., into quantifiers, but to think of classes and relations rather as among the values of the regular variables of quantification '*x*', '*y*', etc.; cf. my *Mathematical Logic*, §§22–23, and *Elementary Logic* (1941), §56.

The so-called "algebra" or "calculus" of classes and that of relations, as well as much else that is commonly treated in class and relation theory, require no

So 'p', 'q', 'f', 'g', etc., are merely dummy letters, *schematic* letters, in place of which we may imagine any arbitrary statements and predicates. Expressions constructed of such letters, e.g.:

$$(1) \qquad (x)(fx \supset p) \,.\, (\exists x)fx \,.\!\supset p,$$

I call *schemata;* they are imaginary statements, diagrams of statements, and are distinguished from genuine statements in having dummy components such as 'p' and 'fx' in place of genuine components such as 'birds fly' and 'x is red'.[4]

The schemata of quantification theory may be specified thus: they comprise 'p', 'q', etc.; also 'f', 'g', etc., followed each by one or more occurrences of variables 'x', 'y', etc.; also everything that can be built up from these by means of truth functions and application of quantifiers '(x)', '(y)', '$(\exists x)$', '$(\exists y)$', etc., provided that no one of the letters 'f', 'g', etc., occurs twice in a schema with different numbers of occurrences of variables after it.

Matrices are like statements except for containing free variables 'x', 'y', etc., in places appropriate to names; e.g., 'x is red'. Schemata differ fundamentally from these. Matrices are fragmentary expressions capable of occurring, overlaid by quantifiers, as integral parts of statements; schemata, on the other hand, cannot be completed into statements, but are mere diagrams instrumental to the logical study of statements.

Quantification theory can be presented, alternatively, in a *metalogical* style in which we describe and treat statements without this diagrammatic appeal to schemata, and also without use of the notion of predicate.[5] This metalogical method has advantages in some connections, but the method of schemata has a graphic quality which recommends it for general elementary purposes.

2. Validity. Before proceeding further, a few technical terms

---

quantification over classes and relations. We can, if we like, develop these portions of logic as a "virtual" theory of classes and relations which makes no real assumption of such entities and is wholly translatable into the present schematism of quantification theory; cf. my *O Sentido da Nova Lógica*, 218–223, or indeed "A theory of classes presupposing no canons of type," 325.

[4] Whitehead and Russell's use of 'p', 'q', etc., and much of their use of their predicate letters 'ϕ', 'ψ', etc., can be construed as schematic in the above sense, though those authors do not distinguish between this and other interpretations. See §5 of I, above; also my "Ontological remarks on the propositional calculus." The doctrine of schemata is explicit in Cooley, 11, 75, and in my *Elementary Logic* (1941), 40, 90f., 116f., though in these two books the respective words 'form' and 'frame' are used instead of 'schema'.

[5] Such is my procedure in *Mathematical Logic.*

must be defined. A schema will be called *n*-adic if there are no more than *n* consecutive occurrences of variables[6] in it. Thus a monadic schema is one in which '*f*', '*g*', etc., occur only with single variables attached, and a medadic (0-adic) schema is one which is built up of just the letters '*p*', '*q*', etc., by truth functions. A schema is called *closed* if it has no free variables,[6] and it is called a *closure* of another schema which has free variables if it is formed from the latter schema by prefixing universal quantifiers '(*x*)', '(*y*)', etc., corresponding to all the free variables. A statement obtainable from a closed schema by substitution for the schematic letters is called an *instance* of the schema. A closed schema all of whose instances are true is called *valid;* e.g., (1) above. Derivatively, schemata with free variables are called valid if they have valid closures.

For the validity of medadic schemata we have a familiar decision procedure in truth tables. The main business of quantification theory, thought of from the point of view of schematic presentation, is to specify the valid schemata beyond the medadic stage. This may conveniently be done in two stages in turn: specifying the valid monadic schemata and the valid polyadic schemata.

It has long been known that a decision procedure is possible for the validity of monadic schemata.[7] This monadic domain embraces the bulk of what is familiar and most useful in quantification theory, including the theory of the syllogism. It is known, furthermore, that *no* decision procedure is possible for the validity of polyadic schemata.[8] It is therefore reasonable to segregate the monadic domain and take advantage of its amenability to a decision procedure, thus deferring the inferior method of deductive proof to the polyadic domain which admits of nothing better. Actually the tendency in the literature has been rather to merge the monadic with the polyadic and use deductive proof throughout, probably because the known decision procedures for monadic schemata were rather cumbersome; the primary purpose of this paper, however, is to present a decision procedure for monadic schemata which seems convenient enough for practical and pedagogical use. The procedure will be explained in §§3–4 and justified in §5.

[6] This refers only to variables '*x*', '*y*', etc., not to schematic letters.

[7] First shown by Löwenheim. For other decision procedures to the same purpose see Hilbert and Ackermann, 1938, 95–97; also the references to Skolem and Behmann there provided.

[8] See XX, "Church's theorem," below.

Polyadic schemata can be handled afterward very simply. Let us call a schema *monadically valid* if it is obtainable by substitution in a valid monadic schema. Thus a monadically valid schema, though it need not be monadic, has a valid structure capable of depiction in a monadic schema. (Similarly I shall call a schema *medadically valid* if it is obtainable by substitution in a valid medadic schema; hence if it is valid by virtue of its truth-functional structure.) Now it turns out that all the valid polyadic schemata can be derived from the monadically valid schemata by repeated use of this one simple *rule of generalized modus ponens: If a conditional is valid, and its antecedent consists of zero or more quantifiers followed by a valid schema, then its consequent is valid.* Diagrammatically:

from '$(x_1)(x_2) \ldots (x_n)$(- - - -) ⊃ ——' and '- - - -' infer '——'.

The rule amounts to a convenient operation of bracketing out, for deletion, the proved antecedent (including added quantifiers) of a proved conditional. An example of its use, and a proof of the adequacy just now claimed for it, will appear in §7.

3. Reduction to Basic Schemata. A schema will be called a *basic quantification* if it consists of a universal quantifier (say '(x)') followed by a truth function built up of components each of which consists of a predicate letter and a single occurrence of the variable of quantification (thus 'fx', 'gx', etc.). A schema will be called *basic,* more generally, if it is a truth function all of whose components are statement-letters ('p', 'q', etc.) or basic quantifications. Equivalently: a basic schema is a closed monadic schema wherein all quantifications are basic quantifications.

In §4 a method will be explained for testing the validity of basic schemata. In the present section, meanwhile, we shall see how to transform any closed monadic schema into an equivalent which is basic. The combined techniques of the two sections then enable us to test *any* monadic schema for validity, simply by transforming its closure into a basic equivalent and testing the latter for validity.

Consider, to begin with, a quantification '$(x)(\ldots .)$' where '. . . .' is a truth function of components at least one of which is devoid of free occurrences of 'x'. Select such a component, say 'p'. (Instead of 'p' it could just as well be 'fy', or '$(y)(fy \,.\, \sim fz)$', etc.) Find, by truth-function theory, the two expressions to which '. . . .' reduces on the respective assumptions that 'p' is true and that 'p' is false. (An easy graphic way is to put the appropriate truth-value letter, 'T' or 'F', for 'p' throughout '. . . .' and then progressively reduce '$\sim$T' to 'F', '$\sim$F' to 'T', 'T . fx' to 'fx', 'F . fx' to 'F', '$fx \supset$ F' to '$\sim fx$', and so on.) Where the two expressions to which '. . . .' thus reduces are respectively '- - - -' and '——', our original quantification '$(x)(. . . .)$' can now be given the equivalent form:

(2) $$p \,.\, (x)(\text{- - - -}) \,.\vee.\, \sim p \,.\, (x)(\text{——}).$$

If it should happen that '- - - -' or '——' is simply 'T' or 'F', (2) reduces further to one or another of these:

(3) $$p \vee (x)(\text{——}),\quad p \supset (x)(\text{- - - -}),\quad \sim p \,.\, (x)(\text{——}),\quad p \,.\, (x)(\text{- - - -}).$$

If both '- - - -' and '——' are 'T' or 'F', (2) reduces to one or another of:

(4) $$p,\qquad \sim p,\qquad p \,.\sim p,\qquad p \supset p.$$

We thus have a general method for *exporting* 'p' from the quantification; namely, transformation of '$(x)(. . . .)$' into (2), or into its simpler equivalent from among (3)–(4).

Now the method of transforming any closed monadic schema ϕ into a basic equivalent consists merely in continued use of the above exportation technique, starting in the innermost quantifications of ϕ. (Any occurrences of '$(\exists x)$', '$(\exists y)$', etc., are first translated into '$\sim(x)\sim$', '$\sim(y)\sim$', etc., so that we have only universal quantifications.)

For example, let us transform the closure of the monadic schema:

(5) $$(x)(fx \,.\, fy \,.\!\supset gx) \,.\, p \,.\, (x)fx \,.\!\supset gy,$$

namely:

(6) $$(y)((x)(fx \,.\, fy \,.\!\supset gx) \,.\, p \,.\, (x)fx \,.\!\supset gy),$$

into a basic equivalent. Exportation of 'fy' from '$(x)(fx \,.\, fy \,.\!\supset gx)$' gives '$fy \supset (x)(fx \supset gx)$' (answering to the second form in (3)), so that (6) becomes:

(7) $$(y)(fy \supset (x)(fx \supset gx) \,.\, p \,.\, (x)fx \,.\!\supset gy).$$

Exportation of '$p \,.\, (x)fx$' from (7) gives:

(8) $$p \,.\, (x)fx \,.\!\supset (y)(fy \supset (x)(fx \supset gx) \,.\!\supset gy).$$

Exportation of '$(x)(fx \supset gx)$' from the consequent of (8) gives:

$$(x)(fx \supset gx) \,.\, (y)gy \,.\!\vee\!.\, \sim(x)(fx \supset gx) \,.\, (y)(\sim fy \supset gy)$$

(corresponding to (2)), so that (8) becomes the basic schema:

(9) $p \,.\, (x)fx \,.\!\supset:$

$$(x)(fx \supset gx) \,.\, (y)gy \,.\!\vee\!.\, \sim(x)(fx \supset gx) \,.\, (y)(\sim fy \supset gy).$$

As in the above example, so in general, the continued process of exportation beginning in innermost quantifications will always turn a closed monadic schema ϕ eventually into a basic schema ψ. This is seen as follows. Since ϕ is monadic, any innermost quantification in it must consist of a quantifier followed by a truth function whose components are of at most these three kinds: (i) a predicate letter followed by the variable of quantification, (ii) a predicate letter followed by a variable other than that of the quantification, (iii) a statement letter. But components of kinds (ii) and (iii), lacking as they do the variable of quantification, can all be exported. In this way any innermost quantification in ϕ gives way to a schema involving none but basic quantifications. So now the next broader quantifications come to consist each of a quantifier followed by a truth function whose components are of at most four kinds: (i), (ii), (iii), and basic quantifications. But components of kinds (ii) and (iii) can be exported as before; and so also can the basic quantifications, since they are closed and therefore have no free occurrences of the variable of the broader quantification. In this way, progressively broader quantifications give way to schemata involving none but basic quantifications, until finally ϕ is transformed into an equivalent ψ in which all quantifications are basic. Moreover, ψ will, like ϕ, be monadic and closed, since the intervening process of exportation cannot give rise to any polyadic ingredient or free variable not present in ϕ. Thus ψ is basic.

4. Validity Test for Basic Schemata. The validity test for basic schemata which is to be presented consists essentially of a certain combination of the following familiar techniques of truth-function theory:

(i) Constructing a truth table under a complex truth function of given components to see which assignments of truth values to the components would falsify the compound.

(ii) Testing for medadic (or truth-functional) validity or contravalidity. This is done by setting up a table as in (i) and seeing whether none or all of the assignments falsify the compound.

(iii) Testing to see whether one schema, χ, medadically implies another, ω. This is done by setting up a table and seeing whether every assignment of truth values which verifies χ verifies ω.[9]

Now preparatory to testing basic schemata for validity, all their variables are to be rewritten uniformly as 'x'. For example, (9) becomes:

(10) $p \,.\, (x)fx \,.\!\supset:$
$$(x)(fx \supset gx) \,.\, (x)gx \,.\!\vee\!.\, \sim(x)(fx \supset gx) \,.\, (x)(\sim fx \supset gx).$$

Such relettering will never engender conflict, since in a basic schema all occurrences of variables are bound to quantifiers with non-overlapping scopes.

For any basic schema ψ, thus relettered, the validity test is as follows. First set up a truth table under ψ, assigning 'T's and 'F's in all combinations to the statement letters and the quantifications of ψ and calculating, for each row of the table, the value of ψ. Keep only the rows that yield 'F' for ψ. (If there are none, so that ψ is medadically valid, the test is already at an end.) Then determine whether each of these rows meets at least one of the following conditions:

(a) It assigns 'F' to a quantification whose scope is medadically valid.

(b) It assigns 'T' to one or more quantifications whose scope, or the conjunction of whose scopes, is medadically contravalid.

(c) The scope, or conjunction of scopes, of one or more quantifications assigned 'T' medadically implies the scope of a quantification assigned 'F'.

As soon as a row is found to meet one of the conditions (a)–(c), we can drop it and go on to the next row. As soon as a row is found to meet none of (a)–(c), we can stop altogether, having found ψ non-valid. If every row meets one of the conditions (a)–(c), ψ is valid.

The only reason for including (a) and (b) in the routine is to provide for rows where no quantification is marked 'T' or none is marked 'F'; for otherwise (a) and (b) are merely extreme cases of (c).

That the test affords a sufficient condition of validity—i.e., that

[9] Concerning this test there is the following suggestion in *O Sentido da Nova Lógica*, 65f: If χ is simpler than ω, work out the table for χ and then extend the table to ω in just those lines where χ came out true. If ω is simpler, work out the table for ω and then extend it to χ in just those lines where ω came out false.

no basic schema ψ passing the test has a false instance ψ^0—is immediately apparent: every assortment of truth-values for the quantifications of ψ^0 which could conduce to falsehood of ψ^0 is precluded by (a), (b), or (c). That the test also affords a necessary condition of validity will be proved in §5.

Meanwhile let us note some practical shortcuts. Ordinarily it will not be necessary to construct a full truth table under ψ. In practice we can, by inspection, usually sidestep most or all of the rows that verify ψ, rather than working them out and dropping them afterward. In the case of the conditional (10), for example, we simply reflect that the only assignments of truth values capable of falsifying the whole must be such as to verify the antecedent (hence assignment of 'T' to 'p' and '$(x)fx$') and falsify both alternatives of the consequent. Thus the only assignments that make (10) come out false are those shown in the four rows below:

$p\,.$	$(x)fx\,.\supset:$	$(x)(fx \supset gx)\,.$	$(x)gx\,.\vee.\sim(x)(fx \supset gx)\,.$	$(x)(\sim fx \supset gx)$
T	T	T	F	T
T	T	T	F	F
T	T	F	T	F
T	T	F	F	F

(The value assigned to each quantification is marked under the quantifier, and a quantification occurring twice is marked at its first occurrence.) Finally, moving to (a)–(c), we can usually spot the desired case of medadic contravalidity or validity or implication by inspection, without auxiliary tables, if it exists at all. In the above example, the fulfillment of (c) by the first two lines is recognized simply by noting that the conjunction of the scopes 'fx' and '$fx \supset gx$' medadically implies 'gx'; and the fulfillment of (c) by the remaining two lines is recognized by noting that 'fx' medadically implies '$\sim fx \supset gx$'. (10) is valid; hence also (5).

5. Proof That Passing the Test Is Necessary for Validity. It is now to be proved that the test gives a necessary condition of validity of basic schemata. I.e., it is to be proved that every basic schema failing the test has a false instance. Suppose, then, that ψ is a basic schema failing the test, so that there is an assignment A of 'T's and 'F's to the statement letters and quantifications of ψ which yields 'F' for ψ as a whole and yet conforms to none of (a)–(c). Certain substitutions upon the schematic letters of ψ will be specified, for forming an instance ψ^0; and it will be shown that these substitutions turn the statement letters and quantifications of ψ into statements whose truth values realize A, so that ψ^0 is false.

'$0 = 0$', to begin with, is to be substituted for those statement letters of ψ which are marked 'T' in A, and '$0 \neq 0$' for those which are marked 'F'. Clearly these substitutions realize A so far as they go. It remains only to find matrices to substitute for the 'fx', 'gx', etc., of ψ which will cause the quantifications also to realize A.

Let us suppose there are k predicate letters in ψ, and think of them not as 'f', 'g', etc., but as 'f_1', 'f_2', . . . , 'f_k'. Let $\chi_1, \chi_2, \ldots, \chi_m$ $(m \geqq 0)$ be the scopes of those quantifications in ψ which are marked 'T' in A, and let $\omega_1, \omega_2, \ldots, \omega_n$ $(n \geqq 0)$ be the scopes of the others.

Case 1: $n = 0$. Let A_0 be an assignment of 'T's and 'F's to 'f_1x', 'f_2x', . . . , 'f_kx' which makes all of $\chi_1, \chi_2, \ldots, \chi_m$ turn out as 'T'. (There is such an A_0, in view of the fact that (b) fails for A.) Now the matrices substituted for 'f_1x', 'f_2x', . . . , 'f_kx' in forming ψ^0 from ψ are to be '$x = x$' and '$x \neq x$', as follows: for such of 'f_1x', 'f_2x', . . . , 'f_kx' as are marked 'T' by A_0, we substitute '$x = x$'; for the others, '$x \neq x$'. Since this turns $\chi_1, \chi_2, \ldots, \chi_m$ into matrices which hold true for all values of 'x', all the quantifications in ψ^0 are true and hence realize A.

Case 2: $n > 0$. Let A_i, for each i from 1 to n, be a certain assignment of 'T's and 'F's to 'f_1x', 'f_2x', . . . , 'f_kx' causing all of $\chi_1, \chi_2, \ldots, \chi_m$ $(m \geqq 0)$ to come out as 'T' and ω_i as 'F'. (There is such an A_i, for each i, in view of the fact that (a) and (c) fail for A.) Now the matrix to be substituted for 'f_jx', for each j from 1 to k, will be abbreviated as 'f_j^0x' and is to be determined as follows. Consider those assignments, if any, from among $A_1, \ldots, A_n$, in which 'f_jx' is assigned 'T'. If there are none, 'f_j^0x' is to mean '$x \neq x$'. If there are some, say $A_{a_j}, A_{b_j}, \ldots$, but A_n is not among them, then 'f_j^0x' is to mean:

(11) $$x = a_j \,.\!\vee.\, x = b_j \,.\!\vee.\, \ldots\,.$$

If finally A_n is among them, then 'f_j^0x' is to mean:

(12) $$x = a_j \,.\!\vee.\, x = b_j \,.\!\vee.\, \ldots\, .\!\vee.\, x = n \,.\!\vee. \quad x \neq 1 \,.\, x \neq 2 \,.\, \ldots\, .\, x \neq n.$$

So now ψ^0 has been specified for Case 2, and it remains only to show that its quantifications realize A.

Note first that, for each i from 1 to n and each j from 1 to k, the statement 'f_j^0i' has the truth value which is assigned to 'f_jx' by A_i.

For, if that truth value is 'T', then '$f_j{}^0i$' is according to the above specifications a truth of the form:

$$i = a_j . \vee . i = b_j . \vee . \ldots . \vee . i = i . \vee . \ldots .$$

If on the other hand that truth value is 'F', then '$f_j{}^0i$' is a falsehood of one of the three forms:

$i \neq i$,

$i = a_j . \vee . i = b_j . \vee . \ldots$ (where i is not one of $a_j, b_j, \ldots$),

$i = a_j . \vee . i = b_j . \vee . \ldots . \vee . i = n . \vee . i \neq 1 . i \neq 2 . \ldots . i \neq n$ (where i is not one of $a_j, b_j, \ldots, n$ but is one of $1, 2, \ldots, n$).

Now let $\chi_1{}^0, \ldots, \chi_m{}^0, \omega_1{}^0, \ldots, \omega_n{}^0$ be the matrices in ψ^0, corresponding to the $\chi_1, \ldots, \chi_m, \omega_1, \ldots, \omega_n$ of ψ. Since A_i was an assignment of 'T's and 'F's to 'f_1x', . . . , 'f_kx' causing ω_i to come out as 'F', it follows from the preceding paragraph that the number i, as value of 'x', fails to satisfy the matrix $\omega_i{}^0$. Each of the matrices $\omega_1{}^0, \ldots, \omega_n{}^0$ thus fails for at least one value of 'x'. The quantifications '$(x)(\ldots)$' that have the scopes $\omega_1{}^0, \ldots, \omega_n{}^0$ are therefore all false.

Similarly, since A_i was an assignment causing all of $\chi_1, \ldots, \chi_m$ to come out as 'T', it follows that i as value of 'x' fulfills all the matrices $\chi_1{}^0, \ldots, \chi_m{}^0$. This is true for each integer i from 1 to n. Moreover, any value of 'x' other than integers 1 to n will fulfill $\chi_1{}^0, \ldots, \chi_m{}^0$ if n does; for, $\chi_1{}^0, \ldots, \chi_m{}^0$ are truth functions of '$f_1{}^0x$', . . . , '$f_k{}^0x$', and every object other than $1, \ldots, n$ fulfills exactly those of '$f_1{}^0x$', . . . , '$f_k{}^0x$' which n fulfills (viz., those of the form (12)). Hence $\chi_1{}^0, \ldots, \chi_m{}^0$ are fulfilled not only by the integers 1 to n but by any other object as well. Thus the quantifications '$(x)(\ldots)$' having the scopes $\chi_1{}^0, \ldots, \chi_m{}^0$ are true. Since those having the scopes $\omega_1{}^0, \ldots, \omega_n{}^0$ were seen to be false, the proof is complete that the quantifications in ψ^0 realize A.

6. *Illustrations.* All the monadic schemata which ordinarily appear in the books can be put through the present testing routine quickly and easily. Let us begin with some which are not basic.

(A) $(x)fx \supset fy.$

Since this has a free variable, we take its closure '$(y)((x)fx \supset fy)$'. Exportation of '$(x)fx$' by the method of §3 turns this into '$(x)fx \supset (y)fy$'. Relettering to 'x' as at the beginning of §4, we have '$(x)fx \supset (x)fx$'. which is medadically valid. Thus (A) has been found valid through the mere reduction process, without use of the testing method of §4.

The same thing happens with:

(B) $$fy \supset (\exists x)fx,$$

only here we have to translate '$(\exists x)$' into '$\sim(x)\sim$'. Forming the closure '$(y)(fy \supset \sim(x) \sim fx)$' and exporting '$(x) \sim fx$', we have '$(x) \sim fx \supset (y) \sim fy$', which, reletterered to 'x', is medadically valid.

Two more examples:

(C) $$(x)(p \supset fx) \supset . \, p \supset (x)fx.$$

Exportation of 'p' from the antecedent turns (C) into the medadically valid basic schema:

$$p \supset (x)fx \,. \supset . \, p \supset (x)fx,$$

so that again no use is required of the testing method of §4.

(D) $$(x)(fx \supset p) \supset . \, (\exists x)fx \supset p.$$

Translating '$(\exists x)$' into '$\sim(x)\sim$' as usual, and exporting 'p' from the antecedent, we have the medadically valid basic schema:

$$p \lor (x) \sim fx \,. \supset . \sim(x) \sim fx \supset p.$$

Biconditionals corresponding to the conditionals (C) and (D) prove valid, of course, in similar fashion.

The validity of (A) and (B) is affirmed in effect by the metatheorems *104 and *134 of *Mathematical Logic* (1940). These metatheorems are two among thirteen in that book which affirm, in effect, the validity of certain non-basic monadic schemata.[10] All thirteen schemata turn out to reduce, like (A)–(D), to medadically valid basic schemata, so that no use of the testing method of §4 has to be made in connection with any of them.

The rest of the valid monadic schemata which ordinarily appear in the books are already basic and hence can be tested directly by the method of §4. Four examples will be set forth. Under each schema those truth-value assignments are shown which render the whole false; they may be presumed discovered by rapid inspection.

(E) $$\underset{\mathrm{T}}{(x)(fx \supset gx)} \supset . \, \underset{\mathrm{T}}{(x)fx} \supset \underset{\mathrm{F}}{(x)gx}$$

[10] The other eleven are *103, *110, *118, *135, *137, *157–162.

To test this we observe that '$fx \supset gx . fx$' medadically implies 'gx', fulfilling (c) of §4.

(F) $(x)(fx . gx) \equiv . (x)fx . (x)gx$

T	T	F
T	F	T
T	F	F
F	T	T

To test this we observe that the first three rows all fulfill (c), since '$fx . gx$' medadically implies 'gx' and 'fx'; and also that the fourth row fulfills (c), since '$fx . gx$' medadically implies '$fx . gx$'.

(G) $(x)(fx \supset gx) . (x)(gx \supset hx) . \supset (x)(fx \supset hx)$

T	T	F

To test this, which is the principle of the syllogism, we observe that '$fx \supset gx . gx \supset hx$' medadically implies '$fx \supset hx$', fulfilling (c).

(H) $(x)fx \supset \sim(x) \sim fx$

T	T

To test this schema (in which '$(\exists x)$' has been translated into '$\sim(x)\sim$') we observe that '$fx . \sim fx$' is medadically contravalid, fulfilling (b).

The reader will find that all further basic schemata corresponding to metatheorems of *Mathematical Logic*[11] come out as briefly as the above four.

7. *Polyadic Theory.* To derive any further valid schema of quantification theory, we start with monadically valid ones and use the rule of generalized *modus ponens* (§2). A convenient notation is this: Write down the required monadically valid schemata, justifying each by a reference to the valid monadic schema from which it is got by substitution; use reference numerals as abbreviations for any recurrences of valid schemata which have already been numbered; and use brackets to indicate suppression of an antecedent by generalized *modus ponens*.[12] Example:

(I) $(\exists x)(y)fxy \supset (y)(\exists x)fxy$

Proof:	From (B):	$fxy \supset (\exists x)fxy$	(1)
	From (E):	$[(y)1 \supset .](y)fxy \supset (y)(\exists x)fxy$	(2)
	From (D):	$[(x)2 \supset] I$	

[11] Namely, *115, *130, *131, *141–*156.
[12] This notation is already familiar to readers of *Mathematical Logic;* see 92, 94.

In theory there is no need to recognize, over and above generalized *modus ponens* and ordinary substitution, a third operation having to do with relettering of bound variables; for, the effect of such relettering can always be gained by choosing differently lettered monadic schemata in the first place. The citation '(E)' in the above proof, for example, may be understood as referring not to (E) itself but to the different valid monadic schema:

$$(y)(fy \supset gy) \supset . (y)fy \supset (y)gy.$$

The above example (I) is the polyadic schema corresponding to the metatheorem *139 of *Mathematical Logic.* It will now be proved that every valid schema can be derived in similar fashion. To prove this it will be sufficient to show that all schemata demonstrable in the system of Hilbert and Ackermann[13]—which I shall call *H*—can be obtained from monadically valid schemata by generalized *modus ponens.* For Hilbert and Ackermann prove in turn that every valid schema is demonstrable in *H*.[14]

H has by way of axioms the monadic schemata (A) and (B), above, and various valid medadic schemata. The rules of inference are these:

(α) Substitution.

(β) Simple *modus ponens.*

(γ1) In a conditional schema containing 'x' as free variable in the consequent only, insert the quantifier '(x)' to govern the consequent.

(γ2) In a conditional schema containing 'x' as free variable in the antecedent only, insert '$(\exists x)$' to govern the antecedent.

(δ) Relettering of bound variables.

Let us liberalize (γ1) and (γ2) to the extent of allowing them to apply not just to the specific letter 'x' but equally to 'y', 'z', etc. Let us now call them (γ'1) and (γ'2) and call the system H'.

Anything demonstrable in H' is demonstrable in such a way that all use of (α) and (δ) precedes all use of (β), (γ'1), and (γ'2). For, consider any proof involving substitution and relettering intermediately; we can trace the proof back to its starting point in the axioms, do the substituting and relettering rather in these, and then reproduce the old proof step by step carrying along the substituted expressions and new variables in their proper places, since any use of (β), (γ'1), and (γ'2) along the way will apply just

[13] 1938, 56–57.

[14] *Ibid.*, 74–81. (After Gödel.)

as well to the substituted and relettered material.

Hence whatever is demonstrable in *H*′ (or, a fortiori, in *H*) is derivable from monadically valid schemata by (β), ($\gamma'1$), and ($\gamma'2$). This follows from the foregoing paragraph in view of the fact that the axioms are valid monadic schemata and everything got from them by (α) and (δ) is monadically valid.

But anything derivable from monadically valid schemata by (β), ($\gamma'1$), and ($\gamma'2$) is also derivable from monadically valid schemata by generalized *modus ponens;* for, (β) is a special case of generalized *modus ponens*, and ($\gamma'1$) and ($\gamma'2$) yield no more than can be got with help of (C) or (D) as in the last step of the proof of (I) above.

XVIII

A Proof Procedure for Quantification Theory

The purpose of this paper is to present and justify a simple proof procedure for quantification theory. The procedure will take the form of a method for proving a quantificational schema to be *inconsistent*, i.e., satisfiable in no non-empty universe. But it serves equally for proving validity, since we can show a schema valid by showing its negation inconsistent.

Method A, as I shall call it, will appear first, followed by a more practical adaptation which I shall call B. The soundness and completeness of A will be established, and the equivalence of A and B. Method A is from Skolem, 1928.

The reader need be conversant with little more than the fairly conventional use of such terms as 'quantificational schema', 'interpretation', 'valid', 'consistent', 'prenex', and my notation of quasi-quotation.[1]

1. Method A. Where ϕ is any prenex quantificational schema, its *functional normal form* (as I shall call it) is got from it by deleting all existential quantifiers and attaching subscripts to the recurrences of their variables, according to the following scheme: if the universal quantifiers to the left of $\ulcorner(\exists\beta)\urcorner$ are $\ulcorner(\alpha_1)\urcorner, \ldots, \ulcorner(\alpha_n)\urcorner$ in that order, then $\ulcorner(\exists\beta)\urcorner$ is dropped and β is rewritten in the sequel as $\ulcorner\beta_{\alpha_1 \ldots \alpha_n}\urcorner$. No meaning need be associated with the subscript notation.

E.g., the prenex schema:

Reprinted from the *Journal of Symbolic Logic,* Volume 20, 1955. Historical remarks have been improved thanks to Dreben.

[1] See VII and XVII above. 'Prenex' means that the quantifiers are initial.

$$(1) \quad (\exists y)(x)(\exists w)(z)[Fxy \supset -(Fxz \,.\, Fzx) \,.\, -(Fxw \,.\, Fwx) \supset Fxy]$$

has this as its functional normal form:

$$(2) \quad (x)(z)[Fxy \supset -(Fxz \,.\, Fzx) \,.\, -(Fxw_x \,.\, Fw_xx) \supset Fxy].$$

Given now any functional normal form ψ, consider the following class C of terms. C is to contain, to begin with, all those free variables of ψ which carry no subscripts (or 'a', arbitrarily, if there are none). Further, if a letter occurs with subscripts in ψ, then that same letter, with members of C in place of all its subscripts, is to belong in turn to C. This class C, usually infinite, will be called the *lexicon* of ψ. Thus the lexicon of (2) comprises 'y', 'w_y', 'w_{w_y}', and so on. (Where the iteration of subscripts threatens to get out of hand, we may conveniently switch to a linear notation: '$[wy]$' for 'w_y', '$[w[wy]]$' for 'w_{w_y}', etc.)

By a *lexical instance* of a functional normal form ψ will be meant any result of dropping the quantifiers of ψ (which are all universal) and substituting, for the recurrences of the variables of those quantifiers, terms from the lexicon of ψ. (The substitutions must reach all occurrences of the variables, not omitting occurrences within subscripts.) Here, e.g., are two lexical instances of (2):

$$(3) \quad Fyy \supset -(Fyy \,.\, Fyy) \,.\, -(Fyw_y \,.\, Fw_yy) \supset Fyy,$$

$$(4) \quad Fw_yy \supset -(Fw_yy \,.\, Fyw_y) \,.\, -(Fw_yw_{w_y} \,.\, Fw_{w_y}w_y) \supset Fw_yy.$$

Now what I call Method A, for proving the inconsistency of a quantificational schema ϕ, is as follows: put ϕ into prenex form,[2] then get the functional normal form, and finally present a truth-functionally inconsistent lexical instance or conjunction of lexical instances.

E.g., suppose we want to show the inconsistency of:

$$(\exists y)(x)[Fxy \equiv -(\exists z)(Fxz \,.\, Fzx)].^3$$

Expanded, this becomes:

$$(5) \quad (\exists y)(x)[Fxy \supset -(\exists z)(Fxz \,.\, Fzx) \,.\, -(\exists z)(Fxz \,.\, Fzx) \supset Fxy],$$

and thereupon goes into the prenex equivalent (1). But the functional normal form (2) of (1) has the lexical instances (3) and (4), which are together inconsistent by truth table.

[2] This well-known transformation is explained, e.g., in *Methods of Logic*, 227.

[3] When 'F' is taken as 'ϵ', this is the second paradox of a series which begins with Russell's. See my *Mathematical Logic*, 128f.; also "On the theory of types," 127f.

It will be shown in §§4–5 that Method A is sound and complete. Meanwhile let us turn to a convenient variant of A, which I shall call B.

2. Method B. Under this method we show the inconsistency of a conjunction of prenex schemata without first making a single prenex schema of it. For the purpose of formulating this method, I shall need to speak of the "lexicon" not of a single functional normal form ψ, as above, but of a conjunction $\ulcorner\psi_1 \ldots \psi_n\urcorner$ of functional normal forms. The lexicon of $\ulcorner\psi_1 \ldots \psi_n\urcorner$ is to contain all variables which occur free and without subscripts in any of ψ_1, $\ldots$, ψ_n (or '*a*' if there are none); further, if a letter occurs with subscripts in any of $\psi_1, \ldots, \psi_n$ then it with members of the lexicon in place of its subscripts is to belong in turn to the lexicon.

E.g., the conjunction of:

(6) $$(x)(y)(Fxy \vee . Fxz_{xy} . Fz_{xy}y . \vee . Fyz_{xy} . Fz_{xy}x),$$

(7) $$(x)(z) -(Fy_xz . Fzx),$$

(8) $$(y) -Fxy,$$

has as its lexicon the class whose members are '*x*' and, for all members ζ and η of the class, $\ulcorner y_\zeta\urcorner$ and $\ulcorner z_{\zeta\eta}\urcorner$. Note that this lexicon is not simply the sum of the respective lexica of (6), (7), and (8).

By a lexical instance of a conjunction $\ulcorner\psi_1 \ldots \psi_n\urcorner$ of functional normal forms will be meant any expression obtained from any of $\psi_1, \ldots, \psi_n$ by dropping the quantifiers and substituting, for the recurrences of their variables, terms from the lexicon of $\ulcorner\psi_1 \ldots \psi_n\urcorner$.

The conjunction of (6)–(8), e.g., has the following among its lexical instances:

(9) $$Fxy_x \vee . Fxz_{xy_x} . Fz_{xy_x}y_x . \vee . Fy_xz_{xy_x} . Fz_{xy_x}x,$$

(10) $$-(Fy_xz_{xy_x} . Fz_{xy_x}x),$$

(11) $$-Fxy_x,$$

(12) $$-Fxz_{xy_x}.$$

Now Method B, for proving the inconsistency of a conjunction $\ulcorner\phi_1 \ldots \phi_n\urcorner$ of quantificational schemata, is as follows. Put $\phi_1, \ldots, \phi_n$ into prenex normal forms $\phi'_1, \ldots, \phi'_n$, so choosing the variables that none occurs both free and in an existential quantifier, nor twice in existential quantifiers. Then get the respective functional normal forms $\psi_1, \ldots, \psi_n$ of $\phi'_1, \ldots, \phi'_n$, and finally present a truth-functionally inconsistent lexical instance or conjunction of lexical instances of $\ulcorner\psi_1 \ldots \psi_n\urcorner$.

E.g., to prove the inconsistency of the conjunction of:

$$(13) \qquad (x)(y)[Fxy \lor (\exists z)(Fxz\,.\,Fzy\,.\!\lor\!.\,Fyz\,.\,Fzx)],$$

$$(14) \qquad -(\exists x)(y)(\exists z)(Fyz\,.\,Fzx),$$

$$(15) \qquad (\exists x) -(\exists y)Fxy,$$

we first put (13)–(15) into prenex form thus:

$$(x)(y)(\exists z)(Fxy \lor.\, Fxz\,.\,Fzy\,.\!\lor\!.\,Fyz\,.\,Fzx),$$

$$(x)(\exists y)(z) -(Fyz\,.\,Fzx),$$

$$(\exists x)(y) -Fxy,$$

then obtain the corresponding functional normal forms (6)–(8), and finally present the truth-functionally inconsistent conjunction of lexical instances (9)–(12).

To show that a conclusion follows from given premises, we have merely to show by Method B that the premises and the negation of the conclusion are inconsistent. E.g., to show that '$(\exists x)(y)(\exists z)$ $(Fyz\,.\,Fzx)$' follows from (13) and (15), we show (13), (14), and (15) jointly inconsistent as above.

3. Two Strategies. For a second example of Method B, let us show that transitivity and irreflexivity:

$$(16) \qquad (x)(y)(z)(Fxy\,.\,Fyz\,.\!\supset Fxz),$$

$$(17) \qquad (x) -Fxx$$

together imply asymmetry: $(x)(y)(Fxy \supset -Fyx)$. I.e., what is to be shown is the joint inconsistency of (16), (17), and '$-(x)(y)$ $(Fxy \supset -Fyx)$'. This last goes over into prenex form as:

$$(18) \qquad (\exists x)(\exists y) -(Fxy \supset -Fyx).$$

The functional normal forms of (16) and (17) are (16) and (17) themselves; that of (18) is '$-(Fxy \supset -Fyx)$'. The lexicon comprises just 'x' and 'y'. Finally we present three lexical instances:

$$Fxy\,.\,Fyx\,.\!\supset Fxx, \qquad -Fxx, \qquad -(Fxy \supset -Fyx),$$

which are, in conjunction, truth-functionally inconsistent.

As this example illustrates, a finite lexicon is assured when none of our prenex schemata has a universal quantifier to the left of an existential one. When the lexicon is finite, the number of lexical instances is likewise finite; and then an actual decision procedure for inconsistency is at hand, since we can subject the conjunction of *all* lexical instances to a truth-table test.[4] In turning schemata into prenex form it is therefore advantageous to bring existential quantifiers out ahead of universal ones, insofar as we have a choice. This policy is advantageous even when we cannot get all the existential quantifiers out in front; for in any event we minimize the influx of subscripts.

An advantage of Method B over Method A is that any given existential quantifier tends, under Method B, to be preceded by fewer universal quantifiers than under Method A. A more obvious advantage of Method B is that it reduces the complexity of the individual lexical instances. A useful strategy, therefore, is that of maximum fragmentation: where possible, render a schema as a conjunction of shorter schemata and thus exploit the advantages of Method B to the full. Such fragmentation can often be facilitated by these two expedients: (a) Drop all distinctively lettered initial existential quantifiers, these being obviously immaterial to consistency; and (b) Distribute universal quantifiers into conjunctions, where possible, according to the equivalence of '$(x)(Fx \,.\, Gx)$' to '$(x)Fx \,.\, (x)Gx$'.

In the case of (5), e.g., we might have dropped the initial '$(\exists y)$' and distributed the '(x)', thus turning (5) into the conjunction of:

$$(x)[Fxy \supset -(\exists z)(Fxz \,.\, Fzx)],$$

$$(x)[-(\exists z)(Fxz \,.\, Fzx) \supset Fxy],$$

which could thereupon be handled by Method B.

After establishing in §§4–5 the soundness and completeness of Method A, I shall prove in §6 that Method B is equivalent to A and therefore sound and complete as well.

4. Soundness of Method A means that if a prenex schema ϕ is consistent then its functional normal form has no truth-functionally inconsistent conjunction of lexical instances.

Let us think of ϕ as:

(19) $$(\exists x)(y)(z)(\exists u)(v)(\exists w)\ \Phi(x, y, z, u, v, w);$$

[4] Substantially this case of the decision problem was first solved by Bernays and Schönfinkel.

this will typify the general case well enough. Now we are supposing ϕ consistent, hence true under some interpretation $\mathfrak{J}$ in some non-empty universe *U;* and what we want to show is that every conjunction of lexical instances of the functional normal form:

(20) $$(y)(z)(v)\ \Phi(x,\ y,\ z,\ u_{yz},\ v,\ w_{yzv})$$

is truth-functionally consistent.

Let us adopt the interpretation $\mathfrak{J}$, thus supposing (19) simply true. But (19) says there is a particular object, which I shall hereafter call x, such that

(21) $$(y)(z)(\exists u)(v)(\exists w)\ \Phi(x,\ y,\ z,\ u,\ v,\ w).$$

According to (21) there is, for each choice of y and z, an object—which let us call u_{yz}—such that $(v)(\exists w)\ \Phi(x,\ y,\ z,\ u_{yz},\ v,\ w)$. So

(22) $$(y)(z)(v)(\exists w)\ \Phi(x,\ y,\ z,\ u_{yz},\ v,\ w).$$

According to (22) there is, for each choice of y, z, and v, an object—which let us call w_{yzv}—such that $\Phi(x,\ y,\ z,\ u_{yz},\ v,\ w_{yzv})$. So (20), under these provisions, becomes true and hence so do all its instances. But this would be impossible if a conjunction of these instances were truth-functionally inconsistent.[5]

5. *Completeness of Method A* means that if a prenex schema ϕ is inconsistent, i.e., if

(i) ϕ is false under every interpretation in every non-empty universe,

then the functional normal form ψ of ϕ has a truth-functionally inconsistent conjunction of lexical instances.

Let ξ_1, ξ_2, . . . be all the expressions obtainable by applying predicate letters of ψ to terms from the lexicon of ψ. Clearly all the lexical instances of ψ are truth functions of ξ_1, ξ_2, ...

Let *U* be a universe in one-to-one correlation with the lexicon of ψ. If we construe the terms of the lexicon as naming their respective correlates in *U*, then an interpretation of the predicate letters of ψ (with *U* as universe) is fixed by any full assignment of truth values to ξ_1, ξ_2, ... Moreover, any such interpretation makes ψ true if it makes all the lexical instances true; for, given that the

[5] *Note added 1966:* This sketchy argument depends on the axiom of choice, as Dreben has remarked. We can avoid that dependence if we wish, thanks to Löwenheim's theorem, by taking *U* as the universe of positive integers. We can then specify u_{yz} as the *least* u such that $(v)(\exists w)\Phi(x,\ y,\ z,\ u,\ v,\ w)$; and similarly for w_{yzv}. See next footnote.

lexicon names all the objects of U, the lexical instances exhaust the cases of ψ. But ψ in turn implies ϕ; this becomes generally evident if we look back to the quasi-example (20) and observe that it implies (22), which implies (21), which implies (19). By (i), then,

(ii) No assignment of truth values to $\xi_1, \xi_2, \ldots$ makes all lexical instances of ψ true.

Let us speak of a given assignment of truth values to $\xi_1, \ldots, \xi_i$ as *condemning* a given conjunction of lexical instances of ψ if it makes that conjunction come out false for all values of $\xi_{i+1}, \xi_{i+2}, \ldots$. Then let t_i for each i be one or other of the truth values, $\top$ or $\bot$, according to this inductive condition:

(iii) t_i is $\top$ if assignment of $t_1, \ldots, t_{i-1}$, and $\top$ respectively to $\xi_1, \ldots, \xi_i$ condemns no conjunction of lexical instances of ψ; otherwise $\bot$.

Thus t_1, to begin with, is $\top$ if assignment of $\top$ to ξ_1 condemns no conjunction of lexical instances; otherwise $\bot$. The stipulation (iii) fixes t_i for each i, or for each i up to the number of ξ's, according as the ξ's are infinite or finite in number.

By (ii), there is a lexical instance χ of ψ which comes out false when $t_1, t_2, \ldots$ are assigned respectively to $\xi_1, \xi_2, \ldots$. Then, where j is high enough so that none of $\xi_{j+1}, \xi_{j+2}, \ldots$ occurs in χ, it follows that the assignment of $t_1, \ldots, t_j$ respectively to $\xi_1, \ldots, \xi_j$ falsifies χ (and hence, *a fortiori*, condemns χ). Then there is also a *least* h, whether j or less, such that the assignment of $t_1, \ldots, t_h$ to $\xi_1, \ldots, \xi_h$ condemns a conjunction of lexical instances of ψ. (Note that $t_1, \ldots, t_h$ may condemn a conjunction of lexical instances even where h is too small for $t_1, \ldots, t_h$ to condemn any one lexical instance.) For that h, by (iii), t_h must be $\bot$. So

(iv) Assignment of $t_1, \ldots, t_{h-1}, \bot$ respectively to $\xi_1, \ldots, \xi_h$ condemns some conjunction ω of lexical instances of ψ.

But also

(v) Assignment of $t_1, \ldots, t_{h-1}, \top$ respectively to $\xi_1, \ldots, \xi_h$ condemns some conjunction ω' of lexical instances of ψ,

since otherwise, by (iii), t_h would be $\top$. Therefore $h = 1$; for otherwise, by (iv) and (v), the assignment of $t_1, \ldots, t_{h-1}$ to $\xi_1, \ldots, \xi_{h-1}$ would condemn $\ulcorner\omega\omega'\urcorner$, contrary to the leastness of h. But then, taking h as 1 in (iv) and (v), we see that ω and ω' are respectively condemned by assigning $\top$ and $\bot$ to ξ_1, and hence that $\ulcorner\omega\omega'\urcorner$ is a truth-functionally inconsistent conjunction of lexical instances.[6]

6. Reduction of B to A. The soundness and completeness of Method B will now be established by showing that B accomplishes all that Method A accomplishes and nothing more.

Consider any conjunction $\ulcorner\mu_1\phi_1 \,.\,.\,.\,.\,.\, \mu_n\phi_n\urcorner$, where μ_i for each i is a string of quantifiers and ϕ_i is without quantifiers. Suppose further that, in conformity with Method B, no variable occurs both free and in an existential quantifier, nor twice in existential quantifiers. Let $\ulcorner\nu_i\psi_i\urcorner$ be the functional normal form of $\ulcorner\mu_i\phi_i\urcorner$, for each i. Now what is to be shown is that there is a prenex $\ulcorner\mu\phi\urcorner$, equivalent to $\ulcorner\mu_1\phi_1 \,.\,.\,.\,.\,.\, \mu_n\phi_n\urcorner$, whose functional normal form has an inconsistent conjunction of lexical instances if and only if $\ulcorner\nu_1\psi_1 \,.\,.\,.\,.\,.\, \nu_n\psi_n\urcorner$ has an inconsistent conjunction of lexical instances. The equivalence of Methods A and B then becomes evident.

We may assume without loss of generality that the universal quantifiers in $\mu_1, \ldots, \mu_n$ are lettered as we please; for the choice of letters in that quarter obviously has no effect on the lexicon and the lexical instances. Let us suppose then that in each of $\mu_1, \ldots, \mu_n$ the leftmost universal quantifier (if any) is uniformly $\ulcorner(\alpha_1)\urcorner$, the next (if any) is $\ulcorner(\alpha_2)\urcorner$, and so on, where $\alpha_1, \alpha_2, \ldots$ are distinct from the existential variables and the free variables.

By our constructions, any variable which is existentially quantified in μ_i is foreign to $\ulcorner\mu_j\phi_j\urcorner$ for all $j \neq i$. Therefore $\ulcorner\mu_1\phi_1 \,.\,.\,.\,.\,.\, \mu_n\phi_n\urcorner$ is logically transformable by bringing out all those existential quantifiers of μ_i, for each i, which are not preceded in μ_i by $\ulcorner(\alpha_1)\urcorner$, and letting them govern the whole conjunction. Within the conjunction thus governed, each conjunctional component either begins with $\ulcorner(\alpha_1)\urcorner$ or has no occurrences of α_1. But then, in view of the laws '$(x)Fx \,.\, (x)Gx \,.\!\equiv (x)(Fx \,.\, Gx)$' and '$(x)Fx \,.\, p \,.\!\equiv (x)(Fx \,.\, p)$', we can pull out $\ulcorner(\alpha_1)\urcorner$ everywhere and let a single occurrence of $\ulcorner(\alpha_1)\urcorner$ govern the whole conjunction. Next, repeating the process, we can bring forward all those further existential quantifiers of μ_i, for each i, which are not preceded in μ_i by $\ulcorner(\alpha_2)\urcorner$. Next we can pull out $\ulcorner(\alpha_2)\urcorner$ everywhere, in favor of a single occurrence of $\ulcorner(\alpha_2)\urcorner$ governing the whole conjunction; and so on. We end up with a prenex equivalent $\ulcorner\mu(\phi_1 \ldots \phi_n)\urcorner$ of $\ulcorner\mu_1\phi_1 \,.\,.\,.\,.\,.\, \mu_n\phi_n\urcorner$, where μ is composed thus: first come all existential quantifiers of μ_i, for all i,

[6] The above argument is akin to Gödel's completeness argument (1930) as extended by Dreben. See also next paper. The argument incidentally proves Löwenheim's theorem, since U is clearly finite or denumerable.

which were not preceded in μ_i by $\ulcorner(\alpha_1)\urcorner$; then comes $\ulcorner(\alpha_1)\urcorner$; then come all further existential quantifiers of μ_i, for all i, which were not preceded in μ_i by $\ulcorner(\alpha_2)\urcorner$; and so on.

Next let us reflect on the functional normal form $\ulcorner\nu_i\psi_i\urcorner$ of $\ulcorner\mu_i\phi_i\urcorner$. Clearly ν_i, for each i, will be $\ulcorner(\alpha_1)\ \ldots\ (\alpha_{u_i})\urcorner$ where u_i is the number of universal quantifiers in μ_i; and ψ_i will differ from ϕ_i only in that each variable β of ϕ_i which had been existentially quantified in μ_i is decorated in ψ_i with a string of subscripts $\ulcorner\alpha_1\alpha_2\ \ldots\urcorner$ corresponding to all those universal quantifiers $\ulcorner(\alpha_1)\urcorner$, $\ulcorner(\alpha_2)\urcorner$, ... which preceded $\ulcorner(\exists\beta)\urcorner$ in μ_i.

What now of the functional normal form of $\ulcorner\mu(\phi_1\ \ldots\ \phi_n)\urcorner$? Obviously its string of quantifiers will be $\ulcorner(\alpha_1)\ \ldots\ (\alpha_k)\urcorner$ where k is the largest of $u_1, \ldots, u_n$. What comes after the quantifiers will be formed from $\ulcorner\phi_1\ \ldots\ \phi_n\urcorner$ by inserting subscripts. Specifically, within any component ϕ_i of $\ulcorner\phi_1\ \ldots\ \phi_n\urcorner$ the string of subscripts $\ulcorner\alpha_1\alpha_2\ \ldots\urcorner$ which is to be attached to a variable β will correspond to the universal quantifiers which preceded $\ulcorner(\exists\beta)\urcorner$ in μ. But the universal quantifiers preceding $\ulcorner(\exists\beta)\urcorner$ in μ are, by construction, the same as those which preceded $\ulcorner(\exists\beta)\urcorner$ in μ_i. Therefore what $\ulcorner\phi_1\ \ldots\ \phi_n\urcorner$ gives way to is precisely $\ulcorner\psi_1\ \ldots\ \psi_n\urcorner$; so the functional normal form of $\ulcorner\mu(\phi_1\ \ldots\ \phi_n)\urcorner$ is $\ulcorner(\alpha_1)\ \ldots\ (\alpha_k)(\psi_1\ \ldots\ \psi_n)\urcorner$.

We have only to remind ourselves of the definition of 'lexicon' to observe that the lexicon of a functional normal form is uniquely determined once we are told what complex terms (i.e., letters with subscripts) that functional normal form contains, and what free variables without subscripts. Similarly for a conjunction of functional normal forms. But then $\ulcorner(\alpha_1)\ \ldots\ (\alpha_k)(\psi_1\ \ldots\ \psi_n)\urcorner$ and $\ulcorner\nu_1\psi_1\ .\ .\ .\ .\ .\ \nu_n\psi_n\urcorner$ *have the same lexicon*. For, their complex terms are the same, viz., all complex terms of $\ulcorner\psi_1\ \ldots\ \psi_n\urcorner$; and their free variables without subscripts are the same, viz., all those of $\ulcorner\psi_1\ \ldots\ \psi_n\urcorner$ except $\alpha_1, \ldots, \alpha_k$.

Hence each lexical instance of $\ulcorner(\alpha_1)\ \ldots\ (\alpha_k)(\psi_1\ \ldots\ \psi_n)\urcorner$, being a result of substituting in $\ulcorner\psi_1\ \ldots\ \psi_n\urcorner$ for $\alpha_1, \ldots, \alpha_k$ from that lexicon, is a conjunction of lexical instances $\chi_1, \ldots, \chi_n$ of $\ulcorner\nu_1\psi_1\ .\ .\ .\ .\ .\ \nu_n\psi_n\urcorner$; and conversely each lexical instance χ_i of $\ulcorner\nu_1\psi_1\ .\ .\ .\ .\ .\ \nu_n\psi_n\urcorner$ is a conjunctional component χ_i of a lexical instance $\ulcorner\chi_1\ \ldots\ \chi_n\urcorner$ of $\ulcorner(\alpha_1)\ \ldots\ (\alpha_k)(\psi_1\ \ldots\ \psi_n)\urcorner$.

But it then follows that $\ulcorner(\alpha_1)\ \ldots\ (\alpha_k)(\psi_1\ \ldots\ \psi_n)\urcorner$ will have an inconsistent conjunction of lexical instances if and only if $\ulcorner\nu_1\psi_1\ .\ .\ .\ .\ .\ \nu_n\psi_n\urcorner$ has, q.e.d.

XIX

Interpretations of Sets of Conditions

The celebrated theorem of Löwenheim and Skolem tells us that *every consistent set S of quantificational schemata* (i.e., every set of well-formed formulae of the lower predicate calculus admitting of a true interpretation in some non-empty universe) *admits of a true numerical interpretation* (i.e., an interpretation of predicate letters such that all schemata of S come out true when the variables of quantification are construed as ranging over just the positive integers).

Later literature goes farther, and shows how, given S, actually to *produce* a numerical interpretation which will fit S in case S is consistent. The general case is covered by Kleene.[1] The special case where S contains just one schema (or any finite number, since we can form their conjunction) had been dealt with by Hilbert and Bernays. Certain extensions, along lines not to be embarked on here, have been made by Kleene, Kreisel, Hasenjaeger, and Wang (1951).

My present purpose is expository: to make the construction of the numerical interpretation, and the proof of its adequacy, more easily intelligible than they hitherto have been. The reasoning is mainly Kleene's, though closer in some ways to earlier reasoning of Gödel.

1. The General Numerical Interpretation. Our task here is to

Reprinted from the *Journal of Symbolic Logic*, Volume 19, 1954.

[1] 1952, 389–398; also 431, lines 22–26.

present a numerical interpretation of any consistent class S of quantificational schemata. We may think of the membership of S as making up an infinite progression of schemata, ordered in familiar lexicographic fashion. The case of a finite S can be accommodated by supposing repetition, say with arbitrary relettering of bound variables, from the last schema onward. (Also the finite case can, of course, be treated separately and more simply, as noted in §3.) We may without loss of generality suppose the schemata closed (i.e., devoid of free variables aside from predicate letters) and prenex (i.e., with all quantifiers initial) and wholly unlike one another in the choice of letters for the bound variables. Thus the members of S are $\ulcorner \mu_1\phi_1 \urcorner$, $\ulcorner \mu_2\phi_2 \urcorner$, . . . where μ_1, μ_2, . . . are strings of quantifiers and ϕ_1, ϕ_2, . . . lack quantifiers and, for each m, the conjunction $\ulcorner \mu_1\phi_1 . \ldots . \mu_m\phi_m \urcorner$ is equivalent to $\ulcorner \mu_1 \ldots \mu_m(\phi_1 \ldots \phi_m) \urcorner$. Let us suppose further that μ_1 begins with a universal quantifier; such a quantifier can always be trivially prefixed.

We shall need the auxiliary notion of a *substitution sequence* for a string of quantifiers. To begin with, suppose positive integers, same or different, arbitrarily assigned to all the universal quantifiers in the string. Then to the jth existential quantifier in the string, for each j, we assign (following Kleene) the number $2^j \cdot 3^{a_1} \cdot 5^{a_2} \cdot \ldots \cdot p_r^{a_r}$, where a_1, a_2, . . . , a_r are the respective numbers assigned to the preceding universal quantifiers and p_r is the rth prime number after 2. Thus for each string of quantifiers there are substitution sequences corresponding to all the ways of assigning numbers to the universal quantifiers; and there are infinitely many such ways, if a universal quantifier is present at all. So, for any string of quantifiers one at least of which is universal, we can speak of the first, second, . . . substitution sequence, according to a lexicographic ordering.

Now let ψ_m^n, for each m and n, be what we get from $\ulcorner \phi_1 \ldots \phi_m \urcorner$ by substituting numerals for variables according to the nth substitution sequence for $\ulcorner \mu_1 \ldots \mu_m \urcorner$. (Since μ_1 has a universal quantifier, ψ_m^n exists for every n.) Thus ψ_m^n for each m and n is a truth function of atomic formulae ω_1, ω_2, . . . each of which consists of a predicate letter in application to one or more numerals.

Where ω_1, ω_2, . . . *ad infinitum* are, in a lexicographic ordering, all the formulae that can be formed by applying predicate letters to numerals, clearly any assignment of truth values to ω_1, . . . , ω_r will either verify or falsify $\ulcorner \psi_m^1 \ldots \psi_m^n \urcorner$ if r is high enough so that ω_1, . . . , ω_r exhaust the atomic formulae in $\ulcorner \psi_m^1 \ldots \psi_m^n \urcorner$.

If on the other hand r is not that high, then an assignment of truth values to $\omega_1, \ldots, \omega_r$ may still verify or falsify $\ulcorner \psi_m{}^1 \ldots \psi_m{}^n \urcorner$ outright (for all values of the further atomic formulae in $\ulcorner \psi_m{}^1 \ldots \psi_m{}^n \urcorner$), or it may do neither (pending assignment of values to the further atomic formulae in $\ulcorner \psi_m{}^1 \ldots \psi_m{}^n \urcorner$). Let us call an assignment of truth values to $\omega_1, \ldots, \omega_r$ *innocuous* if there are no m and n such that it falsifies $\ulcorner \psi_m{}^1 \ldots \psi_m{}^n \urcorner$ outright.

To specify a numerical interpretation of S, or $\{\ulcorner \mu_1 \phi_1 \urcorner, \ulcorner \mu_2 \phi_2 \urcorner, \ldots\}$, it is necessary and sufficient to say what numbers or number sequences, as arguments, are to verify and falsify the several predicate letters. In short, it is necessary and sufficient to give truth values to $\omega_1, \omega_2, \ldots$. We are now ready to specify, in that way, a numerical interpretation $\mathfrak{J}$ which fits S if S is consistent. It is this: *for each r, ω_r is to be true if and only if there is an innocuous assignment to $\omega_1, \ldots, \omega_r$ and it, or the earliest such if there are several, assigns truth to ω_r.* "Earliest" here is to be understood in terms of the familiar ordering:

$$\top \ldots \top\top\top, \quad \top \ldots \top\top\bot, \quad \top \ldots \top\bot\top, \quad \top \ldots \top\bot\bot, \quad \ldots, \quad \bot \ldots \bot\bot\bot$$

2. Proof that $\mathfrak{J}$ Fits S if S Is Consistent.

LEMMA 1. *If $\ulcorner \mu\phi \urcorner$ is a closed prenex consistent schema and ψ^n for each n is the result of substituting numerals in ϕ according to the nth substitution sequence for μ, then, for each n, $\ulcorner \psi^1 \ldots \psi^n \urcorner$ is truth-functionally consistent.*

Proof. Where μ has k quantifiers, let χ_i for each i from 1 to k be formed from $\ulcorner \mu\phi \urcorner$ by dropping the first i quantifiers and making substitutions for the recurrences of the variables of the dropped quantifiers according to the first substitution sequence for μ; using, however, new and distinct variables $\alpha_1, \alpha_2, \ldots$ instead of '1', '2', $\ldots$. In like fashion let $\chi_{k+i}, \chi_{2k+i}, \ldots$ be formed according to the second, third, $\ldots$ substitution sequence. Let χ_0 be $\ulcorner \mu\phi \urcorner$. For each $j \geqq 0$, therefore, χ_{j+1} is got from χ_j (or perhaps from χ_0) by dropping the first quantifier and putting α_r (for some r) for the recurrences of the variable of that quantifier. There are three possible Cases: (1) the dropped quantifier is universal, (2) it is existential and α_r is foreign to $\chi_1, \ldots, \chi_j$, or (3) it is existential and α_r occurs somewhere in $\chi_1, \ldots, \chi_j$. In Case 1, $\ulcorner \chi_0 \ldots \chi_j \urcorner$ implies χ_{j+1}; in Case 2, $\ulcorner \chi_0 \ldots \chi_j \urcorner$ implies $\ulcorner (\exists\alpha_r)(\chi_0 \ldots \chi_{j+1}) \urcorner$; and in Case 3, χ_{j+1} is a mere repetition of one of $\chi_1, \ldots, \chi_j$ (by virtue of the structure of substitution sequences). In all three cases, therefore, the *existential closure* of $\ulcorner\chi_0 \ldots \chi_j\urcorner$ (formed by prefixing existential quantifiers for all free variables) implies that of $\ulcorner\chi_0 \ldots \chi_{j+1}\urcorner$. This happens for all j. Hence χ_0 (which is, vacuously, its own existential closure) implies the existential closure of $\ulcorner\chi_0 \ldots \chi_{nk}\urcorner$. Hence, if χ_0 is consistent, $\ulcorner\chi_0 \ldots \chi_{nk}\urcorner$ is truth-functionally consistent; then so is $\ulcorner\chi_k\chi_{2k} \ldots \chi_{nk}\urcorner$; and then so is $\ulcorner\psi^1 \ldots \psi^n\urcorner$, this being the same thing with '1', '2', . . . in place of $\alpha_1, \alpha_2, \ldots$.

Hereafter (though not in the above lemma) the notation refers back to §1.

LEMMA 2. *If $m > i$, then for every j there is an n such that $\psi_m{}^n$ implies $\psi_i{}^j$ truth-functionally.*

Proof. The assignment of numbers to universal quantifiers which is made in the jth substitution sequence for $\ulcorner\mu_1 \ldots \mu_i\urcorner$ is made again in some substitution sequence, say the nth, for $\ulcorner\mu_1 \ldots \mu_m\urcorner$. Moreover the assignments to existential quantifiers of $\ulcorner\mu_1 \ldots \mu_i\urcorner$ will be the same in both, since such assignments depend in no way on $\mu_{i+1}, \ldots, \mu_m$. Therefore $\psi_m{}^n$ will consist simply of $\psi_i{}^j$ in conjunction with some result of substitution on $\ulcorner\phi_{i+1} \ldots \phi_m\urcorner$.

LEMMA 3. *For any h, i, j, and k there are m and n such that $\ulcorner\psi_m{}^1 \ldots \psi_m{}^n\urcorner$ implies $\ulcorner\psi_h{}^1 \ldots \psi_h{}^k\psi_i{}^1 \ldots \psi_i{}^j\urcorner$ truth-functionally.*

Proof. Take m as $h + i$. Then, by Lemma 2, each of $\psi_h{}^1, \ldots, \psi_h{}^k, \psi_i{}^1, \ldots, \psi_i{}^j$ is implied by one or another of $\psi_m{}^1, \psi_m{}^2, \ldots$. Thus there is a set of $j + k$ or fewer formulas, from among $\psi_m{}^1, \psi_m{}^2, \ldots$, such that their conjunction implies $\ulcorner\psi_h{}^1 \ldots \psi_h{}^k\psi_i{}^1 \ldots \psi_i{}^j\urcorner$. Then, where $\psi_m{}^n$ is the last formula of such a set, $\ulcorner\psi_m{}^1 \ldots \psi_m{}^n\urcorner$ implies $\ulcorner\psi_h{}^1 \ldots \psi_h{}^k\psi_i{}^1 \ldots \psi_i{}^j\urcorner$.

For purposes of the next lemma we adopt the following convention. Where $\mathfrak{A}$ is an assignment of truth values to $\omega_1, \ldots, \omega_r$, let us understand $\mathfrak{A}^+$ as consisting in the assignment of $\mathfrak{A}$ to $\omega_1, \ldots, \omega_r$ and truth to ω_{r+1}; and let us understand $\mathfrak{A}^-$ as consisting in the assignment of $\mathfrak{A}$ to $\omega_1, \ldots, \omega_r$ and falsity to ω_{r+1}.

LEMMA 4. *If $\mathfrak{A}$ is the earliest innocuous assignment to $\omega_1, \ldots, \omega_r$, then $\mathfrak{A}^+$ or $\mathfrak{A}^-$ is the earliest innocuous assignment to $\omega_1, \ldots, \omega_{r+1}$.*

Proof. If neither $\mathfrak{A}^+$ nor $\mathfrak{A}^-$ is innocuous, then $\mathfrak{A}^+$ falsifies $\ulcorner\psi_h{}^1 \ldots \psi_h{}^k\urcorner$ and $\mathfrak{A}^-$ falsifies $\ulcorner\psi_i{}^1 \ldots \psi_i{}^j\urcorner$ for some h, i, j, and k. But then $\mathfrak{A}$ falsifies $\ulcorner\psi_h{}^1 \ldots \psi_h{}^k\psi_i{}^1 \ldots \psi_i{}^j\urcorner$. Then, by Lemma 3, $\mathfrak{A}$ falsifies $\ulcorner\psi_m{}^1 \ldots \psi_m{}^n\urcorner$ for some m and n. But this is impossible, since $\mathfrak{A}$ is innocuous. Therefore $\mathfrak{A}^+$ or $\mathfrak{A}^-$ is innocuous. Moreover, by the definition of earliness of assignments, any assignment to $\omega_1, \ldots, \omega_{r+1}$ earlier than $\mathfrak{A}^+$ must be $\mathfrak{B}^+$ or $\mathfrak{B}^-$ for some $\mathfrak{B}$ which is earlier than $\mathfrak{A}$ and hence not innocuous. But, by the definition of innocuousness, if $\mathfrak{B}$ is not innocuous then neither is $\mathfrak{B}^+$ nor $\mathfrak{B}^-$. Therefore $\mathfrak{A}^+$ or $\mathfrak{A}^-$ is the earliest innocuous assignment to $\omega_1, \ldots, \omega_{r+1}$.

From here on to the end of the section, all arguments are to be understood as subject to the

HYPOTHESIS. *S is consistent.*

LEMMA 5. *For each m and n,* $\ulcorner\psi_m{}^1 \ldots \psi_m{}^n\urcorner$ *is truth-functionally consistent.*

Proof. For any m, by Hypothesis, $\ulcorner\mu_1 \ldots \mu_m(\phi_1 \ldots \phi_m)\urcorner$ is consistent. But this formula is related to $\ulcorner\psi_m{}^1 \ldots \psi_m{}^n\urcorner$ as is $\ulcorner\mu\phi\urcorner$ in Lemma 1 to $\ulcorner\psi^1 \ldots \psi^n\urcorner$.

LEMMA 6. *For each r there is an innocuous assignment to* $\omega_1, \ldots, \omega_r$.

Proof. Suppose neither the assignment of truth nor the assignment of falsity to ω_1 is innocuous. For some h, i, j, and k, then, assignment of truth to ω_1 falsifies $\ulcorner\psi_h{}^1 \ldots \psi_h{}^k\urcorner$ and assignment of falsity to ω_1 falsifies $\ulcorner\psi_i{}^1 \ldots \psi_i{}^j\urcorner$. Then $\ulcorner\psi_h{}^1 \ldots \psi_h{}^k\psi_i{}^1 \ldots \psi_i{}^j\urcorner$ is truth-functionally inconsistent. Then, by Lemma 3, $\ulcorner\psi_m{}^1 \ldots \psi_m{}^n\urcorner$ is truth-functionally inconsistent for some m and n. But this contradicts Lemma 5. Therefore Lemma 6 holds when r is 1. From Lemma 4, then, it follows by mathematical induction that Lemma 6 holds for all r.

LEMMA 7. *$\mathfrak{J}$ makes $\psi_m{}^n$ true for all m and n.*

Proof. Let k be the highest number such that ω_k occurs in $\psi_m{}^n$. By Lemma 6 and the definition of $\mathfrak{J}$, $\mathfrak{J}$ agrees on ω_r (for each r) with the earliest innocuous assignment to $\omega_1, \ldots, \omega_r$. By Lemma 4, then, $\mathfrak{J}$ agrees on each of $\omega_1, \ldots, \omega_k$ with the earliest innocuous assignment to $\omega_1, \ldots, \omega_k$. But that assignment makes $\psi_m{}^n$ true.

THESIS. *For each m, $\mathfrak{J}$ makes* $\ulcorner\mu_m\phi_m\urcorner$ *true.*

Proof. $\ulcorner\mu_1 \ldots \mu_m\urcorner$ has the form $\ulcorner(\alpha_1) \ldots (\alpha_a)(\exists\beta_1) \ldots (\exists\beta_b)(\gamma_1) \ldots (\gamma_c)(\exists\delta_1) \ldots (\exists\delta_d) \ldots\urcorner$. Hence truth of $\ulcorner\mu_1 \ldots \mu_m(\phi_1 \ldots \phi_m)\urcorner$ (in the universe of positive integers) amounts, by the meaning of quantification, to this: for each choice of numerical substitutions for $\alpha_1, \ldots, \alpha_a$ there are numerical substitutions for $\beta_1, \ldots, \beta_b$ such that for each choice of numerical substitutions for $\gamma_1, \ldots, \gamma_c$ there are (and so on) such that $\ulcorner\phi_1 \ldots \phi_m\urcorner$ comes out true. But, by the definition of substitution sequence, some substitution sequence for $\ulcorner\mu_1 \ldots \mu_m\urcorner$ realizes any desired substitutions on $\alpha_1, \ldots, \alpha_a$ followed by some on $\beta_1, \ldots, \beta_b$ followed by any whatever on $\gamma_1, \ldots, \gamma_c$ followed by, etc. So $\ulcorner\mu_1 \ldots \mu_m(\phi_1 \ldots \phi_m)\urcorner$ will be true if $\ulcorner\phi_1 \ldots \phi_m\urcorner$ comes out true under substitution according to every substitution sequence for $\ulcorner\mu_1 \ldots \mu_m\urcorner$; hence if $\psi_m^1, \psi_m^2, \ldots$ are all true. But, by Lemma 7, $\mathfrak{J}$ makes $\psi_m^1, \psi_m^2, \ldots$ all true. Therefore $\mathfrak{J}$ makes $\ulcorner\mu_1 \ldots \mu_m (\phi_1 \ldots \phi_m)\urcorner$ true. Therefore $\mathfrak{J}$ makes $\ulcorner\mu_m\phi_m\urcorner$ true.

3. The Finite Case. Completeness. If we are interested in the case not of an infinite S but merely of a single schema $\ulcorner\mu\phi\urcorner$ (or any finite number, since we can form their conjunction), then we can greatly simplify §§1–2 as follows. We drop all subscripts from 'μ', 'ϕ', and 'ψ', thus speaking simply of μ, ϕ, and ψ^n instead of $\ulcorner\mu_1 \ldots \mu_m\urcorner$, $\ulcorner\phi_1 \ldots \phi_m\urcorner$, and ψ_m^n. The Hypothesis and Thesis become:

$\ulcorner\mu\phi\urcorner$ is consistent, $\mathfrak{J}$ makes $\ulcorner\mu\phi\urcorner$ true,

and Lemmas 5 and 7 become:

LEMMA 5′. *For each n, $\ulcorner\psi^1 \ldots \psi^n\urcorner$ is truth-functionally consistent,*

LEMMA 7′. *$\mathfrak{J}$ makes ψ^n true for all n.*

Similar editing takes place uniformly in the proofs of Lemmas 4, 6, and 7′ and of the Thesis. Moreover, we can now drop the citation of Lemma 3 in the proofs of Lemmas 4 and 6, simply taking n at those points as the larger of j and k; so Lemmas 2–3 can be omitted altogether. The proof of Lemma 5′ reduces to mere citation of Lemma 1. Lemma 1 itself, and its proof, remain unchanged.

The simplified line of reasoning which is thus arrived at can be slightly varied in turn to give a proof of the completeness and soundness of a system of quantification theory. For this purpose we drop the hypothesis that $\ulcorner\mu\phi\urcorner$ is consistent, and let Lemma 5′ itself stand as hypothesis. Now the conditional whose hypothesis is Lemma 5′, and whose thesis is that $\mathfrak{J}$ makes $\ulcorner\mu\phi\urcorner$ true, implies the converse of Lemma 1. So our proofs, thus rearranged, comprise in effect simply a proof of Lemma 1 and its converse; a proof, in short, that $\ulcorner\mu\phi\urcorner$ *is consistent if and only if* $\ulcorner\psi^1 \ldots \psi^n\urcorner$

is truth-functionally consistent for each n. This establishes the completeness and soundness of a system of quantification theory in which a proof of $\ulcorner \sim \mu\phi \urcorner$ consists simply in citing a number n for which $\ulcorner \psi^1 \ldots \psi^n \urcorner$ is inconsistent by truth tables.

The notion of a substitution sequence can be simplified, for purposes of this system, to the point of practicability: we can number the existential variables in the economical way in which Dreben numbered his universal ones, instead of bringing in Kleene's big numbers (which, however, were needed in §§1–2, in order to get Lemma 2). The whole theory determined by this present §3 is implicit in Dreben's paper, but the argument here indicated is simpler.

XX

Church's Theorem on the Decision Problem

1. Program. Church showed in 1936 that there can be no decision procedure for quantification theory.[1] My purpose in this expository paper is to present a more perspicuous and self-contained account of this important proof than has thus far been available in print. The argument is substantially that which I have used in the classroom from 1949 onward.

The theorem, roughly stated, is that

(I) *The class of valid quantificational schemata is not effective;*

i.e., that there is no general mechanical method for deciding membership in that class. Now such a result is demonstrable only insofar as the impressionistic idea of "effectiveness" is made sharp and explicit. The sharp concept to this purpose is that of *recursiveness* (§2), in terms of which Church's theorem may be stated thus strictly:

(II) *The class of Gödel numbers* (cf. §2) *of valid quantificational schemata is not recursive.*

However, (II) mainly interests us only as evidence for (I), and hence only insofar as we are persuaded of this ancillary "Thesis":[2]

This paper, mimeographed in 1954 for the use of my pupils, appears in print for the first time.

[1] Turing independently proved the same. See also Hilbert and Bernays, Vol. 2, 416–421.

[2] So called by Kleene.

(III) *All effective classes of numbers are recursive.*

Now it turns out that by use of (III) and its dyadic analogue:

(IV) *All effective relations of numbers are recursive*

we can get to (I) with much less labor than it takes to prove (II) without (III)–(IV). Such is the plan of this paper. But let me not thereby seem to belittle the important fact that (II) *can* be proved without (III)–(IV).

Recursiveness will be defined and examined in §2, less for reasons of unfamiliarity than in order to have certain details explicitly before us for reference. In §3 a small theory of functions will be developed; it is needed in order to forge a link between substitution operations and quantification theory, a link which is essential to the proof of (I) or (II). Finally, in §4, (I) will be proved with help of (III) and (IV). Meanwhile the intuitive term "effective" and the technical term "recursive" will be kept apart, no use of (III) or (IV) being made till the very end.

2. Recursiveness. An equation will be called *rudimentary* if built up of just these materials: '0', 'S' (for successor), '=' (for identity of numbers), variables 'x', 'y', . . . (for positive integers and 0), variables 'f', 'g', . . . (for numerical functions), and parentheses (to set off complex arguments of functions). Examples:

$$0 = 0, \quad 0 = S0, \quad f(gx)(fyx) = g(S(fx0)).$$

Each of '0', 'S0', 'SS0', etc., will be called a *numeral.* Where ρ is a function variable and $\mu, \mu_1, \ldots, \mu_n$ are numerals, the equation $\ulcorner \rho\mu_1 \ldots \mu_n = \mu \urcorner$ will be called an *evaluation* of ρ. Specifically it will be called an evaluation of ρ *for* $x_1, \ldots, x_n$ as arguments, where $x_1, \ldots, x_n$ are the numbers named by $\mu_1, \ldots, \mu_n$. Example: 'f(S0)(SS0) = SSS0' is an evaluation of 'f' for 1 and 2 as arguments. An evaluation will be called *positive* when, as in this example, the right side is not '0'; otherwise it will be called a *zero evaluation.*

By a *recursive derivation* of an equation ψ from a conjunction ϕ of equations is meant a conjunction of rudimentary equations beginning with ϕ and ending with ψ and such that each of the equations after ϕ is got, from equations further left, by one or the other of these operations: (A) substituting numerals for variables, and (B) putting one side of an equation for the other in an equation. When such a recursive derivation exists, ψ is called *recursively derivable* from ϕ. A conjunction ϕ is called a *recursion* if just one evaluation of each function letter of ϕ, for each choice of numbers as arguments, is recursively derivable from ϕ.

A class of numbers is called *recursive* if there is a recursion ϕ such that zero evaluations of '*f*' are recursively derivable from ϕ for all and only those arguments belonging to the class. (The singling out of the letter '*f*' for this key role is of course arbitrary and inessential.) A dyadic relation of numbers is called recursive under parallel circumstances; simply reread "arguments" now as "pairs of arguments."[3]

To expressions built up of an alphabet of nine or fewer signs, we may conveniently assign *Gödel numbers* as follows: we assign the numbers 1, 2, etc., to the individual signs, and then to any compound expression ξ we assign the number whose arabic numeral is got by concatenating the digits '1', '2', etc., to match the concatenation of signs in ξ. Alphabets in excess of nine signs can artificially be reduced to nine for these purposes. E.g., the alphabet used in recursions and recursive derivations may, for purposes of Gödel numbering, be conceived as comprising just '0', 'S', '*f*', '*x*', '=', the two parentheses, the dot of conjunction, and an accent '′'; for we may treat '*g*', '*h*', etc., as '*f*′', '*f*″', etc., and '*y*', '*z*', etc., as '*x*′', '*x*″', etc.

Consider now the relation K of any number x to any number y such that y is the Gödel number of a recursive derivation, from a conjunction whose Gödel number is x, of a positive evaluation of '*f*' for x as argument. Clearly K is effective—i.e., effectively decidable for any specific numbers x and y given by numerals. Yet the domain of K is not recursive. For suppose it were. Then, according to the definition of recursiveness, there would be a recursion ϕ such that zero evaluations of '*f*' would be derivable from ϕ for all and only those arguments x belonging to the domain of K. But this situation is seen to be impossible when x is taken in particular as the Gödel number of ϕ; for, by the definition of K, x belongs to the domain of K if and only if a *positive* evaluation of '*f*', for x as argument, is derivable from a conjunction whose Gödel number is x.[4]

3. Schematic Function Theory. A theory will now be set forth which uses '*x*', '*y*', etc., as quantifiable variables and '*f*', '*g*', etc., as

[3] The terminology and definitions of the past two paragraphs are adapted from Kleene, 1943, 43–45.

[4] I have adapted K and the attendant argument from Kleene, 1943, 48–49.

function letters not subject to quantification. Because unquantified, these latter letters are best viewed as schematic, and the formulas of the theory as schemata, valid if true for all functions as interpretations. The universe of quantification may, but need not, be taken as comprised of numbers. The functions appropriate as interpretations of the function letters are, at any rate, any functions having values in that universe for all arguments in that universe. Each function letter is to be thought of as n-ary (i.e., as taking arguments n at a time) for some $n \geqq 0$, varying only from letter to letter; where n is 0 the letter behaves as a schematic constant, or parameter.

The class of *terms* is explained inductively thus: quantifiable variables are terms of order 0; and an n-ary function letter followed by n terms, some of order i and none higher, is a term of order $i + 1$. A nullary function letter counts as of order 1.

In describing the formulas of this theory let us use 'α', 'β', and 'γ' to refer to quantifiable variables 'x', 'y', etc.; let us use 'ρ' to refer to 'f', 'g', etc.; and let us use 'ζ', 'η', and 'θ' to refer to any terms.

Equations $\ulcorner\zeta = \eta\urcorner$ will be arbitrarily required to have a term η of positive order, rather than just a variable α, as right side;[5] thus every equation has the form $\ulcorner\zeta = \rho\eta_1 \cdots \eta_n\urcorner$, where $n \geqq 0$. The shown occurrences of $\zeta, \eta_1, \cdots, \eta_n$ here will be called the *principal* occurrences of terms in the equation.

An equation will be called a *primitive* equation if it has the form $\ulcorner\alpha = \rho\beta_1 \cdots \beta_n\urcorner$; in other words, if all principal occurrences in it are of order 0. The atomic formulas of our theory are to be thought of as such equations exclusively; and the formulas generally (pending supplementation by an imminent abbreviative definition) are just what can be built from those primitive equations by truth functions and quantification. Thus other equations, and terms of order above 1, have no place in our initial notation. But they are brought in by the following contextual

Definition. If ψ is an equation with just k principal occurrences of terms of positive order, and these are occurrences respectively of ζ_1, . . . , ζ_k, then ψ is short for $\ulcorner(\exists\alpha_1) \ldots (\exists\alpha_k)(\alpha_1 = \zeta_1 \,.\, \alpha_2 = \zeta_2 \,. \ldots .\, \alpha_k = \zeta_k \,.\, \phi)\urcorner$, where $\alpha_1, \ldots, \alpha_k$ are new and distinct and ϕ is like ψ except for having $\alpha_1, \ldots, \alpha_k$ in place of the respective principal occurrences of $\zeta_1, \ldots, \zeta_k$.

[5] This restriction simplifies the theory somewhat, without significantly impoverishing it. Equations of the excluded form $\ulcorner\zeta = \alpha\urcorner$ can always be rendered $\ulcorner\alpha = \zeta\urcorner$, barring only the useless species $\ulcorner\beta = \alpha\urcorner$.

Any non-primitive equation can be expanded into primitive notation by repeated application of the above definition. Each application turns an equation ψ into a formula in which no equation contains principal occurrences of terms of as high order as ψ did.

The theory is to comprise two classes of *axioms*. The first consists of all formulas $\ulcorner(\exists\alpha)(\alpha = \zeta)\urcorner$ such that ζ is a term of order 1 lacking α. The second consists of all formulas $\ulcorner\alpha = \zeta \,.\, \beta = \zeta \,.\!\supset\!.\, \phi_\alpha \equiv \phi_\beta\urcorner$ such that ζ is of order 1 and ϕ_α and ϕ_β are primitive equations which are alike except that ϕ_α has α in one or more places where ϕ_β has β.

The theorems comprise all the consequences of the axioms [better: of their universal closures] by quantification theory. No use is made of identity theory, beyond what the axioms themselves provide. We turn now to seven metatheorems.

M1. If α and β are numerical variables, ζ is a term of order 1 lacking α, ϕ_α is a primitive equation, and ϕ_β is ϕ_α with β for all α, then $\ulcorner\beta = \zeta \,.\!\supset\!.\, \phi_\beta \equiv (\exists\alpha)(\alpha = \zeta \,.\, \phi_\alpha)\urcorner$ *is a theorem.*

Proof. The formula is implied by an axiom of the second class, viz., $\ulcorner(\alpha)(\gamma)(\alpha = \zeta \,.\, \gamma = \zeta \,.\!\supset\!.\, \phi_\alpha \equiv \phi_\gamma)\urcorner$ where γ is a new variable. The form of the implication is:

$$(x)(y)(Fx \,.\, Fy \,.\!\supset\!.\, Gx \equiv Gy) \supset: Fz \supset\!.\, Gz \equiv (\exists x)(Fx \,.\, Gx),$$

which, being a monadic quantificational schema, can be checked for validity in known ways.

M2. If ζ is of order 1 and ϕ_β and ϕ_ζ are equations which are alike except that ϕ_β has a principal occurrence of β where ϕ_ζ has one of ζ, then $\ulcorner\beta = \zeta \,.\!\supset\!.\, \phi_\beta \equiv \phi_\zeta\urcorner$ *is a theorem.*

Example: $y = fxz \,.\!\supset: gx = hy(fww) \,.\!\equiv\!.\, gx = h(fxz)(fww)$. By our Definition, this expands into:

$$y = fxz \,.\!\supset\!.\, (\exists u)(\exists v)(u = gx \,.\, v = fww \,.\, u = hyv) \equiv \\ (\exists u)(\exists t)(\exists v)(u = gx \,.\, t = fxz \,.\, v = fww \,.\, u = htv).$$

But the formula, thus expanded, is clearly a consequence (by quantification theory) of this case of M1:

$$y = fxz \,.\!\supset: u = hyv \,.\!\equiv (\exists t)(t = fxz \,.\, u = htv).$$

Any other example of M2 is similarly provable.

M3. If ζ is of order 1 and ψ_β and ψ_ζ are formulae which are alike *except that* ψ_β *has some free occurrences of* β *where* ψ_ζ *has free occurrences of* ζ,[6] *then* $\ulcorner\beta = \zeta\ .\supset.\ \psi_\beta \equiv \psi_\zeta\urcorner$ *is a theorem.*

Proof. Case 1: Only one occurrence of β in ψ_β gives way to ζ in ψ_ζ. Let ϕ_β be the equation within ψ_β which contains that occurrence of β. Correspondingly for ϕ_ζ.

Subcase 1a: The occurrence of β is principal in ϕ_β. Then $\ulcorner\beta = \zeta\ .\supset.\ \phi_\beta \equiv \phi_\zeta\urcorner$ is a theorem by M2, and $\ulcorner\beta = \zeta\ .\supset.\ \psi_\beta \equiv \psi_\zeta\urcorner$ follows in view of the principle, in quantification theory, of the substitutivity of the biconditional.[7]

Subcase 1b: The occurrence is not principal in ϕ_β. Then let η_β be the term which immediately contains that occurrence of β; and let η_ζ be the corresponding part of ϕ_ζ. Expansion of ϕ_β, by repeated application of the Definition, eventually gets this occurrence of η_β over into the context $\ulcorner\alpha = \eta_\beta\urcorner$ for some variable α; and parallel expansion of ϕ_ζ gets the occurrence of η_ζ over into the context $\ulcorner\alpha = \eta_\zeta\urcorner$. But the occurrence of β in $\ulcorner\alpha = \eta_\beta\urcorner$ is principal, so we are back in Subcase 1a.

Case 2: Many occurrences of β in ψ_β give way to ζ in ψ_ζ. Then there is a chain of formulas, the first of which is ψ_β and the last of which is ψ_ζ, such that each is turned into the next by putting ζ once for β; so $\ulcorner\beta = \zeta\ .\supset.\ \psi_\beta \equiv \psi_\zeta\urcorner$ is deducible from a series of instances of Case 1.

M4. If ψ_ζ *is like* ψ_α *except for having free* ζ *in place of all free occurrences of* α, *then* $\ulcorner(\alpha)\psi_\alpha \supset \psi_\zeta\urcorner$ *is a theorem.*

Proof. Case where ζ is of order 0: Here $\ulcorner(\alpha)\psi_\alpha \supset \psi_\zeta\urcorner$ holds by pure quantification theory.

Case where ζ is of order 1: Taking β as a new variable, we have $\ulcorner\beta = \zeta\ .\supset:(\alpha)\psi_\alpha \supset \psi_\beta\ .\equiv.\ (\alpha)\psi_\alpha \supset \psi_\zeta\urcorner$ as a case of M3. But the part $\ulcorner(\alpha)\psi_\alpha \supset \psi_\beta\urcorner$ holds by pure quantification theory; so we are left with $\ulcorner\beta = \zeta\ .\supset.\ (\alpha)\psi_\alpha \supset \psi_\zeta\urcorner$, and hence $\ulcorner(\exists\beta)(\beta = \zeta) \supset.\ (\alpha)\psi_\alpha \supset \psi_\zeta\urcorner$. But $\ulcorner(\exists\beta)(\beta = \zeta)\urcorner$ can be dropped, being an axiom.

Case where ζ is of order 2: Here an example will suffice to show the reasoning. Let us take ζ as '$f(gyv)w$', and represent ψ_α as '$\ldots x \ldots$'. Suppose 'u' is foreign to '$\ldots x \ldots$'. By the preceding Case (ζ of order 1), these are theorems:

$$(1) \qquad (x)(\ldots x \ldots) \supset.\ \ldots fuw \ldots,$$

[6] A free occurrence of ζ in ψ_ζ is one within which no occurrences of variables are bound in ψ_ζ. Cf. *Mathematical Logic*, 142f.

[7] *Ibid.*, *121.

(2) $(u)[(x)(\ .\ .\ .\ x\ .\ .\ .\ ) \supset .\ .\ .\ .\ fuw\ .\ .\ .\ ] \supset .$
$(x)(\ .\ .\ .\ x\ .\ .\ .\ ) \supset .\ .\ .\ .\ f(gyv)w\ .\ .\ .\ .$

Hence so is:

(3) $(x)(\ .\ .\ .\ x\ .\ .\ .\ ) \supset .\ .\ .\ .\ f(gyv)w\ .\ .\ .\ .$

Case where ζ is of order 3, say '$f(gy(hzw))w$': Proof similar, starting with (3) instead of (1).

Any higher order can be reached by continuing the process.

M5. If ζ is of positive order and ψ_β and ψ_ζ are alike except that ψ_β has some free occurrences of β where ψ_ζ has free occurrences of ζ, then $\ulcorner \beta = \zeta . \supset . \psi_\beta \equiv \psi_\zeta \urcorner$ is a theorem.

Proof. ζ has the form $\ulcorner \rho\eta_1\ .\ .\ .\ \eta_k \urcorner$. Let $\gamma_1, \ldots, \gamma_k$ be new and distinct, and let θ_i for each i from 0 to k be $\ulcorner \rho\eta_1\ .\ .\ .\ \eta_i\gamma_{i+1}\ .\ .\ .\ \gamma_k \urcorner$. By M4 we have

$$\ulcorner (\gamma_i)(\beta = \theta_{i-1} . \supset : \psi_\beta \equiv \psi_{\theta_{i-1}}) \supset : \beta = \theta_i . \supset . \psi_\beta \equiv \psi_{\theta_i} \urcorner$$

as a theorem for each i from 1 to k. But we also have $\ulcorner \beta = \theta_0 . \supset . \psi_\beta \equiv \psi_{\theta_0} \urcorner$, by M3. So we get $\ulcorner \beta = \theta_k . \supset . \psi_\beta \equiv \psi_{\theta_k} \urcorner$, which is $\ulcorner \beta = \zeta . \supset . \psi_\beta \equiv \psi_\zeta \urcorner$.

M6. If η is of positive order and ψ_ζ and ψ_η are alike except that ψ_ζ has some free occurrences of ζ where ψ_η has free occurrences of η, then $\ulcorner \zeta = \eta . \supset . \psi_\zeta \equiv \psi_\eta \urcorner$ is a theorem.

Proof. Let β be new. Then $\ulcorner \beta = \eta . \supset . \psi_\beta \equiv \psi_\eta \urcorner$ is a theorem by M5, and

$$\ulcorner (\beta)(\beta = \eta . \supset . \psi_\beta \equiv \psi_\eta) \supset : \zeta = \eta . \supset . \psi_\zeta \equiv \psi_\eta \urcorner$$

is a theorem by M4; so $\ulcorner \zeta = \eta . \supset . \psi_\zeta \equiv \psi_\eta \urcorner$ follows.

M7. If ψ_ζ is like ψ_α except for having free ζ in place of all free occurrences of α, then $\ulcorner \psi_\zeta \supset (\exists\alpha)\psi_\alpha \urcorner$ is a theorem.

Proof from $\ulcorner (\alpha)\ -\psi_\alpha \supset -\psi_\zeta \urcorner$, which is a theorem by M4.

4. Church's Theorem. I shall next establish the following

LEMMA. *If the class of valid quantificational schemata is effective then every recursive dyadic relation has an effective domain.*

Let R be a recursive dyadic relation. Then, by the definition in §2, there is a recursion ϕ such that any numbers m and n stand in R if and only if a zero evaluation of 'f', for m and n as arguments, is recursively derivable from ϕ.

In §3 a schematic function theory was developed in which nothing was stipulated concerning the number of function letters. Let us now fix those function letters as comprising just a binary 'f', a singulary 'S', a nullary '0', and whatever of 'g', 'h', etc., there may be in ϕ. The two axiom classes specified in §3 then come to be finite (if we omit, as redundant, those variant axioms which differ only in the alphabetical choice of 'x', 'y', etc.). Let ψ be the conjunction of this finite stock of axioms.

The Lemma will now be proved by showing how, for any number m, a formula is effectively specifiable which is *quantificationally valid* (i.e., which has the form of a valid schema of quantification theory, with primitive equations in the role of atomic components) *if and only if m is in the domain of R.* The formula in question is the expansion, by the Definition in §3, of $\ulcorner \phi\psi \supset (\exists y)(f\mu y = 0)\urcorner$ where μ is '0' preceded by m occurrences of 'S'.

For suppose the expansion of $\ulcorner \phi\psi \supset (\exists y)(f\mu y = 0)\urcorner$ is quantificationally valid. Then, since ϕ is a recursion and therefore true for certain interpretations of 'f', 'g', etc., and ψ is true for all, we must conclude that $\ulcorner(\exists y)(f\mu y = 0)\urcorner$ is true for the interpretation of 'f' which fulfills ϕ, and hence that m belongs to the domain of R.

Conversely, if m belongs to the domain of R then $\ulcorner f\mu\nu = 0\urcorner$, for some numeral ν, is recursively derivable from ϕ; i.e., derivable by (A) and (B) of §2 from ϕ. But M6 and M4 show that whatever can be got from ϕ by (A) and (B) can be got from $\ulcorner\phi\psi\urcorner$ by pure quantification theory, together with the Definition in §3; and, once $\ulcorner f\mu\nu = 0\urcorner$ is got, M7 shows that $\ulcorner(\exists y)(f\mu y = 0)\urcorner$ can be deduced in turn. Hence $\ulcorner\phi\psi \supset (\exists y)(f\mu y = 0)\urcorner$, expanded by the Definition, must be quantificationally valid.

From the Lemma, finally, we argue to (I) of §1 as follows. In §2 we noted an effective relation K whose domain was not recursive. It follows by (IV) and (III) of §1 that K is a recursive relation whose domain is not effective. In view of the Lemma, then, (I) holds.

XXI

Quantification and the Empty Domain

Quantification theory, or the first-order predicate calculus, is ordinarily so formulated as to provide as theorems all and only those formulas which come out true under all interpretations in all *non-empty* domains. There are two strong reasons for thus leaving aside the empty domain.

(i) Where D is any non-empty domain, any quantificational formula which comes out true under all interpretations in all domains larger than D will come out true also under all interpretations in D.[1] Thus, though any small domain has a certain triviality, all but one of them, the empty domain, can be included without cost. To include the empty one, on the other hand, would mean surrendering some formulas which are valid everywhere else and thus generally useful.

(ii) An easy supplementary test enables us anyway, when we please, to decide whether a formula holds for the empty domain. We have only to mark the universal quantifications as true and the existential ones as false, and apply truth-table considerations.

Incidentally, the existence of that supplementary test shows that there is no difficulty in framing an *inclusive* quantification theory (i.e., inclusive of the empty domain) if we so desire. A proof in this theory can be made to consist simply of a proof in the exclusive (or usual) theory followed by a check by the method of (ii). We may, however, be curious to see a more direct or autonomous formula-

Reprinted from the *Journal of Symbolic Logic*, Volume 19, 1954.

[1] Cf. Hilbert and Ackermann, 1938, 92.

tion: one which does not consist, like the above, of the exclusive theory plus a rule of expurgation. And, in fact, such formulations have of late been forthcoming: Mostowski, Hailperin (1953), and, as part of a broader context, Church.[2] I shall not presuppose acquaintance with these papers, except in my final paragraph (and then only with Hailperin's).

Quantification theory may or may not be so fashioned as to accord significance to *vacuous* quantification, i.e., to the attachment of a quantifier to a formula lacking free occurrences of the variable of the quantifier. The three versions cited above all do recognize vacuous quantification. Now admission of the empty domain raises a question regarding the vacuous universal quantification '$(x)f$' of a falsehood 'f': Should we regard this quantification as false for the empty domain (on the ground that a vacuous quantifier is always simply redundant and omissible), or as true for the empty domain (on the ground that all universal quantifications are true for the empty domain)? Hailperin points out that Mostowski implicitly elected the first alternative, but that a more elegant system can be obtained by electing rather the second.

Hailperin is right, except that he has understated his case. If a general semantical characterization of the truth conditions of quantification over a domain is phrased along natural lines, without special mention of vacuousness of quantification or emptiness of domain, the verdict of truth of '$(x)f$' for the empty domain is pretty sure to follow. Moreover, this verdict is mandatory if, in general, the vacuous quantification '$(x)p$' is equated to '$(x)(p \,.\, Fx \supset Fx)$'; and we *must* so equate it if we are to preserve extensionality, since '$p \equiv . \, p \,.\, Fx \supset Fx$' is tautologous.

Hailperin recognizes a close kinship of his system of inclusive quantification theory to Church's. But in developing his system and establishing its properties he refers in detail to a system of exclusive quantification theory in my *Mathematical Logic*. Now this exclusive system runs, in the revised edition, as follows:

(1) If ϕ is tautologous (by truth tables), $\vdash \phi$.

(2) $\vdash \ulcorner (\alpha)(\phi \supset \psi) \supset . \, (\alpha)\phi \supset (\alpha)\psi \urcorner$.

(3) If α is not free in ϕ, $\vdash \ulcorner \phi \supset (\alpha)\phi \urcorner$.

(4) $\vdash \ulcorner (\alpha)\phi \supset \phi^{\beta}_{\alpha} \urcorner$.

(5) If $\ulcorner \phi \supset \psi \urcorner$ and ϕ are theorems, so is ψ.

[2] "A formulation of the logic of sense and denotation," 17f.

Here ϕ^{β}_{α} is understood as like ϕ except for containing free β in place of all free α; and '$\vdash \phi$' means that the *closure of* ϕ is a theorem. Free variables are not allowed in theorems.

In the first edition a further principle was included, viz.:

(6) $$\vdash \ulcorner(\alpha)(\beta)\phi \supset (\beta)(\alpha)\phi\urcorner.$$

However, Berry showed that, by modifying an arbitrary detail in the underlying definition of closure, we can dispense with (6). This simplification, which I adopted in the revised edition, is a particularly striking one when we reflect that (6) was the only polyadic axiom form in the lot.

Taking the system of my first edition as point of departure, hence (1)–(6), Hailperin builds his system of inclusive quantification theory from it by changing (4) to:

(7) $$\vdash \ulcorner(\alpha)\phi \supset (\beta)\phi^{\beta}_{\alpha}\urcorner$$

and adding:

(8) If α is not free in ϕ, $\vdash \ulcorner\phi \supset (\alpha)\psi \,.\!\supset (\alpha)(\phi \supset \psi)\urcorner$.

Now the main point which I want to make is that Hailperin's inclusive theory, simpler though it is than Mostowski's, can be much simplified in turn. We can drop (6) by Berry's expedient. Also we can drop (8) if, instead of changing (4) to (7), we merely weaken (4) by prefixing the hypothesis that α is free in ϕ.

The resulting system of inclusive quantification theory is simply the exclusive system (1)–(5) with the words "If α is free in ϕ" inserted in (4). This insertion is wanted so as to except '$(x)f \supset f$', which fails for the empty domain.

The completeness of this system of inclusive quantification theory can be seen by substantially Hailperin's proof, which is easily adaptable to this system. Another fact which Hailperin establishes about his system, viz., that it can be strengthened to exclusive quantification theory by adding '$\vdash \ulcorner\sim(\alpha)f\urcorner$' (or say '$\vdash \ulcorner\sim(\alpha)(\phi \,.\, \sim\phi)\urcorner$'), is also demonstrable for our simpler system, again by substantially Hailperin's proof.

The required adaptation of Hailperin's proofs is twofold, involving not only a switch from his system to our new one, but a switch also from the first edition of *Mathematical Logic*, which he cites for certain proof patterns, to the revised edition. In detail the changes are as follows. In his proofs of his Lemma 1 and Theorem 1, change

"*104" to "*103." (This change merely reflects a change of numbering in the revised edition.) In his proof of Theorem 1, drop the proof of Case 1 in favor of a mere citation of our weakened (4) above. In his proof of Lemma 3, change "*112" to "*115" and cite our weakened (4) instead of QE1. (These changes in the proof of Lemma 3 reflect both a change of numbering and a radical change of proofs in the revised edition.) In his proof of Theorem 2, read "QE0–6" as excluding QE1 and QE4–5 and as including the weakened (4).

Note added in 1993: It has been pointed out to me, by Hugues Leblanc for one, that (6) must be retained here. Berry's elimination of it, valid for standard logic, does not carry over to the empty domain. Thus corrected, my system improves on Hailperin's only modestly, reducing (7) and (8) to (4) with free α.

XXII

Reduction to a Dyadic Predicate

Consider any interpreted theory Θ, formulated in the notation of quantification theory (or lower predicate calculus) with interpreted predicate letters. It will be proved that Θ is translatable into a theory, likewise formulated in the notation of quantification theory, in which there is only one predicate letter, and it a dyadic one.[1]

Let us assume a fragment of set theory, adequate to assure the existence, for all x and y without regard to logical type, of the set $\{x, y\}$ whose members are x and y, and to assure the distinctness of x from $\{x, y\}$ and $\{\{x\}\}$. ($\{x\}$ is explained as $\{x, x\}$.) Let us construe the ordered pair $x;y$ in Kuratowski's fashion, viz., as $\{\{x\}, \{x, y\}\}$, and then construe $x;y;z$ as $x;(y;z)$, and $x;y;z;w$ as $x;(y;z;w)$, and so on. Let us refer to w, $w;w$, $w;w;w$, etc., as $1w$, $2w$, $3w$, etc.

Suppose the predicates of Θ are 'F_1', 'F_2', . . . , finite or infinite in number, and respectively d_1-adic, d_2-adic, ... Now let Θ' be a theory whose notation consists of that of quantification theory with just the single dyadic predicate 'F', interpreted thus:

Reprinted from the *Journal of Symbolic Logic*, Volume 19, 1954.

[1] This result is reminiscent of, but distinct from, two others in the literature. One is Löwenheim's and Kalmár's, which has to do not with the translatability of an interpreted theory, but with the likeness of quantificational schemata in point of consistency or inconsistency. The other is that of Church, Craig, and Quine, which assures reducibility not merely to a dyadic predicate but to a symmetric one; it differs from the present result in supposing the universe to consist of natural numbers. See Kalmár, 1936; Church and Quine; Craig and Quine.

(1) $Fxy \equiv: (\exists z)(x = \{y, z\}) \vee . x = y . (\exists n)(\exists w_1) \ldots (\exists w_{d_n})(F_n w_1 \ldots w_{d_n} . x = nw_1;w_1;w_1;w_2;w_3; \ldots ;w_{d_n})$.

The universe of Θ' is to comprise all objects of the universe of Θ and, in addition, $\{x, y\}$ for every x and y in the universe of Θ'. (Of course the universe of Θ may happen already to comprise all this.)

Now I shall show how the familiar notations '$x = y$', '$x = \{y, z\}$', etc., and ultimately the desired '$F_1 w_1 \ldots w_{d_1}$', '$F_2 w_1 \ldots w_{d_2}$', etc., themselves can all be defined within Θ'. The arrow '$\rightarrow$' is used as a sign of definition.

DEFINITION. $x = y \rightarrow (z)(Fzx \equiv Fzy)$.

Justification. Obviously $(z)(Fzx \equiv Fzy)$ where x is y. So it will suffice to establish the converse: to *assume* that $(z)(Fzx \equiv Fzy)$, and show that $x = y$ in the ordinary sense of '='. Since $\{x\}$ is $\{x, x\}$, clearly $(\exists z)(\{x\} = \{x, z\})$ and hence, by (1), $F\{x\}x$. Then, by our assumption, $F\{x\}y$. Then, by (1), either $(\exists z)(\{x\} = \{y, z\})$ (whereat $x = y$) or else $\{x\} = y$. The same argument with 'x' and 'y' switched shows that $x = y$ or $\{y\} = x$. Combining,

$$x = y . \vee . \{x\} = y . \{y\} = x.$$

Hence x is either y or $\{\{x\}\}$. But x cannot be $\{\{x\}\}$.

DEFINITION.[2] $x = \{y, z\} \rightarrow (w)(w \neq x . Fxw . \equiv : w = y . \vee . w = z)$.

Justification. We see from (1) that

$$w \neq x . Fxw . \equiv (\exists u)(x = \{w, u\}).$$

But clearly

$$x = \{y, z\} . \equiv (w)[(\exists u)(x = \{w, u\}) \equiv : w = y . \vee . w = z].$$

DEFINITIONS. $x = y;z \rightarrow (\exists u)(\exists w)(x = \{u, w\} . u = \{y, y\} . w = \{y, z\})$,

$x = y;z;w \rightarrow (\exists u)(x = y;u . u = z;w)$,

$x = y;z;w;u \rightarrow (\exists v)(x = y;v . v = z;w;u)$,

and so on. Further

$$y = 1w \rightarrow y = w,$$
$$y = 2w \rightarrow y = w;w,$$

and so on. *Justifications* obvious.

[2] The preceding definition of '$x = y$' applies only to simple variables, and thus does not overlap the present definition or succeeding ones.

DEFINITION (for each fixed n and d_n).

$$F_n w_1 \ldots w_{d_n} \rightarrow (\exists x)(\exists y)(Fxx \,.\, y = nw_1 \,.\, x = y;w_1;w_1;w_2;w_3; \ldots ;w_{d_n}).$$

Justification. The definiens here amounts to:

$$F(nw_1;w_1;w_1;w_2;w_3; \ldots ;w_{d_n})(nw_1;w_1;w_1;w_2;w_3; \ldots ;w_{d_n}), \tag{2}$$

and we want to show it equivalent to '$F_n w_1 \ldots w_{d_n}$'. By (1), since $x \neq \{x, z\}$,

$$Fxx \equiv (\exists m)(\exists u_1) \ldots (\exists u_{d_m})(F_m u_1 \ldots u_{d_m} \,.\, x = mu_1;u_1;u_1;u_2;u_3; \ldots ;u_{d_m}).$$

Taking x here as $nw_1;w_1;w_1;w_2;w_3; \ldots ;w_{d_n}$, we infer that (2) is equivalent to:

$$(\exists m)(\exists u_1) \ldots (\exists u_{d_m})(F_m u_1 \ldots u_{d_m} \,.\, nw_1;w_1;w_1;w_2;w_3; \ldots ;w_{d_n} = mu_1;u_1;u_1;u_2;u_3; \ldots ;u_{d_m}). \tag{3}$$

Recalling our convention of parentheses, we see that the equation contained in (3) equates certain ordered triples, thus:

$$nw_1;w_1;(w_1; \ldots ;w_{d_n}) = mu_1;u_1;(u_1; \ldots ;u_{d_m}),$$

and implies therefore that $nw_1 = mu_1$ and $w_1 = u_1$, and hence also that $m = n$. So (3) reduces to:

$$(\exists u_1) \ldots (\exists u_{d_n})(F_n u_1 \ldots u_{d_n} \,.\, nw_1;w_1;w_1;w_2;w_3; \ldots ;w_{d_n} = nu_1;u_1;u_1;u_2;u_3; \ldots ;u_{d_n}),$$

and hence to:

$$(\exists u_1) \ldots (\exists u_{d_n})(F_n u_1 \ldots u_{d_n} \,.\, w_1 = u_1 \,.\, w_2 = u_2 \,.\, \ldots \,.\, w_{d_n} = u_{d_n}),$$

and hence to '$F_n w_1 \ldots w_{d_n}$'.

XXIII

Variables Explained Away

As x increases, we are told, $2/x$ decreases. Since numbers never increase or decrease, such talk of variables must be taken metaphorically. The meaning of this example is of course simply the general statement that if $x > y$ then $2/x < 2/y$. Indeed logicians and mathematicians nowadays use the word 'variable' mostly without regard to its etymological metaphor; they apply the word merely to the essentially pronominal letters 'x', 'y', etc., such as are used in making general statements and existence statements about numbers. A characteristic use of such letters is seen in the generality prefix 'every number x is such that', followed by some sentence, usually of the conditional or 'if–then' form, containing the letter 'x'. Another characteristic use of such letters is seen in the existence prefix 'some (at least one) number x is such that'.

The familiar form of stipulation 'Let x be thus and so' is usually best construed as amounting to a generality prefix and an 'if'-clause. Ordinarily the stipulation prefaces some passage of mathematical reasoning; and this whole combination can be treated as a generalized conditional sentence beginning 'Every number x is such that if x is thus and so then'—and continuing with the main body of the passage of reasoning in question.

The use of 'x' as an unknown in mathematical problems comes

This paper was read by invitation to the American Philosophical Society in April 1960. It was promptly published in the *Proceedings* of the Society and is reprinted here by permission. An abstract of it appeared also in the *Journal of Symbolic Logic* for 1959, under the title "Eliminating variables without applying functions to functions." In that same year, as I afterward learned, a construction by Bernays to the same purpose appeared ("Über eine natürliche Erweiterung des Relationenkalküls"). I think my scheme more elegant than his, but his paper goes beyond mine in that it gives axioms.

to the same thing. Such a problem starts out with some initial condition on x. Solving such a problem consists in finding an equation, '$x = \ldots$', worthy of standing as the 'then'-clause of a generalized conditional sentence whose 'if' clause states the given initial condition.

Mathematicians often introduce further letters in the role of unspecified constants or so-called parameters, in explicit contrast to the so-called variables such as 'x' and 'y'. Logically these parameters can be looked upon still as variables, and contrasted with 'x' and 'y' merely in respect of how much text the general sentences or existence sentences take in. A typical page involving 'a' as a so-called parameter, and 'x' as a variable explicitly so-called, might be analyzed in the following fashion. The whole is governed by the implicit generality prefix 'every number a is such that'. Then one or more briefer subsidiary clauses are governed by more transitory prefixes 'every number x is such that' or 'some number x is such that'. Typical talk of parameters can be construed along this line without essential difficulty.

Variables, of course, lend themselves to discourse not only of numbers but of objects of any sort. The non-numerical prefixes 'every set x is such that', 'every person x is such that', 'some country x is such that', have equal rights with the prefixes that talk of numbers.

Nor are variables necessarily tied up with generality prefixes or existence prefixes at all. Basically the variable is best seen as an abstractive pronoun: a device for marking positions in a sentence, with a view to abstracting the rest of the sentence as predicate. Thus consider the existence statements 'Some number x is such that x is prime' and 'Some number x is such that $x^3 = 3x$'. The variable is conveniently dropped from the first: we may better say simply 'Some number is prime', because in 'x is prime' the predicate 'is prime' is already nicely segregated for separate use. The variable can be eliminated also from the second example, but less conveniently: we could say 'Some number gives the same result when cubed as when trebled', thus torturing the desired complex predicate out of '$x^3 = 3x$' with a modicum of verbal ingenuity. In more complex examples, finally, use of 'x' is the only easy way of abstracting the jagged sort of predicate which we are trying to say that some number fulfills. Where the variable pays off is as a device for segregating or abstracting a desired predicate by exhibiting the predicate sentencewise with the variable for blanks.

The variable is invaluable still as abstractive pronoun in places where generality and existence are not the point. Thus consider singular descriptions, as logicians call them: phrases beginning with the singular 'the'. We say 'the square of 2', 'the author of *Waverley*', without variables; but in 'the number x such that', followed by some complex condition on 'x', we need the variable as abstractive pronoun just as urgently as in the corresponding existence statement.

As a point now of theory and not of practical convenience, it can be interesting to inquire whether the variable is in principle dispensable. We were able to avoid the variable as abstractive pronoun in the case of '$x^3 = 3x$' by torturing '$x^3 = 3x$' into 'x gives the same result when cubed as when trebled'. Once we had coaxed the dummy letter 'x' thus into suitable position and segregated the rest, we ceased to need the 'x'. In this example the coaxing depended on such auxiliary words as 'gives', 'result', and 'when', along with participial endings of verbs. Now my question is whether a general, finite battery of such auxiliary operators can be assembled that will enable us always to coax variables thus into positions where we can dispense with them.

The answer is affirmative, as I shall show. The interest in carrying out the elimination is that the device of the variable thereby receives, in a sense, its full and explicit analysis. There is no thought of denying ourselves the continuing convenience of variables in practice.

I shall need henceforward to talk continually of *predicates* and *predication* in the following regimented way. An n-place predicate is a sign that attaches to a string of n subjects to make a sentence; and a sentence so formed is called a predication. Thus we may have a three-place predicate 'F' of distance comparison, where the predication '$Fxyz$' means that x is farther from y than from z. We may have a two-place predicate 'B' of biting, where the predication 'Bxy' means that x bites y. We may have a one-place predicate 'D' of doghood, where 'Dx' means that x is a dog. A no-place predicate, if we may force our terminology a bit, would be a sentence as it stands.

Given the two-place predicate 'B', which is the transitive verb 'bites', let us now contrast two styles in which we might say that x bites something. The one style uses an existence prefix; the other style uses a certain operator on predicates. The one style is familiar, and consists in two steps: first we form a predication 'Bxy' and then we apply to it the existence prefix 'Something y is such that'. The other style is opposite in order: first we make a new predicate, a one-place predicate meaning 'bites something', and then we use it and 'x' to form a predication 'x bites something'. For this style we need an operator which can be applied to a two-place predicate or transitive verb 'B', 'bites', to produce a one-place predicate 'bites something'. Let us call this operator that of *derelativization* and write it 'Der'. Thus 'Der B' is the one-place predicate or intransitive verb of biting, or biting something, and the predication '(Der B) x' means that x bites something.

I remarked that the essential utility of variables is that they mark positions. This point becomes vivid when we contrast the derelativization operator with the existence prefix, which used a variable 'y'. The two devices are alike in enabling us to say that x bites something. But the existence prefix with its variable has the advantage of enabling us to say also such further things as that

Something x is such that something y is such that Bxy,
Something y is such that Byx,
Something y is such that Byy,

whereas our derelativization operator only takes care of the case 'Something y is such that Bxy'. To make the derelativization operator suffice in lieu of existence prefixes and variables, what are needed are certain further operators capable of coaxing a variable into the right position. Also an extension of the derelativization operator itself is needed; let me begin with that.

So far I have explained derelativization as applying to a two-place predicate 'B', 'bites', to produce a one-place predicate 'Der B', 'bites something'. Let us now explain it as applying similarly to a one-place predicate to produce a no-place predicate, or sentence, which simply affirms existence: 'Der D' means simply that there are dogs. Then, since '(Der B)x' means that x bites something, 'Der Der B' means that something bites something. This disposes of our example 'Something x is such that something y is such that Bxy'.

With an eye now to the next of the above examples, 'Something y is such that Byx', we add an operator of *inversion*. This operator may be described as turning a transitive verb or two-place predicate from active to passive: '(Inv B)xy' means that Byx. Thus equipped, we can rectify 'Something y is such that Byx' to read

'Something y is such that (Inv B)xy', whereupon we can bring derelativization to bear; the whole gets translated as '(Der Inv B)x', devoid of the existence prefix and its 'y'.

Our further example 'Something y is such that Byy' prompts the adoption of yet a third operator, that of *reflection*. It turns the two-place predicate 'B', 'bites', into the one-place predicate 'Ref B', 'bites self'. Thus '(Ref B)y' means 'Byy'. Then instead of 'Something y is such that Byy' we can write 'Something y is such that (Ref B)y' and hence simply 'Der Ref B'.

These simple examples already illustrate the essential trick of the general elimination of variables. Let us now generalize.

Our three operators—'Der', 'Inv', 'Ref'—need to be generalized for application to predicates of more than two places. I shall generalize them in the least imaginative way, simply supplying the extra places as inert background. Even so, there are in the case of inversion two such generalizations both of which will be wanted. Altogether, then, our four operators on predicates may be described succinctly as follows, where 'P' represents any n-place predicate:

Derelativization: (Der P)$x_1 \ldots x_{n-1}$ if and only if there is something x_n such that $Px_1 \ldots x_n$.

Major inversion: (Inv P)$x_1 \ldots x_n$ if and only if $Px_nx_1 \ldots x_{n-1}$.

Minor inversion: (inv P)$x_1 \ldots x_n$ if and only if $Px_1 \ldots x_{n-2}x_nx_{n-1}$.

Reflection: (Ref P)$x_1 \ldots x_{n-1}$ if and only if $Px_1 \ldots x_{n-1}x_{n-1}$.

We saw that 'Something y is such that Bxy' and the three kindred examples could be rendered respectively as '(Der B)x', 'Der Der B', '(Der Inv B)x', and 'Der Ref B'. Let us now try our four generalized operators on the more serious example:

Something x is such that something y is such that $Pyxyx$.

By transforming the part '$Pyxyx$' first into '(inv P)$yxxy$', thence into '(Inv inv P)$xxyy$', and thence into '(Ref Inv inv P)xxy', we reduce the whole sentence to:

Something x is such that (Der Ref Inv inv P)xx,

which reduces in turn to:

Der Ref Der Ref Inv inv P.

More generally, we can claim this of our four operators: they enable us to get rid of existence prefixes and their variables whenever, as in the above example, there are only the existence prefixes and one predication. The reasoning is as follows. It is easily seen that major and minor inversion suffice to permute any number of subjects into any desired order; and then reflection suffices to resolve repetitions, when they are permuted to terminal position. Finally derelativization takes care of each existence prefix and its variable in terminal position.

We have still to worry about existence prefixes governing sentences which are compounded of predications, e.g., in the fashion '*Bxy* and not *Fwxz*'. To handle such cases, we need these two further operators on predicates:

Negation: (Neg $P)x_1 \ldots x_m$ if and only if not $(Px_1 \ldots x_m)$.
Cartesian multiplication: $(P \times Q)x_1 \ldots x_m y_1 \ldots y_n$ if and only if $Px_1 \ldots x_m$ and $Qy_1 \ldots y_n$.

Using these, we can express our example '*Bxy* and not *Fwxz*' as a single predication '($B \times$ Neg $F)xywxz$'. (In reading this we have to know, of course, that '*B*' is two-place and '*F*' is three-place.)

Our operators on predicates are now six. They enable us to get rid of an existence prefix and its associated variable when what the prefix governs is constructed by 'not' and 'and', as complexly as you please, from any number of predications.

I can put this more strongly. Suppose we have a language of the following form. Its simple sentences are predications, formed of predicates and strings of variables. Its compound sentences are built up of such predications by repeated use of just three devices: 'not', 'and', and existence prefixes. These prefixes are 'something *x* is such that', 'something *y* is such that', etc., with no restriction of the objects to special categories such as numbers or persons; the universe may be conceived widely or narrowly, but it is to be the same for every existence prefix. A language thus simply constituted I shall call *standard.* Standard languages differ from one another only in their stock of predicates and in how the universe is chosen. Now we can say this of our six operators on predicates: these, if added to a standard language, enable us to rid the language of existence prefixes and variables altogether. Given any sentence of a standard language, we go to work on an *innermost* existence prefix: one whose governed clause contains no existence prefixes. Our six operators on predicates enable us to eliminate it and its variable. Then we deal with any surviving innermost existence prefix, and, working thus outward, eventually make a clean sweep of all existence prefixes and their variables.

Thus consider the sentence 'Some men read no books'. In standard language it is:

Something x is such that (Mx and not something y is such that By and Rxy),

for obvious interpretations of 'M', 'B', and 'R'. Now the part 'By and Rxy' can be transformed successively thus:

$$(B \times R)yxy, \qquad [\text{Inv}(B \times R)]xyy, \qquad [\text{Ref Inv } (B \times R)]xy.$$

The whole sentence 'Some men read no books' then becomes:

Something x is such that $\{Mx$ and not $[\text{Der Ref Inv}(B \times R)]x\}$,

which can be further transformed into:

Something x is such that $[M \times \text{Neg Der Ref Inv } (B \times R)]xx$,

and finally into:

$$\text{Der Ref}[M \times \text{Neg Der Ref Inv}(B \times R)].$$

This, it will be said, is an illustration in miniature of how variables might be eliminated from serious theories. Actually it is more: it is already a solution of the general case.[1] For there is evidence that what I have called the standard form of language is, despite its apparent poverty, an adequate medium for scientific theories generally. Some illustrative translations will clarify this point.

Existence prefixes suffice to the exclusion of generality prefixes. Thus consider the generality prefix 'every number x is such that'. Using 'not' and an existence prefix, we can paraphrase it as 'not some number x is such that not'.

[1] The first general elimination of variables was due to Schönfinkel, 1924. His operators operate on themselves and one another, whereas our six operate only on the original predicates and on the predicates thence derived by the operators. His presuppose an abstract universe equivalent to that of higher set theory, whereas ours make no ontological demands, being even retranslatable into 'not', 'and', and existence prefixes. An apparatus equivalent in scope to ours is Tarski's cylindrical algebra, when the number of its dimensions is taken as infinite but locally finite; see Henkin, "The representation theorem for cylindrical algebras." But here again there is a radical difference in approach. In a way our operators are reminiscent also of the axioms of class existence in von Neumann, 1925, despite dissimilarity of purpose. See also my "Toward a calculus of concepts." Along Schönfinkel's line much research has meanwhile been done, mainly by Curry.

Existence prefixes suffice to the exclusion also of the prefixes of singular description. Thus consider the singular description 'the number x such that $x + x = x$'. Whenever it is used, it is used in one or another sentence that says something further about the described number; e.g., that it is less than 1. Now instead of saying that *the* number x, such that $x + x = x$, is less than 1, we can resort to an existence prefix and say merely that *some* number x is such that $x + x = x$ and $x < 1$. If with an eye to the 'the' of singular description we want also to affirm uniqueness—that only one number x is such that $x + x = x$—we can add a further sentence to that effect. It too can ultimately be formulated without using variables otherwise than in connection with existence prefixes.[2]

I urged earlier that the variable is best understood as an abstractive pronoun. Still one finds, as in these examples, that all contexts which call for variables can be warped around into ones in which variables are used solely with existence prefixes. Alternative paraphrases are available too, herding the variables into other types of construction; but we *can* rest with the existence prefixes.

We can do better: we can adhere to the unrestricted form of existence prefix 'something x is such that', as against the restricted form 'some number x is such that' and the like. For, 'some number x is such that' can be paraphrased as 'something x is such that x is a number and'. Such, indeed, was our treatment of men and books in transforming 'Some men read no books'.

This much suffices perhaps to illustrate that the standard form of language is adequate so far as the role of variables is concerned. Variables can be seen as adjuncts purely of existence prefixes, and unrestricted ones at that.

Another economy of standard language was that apart from existence prefixes it recognizes only 'not' and 'and' as means of building sentences from sentences. Ways have long been familiar whereby 'not' and 'and' can be made to do the work of various further sentence connectives: 'p or q' can be rendered 'not (not p and not q)', and 'if p then q' can be rendered 'not (p and not q)'.

These and further reductions to what I have called the standard form are familiar to logicians.[3] All branches of classical mathemat-

[2] Not some number x is such that [$x + x = x$ and some number y is such that ($x \neq y$ and $y + y = y$)].

[3] The modern logic of *quantifiers*—i.e., generality prefixes and existence prefixes—dates from Frege, 1879. So do the various reductions noted in the past few paragraphs, except that the eliminability of singular descriptions was noted rather by Russell, 1905.

ics can be put into standard form, and so can all other branches of theory that would be at all generally regarded as having attained to explicit scientific formulation. This is abundantly borne out by literature on the logical regimentation of mathematics and other scientific discourse.

Singular terms seem a mainstay of language. We continually use proper names, and also complex singular terms such as 'the author of *Waverley*' and '$x + y$'. It is worth noticing, then, that our standard form has none of these—no singular terms except the simple variables themselves. It has long been known that by suitable choice of predicates we can dispense with singular terms other than variables. The main step in that argument is the elimination of singular descriptions that was illustrated above.

And now our new reduction dispenses even with the variables. There cease to be singular terms at all; there remain only the predicates themselves and our six fixed operators upon them. Each sentence fares substantially as our example 'Some men read no books' was seen to fare.

It will be said that there may still survive, in examples other than that one, the sentential operators 'not' and 'and'. But we can disclaim these, for they are best viewed as merely those cases of 'Neg' and '$\times$' where the predicates to which 'Neg' and '$\times$' are applied happen to be no-place predicates, i.e., sentences.

We end up with a universal algebra purely of predicates, comprising just our six operators and any arbitrary predicates as generators for them to operate on. This is a general logical notation. It is devoid of variables, yet theoretically adequate as a framework for theories generally, mathematical and otherwise. To fix it as a notation for any specific subject matter we merely supply the appropriate vocabulary of specific predicates, leaving the outward framework unchanged; and that framework consists of our six operators, nothing more.

XXIV

Truth, Paradox, and Gödel's Theorem

1. *Background.* Gödel's epoch-making theorem of 1931 is that there can be no complete proof procedure for elementary number theory. One constraint on what qualify as proof procedures is that they be specified by appeal only to sameness and difference of strings of signs, using first-order logic—hence without appeal to what the strings mean. *Protosyntax* is my word for that formal apparatus. The further constraint is that there be an *effective* or mechanical test of whether a purported proof of a formula is indeed a proof of it.

Few of us would have been surprised to learn that there is no algorithm—no effective criterion, no outright test—for truth in elementary number theory. Such a test would make short work of unsolved problems such as Goldbach's conjecture and Fermat's Last Theorem; too good to be true. On the other hand Gödel's theorem came as a shock, for we supposed that truth in mathematics *consisted* in demonstrability.

Actually this contrast was unreasonable, as we see by a zigzag argument due to S. C. Kleene (p. 284). Whenever there is so much as a complete proof procedure for a theory couched in sentences subject to negation, there is also an outright mechanical test. Just program a computer to grind out all possible proofs of anything and everything in order of length, and alphabetically within each length. If the proof procedure is complete, the machine will eventually grind out a proof of the desired formula or its negation, thus

This is a lecture that evolved through Lehigh, Girona, Lethbridge, and Boston Universities in 1990–1992.

deciding its truth value. The decision cannot be expected within what computer engineers call polynomial time, but that is merely a practical point.

Substantially the same argument that establishes Gödel's theorem, however, establishes something stronger: that truth for elementary number theory cannot be defined in protosyntax at all, either by proof procedure or otherwise.

We may well ask whether this apparent strengthening is really a strengthening. Can an interpreted system admit of a protosyntactic truth definition but no complete proof procedure? Warren Goldfarb, pursuant on a suggestion of Hilary Putnam's, has shown me just such a system. Reworked to facilitate exposition, the idea is in effect as follows.

Gödel's systematic numbering of strings of signs will be helpful. Any effective one-to-one assignment will do, as long as it reaches all desired strings. The system *L*, then, is to have a single predicate '$\overline{\text{V}}$', interpreted as true of all and only the Gödel numbers of *non*-valid schemata of first-order predicate logic. Also it has the numeral '0' and the successor operation for deriving the positive integers. So the sentences of *L* are just '$\overline{\text{V}}0$', '$\overline{\text{V}}1$', '$\overline{\text{V}}2$', and so on. Now Gödel showed in 1930 that we have complete proof procedures for the validity of schemata of first-order logic. Therefore validity of these schemata is protosyntactically definable, and so also, thanks to negation, is non-validity. So there is a protosyntactic truth definition for *L*.

But there is no complete proof procedure for *L;* for, if there were, Kleene's zigzag argument would produce an effective decision procedure for first-order logic, and this was shown impossible by both Alonzo Church and A. M. Turing in 1936–37. Conclusion: *L* admits of a protosyntactic truth definition but no complete proof procedure. So the apparent strengthening of Gödel's theorem is real.

If you find *L* unrepresentatively trivial in lacking truth functions, quantifiers, and variables, then feel free to add them. Since there is only a one-place predicate, any quantifiers scattered through a complex truth function can be driven inward by the familiar rules of passage until each governs just an atomic formula. Thus every closed sentence comes down to a truth function of various of '$\overline{\text{V}}0$', '$\overline{\text{V}}1$', etc. and '$\exists x\ \overline{\text{V}}x$' and '$\forall x\ \overline{\text{V}}x$'. But these last two are respectively true and false, and so can be resolved out, leaving just a truth function of '$\overline{\text{V}}0$', '$\overline{\text{V}}1$', etc. The truth definition for the original system L readily extends to these compounds, while the lack of a complete proof procedure carries over *a fortiori.*

The broader version of Gödel's theorem was already implicit in Alfred Tarski, 1935, Theorem I, and in the last chapter of my *Mathematical Logic,* 1940. It is a major simplification, for it bypasses the notion of a proof procedure. This is a relief, for it spares us the notion of an effective check. Effectiveness is a notion whose three rigorous explications—"recursiveness," "lambda definability," "Turing computability"—all take a good deal of explaining. They hinge, moreover, on a sort of conjecture, though quite an acceptable one, called Church's thesis. All these matters are swept aside by the widening of Gödel's theorem. It now simply says that number-theoretic truth is protosyntactically indefinable.

The novelty of my 1940 treatment was that instead of modeling protosyntax in number theory, by Gödel numbering, and then showing the number-theoretic indefinability of number-theoretic truth, I showed the protosyntactic indefinability of protosyntactic truth itself and then transferred the result to number theory on the strength of the reinterpretability (Paper V in this volume) of number theory and protosyntax in each other. But my 1940 treatment was a headache, because of some pedantry. I applied my argument to the primitive notation of the main body of the book, and in that notation there were no singular terms but bound variables. I had to make an unintuitive detour through what I called identity matrices. In 1957, with acknowledgment to me, Raymond Smullyan presented the argument in admirable simplicity. My purpose in the present purely expository paper is to sketch the same argument in the broader setting and perhaps more intuitively still.

2. *The Argument.* The notation of protosyntax may be taken to comprise these thirteen signs:

$$\sim,\ \&,\ \exists,\ x,\ y,\ z,\ ',\ =,\ (,\ ),\ \frown,\ \mathrm{I},\ \Delta.$$

The first ten cover the truth functions, quantification, and identity. The accent, seventh in the sequence, is for attaching to the three variables to generate further variables. The eleventh is the concatenation sign, for spelling out strings of signs, and the twelfth, 'I', is a name of the first sign of the object alphabet, whatever that may be. The last sign, 'Δ', is for alphabetic successor.

Attached to the name of any sign in the object alphabet, it forms the name of the next sign in that alphabet if such there be.

Since we are to apply protosyntax to itself, the object alphabet will now comprise those same thirteen signs, designated respectively by these thirteen names:

$$\mathrm{I},\ \Delta\mathrm{I},\ \Delta\Delta\mathrm{I},\ \ldots,\ \Delta^{11}\mathrm{I},\ \Delta^{12}\mathrm{I}.$$

To prove that protosyntactic truth is not definable in protosyntax, we show that 'True x' is not so definable as to fulfill Tarski's disquotational schema

(1) True '. . . .' ≡ . . . .

for all closed sentences of protosyntax in the blank '. . . .'.

The strategy hinges on a version of the truth paradox, or paradox of the liar. Given any open sentence in one free variable 'x', let us substitute for 'x', in it, a name of that sentence itself. The result is the *self-predication* of the original sentence. Thus the self predication of the sentence 'x is long,' briefly SP 'x is long,' is

'x is long' is long.

We are evidently on our way to Kurt Grelling's familiar paradox of denotation, the Heterological. But I take a different turning for my truth paradox:

(2) SP 'SPx is false' is false.

This tells us that a certain sentence is false, namely the sentence obtained by putting the quotation in place of 'x' in the quoted sentence itself. But if we make this substitution we get (2) all over again. So (2) denies itself. Self satisfaction ends in self denial.

Rewritten in terms of truth, our truth paradox (2) is this:

(3) ~True SP'~True SPx'.

We want to use it to prove that any protosyntactically definable predicate 'True' is bound to violate the disquotational schema (1) for some closed protosyntactic sentence in the blank '. . . .'.

Once we have protosyntactically defined 'SP' and quotation, the argument proceeds as follows. By the definition of self predication, (3) is the self predication of '~True SPx'.

(3) = SP '~True SPx'.

Therefore

True (3) .≡. True SP '~True SPx'.

That is, writing (3) out,

(4) True '~True SP '~True SPx'' .≡. True SP '~True SPx'.

If (1) held, we could reduce the left side of the biconditional (4) by canceling its first 'True' and outermost quotes. The result would be a self-contradiction of the form '$\sim p \equiv p$'. Therefore (1) fails, and the supposed truth definition was unsuccessful, q. e. d.

What remains to be done, then, in proving the protosyntactic incompletability of protosyntax, is to fill in the missing definitions of 'SP' and quotation. The latter is immediate: any quotation can be spelled out by naming the successive signs of the quoted expression and then joining the names by the concatenation sign. But note that the quotations in the above argument must not be understood as naming the expressions actually shown between the quotation marks; they name rather the definitional expansions of those expressions into the primitive protosyntactic alphabet.

Definition of 'SP', then, is the remaining problem. There is drudgery here that I shall pass over, sketching only enough to show the hurdles and how to cope. Related constructions have been painfully carried out in the aforementioned chapter of *Mathematical Logic,* as well as in Gödel's original paper.

The self-predication of an open sentence in 'x' is the result of *substituting* the *name* of the sentence for 'x' (that is, for ΔΔΔI) in the sentence. *Name of* is the first sticking point here. We can name any given string by spelling, but now we have to refer to the name of a string that is not given. We have to define 'y is name of string z'.

To begin with we can define 'y is the name of *sign* z' by exhaustion of thirteen cases. If z is I (that is, '~'), y is Δ^{11}I (that is, 'I'); if z is ΔI (that is, '&'), y is $\Delta^{12}\text{I}^\frown\Delta^{11}$I (that is, 'ΔI'); and so on. Next it is a routine matter to define the name of a string as a function of the names of any two shorter strings of which it is the concatenate.

Thereupon we have the basis for a recursion: y is the name of z if it can be paired with z by a series of steps from the thirteen initial cases, each step moving us from the names of two concatenands to the name of their concatenate. The explicit definition is fussy, so let me just recall the underlying principle for embodying such a recursion in a formal definition.

The underlying idea is the *ancestral* of a relation. It gets its name from its familiar case: ancestor is the ancestral of parent. One's ancestor is a parent of a parent . . . of a parent of oneself. The general definition of the ancestral, due to Frege, is evident from this example: to be an ancestor of mine is to belong to every class that contains me and the parents of all its members. But the ancestral so defined is not available to protosyntax, for it quantifies over classes.

Happily there is another way of defining the ancestral, using finite sequences. To be an ancestor of mine is to belong, with me, to a finite sequence in which everybody except me is parent of some earlier member. Now finite sequences, unlike classes, can be simulated in protosyntax. The objects in protosyntax are strings of signs, and the ones that ordinarily matter are well-formed formulas. What are wanted for defining the ancestral, here, are sequences of formulas. We can simulate such sequences by exploiting the *ill*-formed: by using '()' as a separator, since '()' never occurs in a formula. We can take a sequence as a string, and its members as its segments from one '()' to the next. So the ancestral is available, and '*y* is the name of string *z*' can be defined.

The other needed component of the definition of 'SP' is substitution for '*x*'. This again proceeds by recursion in straightforward fashion.

XXV

Immanence and Validity

The contrast between object language and metalanguage plays a prominent role in mathematics, or metamathematics, for good reasons. It is inevitable when we study an uninterpreted formalism, as in abstract algebra. Here our normal language is the metalanguage, and the object language is alien. Again there are the semantic paradoxes of truth and denotation, or satisfaction. These have driven us from our own language as object language into a metalanguage, stronger in set theory, in which to express truth and denotation for our language. The semantics of the metalanguage calls in turn for a metametalanguage, if we care about it, and so on up.

I propose to contrast this *transcendent* style of metatheory, as I call it, with the *immanent* style, in which we express the metatheory as best we can within the language of the theory itself. The attraction is a sort of absolutism: thinking of our language as our serious all-purpose language, and thinking of its set theory as the theory of just the sets that there really are. This attracts me because of my philosophy of mathematics, of which I'll offer a partial sketch.

The variables of quantification in natural science range over physical objects and over numbers, functions, and other sets. All these are equally assumed in the only sense that I understand. The scientific theory stands or falls by the success or failure of its predictions, but these predictions are implied jointly by the mathe-

This paper evolved from my Alfred Tarski Lecture at Berkeley, March 1990. I presented a revised version at a symposium of the F. Gonseth-Vereinigung in Biel two months later, and it appeared with further changes in *Dialectica,* Volume 45, 1991. It is reprinted here with omissions and emendations.

matical and nonmathematical sentences. In this participatory way mathematical objects qualify as real on a par with the other values of the variables.

What then of mathematical truths or hypotheses that don't figure in natural science? What of the extravagant flights of higher set theory? We reckon such sentences still as meaningful because they are constructed grammatically from lexicon that is also needed in applicable mathematics. Their exclusion from the language would require an excessive gerrymandering of the grammar. Which of them to retain as true, then, and which false? This can still be tentatively settled, up to a point, by considerations that also figure familiarly at the theoretical edge of natural science: considerations of economy and simplicity.

On these grounds the inaccessible numbers, other than ω, get a resounding negative. Gödel's so-called axiom of constructibility, '$V = L$', on the other hand, is welcomed with open arms.[1] Working in the classical Zermelo-Fraenkel set theory, Kurt Gödel formulated a complex condition on sets which he called constructibility; and what the axiom says is that all sets are constructible. Gödel proves that it is consistent with the Zermelo-Fraenkel system if that is self-consistent; and it declares for economy across the board. In particular it implies the axiom of choice and the continuum hypothesis.

We can still condone the more extravagant reaches of set theory as a study merely of logical relations among hypotheses, on a par with studies of abstract algebras. We just withhold truth claims after a point.

So I like the fiction of an all-purpose scientific language, final until further notice, in which we treat of truth and models and logical validity in terms of real sets, as real as apples and neutrinos.

Now let us see how the truth predicate fares, treated immanently. Our syntactical and set-theoretic vocabularies are now parts of our single language. Instead of a hierarchy of metalanguages, each providing a truth predicate applicable to sentences in each lower language, we now settle for a hierarchy of truth predicates within our single language. Each of them behaves as a truth predicate should as long as it is affirmed of sentences that do not

[1] We need not pause over the content of the axiom. Readers familiar with it should note that what I say of it here and later hinges on the earlier of Gödel's presentations, namely "Consistency proof for the generalized continuum hypothesis."

themselves contain truth predicates of that or higher levels, or predicates such as satisfaction that are akin to truth predicates. It is a hierarchy of better and better truth predicates, with no best.

Another place where we find the immanent and the transcendent approaches in clear contrast is in defining, more specifically, *logical* truth. A logical truth is a sentence whose logical structure is such that all sentences with that structure are true. And what is logical structure? We can shift that question of structure to vocabulary, if we are prepared to enumerate the logical vocabulary of our language, which is to say, the connectives and other constants and variables of our symbolic logic. Then a logical truth is a sentence that stays true under all uniform substitutions for its nonlogical components. It contains only logical signs *essentially,* all other expressions vacuously. This definition has been pretty well recognized as far back at least as Bernard Bolzano.

The contrasts between first-order logic and set theory run so deep, as we now know them, that it becomes natural to mark them by limiting the term 'logic' at that point. Unlike set theory, logic in this sense is completable. And unlike logic, which is ontologically indiscriminate, set theory deals with distinctive objects.

In generating logical truths, and testing for them, it is convenient and usual to resort to logical schemata, as we well know; that is, to formulas of sentential form built of logical signs and schematic letters, these standing in place of extralogical constituents. Then a logical truth is any substitution instance of a logical schema all of whose substitution instances are true. The schema is a diagram of a logical structure, we may say, and then we are back to saying again, more intelligibly than at first, that a logical truth is any instance of a logical structure all of whose instances are true.

From a transcendental point of view, the definition of logical truth now before us would be seen as applying to any object language with our specified logical framework. At that point, doubts arise. Some such object language could be so poor in extralogical vocabulary that it could produce only true substitution instances of some logical schema that is nevertheless falsified by substitutions from some richer object language and hence not valid.

Before tackling this difficulty, let us be more specific about our logical schemata. The logical signs are the truth-function signs, the quantifiers, the variables of quantification, and the identity sign. Our schemata are built of these signs filled out with schematic letters. For convenience of application these letters should be of three kinds: letters for predicates, letters for names, and letters for name functors such as 'log' or 'plus.' But a more economical notation is helpful when we are concerned only to treat of our formulas metalogically and not to apply them. Ways are well known of so paraphrasing our sentences, however awkwardly, as to dispense with names and name functors and make do with just predicates and the logical signs. Let us suppose this done. So the only schematic letters in our schemata, now, are the predicate letters.

Under this regimentation, the question of richness and poverty of object languages boils down to differences in predicate lexicon. We can rise above these differences, following Tarski, by recourse to *models.* A model, for our purposes, is a sequence of sets. A model *of* a given logical schema consists of a set providing the range of the variables, followed by a subset of that set for each one-place predicate letter of the schema, and then correspondingly for each two-place letter, and so on. So now, instead of a schema's being said to come out true under all substitutions from one or another object language, it can be said to be satisfied by all its models. The substitution instances of such a schema in any particular object language, then, qualify as logically true regardless of poverty of that language in respect of predicates. The models belong to the real universe of sets assumed by the unformalized metalanguage.

Turning now from that transcendental line to an immanental one, we might adhere to the same formulation but take both object language and metalanguage as our own serious all-purpose language of the day, and take the models as sequences of sets within the set theory of our current choice or conviction. The reason for adhering still to models rather than substitution, despite the richness of our own lexicon of predicates, is that no language can be rich enough in predicates to specify every set. This follows from Georg Cantor's proof that any set has more subsets than members; for then in particular the set of all expressions has more subsets than there are expressions.

However, let us not despair so quickly. Granted that there are sets unspecifiable in our language, maybe they don't matter to the validity of logical schemata. Maybe when a logical schema is satisfied by all the sets specifiable in *our* rich language, it is satisfied by all the other sets as well. How rich would our language have to be?

The question can be answered in two words: not very. It has only to be rich enough for elementary number theory. I speak of expression, not proof. If the language accommodates elementary number theory, any logical schema true under all substitutions will also be satisfied by all its models, however unspecifiable these be. This is an extension by S. C. Kleene of a theorem of David Hilbert and Paul Bernays,[2] which is in turn a strengthened consequence of the Löwenheim-Skolem theorem. Thus there is no pertinent intrusion of Cantor's ineffable.

So the purely substitutional criterion of validity of logical schemata, and hence of logical truth, is vindicated, and with little credit to our all-purpose language; for elementary number theory requires only the means of expressing addition, multiplication, and quantification over natural numbers.

The modesty of elementary number theory can be put also another way: we need only the number 1 and the algebraic operation of Arabic numeration, along with first-order logic.[3] By the algebraic operation of Arabic numeration I mean the operation of concatenation which, applied say to the numbers 53 and 406, yields the number 53406.

So I settle happily for the immanent definition of logical truth. A logical truth is a substitution instance of a logical schema all of whose substitution instances are true. This does depend on a prior specification of what to count as logical schemata and hence as logical vocabulary, but the rest of our language can be taken for granted and goes without saying. That after all was the status also of a metalanguage, on the transcendental approach.

Next let us see how the immanental and transcendental approaches might fare in set theory itself. We have been dealing with logical schemata, but we can also look to set-theoretic schemata. The vocabulary of set theory, reduced to its economical minimum, is just that of first-order logic with '$\in$' instead of '='. We can skip '=', for it is definable in terms of '$\in$'.

Schemata dominate one's work in logic, but they play only a minor role in set theory. The sentences that can be written in *logical* vocabulary don't go far; '=' is the only predicate, and identity theory is meager. What can be done in sentences of set theory, on

[2] Needlessly restating the theorem at this point in the original printing of the present paper in *Dialectica,* I unaccountably fumbled it. But the full treatment is in XIX of the present volume.

[3] See V in the present volume.

the other hand, with '$\in$' as sole predicate, is as wide as mathematics. It is only at a few points that set theory is profitably eked out with a schema. One case is the axiom schema of class abstraction, or comprehension, or its variant, the schema of separation. Another is the axiom schema of replacement. Still it can be amusing to pause over the validity of other set-theoretic schemata, for instance this:

(1) $$\exists x(Fx \text{ iff } x \in x).$$

We have worried about schemata that might be declared valid by the substitutional criterion but invalid by models, because of unspecifiable sets. But (1) is an opposite example. It is invalid by substitution, since substitution yields the falsehood

(2) $$\exists x(x \notin x \text{ iff } x \in x).$$

Yet it is valid by models. Any and every set y as model satisfies (1) as interpretation of 'F', since

(3) $$\exists x(x \in y \text{ iff } x \in x).$$

We prove (3) by existentially generalizing the tautology

(3) $$y \in y \text{ iff } y \in y.$$

Tarski would have risen above this in his transcendental way. In the tacit theory of real sets in his unformalized metalanguage there would be a set y falsifying (3), but not accessible to the object language as value of 'y' in (3); namely, the set of all the sets in the universe of the object language that are not members of themselves. Such is the transcendental escape hatch. But it is in the immanent setting that the symmetry emerges between set shortage and predicate shortage. It is a symmetry between Russell's paradox, which tells us that some formulable membership conditions determine no sets, and Cantor's theorem, which tells us that some sets are determined by no formulable membership conditions.

It is remarkable that Russell's paradox and Cantor's theorem are opposite in effect, for they are identical in origin. Russell got his paradox by taking the given set in Cantor's proof as the universe and taking the function in Cantor's proof as identity.

The sentences (2) and (3) illustrate the set shortage. The schema (1) is fulfilled by all sets y, as seen in (3), and yet not by all predicates or open sentences, (2) being false. The opposite shortage is less easily illustrated. We may wonder again, as we did in the case of logical truth, whether the excess of sets over expressions really interferes with the substitutional approach. Is every satisfiable condition in set theory satisfied by a specifiable set? I turn to an argument to just that effect, with thanks to Hilary Putnam.

It means turning again to Gödel's axiom of constructibility. Gödel showed, on the basis of the Zermelo-Fraenkel set theory plus his axiom, how the whole universe of sets could be *well-ordered.* This means that among any lot of sets there is a first, with respect to that order. There are no infinite descents. Moreover, this firstness can be expressed in the set-theoretic notation. Now the application to the problem of unspecifiable sets is this. Whenever there is a set y at all, even unspecifiable, satisfying a condition 'Fy', there is also a *first* such set, and it *is* specifiable as *the first* x *such that* Fx. This specification is translatable into Zermelo-Fraenkel notation. I shall write it '$\mu_x Fx$', borrowing a notation from Hilbert and Bernays. It designates the first x, if any, such that Fx, and otherwise, by default, the empty set.

So we see that any condition 'Fx' that is satisfied at all is satisfied by a specifiable set $\mu_x Fx$. But we can also apparently go on to establish the contrary: the condition 'x is unspecifiable' is itself satisfied, but by no specifiable sets. Finally we can encapsulate the paradox by merging the two arguments:

$$\mu_x(x \text{ is unspecifiable}) \text{ is unspecifiable.}$$

The trouble lies with 'unspecifiable' and 'specifiable.' They are semantic predicates like 'true', and like 'true' they must be dissected into a hierarchy of levels to avert this kind of thing.

So the firstness construction carries the day; every satisfiable condition is satisfied by a specifiable set. But it is a hollow victory; we can learn that the set satisfies the condition only by learning that something does. Moreover, 'V = L' is essential here. Without it, there are conditions that are demonstrably satisfied in Zermelo-Fraenkel set theory but by no specifiable set. Putnam has shown me one such condition, unpublished, and George Boolos has shown me another, both hinging on recondite theorems. Forster (p. 76) has produced one in the set theory of my "New foundations," hinging on my odd treatment of singletons in that system.

The contrast between mere existence and specifiability is reflected in two versions of quantification itself: the *objectual* version and the *substitutional*. Objectually construed, an existential quantification is true if and only if the open sentence thus quantified is true for some object as value of the variable. Substitutionally construed, it is true if and only if the open sentence is true under some substitution for the variable.

The symmetric shortages of sets and predicates obtrude again when we compare objectual and substitutional quantification. A quantification might fail objectually for lack of a suitable set but still come out vacuously true under substitution of a failed set abstract such as '$\{x\colon x \notin x\}$'. We could prevent this by somehow screening out empty terms. Conversely, predicate shortage could render a quantification false substitutionally though still true objectually. But we can prevent this, as we saw, by accepting '$V = L$'.

The substitutional account of quantification over abstract objects such as sets is attractive philosophically if it can be made to suffice. As Charles Parsons writes, "It fits the idea that the classes involved are not 'real' independently of the expressions for them." On the other hand substitutional quantification over individuals is not appealing. It is unnatural or absurd to imagine a substitutable singular term for each animal or star or particle. So Parsons has propounded a two-style quantification theory. Rules are provided for the overlaps of the two styles, as well as for the semantics of substitutional quantifications that contain free variables.

Substitutional quantification still faces a difficulty, however, of a different sort: its truth condition can sometimes end up in a vicious circle. Thus consider an existential quantification whose only substitution instances that come out true are ones where the substituted terms are set abstracts that contain quantifiers in turn. Then the substitution instances will contain those new quantifiers, not present in the original quantification whose quantifier we were eliminating. Thus the truth condition may fail to wind down. We could still resort to Tarski's truth definition, but then it is not clear by what right we accounted the quantification substitutional.

This difficulty does not arise if we restrict our set abstraction, or comprehension laws, by permitting membership conditions to contain quantifiers only of lower logical type than the set we are defining. Such a membership condition is called *predicative*. Parsons was explicit on all this.

Predicative set theory accommodates both problems regarding substitutional quantification over sets: both the circularity problem and the question of unspecifiable sets. It is too weak for Cantor's theorem. That's the good news. But the bad news is that it is too weak also for classical analysis, the classical mathematics of real numbers, which is so much a part of the scientist's equipment.

Sanguine spirits there have been, and Solomon Feferman and Hao Wang are two of them today, who hope to show that enough mathematics can be derived for purposes of natural science without going beyond predicative set theory. This would be a momentous result. It would make a clean sweep of the indenumerable infinites and unspecifiable sets, and incidentally it would make substitutional quantification adequate for all the residual abstract objects.

XXVI

MacHale on Boole

Modern logic—*alias* symbolic, *alias* mathematical—surpasses mediaeval logic somewhat as modern physics surpasses mediaeval conceptions of nature. Unlike physics, however, logic scarcely stirred from its mediaeval torpor until the nineteenth century. George Boole, *fl. ca.* 1850, is commonly singled out as the awakener, and this is what his name means to many of us today. Algebraists and computer engineers know his name as the stem of an adjective, for Boolean algebra has figured in their work. It stems from Boole's logic.

We learn from Desmond MacHale's biography that Boole left more to the mathematicians than logic. An early and important contribution was the theory of operators, a philosophically interesting flight of mathematical abstraction. Various operators are familiar to us all: the minus sign, the square-root sign, the operator "log" of logarithms, the "sin," "cos," and "tan" of trigonometry. Now operator theory is a matter of so handling certain operators as to simulate multiplication, as if $-x$, $\sqrt{x}$, $\log x$, and $\sin x$ were products like $5x$. The fiction would be unproductive in these cases, but it works neatly for operators in the differential calculus, short-cutting manipulations and abetting intuition.

This was one of various contributions of Boole's to the differential calculus, on which he produced two books. A related topic on which he wrote an influential book late in his short life was the calculus of finite differences. MacHale sees Boole also as the founder of the mathematical theory of invariants, which somewhat underlay Arthur Cayley's group theory and matrix theory, not to mention Felix Klein's Erlanger program.

Reprinted from *Times Literary Supplement*, London, 1985, p. 767, with permission.

MacHale treats fairly sparingly of mathematics and generously, as we shall see, of the human side. He falls in with the tradition, however, of representing Boole as the father of modern logic. It is a tradition that had its beginnings almost in Boole's day, but we are able nowadays to view matters in a truer perspective.

Boole's logic—*Laws of Thought,* 1854—was an algebra of classes modeled on arithmetic. The product xy of classes x and y was their common part. Their sum, $x + y$, was the aggregate of all members of either, provided that they had none in common. Their difference, $x - y$, comprised the members of x not in y, provided that y was part of x. Zero was the empty class, and 1 was the class of everything.

Leibniz had already been tinkering with symbols to somewhat the same effect before 1700, and in the intervening six generations the idea had been taken up by Bernoulli, Castillon, Holland, Lambert, Ploucquet, Segner, and Tönnies in varying degrees. (Source: C. I. Lewis, 1918.)

Boole's algebra was better than its precursors, but it had its faults. Boole was trapped in arithmetical analogies. The solving of equations for an unknown was for him a major concern. In logic the solution is usually marred by an indefinite residue, reminiscent of the integral calculus. Fractions entered into Boole's solution procedures (x/y, 0/0, 1/0), arithmetical vestiges without straightforward logical interpretation. Boole carried indefinite terms to bizarre lengths when he formulated 'All y are x' as '$y = vx$' and explained v as an indefinite class, because a clear formulation of 'All y are x' was already available in '$y = yx$.' Or, if he wanted to exclude the case where y exhausts x, he could have added '$y \neq x$'; curiously, however, he held to equations and shunned inequalities.

Boole's deference to arithmetical analogy is most conspicuous in his restrictions on logical addition and subtraction: by allowing only mutually exclusive classes as addends and only subclasses as subtrahends, he ensured that the size of the class $x + y$ be the arithmetical sum of the sizes of the classes x and y, and that the size of $x - y$ be their arithmetical difference.

The logically useful versions of $x + y$ and $x - y$ are free of those restrictions; $x - y$ simply comprises all members of x not in y, and $x + y$ comprises everything in x or y or both. This version of $x + y$ had already been entertained before Boole, and it was reinstated by William Stanley Jevons when he improved Boole's logic ten years later. It engenders the symmetries so characteristic of our familiar Boolean algebra. We only then get "$x + x = x$," parallel to Boole's prized "$xx = x$," and we only then get the full pair of De Morgan's laws, namely, that the negation of the class $x + y$ is the negation of x times that of y, and the negation of xy is the negation of x plus that of y. Jevons transmuted Boole's algebra into Boolean algebra.

But MacHale looks askance: "Jevons' attitude toward mathematics was a very narrow one and in fact he never quite got away from the mistaken impression that symbolic algebra is merely a representation of numerical arithmetic" (236). Jevons showed mathematical sensitivity, I protest, in appreciating how Boole was hobbled by numerical analogy.

There is an important and enduring feature of Boolean algebra, however, to which Boole was led by numerical analogy, namely, his *law of development*. It serves to resolve the terms of a Boolean polynomial into their minimal intersections, and it was suggested to Boole by Taylor's theorem in algebra. Happily Boole's unfortunate restriction on logical addition was no obstacle to the law of development.

Boole noted that his algebra of classes could be reinterpreted as a logic of sentences by construing the product, sum, and difference as expressing the compounding of sentences by the conjunctions "and," "or," and "but not." He linked this interpretation to the class interpretation by lamely associating each sentence with a class of moments: the times when it is true. There is a better way of linking the interpretations: we can associate each class with a sentence affirming membership in it.

The Boolean algebra of sentences, when cleared of crotchets and limbered up in sundry ways, is the truth-function logic that occupies the first two weeks of a modern logic course. If my earlier remarks have blurred Boole's father image, the prehistory of truth-function logic blurs it further. The Stoics were pretty well embarked on truth-function logic in the third century B.C., and their ideas were pushed further by Scholastics of the thirteenth and fourteenth centuries. Petrus Hispanus and William of Ockham even stated De Morgan's laws, for sentences. But the nineteenth-century historians misinterpreted these developments, and the nineteenth-century logicians were unaware of them. Łukasiewicz set the record straight in 1935.

Boole's sentence logic and class logic were parallel interpretations, and he kept them apart. His equations in class logic were themselves sentences, but he kept them clear of the sentential operations, never so much as writing the negation of an equation. If instead we apply the one system to the other, we get truth functions of Boolean equations. This makes for a very substantial chapter of modern logic, outrunning Boolean algebra proper; it is tantamount to monadic quantification theory, or the logic of one-place predicates. In his *Begriffsschrift,* 1879, Gottlob Frege covered all that and much more. The whole of quantification theory or predicate logic, monadic and polyadic, sprang full grown from Frege's brow. Influence upon Frege of Boole and his followers is not evident.

General quantification theory is the full technique of "all," "some," and pronominal variables, and it is what distinguishes logic's modern estate. Charles Sanders Peirce arrived at it independently four years after Frege. Peirce's work did indeed take off from that of Boole, Augustus De Morgan, and Jevons. Ernst Schröder and Giuseppe Peano built in turn on Peirce's work, while Frege's continued independently and unheeded.

The avenue from Boole through Peirce to the present is one of continuous development, and this, if anything, is the justification for dating modern logic from Boole; for there had been no comparable influence on Boole from his more primitive antecedents. But logic became a substantial branch of mathematics only with the emergence of general quantification theory at the hands of Frege and Peirce. I date modern logic from there.

Frege got there first. His initial and succeeding contributions were richer and more refined, moreover, than any other logical work until the present century, when the current from Boole through Peirce and the current from Frege converged. Thus I have long hailed Frege as the founder of modern logic, and viewed Boole, De Morgan, and Jevons as forerunners. John Venn and Lewis Carroll also belong back with them, though coming on the scene only after the great event.

The differences concerned here are vast. Monadic quantification theory, though transcending Boole's logic, cannot cope with inferences that depend essentially on relations, as opposed to classes; it cannot derive "Heads of horses are heads of animals" from "Horses are animals," to cite De Morgan's example. Moreover, monadic quantification theory is meager enough to admit of a complete algorithm; that is, formulas can be mechanically checked for validity (Löwenheim, 1915). However, general quantification theory takes relational reasoning in its stride, and that is where true logical complexity lurks. Like other rich branches of mathematics, it is demonstrably insusceptible of a complete algorithm. (Turing, 1938; Church, 1936). The escarpment between what I am calling modern logic and what went before is bold indeed.

MacHale does more than justice to Boolean algebra: "Within mathematics and logic the Boolean algebra . . . encompasses and unifies such topics and concepts as sets, binary numbers, truth tables, probability spaces, syllogisms, two-state systems, electronic circuits and computer technology. Wittingly or unwittingly, Boole had discovered a new kind of mathematics—a kind of mathematics suitable for, and indeed essential for, computers, information storage and retrieval, and a wide range . . ." (136). He quotes Garrett Birkhoff in a similar if more restrained vein.

In the case of electric circuits the debt to Boolean algebra is clear enough: Claude Shannon's correlation of electric circuits with Boolean polynomials or truth functions enables engineers to simplify circuits by simplifying the polynomials.[1] Computer programming is likewise beholden to Boolean algebra, as to further reaches of logic. But much of what MacHale ascribes to Boolean algebra is just the perennial service of our ubiquitous "and," "or," and "not," available independently of the codification of those three particles under the name of Boolean algebra.

The thriving field of abstract algebra developed largely from Boole's work, first in the theory of invariants and then in logic. Boolean algebra lives on as a handy specimen for abstract algebraists, being so simple a structure and so easily modeled. Ironically, its very familiarity in those circles led ill-informed mathematicians to belittle modern logic as a trivial pursuit, unaware as they were of the logical edifice to which Boolean algebra is the merest vestibule.

There was more in Boole's *Laws of Thought*. There was a probability calculus, which fitted neatly with his logic. Just as 0, 1, and $1 - x$ in his logic were the empty class, the universe, and the negation or complement of the class x, so in probability theory they were impossibility, certainty, and the probability complementary to the probability x. Sums and products fell nicely into place as compounded probabilities. Much of the book, moreover, is given over to inconclusive psychological generalities; for the declared overall purpose was an analysis of rational thinking.

[1] See below, pp. 263f.

So much for science, in which I have strayed widely from MacHale's report. The rest is history.

Boole was born of poor and honest parents in Lincoln in 1815. His father was a shoemaker and an earnest student of science, mathematics, and languages. Thus encouraged, young George was a voracious reader of science, history, fiction, and poetry. He had vigorous schooling, strong in Latin and Greek, and became a schoolmaster. The need of supporting his parents and sisters, after his father became incapacitated, precluded a university education. He developed strong ideas on education and at length established a school of his own.

From boyhood onward he wrote verse. He published five stanzas of translation from the Greek that seemed too good for a boy of fourteen, and was consequently accused of fraud. A vitriolic exchange ensued in the newspaper between able young Boole and his unjust accuser, continuing longer than one could wish. It was not Boole's last involvement in hostile exchanges.

MacHale presents ample samples of Boole's early and late verse and quotes the critic and poet Seán Lucy at length to supplement his own critical judgment of them. They are decidedly competent, sometimes successfully lyrical, often sentimental, usually moralistic and religious. Boole was much concerned with religion and came near to choosing the career of Protestant minister. There is a chapter on theology in *Laws of Thought*. He was active in civic affairs and organizations, and his addresses on public occasions have the ring of sermons.

In 1849 he moved to Ireland as professor of mathematics at the newly established Queen's College in Cork. The president of the college got on badly with some of the professors, and Boole was impelled by his sense of righteousness to take the lead in the dispute. There ensued, again, a scandalous exchange in the newspaper, and a royal inquiry. Otherwise his fifteen years at Cork were successful, productive, rich in honors, and marked by a happy and prolific marriage to Mary Everest, niece of the eponym of the celebrated mountain. Boole sickened and died at the age of forty-nine.

Over the years he conferred and corresponded frequently with learned contemporaries, especially Cayley and De Morgan. MacHale provides biographical sketches of these and a fascinating account of Boole's widow, whose collected works fill four volumes. She was learned, opinionated, eccentric, religious, and something of a mystic. She espoused homeopathic medicine and dabbled in mesmerism.

We are given an impressive record also of Boole's five daughters and their husbands and progeny to the fourth and current generation. They include three mathematicians of some distinction, the Marxist biologist Howard Everest Hinton, and the physicist Sir Geoffrey Ingram Taylor. The best known of the clan was Boole's youngest daughter, Ethel Lilian Voynich. Her long and adventurous life, 1864–1960, peaked in a spectacularly successful novel, *The Gadfly*. We are told that it has sold five million copies in the Soviet Union alone, and has been translated into thirty-odd languages.

XXVII

Peirce's Logic

If we conceive of time multidimensionally, and then limit our attention to a single strand of it, we can trace out a chain of development of logic from Boole up through De Morgan, Mitchell, Peirce, Schröder, Peano, Russell, and Whitehead, to logic in its modern estate. Where the inception of mathematical logic comes in this chain is in 1883, when quantification becomes clearly articulated by C. S. Peirce. Even the terms 'quantifier' and 'quantification,' thus applied, are his.

However, real time is linear. In real time the publication of Gottlob Frege's little monograph the *Begriffsschrift* in 1879 was when the predicate calculus emerged, complete with quantification. It emerged full grown from Frege's brow, four years before it was achieved by Peirce.

Frege scooped Peirce in quantification, he scooped Richard Dedekind and Peirce in the theory of chains, and later he scooped Giuseppe Peano in class abstraction and Alonzo Church in function abstraction. But the *Begriffsschrift* was scarcely noticed except for an unappreciative review by Ernst Schröder. Frege's important *Grundlagen der Arithmetik* of 1884 and *Grundgesetze der Arithmetik* of 1893 fared little better. The three logic volumes of Peirce's papers contain no mention of Frege, to judge from the indices.

It is not until Alfred North Whitehead and Bertrand Russell's great *Principia Mathematica,* 1910–1913, that Frege's influence perceptibly enters the mainstream. Even here there is less explicit

---

Presented in a symposium at Harvard, September 1989, celebrating the sesquicentenary of Charles Sanders Peirce's birth. It will presumably appear in the eventual symposium volume, along with two opening paragraphs and four toward the end that I am omitting because of coverage by XXVI and XXVIII.

borrowing than unwitting duplication of effort. Moreover the austere and unwavering formalism that was characteristic already of the *Begriffsschrift,* and has proved indispensable nowadays in computer theory, proof theory, and the philosophy of mathematics, was not recaptured even in *Principia Mathematica.*

It was in 1939, when I was preparing historical inserts for my otherwise completed book *Mathematical Logic,* that I came fully to appreciate Frege's firsts. I could not find a copy of the *Begriffsschrift,* but some faithful notices by P. E. B. Jourdain were good secondary sources. I then proceeded to tout Frege as the father of modern logic.

But it remains instructive to trace the slightly subsequent and independent emergence of quantification through Peirce's writings. Frege affords no such genetic insight, since quantification is already full fledged in his maiden publication. In an important sense, moreover, Peirce and not Frege was indeed the founding father; for Peirce's influence was continuous through Schröder's work, with side channels into Peano, culminating in *Principia Mathematica.* Frege had been a voice crying in the wilderness.

To begin with, in 1867 (3.20–.41)[1] Peirce modified George Boole's logical algebra into what we now call Boolean algebra. It was a needed rectification, but anticipated by W. S. Jevons in 1864. In 1870 Peirce followed up with a notable seventy-page monograph, "A notation for the logic of relatives" (3.45–.149), in which he transformed Augustus De Morgan's relation logic, a haphazard affair, into something foreshadowing the smooth algebra of relations in *Principia Mathematica.* An unproductive preoccupation of Boole's continues to dominate much of this monograph, namely the procrustean forcing of analogies with themes and theorems of classical mathematics. But what is especially interesting in this monograph is Peirce's atomistic approach to relations as sums or aggregates of what he called simple relatives—what we may think of as ordered pairs (or triples or quadruples as the case may be). It was this feature that was destined to evolve into quantification through Peirce's writings of ten to thirteen years later.

As just noted, he handled relations, or relatives, as sums or aggregates of simple relatives. "All right, which is it: sums or aggregates?" That is our natural response, but it is anachronistic. A relation, we say, is a class of ordered pairs (or triples, etc.), and

[1] Numerical references are to *Collected Papers.*

the question is whether to see Peirce's so-called simple relative as an ordered pair or as the unit class of an ordered pair. The question is anachronistic because the idea of a unit class seems not to have emerged until 1890 in a paper by Peano. It will not matter which way we think of Peirce's simple relatives.

Another distinction that calls for a passing gesture, if only of dismissal, is that between relations and relatives. We talk nowadays of relations as against properties; Peirce, De Morgan, and their predecessors talked of relative terms—'father of'—as against absolute terms such as 'house' or indeed 'father'. The relative term denoted not the pairs but the bearers of the relation, *as bearing* it. This 'as' is vague and unproductive. Nothing will be lost by taking the relatives as relations, classes of pairs.

Peirce went on to draw uninteresting distinctions galore, for he made a hobby early and late of taxonomic terminology. We have self-relatives, aliorelatives, cyclic relatives, equiparants, disquiparants, concurrents, opponents, and copulatives.

Peirce's atomistic approach to relations was evidently meant merely to facilitate the exposition and study of the operations of relation algebra, such as converse, relative product, and cross-product, with no inkling that it would evolve into quantification. He rightly criticized a fumbling attempt by Boole to meet the needs of existence statements by weaving an indefinite singular term 'something' into the algebra of logic, but then Peirce succumbs to a similar attempt himself (3.73).

In the last third (3.214–.251) of the long article "On the algebra of logic" in the *American Journal of Mathematics* of 1880, Peirce gets back to simple relatives, which he now calls individual relatives. Confusingly, he now puts his old term 'simple relative' to an opposite use: the complement of an individual relative. The pair of Abraham and Isaac is an individual relative; the sum or class of all pairs except that one he now calls a simple relative.

He adopts the Greek capital letters 'Σ' and 'Π' from their familiar use in mathematics, where they express summation and productation over a class of numbers. Subscripts are appended, as usual, as indices of summation and productation. Peirce uses the notation for logical sums and products of relatives. Any relation, say the father-son relation, is the logical sum or union of all its component individual relatives, and the logical product, or intersection, of all the corresponding simple relatives. In this adoption of 'Σ' and 'Π', with appended indices, Peirce took another significant step toward quantification. Still, for him at the time it was just a means of further streamlining and generalizing his algebraic manipulation of relations.

The device recurs in a short paper of 1882, "Brief description of the logic of relatives" (3.306–322), perhaps privately printed. The paper is obscure, but comes no closer to quantification. A year later, however, in "The logic of relatives" (3.328–.358), quantification emerges. The paper appeared in a volume by Johns Hopkins philosophers, 1883, edited by Peirce.

Here we may think of all individuals as arbitrarily numbered, and we may think of l_{ij} as 1 or 0 according as person number i does or does not love person j. Then $\Sigma_j l_{ij}$ will be a number, a strictly arithmetical sum of ones and zeroes: a one for each person whom person number i loves. So $\Sigma_j l_{ij}$ is how many people person number i loves. So $\Sigma_j l_{ij} > 0$ if and only if person number i loves some people. Quantification dawns.

Now let us get 'Π', productation, into the act. What of the product $\Pi_i \Sigma_j l_{ij}$? It will be $\Sigma_j l_{1j}$ times $\Sigma_j l_{2j}$ times $\Sigma_j l_{3j}$ times etc.—hence how many the first person loves times how many the second person loves times etc. The product of all these numbers will be large if there are no misanthropes, but a single misanthrope would reduce the whole product to 0. Conclusion: $\Pi_i \Sigma_j l_{ij} > 0$ if and only if everyone loves somebody or other. Quantification is running on both cylinders.

We can leave the '>0' tacit, Peirce observed (3.351–.354), and read '$\Pi_i \Sigma_j l_{ij}$' no longer as a number but simply as 'For all i, for some j, i loves j'. The variables cease to refer to numbers and come to refer directly, in this case, to persons. The 'Π' and 'Σ' come then no longer to express arithmetical product and sum of numbers, nor even logical product and sum of classes, but direct quantification over, in this case, persons.

The example hinged on a two-place predicate, 'loves.' Predicates of one and many places fare similarly, and indeed open sentences generally, of whatever form and however many variables. This becomes explicit in a paper of 1885. Our full, familiar quantification is then at hand.

I see in the Peirce story a fascinating interplay of quest and serendipity. Already in 1870, in his criticism of Boole's treatment of 'something', Peirce showed awareness of the inadequacy of logical theory in matters of 'some' and 'all'. But the successive innovations that led him at last to quantification were not laid out with that happy ending in mind. First he atomized relatives, next he imported 'Σ' and 'Π' to express logical sums and products, and finally he restored 'Σ' and 'Π' to their numerical use, reckoning up the numbers of lovers and loved ones. These two magic letters ended up as the signs of quantification, and they continued in that use through the writings of Schröder and his followers, as a fossil record of its evolution. They have turned up as late as 1940, though superseded in most quarters by notations of Peano and *Principia Mathematica* and subsequent variants.

Actually the two symbols are appropriate for quantification also apart from this erratic history. If in the Boolean tradition we think of the alternation of sentences as logical addition, and of conjunction as logical multiplication, then existential and universal quantification are indeed aptly rendered as logical summation and productation, Σ and Π. Such could, one feels in retrospect, have even been the simple history of quantification, but it was not.

The state of the art at the time of Peirce's breakthrough—Frege apart—is instructively reflected in a paper by O. H. Mitchell in that same Johns Hopkins volume of 1883. Like Peirce as of that and previous years, Mitchell focuses on relatives, primarily dyadic ones, rather than on open sentences in general. He has quantifiers of a sort, universal and existential, but they enjoy no flexibility of scope. There consequently remains the crucial problem of distinguishing between everyone's loving somebody or other and there being someone loved by all. He copes with it lamely by adopting two kinds of existential quantifier, one of which implies identity of the object from case to case. His quantifiers submit poorly to any nesting.

Quantification as we know it goes fairly smoothly into ordinary language, scope and all. We say on the one hand that everybody loves somebody, and on the other hand that somebody is loved by everybody, and we are apt to feel that the mere order of these verbal quantifiers helps to settle the vital distinction of scope. Granted, we touch up our words to stress the contrast: 'Everybody loves somebody *or other*' versus 'Somebody is loved by *all*.' But in the complacency of our hindsight we have trouble imagining how people—logicians, even—a scant century ago could fail to see that mere grammatical scope, at least hinted by word order, is all it takes to make the difference. I draw two morals: that predicate logic is instructive, and that history is broadening.

Quantification made its way into the logic literature again after

Peirce by another route, and I find it interesting to contrast the two lines of thought: Peirce's and Peano's. As I said, there is no tracing the evolution of quantification in Frege's mind; but we can trace it in Peano's.

Boolean algebra at its most primitive readily expresses the non emptiness and the all-inclusiveness of a class α: thus $\alpha \neq \Lambda$ and $\alpha = V$. Invent class abstraction, then, '$\{x: Fx\}$', and you have quantification.

$$\exists x Fx \equiv \{x: Fx\} \neq \Lambda,$$

$$\forall x Fx \equiv \{x: Fx\} = V.$$

This was how Peano came to quantification in 1888. It was a decade when quantification was breaking out all over. Peano's way into quantification was an obvious way, but it had not been open to Peirce, for Peirce did not have class abstraction. Frege did not have it either, when he achieved quantification by pure unimplemented thought in 1879. He introduced abstraction only in 1884, and Peano came out with it independently, it would seem, in 1888. Peano was meticulous with his references and credits, but there were none to Frege.

We have seen two routes to quantification. One, Peirce's, was through the summation and productation operators of arithmetic. The other, Peano's, was through the 'such that' construction. This is the shorter route from ordinary language. It is remarkable that the key to it, the abstraction operator, made its way into mathematical logic only after both Frege and Peirce had arrived at quantification.

Such is my story of quantification. Of Peirce's lesser efforts in logic, one worth mentioning is his long-unpublished anticipation of Sheffer's stroke. He pointed out in a manuscript of about 1880 (4.12) that all the truth functions can be generated from 'neither-nor,' and in 1902 he noted further (4.264) that the function 'not both' would serve as well.

Another anticipation on Peirce's part, noted by Arthur Burks, was his anticipation of Claude Shannon's discovery in 1938 of a correspondence between truth functions and electric circuits. Picture two terminals and two intervening switches. If the switches are connected in parallel, the current is on just in case the one switch *or* the other is closed. If they are connected in series, the current is on just in case the one *and* the other is closed. Such are the roles of alternation and conjunction. As for negation, it answers to the throwing of a switch. Thanks to the resulting correspondence between truth-functional formulas and complicated circuits, the logical techniques for reducing complicated truth-functional formulas to simplest equivalents afforded a cheap way of designing the simplest possible electric circuits for complicated purposes. Minimization of complex truth-functional formulas can itself prove more laborious than one would expect, but electrical engineers found it worthwhile to compile and publish the simplest equivalents of the 65,536 truth functions of four variables. All this happened pursuant on Shannon's discovery. Peirce's anticipation decades earlier had had little notice, for complex circuits had not as yet played a role in industry.

The logical enterprise to which Peirce devoted most attention and attached most importance in later years was his evolving system of "entitative" or "existential" graphs (1897, 1903). It is a complex and cumbersome apparatus, and seems anachronistic at so late a date, when Peano's transparent and efficient logical notation was already inspiring Whitehead and Russell to embark on *Principia Mathematica* and Peirce's equally efficient notation of 'Σ' and 'Π' had long since inspired Schröder.

The conventions governing Peirce's graphs are somewhat as follows. All formulas written are affirmed, unless encircled by a closed loop. The loop denies that all the formulas within it are true; it affirms that there is a falsehood somewhere within it. So an empty loop is itself a flat falsehood, professing as it does to encircle a falsehood when in fact it encircles nothing. Accordingly a loop encircling an empty loop forms a logical truth. Attaching a dash or open curve to a predicate says something fulfills the predicate; hence existential quantification. Attaching that existential curve to two predicates, or branching it to touch three or more, says that something fulfills them all. The curve thus figures as an existential quantifier and bound variable, and indeed graphically as the bond itself. By encircling then we can get negations of existential quantification, hence universal negative quantifications.

There is no way in this system of expressing an open sentence in isolation, since we have only the predicates and the existential curves. A consequence is that there is no way of negating an open sentence before existentially quantifying it. We must approach the existential negative rather as a negated universal, after getting the universal somehow from scratch. Peirce gets it, and eventually the various complex nestings of universal and existential quantifiers, by sundry conventions governing the intersecting of the existential curves with the loops of negation.

His graphs do suffice in the end to depict any closed formula of first-order predicate logic, including identity. Peirce formulates rules of proof, some of which are far from obvious. It is interesting to think them through for validity, since the system diverges so substantially from our familiar patterns of formulation and proof. One does find them valid, and Don Roberts has gone on to provide a completeness proof.

XXVIII

Peano as Logician

Giuseppe Peano's first significant contribution to the infant science of mathematical logic appeared in 1888, in the introductory pages of his book *Calcolo geometrico.* One of the novelties of that short piece was an innovation of notation—a slight matter in itself, but of lasting influence. I must fill in the background.

Around 1850, George Boole developed an elementary little algebra of terms, or classes, in close analogy to the ordinary algebra of numbers. He used the notations of addition and multiplication to express the union and intersection of classes, and the numerals '0' and '1' for the empty class and the universe. For the union of two classes, or logical sum, he required the classes to be mutually exclusive—simply in order to enhance the parallelism with arithmetical addition. This was a foolish restriction, and was dropped by succeeding logicians—W. Stanley Jevons, Charles Sanders Peirce, Ernst Schröder, John Venn. All these logicians still followed Boole, however, in writing their symbolic logic in arithmetical notation. It was left to Peano, in 1888, to cut the arithmetical leading strings and adopt distinctive logical signs. His reason was that he wanted to apply logic to arithmetic, and accordingly needed to distinguish the notations to avoid confusion. His signs for the intersection and union of classes became standard in set theory and have continued so to this day: $x \cap y$ and $x \cup y$.

This paper was presented in October 1982 at a conference at the Accademia delle Scienzie in Turin and published in 1986 in their proceedings, *Celebrazione in memoria di Giuseppe Peano,* by the mathematics department of the University of Turin. It was reprinted with emendations in *History and Philosophy of Logic,* Volume 8, 1987. I am grateful to both publishers for permitting my present use of it; also to Warren Goldfarb and Ivor Grattan-Guinness for correcting me on a historical point, and to the latter also for bibliographical help.

Another novelty of those introductory pages of the *Calcolo geometrico* was Peano's adoption of an explicit notation of class abstraction. Given an equation in 'x', he would express the class of the roots of the equation by writing the variable 'x', a colon, and the equation. More generally, 'x' followed by a colon and any formula in 'x' constituted a name of the class of all objects satisfying the formula. Thus x: Fx was the class of all the values of 'x' that fulfill the condition 'Fx'. These expressions have a modern look if we put curly brackets around them; they are class abstracts in the current notation of set theory.

The 'x' of class abstraction is a bound variable, and Peano stressed its distinctive status in this respect. He generalized his notation of class abstraction to polyadic cases, prefixing '(x, y):', '(x, y, z):', etc. for the abstraction of relations. By means of class abstraction he expressed quantification, both universal and existential. He rendered the universal quantification '$\forall x\ Fx$' as 'x: $Fx = ●$' and the existential quantification '$\exists x\ Fx$' as 'x: $Fx \neq ○$', ● being the universe and ○ the empty class.

Gottlob Frege had already severed ties with arithmetic and propounded a distinctive notation for logic in his *Begriffsschrift* of 1879. A bizarre two-dimensional notation it was, and typographically forbidding. Ernst Schröder reviewed the work promptly, and criticized Frege for breaking a thirty-year tradition of arithmetical notation in logic. Peano, however, evidently remained unaware of these writings for ten years. In the *Begriffsschrift* Frege also showed full appreciation of the status of what we now call bound variables. Peano, however, was still the pioneer in class abstraction. Frege's bound variables figured directly in quantification, unmediated by class abstraction.

Peano's revised notation for logic was meant to clear the way, as I said, for the application of logic to arithmetic. The application was realized the very next year, 1889, in Peano's *Arithmetices principia.* Here the foundations of the arithmetic of natural numbers are laid down as explicit axioms, expressed in arithmetical and logical symbols, and the theorems are derived by explicit formal proofs. The impact of this monograph is attested by the phrase 'Peano's axioms', so familiar down the decades despite Peano's subsequent discovery and acknowledgment (1896, p. 243) that he had been anticipated by Richard Dedekind.

This set of axioms has come to play a more prominent role than ever in consequence of Kurt Gödel's great incompleteness theorem of 1931. What Gödel proved is that elementary number theory, which is to say the first-order arithmetic of natural numbers, does not admit of a complete proof procedure. For many purposes in proof theory and model theory and abstract algebra the need consequently arises to mark out a specific subclass of arithmetical truths that do cohere as a deductive system; and the subclass chosen is the so-called Peano arithmetic, defined by the Peano axioms.

A distinction that is drawn conspicuously in *Arithmetices principia,* and has since dominated set theory, is the distinction between membership and inclusion. I must lead up to it with some history.

In the mediaeval tradition, 'Socrates is mortal' was treated as on a par with 'Men are mortal'. Each of these sentences subsumed one term, 'Socrates' or 'men', under another term, 'mortal'. It just happened that the term 'men' was true of many individuals and 'Socrates' was true of only one. In his *Begriffsschrift* of 1879, Frege handled the two cases distinctively. He wrote 'Fx' to represent any sentence about an object x, for instance 'Socrates is mortal', where x is Socrates. On the other hand he recognized 'Men are mortal' as a universally quantified conditional, '$Gx \supset_x Fx$': everything is such that, if it is a man, it is mortal. I have translated Frege's notation for quantification and the conditional, but the 'Fx' and 'Gx' are his.

Peano, unaware of Frege's work, drew the same distinction independently in *Arithmetices principia,* but in another form. The notation 'Fx', for an arbitrary sentence about x, was never Peano's: I use it in these pages in expounding Peano, but it is my imposition. Peano wrote '$x \in y$' rather than 'Fx', and thought of y as a class. 'Socrates is mortal' is '$x \in y$', 'x is a *member* of y', where x is Socrates and y is the class of mortals. But 'Men are mortal' is an inclusion, '$z \supset y$', where both z and y are classes, that of men and that of mortals.

Peano took epsilon as his symbol for membership because it is the initial of the Greek singular copula 'ἐστί, which is the 'is' of 'Socrates is mortal'. It has figured as the basic symbol in set theory ever since. In most systems of set theory it suffices as the only distinctive symbol, over and above the logical notations for quantification and the truth functions.

Peano remained unaware at that time of the notion of unit classes, classes with single members. Formula 56 in *Arithmetices principia* conflates the unit class with its member.[1] The notion of unit classes seems to have first become explicit in his "Démonstration de l'integrabilité des équations différentielles ordinaires," 1890.

It becomes imperative to distinguish between a unit class and its member when the member is itself a class. For instance the empty class has no members, whereas its unit class has one. The class of the Apostles or the Muses or the months has twelve members, whereas its unit class has one. Still, no such distinction is forced on us when the member is an individual. There has been no call to affirm or deny membership in an individual, so no conflict arises if we identify the individual with its unit class and agree to say thereafter that the individual does indeed have one member, namely, itself. The fashion has been, however, to distinguish unit classes from their members in all cases. The distinction is mandatory where the members are classes of many members or none, so, for uniformity, it has been maintained across the board.

Yet there are important advantages in adhering to the contrary course: in refusing to distinguish a unit class from its member when the member is an individual. The advantage is going to take some explaining, and I must ask you to bear with me. It has to do with making the two-place predicable epsilon suffice as the sole primitive term of set theory.

Individuals, if seen as distinct from their unit classes, are presumably like the empty class in having no members. Then how, in terms of epsilon, are they to be distinguished from the empty class? Either we must adopt an additional undefined predicable for the purpose, to be given the meaning 'is an individual' or perhaps 'is the empty class', or else we must adopt an undefined name 'Λ' designating the empty class, or else we must admit two styles of bound variables, one style for classes and one for individuals. The law of extensionality, so central to set theory, would play havoc with individuals unless some such uneconomical provision were made. It is the law that

$$x \in y \,.\!\equiv_x.\, x \in z \,:\supset.\, y = z.$$

If y and z have no members, then the antecedent in this conditional is vacuously true, implying that $y = z$. Hence individuals have to

[1] This observation is due to van Heijenoort, p. 84.

be explicitly exempted from this law, in one way or another, lest they all get identified with one another and with the empty class. Individuals, as distinct from the empty class, would disappear.

It became customary, therefore, for set-theorists to follow one or another of the three uneconomical alternatives above, usually in an implicit and informal way, and to forgo the economy of a single constant, epsilon, and a single style of variables. A fourth and more drastic alternative was adopted by Abraham Fraenkel in 1928: that of leaving the principle of extensionality unprotected and just accepting the consequence: that there be no individuals at all, as distinct from the empty class. This was the birth of *pure* set theory: set theory without individuals. There was the empty class, its unit class, the class of these two, and so on; also infinite classes of these classes, and so on. A full-strength set theory is forthcoming, but it stays idly aloof from mundane applications; it cannot be embedded in non-set-theoretic contexts without restoring individuals, contrary to the unrestricted law of extensionality.

From 1936 onward I have urged the advantage of reverting halfway to Peano's early attitude, and letting individuals be identical with their unit classes. The trouble over the law of extensionality is then resolved; individuals come to differ from the empty class in having members, namely themselves, and to differ from one another in having different members, namely themselves. No ill consequences ensue, for classes of many members or none continue to be distinct from their unit classes, and their unit classes in turn continue to be distinct from their own unit classes. Set theory can thenceforward be pursued with homogeneous variables and no primitive term but epsilon. Individuality becomes definable: x is an individual if and only if $x = y{:}(y = x)$. Whether there are individuals, and how many, can still be left open.

Peano was recognizing the unit class by 1897, and rendering it ιx. He chose iota as the initial of 'ίσος, 'same'; for ιx is the class of whatever is the same as x. From 1894 onward he had also been using an overline to mark the inverse of an operation; so, applying this to his iota, he came out with $\bar{\iota} y$ for the sole member of y. In 1899 he switched to a more graphic notation for inversion, consisting in inversion of the sign itself; so the sole member of y came to be rendered ℩y. Thus $x =$ ℩ιx and ι℩$y = y$. Frege had a symbol for sole member already in 1893, but Peano's inverted iota is more expressive, and it comes down to us in the standard notation of singular description.

Peano applied his inversion strategy likewise to his epsilon. Membership and class abstraction are mutual inverses, cancelling each other:

$$x \in x{:}Fx \mathrel{.{\equiv}} Fx, \qquad x{:}(x \in y) = y.$$

Accordingly, applying his overline of inversion, he took to rewriting his abstraction prefix '$x{:}$' as '$\overline{x \in}$'. From 1898 onward, expressing inversion by inversion, he wrote it as '$x \ni$'; thus '$x \ni Fx$'.

Peano's sign for class inclusion, '$\supset$', was itself a result of expressing inversion by inversion. J. D. Gergonne had chosen 'C' as the initial of 'contains' or its cognates in Romance languages, and then Peano inverted it for 'is contained in'. In Whitehead and Russell's *Principia Mathematica* the sign got inverted back again and distorted, appearing as '$\subset$' and becoming the standard sign for inclusion to this day in set theory. The reinversion and distortion are due to the analogy of the sign '$<$' of arithmetic.

Peano's neat exploitation of inverses reflects his sensitivity to the inner logic of natural language. Another speaker will treat of Peano on language, but I would mention one characteristic observation that Peano made in his "Algebra de grammatica." He observed that the copula and the present participial ending are mutual inverses; 'es' is inverse to '-ente'. Thus *arde* = *es ardente*. The language here is Interlingua, the transparent neutral Romance language of Peano's devising.

Despite his sensitivity to linguistic structure, Peano seems not to have appreciated the distinction stressed by John Stuart Mill between concrete general and abstract singular terms. It is the difference between the predicable 'man', or 'is a man', or 'human', and the class name 'mankind'. Ontologically the distinction is vital. The general term or predicable denotes each man but makes no reference to a class, whereas the singular term or name postulates a class, an abstract object. Peano, however, treated his epsilon indifferently as a two-place predicable of class membership belonging between two singular terms or variables, and as an innocent copula joining a singular term with a general term. He used it regularly before singular terms and variables, but he read it as a mere copula 'is', 'est', 'è', 'ἐστί.

The same ambiguity invested his abstraction prefix '$x{:}$' or '$x \ni$', as well it might, the inverted epsilon being the inverse of epsilon. I have been calling the abstraction expression a class abstract, hence a class name, an abstract singular term. By allowing himself to substitute the expression for variables, Peano accounted it a class name beyond peradventure. Still, when epsilon is given the reading of an innocent copula and is followed by an abstraction expression, the abstraction expression takes on the status rather of an innocent general term, a predicable, indeed a relative clause of the 'such that' form; '$y \in x \ni Fx$' says that y is an x such that Fx, y is an x that does such and such, and there is no presumption of a class. Peano was reading his abstraction expression in this way when he pronounced his inverted epsilon as 'such that' ('tel que').

He showed no awareness of this duality, and it has come down to us oddly in later years. His epsilon now figures in set theory unequivocally as the two-place predicable of class membership. His early notation of abstraction, modified only to the extent of the curly brackets, figures in set theory unequivocally as class abstraction. His inverted epsilon, however, which was his later symbol of abstraction, has gone the other way. For decades now it had been used informally as shorthand for 'such that', innocent of reference to an abstract object. The inverted epsilon and its right-side-up mate have been divorced.

Peano's early symbol for the empty class, an empty circle, gave way the very next year to the capital lambda, 'Λ'. The companion symbol for the universe, 'V', soon followed. Both symbols have come down from Peano to latter-day logic through Whitehead and Russell's *Principia Mathematica.* The 'V' is invariably used today for the universe, and the 'Λ' is one of two customary signs for the empty class. Peano's early way of expressing universal and existential quantification, namely by equating the appropriate class abstract to the universe and by disequating it to the empty class, was also soon superseded in Peano's writings by another style. In the 1894 introduction to the *Formulaire de mathématiques* we find his universally quantified conditional sign, '$\supset_x$'. It is instructive to reflect that from then on this and the universally quantified biconditional sign '$\equiv_x$' were the only uses Peano saw fit to make of universal quantification. After all, we never do seem to want universal quantification in practical application except over a domain that has been clearly limited either by the antecedent of a conditional or biconditional or by a prior stipulation of subject matter.

By 1897, in his "Studii di logica matematica," we find Peano's enduring latter-day way of expressing existential quantification:

by prefixing '∃' to the appropriate class abstract. Thus quantification, existential as well as universal, has ceased to be expressed by means of equations. The dominance of equations has passed, and therewith the last vestige of arithmetical analogy.

Peano's '∃' was a one-place general term or predicable, affirming nonemptiness. '$\exists y$' meant that y had members. Peano's resulting notation for existential quantification, '$\exists(x \ni Fx)$', was adopted by Russell in the modified form '$(\exists x)Fx$'. Thus '∃' ceased to be a term and class abstraction ceased to be involved in the quantification. '$(\exists x)$' became rather a single variable-binding operator coordinate grammatically with Peano's variable-binding prefix '$x \ni$' of class abstraction. Russell adopted Peano's inverted iota subject to a parallel modification. It had been an operator on singular terms: ιy was the sole member of y. Thus, applied to a class abstract, it produced a singular description '$\iota(x \ni Fx)$', 'the x such that Fx'. Russell rewrote the description as '$(\iota x)Fx$', so that again class abstraction ceased to be involved, and the combination '(ιx)' became a single variable-binding operator of singular description. The resulting notations for existential quantification and singular description carried over into Whitehead and Russell's *Principia Mathematica* and continue to prevail today. For uniformity with existential quantification, Russell followed Frege in adopting also a variable-binding prefix for universal quantification; and in one form or another this practice likewise still prevails.

The dissociation of quantification and description from class abstraction has recommended itself on ontological grounds. Quantification and description are accessible to first-order logic and should not be made to presuppose classes. Now these are scruples that I heartily share, but there is more to be said. For consider again the equivocal status of the abstraction notation: as a class name and as an innocent 'such that' clause, essentially a relative clause. These relative clauses are only complex general terms, complex predicables. They are a convenient way of packaging what a sentence says about an object. What the sentence

I saw Tom but he did not see me

says about Tom is isolated in the relative clause

whom I saw but who did not see me

or

x such that I saw *x* but *x* did not see me.

Predicate it of Tom and you recover the original sentence. The clause names no abstract entity in its own right; there is no reference to a class or property. Now if we construe the abstraction expression:

$$x \ni (\text{I saw } x. - (x \text{ saw me}))$$

in this innocent way, we can follow Peano and apply his '∃' and '℩' to it with ontological impunity. We can go back to treating description and existential quantification as '$\iota(x \ni Fx)$' and '$\exists(x \ni Fx)$', and, for uniformity, universal quantification as '$\forall(x \ni Fx)$'.

Moreover, there is good reason to do so. The relative clause then becomes, explicitly, the locus of all binding of variables. This is as it should be, for it is in the relative clause that the bound variable does its purely combinatorial job of rearrangement and cross-reference. Generality and uniqueness then become the separate business of the functors '∃', '∀', and '℩', which are attachable to any general terms. The bound variable has nothing to do with generality or uniqueness, except as a means of forming some of the general terms themselves. Another virtue of this approach is the link that it forges with ordinary language. For the linguistic prototype of the bound variable is, as Peano appreciated, the pronoun; more specifically it is the relative pronoun and the pronouns that refer back to the relative pronoun.

Furthermore there is a technical gain, relating to substitution in logical formulas. Substitution for schematic predicate letters is a complex affair, and logicians from Paul Bernays onward have implemented it with auxiliary devices variously known as *Nennformen* and stencils and predicate schemata. If abstraction expressions are brought to bear within elementary logic, they serve this auxiliary purpose perfectly and most naturally. Logicians have shunned this course because of ontological scruples. The scruples dissolve when the abstraction expressions are recognized as relative clauses, general terms, rather than class names. They become term abstracts rather than class abstracts.

One way to pursue this course would be to retain Peano's notation '$x \ni Fx$' for the term abstract, in keeping with the already familiar reading of '∋' as an informal 'such that', and to reserve the latter-day abstraction notation '$\{x: Fx\}$' for the class name. My own preference is deliberately to slip back into Peano's conflation of the concrete general with the abstract singular, and accordingly to use the same abstraction notation for both. I use the latter-day notation because it is current.

To take this course is to allow general terms to do double duty as class names. We know from the antinomies of set theory, such as Russell's paradox, that we cannot extend this privilege to all of them. We do it selectively, thereby selecting from among the various systems of axiomatic set theory. To say that a given term abstract '$\{x: Fx\}$' qualifies as a class name, or in other words that there is such a class, is simply to say:

$$(\exists y)(y = \{x: Fx\}),$$

which is to say:

$$\exists\{y: y = \{x: Fx\}\}.$$

The distinction between term abstracts that qualify as class names and those that do not is just that the former qualify for substitution in the instantiating of quantifications. Classes are values of variables.

This line is attractive philosophically, representing the hypostasis of classes as a hypostasis of designata for general terms. Logic properly so called, first order logic, leaves off and set theory begins just at the point where we first equate an abstract, or indeed any general term, to a variable. Abstracts and other general terms can be substituted only for unquantifiable, schematic predicate letters as long as we stay within logic proper, just as sentences can be substituted only for schematic sentence letters.

Ultimately therefore my only criticism of Peano, on the score of conflation of general with abstract singular, is that he permitted substitution of abstracts for variables indiscriminately and without regard to a separation between logic proper, ontologically innocent, and set theory. We must bear in mind, moreover, that Peano's pioneer work antedated the discovery of the antinomies of set theory. Burali-Forti's paradox emerged only in 1897, and Russell's in 1902. Before that, there was no call to distinguish between membership conditions that determined classes and those that did not.

After Peano and Frege discovered each other, there was some mild rivalry in their public exchanges of criticism. Formal rigor reached a higher pitch in Frege than ever before or for decades after, and it was mainly on points of formal rigor that he criticized Peano. A principal theme in that regard was definition and, in particular, Peano's predilection for conditional definition. For instance Peano would define what it meant for x to be prime, but only on the hypothesis that x is a number. This sort of definition is indeed natural, and quite adequate when the purpose of definition is the usual one of elucidating a new expression; but it has the formal drawback of not enabling us in general to rid a page of all its defined signs in favor of full primitive notation. Definitions in formal systems are best thought of as correlating two languages, one of them economical and the other conveniently redundant, and showing that the economical one is theoretically adequate. Conditional definition does not accomplish this.

Conditional definition plays a crucial role in the case of ιx, or singular description. Peano can define ιx conditionally simply as y, the condition being that $z \in x \,.\!\equiv_z .\, z = y$, and not worry about ιx if x has no members or many. Frege, on the other hand, had to devise an arbitrary interpretation for those waste cases.

By Frege's high standards of formal rigor, we see, Peano's work left something to be desired. Yet Peano's work inspired Russell to standards of rigor and logical explicitness that he, Russell, had not thitherto conceived. Peano excelled all his predecessors, moreover, in the flexibility and perspicuity of his notation. It was adopted by Russell with only incidental modifications, such as I have been noting, and it continued thus into Whitehead and Russell's great *Principia Mathematica,* where it became established as the dominant style.

From the beginning, evidently, Peano was interested in logic as a tool for exploring the foundations of mathematics: witness his *Calcolo geometrico,* 1888, and *Arithmetices principia,* 1889. In view of his interest in the foundations of the arithmetic of natural numbers, it is strange that he did not respond with enthusiasm to Frege's reduction of natural numbers to set theory. But he rejected it, protesting, cryptically, that "ils ont des propriétés différentes." Yet in his *Formulario di matematica* over the years he contributed valuably to the construction of the arithmetic of integers, ratios, and real numbers on the basis of that of natural numbers, thereby laying much of the groundwork for the development of these matters in *Principia Mathematica.* As late as 1911 he presented his version of functions as classes of ordered pairs—a version that was missed by *Principia Mathematica* but is now generally adopted in foundational studies. Peano's ideas, like his symbols, continue to do their central and conspicuous work in mathematical logic and the foundations of mathematics. We encounter them at every turn.

XXIX

Free Logic, Description, and Virtual Classes

Quantification theory is home ground for bound variables. Since to be is to be the value of a bound variable, existential considerations are of the essence here. First they obtrude in the law of smaller universes, according to which any formula that is valid for all universes of one size is valid also for all smaller universes except perhaps the empty one. We can blithely apply quantification theory without regard to the limits or extravagance of our universe of discourse, but we must take care that something exist in it.

Existential considerations obtrude into quantification theory again when we use constant singular terms to instantiate quantifications. The move is dependable only if, unlike 'Pegasus', the term designates something.

The first of these two existential presuppositions is affirmed in quantification theory in a schema to the effect that something exists: $\exists x(Fx \supset Fx)$. Critics protest that there being anything is not for pure logic to say. The other existential presupposition is implemented by construing quantification theory as accommodating no terms except those that designate. Critics protest that application of quantification theory is hobbled by this restriction. Quite commonly we want to reason with singular terms whose designation is problematic.

These two objections have motivated *free* logic, in the broad

Written for a symposium held at the Université de Québec in Montreal, March 1994, to celebrate Hugues Leblanc's seventieth birthday. It will perhaps be published concurrently in the proceedings of the symposium.

sense in which the term has been used by Hugues Leblanc and Rolf Schock. It countenances only logical laws that are independent of the requirement that something exist and the requirement that every singular term designate something.

Let us now look more closely at the first issue, that of the empty universe. A basic technique in quantification theory is transformation of a formula in such a way as to bring all its quantifiers out to the beginning *(prenexing)* or, alternatively, to drive every quantifier in so that it governs only clauses in which its variable recurs *(purifying)*. The transformations depend on eight familiar equivalences, called the rules of passage:

(1) $\exists x(p \,.\, Fx) \equiv .\, p \,.\, \exists x\, Fx,$

(2) $\forall x(p \,.\, Fx) \equiv .\, p \,.\, \forall x\, Fx,$

(3) $\exists x(p \vee Fx) \equiv .\, p \vee \exists x\, Fx,$

(4) $\forall x(p \vee Fx) \equiv .\, p \vee \forall x\, Fx,$

(5) $\exists x(p \supset Fx) \equiv .\, p \supset \exists x\, Fx,$

(6) $\forall x(p \supset Fx) \equiv .\, p \supset \forall x\, Fx,$

(7) $\exists x(Fx \supset p) \equiv .\, \forall x\, Fx \supset p,$

(8) $\forall x(Fx \supset p) \equiv .\, \exists x\, Fx \supset p.$

Four of these eight fail for the empty universe. Only (1), (4), (6), and (8) carry over. In practice the resulting obstacle to prenexing and purifying is unacceptable, since we are usually safe in assuming that the universe of discourse with which we are dealing is not empty. In cases where we are not sure of this, we can check for the empty universe in a simple separate move: just mark all universal quantifications true and all existential ones false, in the formula under consideration, and then check the result for truth-functional validity.

Quite apart from practical matters, however, it is interesting to determine just what formulas of quantification theory are valid for all universes including the empty one. (See Paper XXI above.) Then, as Leblanc remarks, we can derive the rest of quantification theory by adding '$\exists x(Fx \supset Fx)$' as a premiss.

Still, the efficient practical course is to set the empty case aside as a separate contingency to be checked swiftly, when it might matter, after reaching tentative conclusions by classical quantification theory. Let me define the classical as comprising as theorems all schemata that are valid in nonempty universes, but contain no identity sign or letters for constant singular terms. Then

I welcome, as an extension of classical quantification theory to singular terms, a *free* extension: one that allows empty terms. This constitutes a free logic in Ermanno Bencivenga's sense—free in its terms—rather than in Leblanc's and Schock's tandem sense, which admits both the empty universe and empty terms.

When working in pure logic, and not in a subject to which the logic is applied, the singular description is a good unifying form within which to organize all singular terms. This does not mean defining descriptions, in Russell's way or otherwise. It just means taking the universal form of singular terms to be '$\iota x\, Fx$,' or briefly 'ιF,' where the inverted iota stands for the words 'the one and only'.

It is sometimes objected that description works only if we have an exclusive feature of the object in mind. Actually this is no restriction. Any singular term yields a purportedly exclusive predicate by combining with identity—thus 'is Socrates', 'is Pegasus'. We just turn the tables by treating this composite predicate as atomic—'socratizes', 'pegasizes'—and then forming the descriptions '$\iota x(x$ socratizes)', '$\iota x(x$ pegasizes)'. Similarly for term functors; thus '$y + z$' becomes '$\iota x\, \Sigma xyz$' where 'Σ' is a three-place predicate of addition: '$x = y + z$'. So we can forget about names and term functors as categories additional to that of singular descriptions. We have to accommodate the descriptions anyway, whether by Russell's method or another. We adopt the convention, in any event, of representing singular terms by simple term letters 'a', 'b', etc. when the context makes no separate use of the insides of the descriptions.

Now a word about Russell's contextual definition of descriptions. The definition can be presented succinctly in two stages. First we define the identity context '$\iota F = x$' as '$\forall y(Fy \equiv .\ y = x)$' and then the general context '$G(\iota F)$' as '$\exists x(Gx\ .\ \iota F = x)$'. The result is indeed a logic of free terms, since a description may or may not designate anything. To say it does is to say that $\exists x(a = x)$, i.e., $\exists x(\iota F = x)$, i.e., $\exists x \forall y(Fy \equiv .\ y = x)$. When the description does not designate, its contexts are declared false by our definition of '$G(\iota F)$'.

The roots of the system, in descriptions, are hidden by the convention of representing the descriptions by term letters, so that the whole looks for all the world like something by Hugues Leblanc. What is gained by its hidden roots is economy: the system stems by uncreative definition and convention from classical quantification theory plus identity, devoid of singular terms. Leblanc's term letters, in contrast, were irreducible additions.

However, the contextual definition on which this economy depended suffers under closer scrutiny. There is a problem of *scope:* how much context to count as the context for purposes of the definition of '$G(\imath F)$'. Thus consider '$\sim H(\imath F)$', 'H' being again a predicate letter. In applying our general definition of '$G(\imath F)$' here, we must decide whether to treat the short context '$H(\imath F)$' or the longer context '$\sim H(\imath F)$' as the '$G(\imath F)$' of the definition. The one choice interprets '$H(\imath F)$' as '$\exists x(Hx \, . \, \imath F = x)$' and hence '$\sim H(\imath F)$' as '$\sim\exists x(Hx \, . \, \imath F = x)$'. The other treats '$\sim H(\imath F)$' outright as '$\exists x(\sim Hx \, . \, \imath F = x)$'. If $\imath F$ does not exist, '$\sim H(\iota F)$' comes out true under the one interpretation and false under the other.

Russell dealt with this ambiguity by introducing prefixes analogous to quantifiers to mark scope. The prefix was a bracketed occurrence of the description—thus '$[\imath F]$'. The two versions of '$\sim$H$(\imath F)$' become '$\sim[\imath F]\, H(\imath F)$' and '$[\imath F] \sim H(\imath F)$'. Then he adopted the convention of leaving the prefix tacit when the scope was minimal. Better to skip the prefixes and just leap to the finish line, settling invariably for the minimal scope, as in effect Russell did. So '$\sim H(\imath F)$' is '$\sim\exists x(Hx \, . \, \imath F = x)$', and true by default unless $\imath F$ exists.

The minimality criterion is the problem. The criterion does not apply to our actual schemata, for we generate valid ones from valid ones by substituting compounds for atoms, thereby disrupting minimalities. The intended minimality is in the unseen sentences, rather, that our formulas depict. If we are using quantification theory to formalize some special discipline, perhaps number theory, set theory, mereology, or Woodger biology, we list our atomic predicates, and then the minimality criterion of scope is straightforward. It is in these enterprises that Russell's contextual definition of description does its job. When quantification theory is applied to otherwise unregimented discourse, however, where so much of its utility lies, minimality makes no sense. An empty term '$\imath F$' or '*a*' may occur in a grammatically atomic clause '*a* is innocent', thereby falsifying that clause, but if we paraphrase the clause as '$\sim$(*a* is guilty)' then what gets falsified is the minimal context '*a* is guilty', so that '$\sim$(*a* is guilty)' comes out true. The minimality criterion of scope fails here for want of a criterion of minimality itself. Paraphrasing disrupts truth values.

For a more broadly applicable treatment of descriptions, then,

I am turned back from Russell to Peano, who first brought descriptions into logic. It was Peano who introduced iota as well as epsilon into logic, both inverted and upright. For him singular description was primitive notation, and my definition of '$\iota F = x$' was for him rather an axiom schema:

$$\iota F = x \; . \equiv \forall y(Fy \equiv . \; y = x).$$

Peano expressed the existence condition as '$\exists x(\iota F = x)$' even as we, and invoked it as a condition whenever he used a singular description. David Hilbert followed him in this.

We can join company with Peano and Hilbert and still adhere to my account of all singular terms as descriptions and my convention to use '*a*', '*b*', etc. as parameters for them all. Formally the resulting logic is the same, I believe, as Leblanc and Theodore Hailperin's logic of free terms, provided that like those authors we extend the logical axioms of identity unconditionally to singular terms.

Frege and others, unlike Hilbert, balked at Peano's free treatment of descriptions and the consequent truth-value gaps. They settled rather on one or another arbitrary fallback, perhaps the empty class or the number zero or even a null individual, as designatum for otherwise empty terms. No free logic theirs.

When we apply quantification theory in formulating set theory, descriptions are a breeze. ιF can be defined simply as the union, or logical sum, of all classes x such that Fx. If there is only one such class, ιF turns out to be it, and we rest content. If there is none, ιF turns out to be the empty class. If there are many, ιF turns out to be one or another substantial class depending on the details of the case, but we no longer care, since we only use 'ιF' when we know or intend there to be but one class x such that Fx. This is pretty, but no longer free logic.

There is a richly productive application of free logic, on the other hand, in the theory of what I call *virtual classes*. It is just classical quantification theory with, instead of the usual predicate letters, just a single predicate: the two-place predicate '$\in$' of class membership. There are no term letters, no descriptions, no identity sign. Such is its notation, pending definitions. It is a dummy set theory to begin with, dummy in that there are as yet no existence assumptions. There is just this axiom of *extensionality:*

$$\forall z(z \in x \; .\!\equiv\!. \; z \in y) \; . \; x \in w \; .\!\supset\!. \; y \in w.$$

So coextensive classes belong to the same classes.

If now we define '$x = y$' as '$\forall z(z \in x .\equiv. z \in y)$', we can derive the full logic of identity. Self-identity '$x = x$' is evident from the definition. The metatheorem of substitutivity '$x = y \,.\, Fx .\supset Fy$' follows from the axiom of extensionality by induction up the tree of truth functions and quantifiers, since the only atomic contexts of 'x' are '$y \in x$' and '$x \in y$' with one or another variable in place of 'y'.

Our definition of identity apparently requires everything to be a class. For, if x and y have no members, the definition declares them identical, thus allowing only one memberless object, the null class. It commits us to what has come to be called pure set theory. Pure set theorists revel in pure set theory, but I chafe, for I want set theory to apply to science generally. As Poincaré put it, "Le mathématicien n'a pas pour but uniquement de contempler son propre nombril."

My remedy for lo these fifty-seven years has been to identify individuals with their singletons, their unit classes. I take self-singletonhood, not nonclasshood, as the distinguishing trait of individuals. Whether there are any is for the axiomatic set-theorist to settle as he pleases. If he has an axiom barring self-membership, he can perhaps still make a place for individuals in my sense by an innocuous exception.[1]

This dummy set theory, with its axiom of extensionality and nothing more, can be parlayed into an elementary but more elaborate set theory by mere definitions and a notational convention. The result, which I call a virtual theory of classes, is an applied free logic—free, that is again, in its terms.

The first definition is a contextual definition of class abstraction. This time there is no problem of scope.

$$y \in \{x: Fx\} .\equiv Fy.$$

Next comes the convention: the parameters 'α', 'β', etc. can stand for abstracts and variables indifferently.

I already defined '$x = y$', but let me waive that as an expository anticipation and do it over more inclusively:

$$\alpha = \beta .\equiv \forall x(x \in \alpha .\equiv. x \in \beta).$$

Now we can complete the contextual definition of abstracts:

[1] For fuller treatment see my immediately preceding paper, p. 270.

$$\{x: Fx\} \in \alpha .\equiv \exists y(y = \alpha \,.\, y = \{x: Fx\}).$$

Class abstracts now make sense in either of the two positions accessible to a free variable, but the position to the left of epsilon implies existence.

One consequence of the definitions is that everything is the class of all its members. For, by our definition of '$y \in \{x: Fx\}$',

$$\forall z(z \in \{y: y \in x\} .\equiv. z \in x),$$

which is to say, by our definition of '$\alpha = \beta$', $\{y: y \in x\} = x$. So we do have a theorem of class existence, without the help of existence axioms; an unproductive one, making everything a class. I already prepared individuals for that eventuality.

Productivity abounds elsewhere, however, without existence. Abstracts generate the algebra of classes. No longer do empty terms perform in unproductive unison. We define:

$$\alpha \subseteq \beta .\equiv \forall x(x \in \alpha .\supset. x \in \beta),$$
$$\alpha \cup \beta = \{x: x \in \alpha .\text{v}. x \in \beta\},$$
$$\alpha \cap \beta = \{x: x \in \alpha \,.\, x \in \beta\},$$
$$\overline{\alpha} = \{x: x \notin \alpha\}.$$

A much richer algebra is forthcoming for virtual relations. Relation abstracts are definable thus:

$$\{xy: Fxy\} = \{z: \exists x \exists y(Fxy \,.\, z = \langle x, y\rangle)\}$$

where the ordered pair is defined in one or another well-known way, e.g. as $\{\{x\}, \{x, y\}\}$. To make the relations work we do at last need an existence axiom: $\exists z(\langle x, y\rangle = z)$. We can then grind out an elaborate algebra of relations before ever broaching the question of existence of relations. Illustrative definitions:

converse: $\breve{\alpha} = \{xy: \langle y, x\rangle \in \alpha\}$,
resultant: $\alpha | \beta = \{xz: \exists y(\langle x, y\rangle \in \alpha \,.\, \langle y, z\rangle \in \beta)\}$,
Cartesian product: $\alpha \times \beta = \{xy: x \in \alpha \,.\, y \in \beta\}$,
image: $\alpha``\beta = \{x: \exists y(\langle x, y\rangle \in \alpha \,.\, y \in \beta)\}$.

And of course the class algebra carries over to relations without further definition, relations being classes.

We thus get the full algebra of classes and relations on the basis of quantification theory without existence assumptions except, in the case of relations, for ordered pairs. This covers most of what is popularly thought of as symbolic logic and elementary set theory.

In pure quantification theory, free or not, there is no actual predicate except, optionally, identity. Hence there is nothing with respect to which empty terms can differ in their behavior from one another—or, for that matter, nonempty terms in theirs. In free logic as applied to classes, on the other hand, we are seeing rich diversity independent of existence. The behavior of would-be classes varies with the defining conditions in their abstracts. We have an applied free logic that exploits its freedom, making as full and discriminate use of its empty terms as it does of its designative ones.

This still goes on when we move into higher set theory, where axioms of class existence are in full force. It continues to be convenient to specify a class by its membership condition and proceed to use it without proving its existence. Often its existence is refutable and still no matter. The most obvious cases are axioms of class existence themselves.

Thus take Ernst Zermelo's *Aussonderung,* which provides that if some expressible condition is fulfilled only by members of a given class, it is also fulfilled by all and only the members of a class. We can now encapsulate the law in the simple schema '$\exists y(x \cap \alpha = y)$' without regard to whether there is any such class as α. Another example is the axiom schema of *replacement,* which implies *Aussonderung.* It says, roughly, that any function applied to the members of a class yields a class, but to avoid trivialization this has to be said without assuming existence of the function. It has evoked awkward circumlocution. Free logic to the rescue:

$$\text{Func}\ \alpha \supset \forall x \exists y (\alpha``x = y).$$

'Func α' just means one-manyness: $\langle x, z\rangle, \langle y, z\rangle \in \alpha \mathrel{.\supset.} x = y$. Nor let us lose sight of the ontological innocence of this mathematical make-believe. Notational conventions aside, this set-theoretic language is still just the austere language of truth functions, membership, and quantification over genuine existent classes. The rest—the free class abstracts with their virtual classes—is laid on by definition and convention.

XXX

The Inception of "New Foundations"

Maurice Boffa has asked me how I came to hit upon "New foundations." In answer I must begin by recalling how I looked upon Bertrand Russell's theory of types in 1935.

By then the theory of types had taken on its simple modern form. The ramified theory had been dropped, and furthermore, thanks to Norbert Wiener's and Casimir Kuratowski's definitions of the ordered pair, the types of relations had been reduced to the simple hierarchy of types of classes. There were just individuals, classes of individuals, classes of such classes, and so on up. This pattern had already been established in 1931, in articles of Alfred Tarski and Kurt Gödel.

Still I was unhappy with types. One unattractive feature was the arbitrary grammatical exclusions. Seemingly intelligible combinations of signs were banned as ungrammatical and meaningless. So I tried in 1935 to legitimize these exclusions by deriving classes and membership from some array of more primitive notions. I hoped to devise contextual definitions that would generate just the formulas that fit the theory of types, while leaving other formulas meaningless in the straightforward sense of not being accounted for by the definitions.

What these more primitive notions might be was the next question. I would have liked to make do with syntactic and semantic notions—thus signs, concatenation, denotation, truth. This plan,

---

Written and circulated after a colloquium that was held at Oberwolfach in February 1987 to mark the fiftieth anniversary of "New foundations."

if successful, would not only legitimize the grammatical restrictions imposed by the theory of types, but would also reduce classes to expressions, to the gratification of nominalistic tastes. But this line failed, as you might expect. The paradoxes of sets merely gave way to semantic paradoxes.

I found a different solution, one lacking the nominalistic virtues. For my primitive notions I adopted a reduced variant of Ernst Zermelo's set theory. Its variables ranged indiscriminately over individuals and classes. I had not yet thought of identifying individuals with their singletons, so the individuals had no members. There was no empty class; any designated individual would have served that purpose, but none was designated. The axiom of extensionality had a nonemptiness clause so as to permit multiplicity of individuals. It is the same weakened extensionality that was to reappear thirty-three years later in R. B. Jensen's amazing theorem about "New foundations."

The only existence assumption in this early system of mine was the schema

$$\exists y \forall x(x \in y \;.\!\equiv\!.\; x \subseteq z \;.\; Fx),$$

which is Zermelo's *Aussonderungsschema* with '$x \subseteq z$' in place of '$x \in z$'. I showed that the theory of types, with indexed variables and an empty class in each type, could be simulated in this theory by contextual definitions. The axiom of infinity, here as in Whitehead and Russell's *Principia Mathematica,* was listed as an optional extra. This was my "Set-theoretic foundations for logic," 1936 (VI in this volume).

I have now described my struggle with one drawback of the theory of types, namely the arbitrariness of the grammatical strictures. Now another unattractive feature of the theory of types was the infinite reduplication of objects: each number, or other mathematical object, had a replica in every higher type. This drawback remained.

Zermelo's system itself was free of both drawbacks, but in its multiplicity of axioms it seemed inelegant, artificial, and ad hoc. I had not yet appreciated how naturally his system emerges from the theory of types when we render the types cumulative and describe them by means of general variables. I came to see this only in January 1954, and set it forth in "Unification of universes in set theory" and *Set Theory and Its Logic.* If I had appreciated it in 1936, I might not have pressed on to "New foundations."

But I might have, still. For I disliked the lack of a universe class in Zermelo's system, and the lack of complements of classes, and in general the lack of big classes. I also disliked the artificiality of having to adopt an axiom of infinity to get arithmetic; and this was a shortcoming equally of the theory of types, a third shortcoming along with the grammatical restriction and the reduplication of mathematical objects.

I wanted a system that would be free of all three of these drawbacks of the theory of types, but would be like the theory of types in having a single comprehensive principle of class existence, and would admit big classes without restriction to type.

Russell's theory of types rested on the unstated intuition that every sentence in one free variable determines a class. This intuition may have owed its stubbornness in part to Russell's vagueness over the distinction between use and mention, hence between sentence and proposition, between open sentence and property or class. Thus it was that, when a class proved untenable, Russell had to banish its membership condition from the language. This trait of the theory of types had carried over into my "Set-theoretic foundations for logic"; there I had merely legitimized the expulsions from the language by suitably crafting my contextual definitions.

It may have been to Zermelo that I owed the insight that a meaningful open sentence may or may not determine a class, and that it can be left to axioms to settle which ones do. Having grasped this point, I was able to look to types as a restriction specifically upon classes and not upon language. The purpose of the theory of types was to bar the paradoxes, and this could be done by using it only to say which open sentences are to be taken to determine classes. Its efficacy for this purpose is a matter of structure, namely, stratification; and this benefit, I conjectured, can be preserved while abandoning the whole notion of a stratified ontology of classes.

So I reconstrued the variables as general, and found new strength accruing at every turn, apparently with impunity. Grammatical restrictions were gone, reduplication of objects was gone, the universe class and the complements of classes were forthcoming, and the existence of infinite classes was evident without an axiom of infinity. Proof of the axiom of infinity within the system awaited Ernst Specker's work of 1953, but one could already show that V existed, that it had all the natural numbers as members, and that each number[1] was distinct from each.

I sent "New foundations for mathematical logic" to *American Mathematical Monthly* in November 1936 and presented the paper at the annual meeting of the Mathematical Association of America in December 1936. I was also presenting it in my course in mathematical logic in the Harvard mathematics department. It was my first year of teaching, after four years of postdoctoral fellowships.

It is evident from *Set Theory and Its Logic* that I do not extol "New foundations" over other set theories. Its extension in my book *Mathematical Logic* has advantages in strength and convenience, but "New foundations" remains a crucial auxiliary in view of Hao Wang's proof that the one system is consistent if the other is. "New foundations" is better than the other for proof-theoretic study because of its greater simplicity. As a working set theory even the system in *Mathematical Logic* is not ideal; there is the inelegance, as Barkley Rosser showed (1952), of requiring an added axiom to assure that the class of all natural numbers be a set. But I am alive to the virtues of these systems, and I am dazzled by the deep and ingenious discoveries that various of you have made regarding "New foundations."

[1] As defined by John von Neumann or Wilhelm Ackermann, not Gottlob Frege (Thomas Forster).

XXXI

Pythagorean Triples and Fermat's Last Theorem

The Pythagorean theorem tells us that going forward three miles and then four miles squarely to the right achieves a net diagonal displacement of five miles; $3^2 + 4^2 = 5^2$. This neat relation cries out for generalization. What triples $\langle x, y, z\rangle$ of positive integers are there, besides $\langle 3, 4, 5\rangle$, such that $x^2 + y^2 = z^2$? More generally, what quadruples $\langle x, y, z, n\rangle$ are there such that $x^n + y^n = z^n$?

A triple $\langle x, y, z\rangle$ such that $x^2 + y^2 = z^2$ is called Pythagorean, and it has long been known that a triple is Pythagorean if and only if it is of the form

$$\langle a^2 - b^2, 2ab, a^2 + b^2\rangle$$

(Ore, pp. 167f). I now offer a very different form to the same effect:

$$(1) \qquad \langle a + \sqrt{2ab}, b + \sqrt{2ab}, a + b + \sqrt{2ab}\rangle.$$

By squaring its three terms and computing, we see that (1) is Pythagorean. To see conversely that $\langle x, y, z\rangle$ is always of the form (1) when $x^2 + y^2 = z^2$, take a as $z - y$, b as $z - x$, and c as $x + y - z$. Then

$$(2) \qquad x = a + c, \qquad y = b + c, \qquad z = a + b + c.$$

Substituting these values in '$x^2 + y^2 = z^2$',

$$(a + c)^2 + (b + c)^2 = (a + b + c)^2.$$

This slight piece is not logic, but to me it has the same appeal.

Multiplying out and canceling, we get $c^2 = 2ab$. So $c = \sqrt{2ab}$. We substitute accordingly in (2), and the result equates $\langle x, y, z\rangle$ to (1).

But the broader generalization, $\langle x, y, z, n\rangle$, presents the more interesting question, indeed the most famous unsolved problem in all of mathematics: Fermat's Last Theorem. Three centuries and more ago Pierre de Fermat claimed to have proved that there are no positive integers x, y, z, and n such that $x^n + y^n = z^n$ if $n > 2$. Mathematicians have tried in vain to confirm or refute this. I shall do neither, but I shall show that Fermat's purported theorem can be colorfully stated in terms of sorting objects into a row of bins some of which are red, some blue, and the rest unpainted. The theorem amounts to saying that when there are more than two objects it can never happen that

(3) the ways of sorting them that shun both colors are equal in number to the ways that shun neither.

To show that this is equivalent to Fermat's Last Theorem, I shall show that (3) boils down to the Fermat equation '$x^n + y^n = z^n$' when n is how many objects there are, z is how many bins there are, x is how many bins are not red, and y is how many are not blue.

There are z choices of bins in which to deposit the first object, and for each such choice there are again z choices of where to deposit the second object, and so on; so altogether there are z^n ways of sorting the n objects into bins. The ways that shun red are x^n in number by similar reasoning, and those that shun blue are y^n in number. So where A is the number of ways that shun both colors, B is the number of ways that shun red but not blue, C is the number of ways that shun blue but not red, and D is the number of ways that shun neither, we have

$$x^n = A + B, \qquad y^n = A + C, \qquad z^n = A + B + C + D.$$

These equations give '$x^n + y^n = z^n$' if and only if $A = D$, which is to say (3).

This minidiscovery lay languishing in my old notebook since 1933, with a long and ugly proof. I turned it up fifty-odd years later and hit upon the present simple proof. I published it in *Quiddities*, pp. 62–63, from which I have just now cribbed a half page with the publishers' permission. Hilary Putnam remarked on reading it that it could be parlayed into a novel formula for Pythagorean triples, and that was the scent that led me to (1).

References

Ackermann. *See* Hilbert.

Benacerraf, P., and H. Putnam, eds. *Readings in the Philosophy of Mathematics.* Englewood, N.J.: Prentice Hall, 1964.

Bencivenga, Ermanno. "Set theory and free logic," *Journal of Philosophical Logic* 5 (1976), 1–15.

Bernays, Paul. "Axiomatische Untersuchungen des Aussagen-Kalkuls der *Principia Mathematica,*" *Mathematische Zeitschrift* 25 (1926), 305–320.

———. "Über eine natürliche Erweiterung des Relationenkalkuls," in A. Heyting, ed., 1–14.

———, and M. Schönfinkel. "Zum Entscheidungsproblem der mathematischen Logik," *Mathematische Annalen* 99 (1928), 342–372.

———. *See also* Hilbert.

Bing, Kurt. "On simplifying truth-functional formulas," *Journal of Symbolic Logic* 21 (1956), 253–254.

Boole, George. *The Mathematical Analysis of Logic.* London and Cambridge, England, 1847.

———. *An Investigation of the Laws of Thought.* London, 1854.

Burks, Arthur. "Logic, computers, and men," *Proceedings of American Philosophical Association* 46 (1972–73), 48f.

Carnap, Rudolf. *The Logical Syntax of Language.* New York and London, 1937.

———. *Meaning and Necessity.* Chicago: University of Chicago, 1947; 2d ed., 1956.

Church, Alonzo. *The Calculi of Lambda Conversion.* Princeton, 1941.

———. "A note on the Entscheidungsproblem," *Journal of Symbolic Logic* 1 (1936), 40–41, 101–102.

———. "Schröder's anticipation of the simple theory of types," preprinted for Fifth International Congress for Unity of Science (Cambridge, Mass., 1939) as from *Journal of Unified Science,* Vol. 9. Owing to a German invasion the volume never came out.

———. Review of Bell, *Journal of Symbolic Logic* 5 (1940), 152.

———. Review of Frege, *Journal of Symbolic Logic* 18 (1953), 93.

———, and W. V. Quine. "Some theorems on definability and decidability," *ibid.* 17 (1952), 179–187.

Cooley, J. C. *A Primer of Formal Logic.* New York, 1942.

Craig, W., and W. V. Quine. "On reduction to a symmetric relation," *Journal of Symbolic Logic* 17 (1952), 188.

Curry, H. B., and R. Feys. *Combinatory Logic.* Amsterdam: North-Holland, 1958.

Davidson, D., and J. Hintikka, eds. *Words and Objections: Essays on the Work of W. V. Quine*. Dordrecht: Reidel, 1969.

Dedekind, Richard. *Stetigkeit und irrationale Zahlen*. Brunswick, 1872.

———. *"Was sind und was sollen die Zahlen."* Brunswick, 1888.

De Morgan, Augustus. *Formal Logic*. London, 1847.

Dreben, Burton. "On the completeness of quantification theory," *Proceedings of National Academy of Sciences* 38 (1952), 1047–1052.

Feigl, H., and W. Sellars. *Readings in Philosophical Analysis*. New York: Appleton, 1949.

Feys. *See* Curry.

Fitch, F. B. *Symbolic Logic*. New York: Ronald, 1952.

Forster, Thomas. *Set Theories with a Universal Set*. Oxford: Clarendon, 1992.

Fraenkel, Adolf. *Einleitung in die Mengenlehre*. 3d ed., Berlin, 1928.

Frege, Gottlob. *Begriffsschrift*. Halle, 1879. Translated in van Heijenoort.

———. *Grundlagen der Arithmetik*. Breslau, 1884. Reprinted with English translation as *The Foundations of Arithmetic*. New York: Philosophical Library; and Oxford: Blackwell's, 1950.

———. *Grundgesetze der Arithmetik*. Vol. 1, 1893; Vol. 2, 1903. Jena.

———. *Translations from the Philosophical Writings of Gottlob Frege* by P. Geach and M. Black. Oxford: Blackwell's, 1952.

Fridshal, R. "The Quine algorithm," *Summaries of Talks at the Summer Institute of Symbolic Logic*. Mimeographed. Cornell, 1957, 211–212.

Geach. *See* Frege.

Gergonne, J. D. "Essai de dialectique rationelle," *Annales de mathématiques pures et appliquées* 7 (1816–17), 189–228.

Ghazala, M. J. "Irredundant disjunctive and conjunctive forms of a Boolean function," *I.B.M. Journal of Research and Development* 1 (1957), 171–176.

Gödel, Kurt. *On Undecidable Propositions of Formal Mathematical Systems*. Mimeographed. Princeton, 1934.

———. "Die Vollständigkeit der Axiome des logischen Funktionenkalküls," *Monatshefte für Mathematik und Physik* 37 (1930), 349–360. Translated in van Heijenoort.

———. "Über formal unentscheidbare Sätze der *Principia Mathematica* und verwandter Systeme," *ibid.* 38 (1931), 173–198. Translated in van Heijenoort.

———. "Consistency proof for the generalized continuum hypothesis," *Proceedings of National Academy of Sciences* 25 (1939), 220–224.

Goodman, Nelson. "Sequences," *Journal of Symbolic Logic* 6 (1941), 150–153.

———. *See also* Leonard.

Hahn, Hans. *Überflüssige Wesenheiten*. Vienna, 1930.

Hailperin, Theodore. "A set of axioms for logic," *Journal of Symbolic Logic* 9 (1944), 1–19.

———. *See also* Leblanc.

Hasenjaeger, Gisbert. "Eine Bemerkung zu Henkins Beweis für die Vollständigkeit des Pradikatenkalküls der ersten Stufe," *ibid.* 18 (1953), 42–48.

Henkin, Leon. *The Completeness of Formal Systems*. Dissertation. Princeton, 1947.

———. "The representation theorem for cylindrical algebras," in Skolem *et al.*

Henle, P., *et al.*, eds. *Structure, Method, and Meaning: Essays in Honor of H. M. Sheffer*. New York: Liberal Arts, 1951.

Herbrand, Jacques. *Recherches sur la théorie de la démonstration*. Warsaw, 1930.

Hermes, Hans. *Semiotik*. Leipzig, 1938. 22 pp.

———, and H. Scholz. *Ein neuer Vollständigkeitsbeweis für das reduzierte Fregesche Axiomensystem des Aussagenkalküls.* Leipzig, 1937. 40 pp.

Heyting, Arend. *Mathematische Grundlagenforschung.* Berlin, 1934.

———, ed. *Constructivity in Mathematics.* Amsterdam: North-Holland, 1959.

Hilbert, David, and Wilhelm Ackermann. *Grundzüge der theoretischen Logik.* Berlin: Springer, 1928; 2d ed., 1938; 3d ed., 1949; 4th ed., 1959. Translation: *Principles of Mathematical Logic.* New York: Chelsea, 1950.

———, and Paul Bernays. *Grundlagen der Mathematik.* Vol. 1, 1934; Vol. 2, 1939. Berlin.

Huntington, E. V. "The fundamental laws of addition and multiplication in elementary algebra." *Annals of Mathematics* 8 (1906), 1–44.

Jensen, R. B. "On a slight (?) modification of Quine's 'New foundations,' " in Davidson and Hintikka, pp. 278–291.

Jevons, W. S. *Pure Logic.* London, 1864.

Jourdain, P. E. B. "The Development of the Theories of Mathematical Logic and the Principles of Mathematics," *Quarterly Journal of Pure and Applied Mathematics* 43 (1912), 219–314.

Kalmár, László. "Über die Axiomatisierbarkeit des Aussagenkalküls," *Acta Litterarum ac Scientiarum Regiae Universitatis Hungaricae Francisco-Josephinae* (Szeged), *Sectio scientiarum mathematicarum* 7 (1935), 222–243.

———. "Zurückführung des Entscheidungsproblems auf den Fall von Formeln mit einer einzigen, binären Funktionsvariablen," *Compositio Mathematica* 4 (1936), 137–144.

Kleene, S. C. *Introduction to Metamathematics.* New York: Van Nostrand, 1952.

———. "Recursive predicates and quantifiers," *Transactions of American Mathematical Society* 53 (1943), 41–73.

Kreisel, Georg. "Note on arithmetic models for consistent formulae of the predicate calculus," *Fundamenta Mathematicae* 37 (1950), 265–285; 2d paper, *Proceedings of XIth International Congress of Philosophy* 14 (Brussels, 1953), 39–49.

Kuratowski, Casimir. "Sur la notion de l'ordre dans la théorie des ensembles," *Fundamenta Mathematicae* 2 (1921), 161–171.

Leblanc, Hugues. *Existence, Truth, and Provability.* Albany: State University, 1982.

———, and Theodore Hailperin. "Nondesignating singular terms." *Philosophical Review* 68 (1959), 239–243. Reprinted in Leblanc.

Lee, O. H., ed. *Philosophical Essays for A. N. Whitehead.* New York, 1936.

Leibniz, G. W. von. *Opera,* Vol. 1. J. E. Erdmann, ed. Berlin, 1840.

Leonard, H. S., and N. Goodman. "The calculus of individuals and its uses," *Journal of Symbolic Logic* 5 (1940), 45–55. Abstract: 2 (1937), 63f.

Lewis, C. I. *A Survey of Symbolic Logic.* Berkeley, Calif., 1918.

———, and C. H. Langford. *Symbolic Logic.* New York, 1932.

Löwenheim, Leopold. "Über Möglichkeiten im Relativkalkül," *Mathematische Annalen* 76 (1915), 447–470. Translated in van Heijenoort.

Łukasiewicz, Jan. "O logice trójwartościowej," *Ruch Filozoficzny* 5 (1920), 169–171.

———. "Ein Vollständigkeitsbeweis des zweiwertigen Aussagenkalküls," *Comptes rendus des séances de la Société des Sciences et des Lettres de Varsovie,* Classe III, Vol. 24 (1931), 153–183.

———. "Uwagi o aksyomacie Nicod'a i o dedukcyi uogólniającej," *Księga Pamiątkowa Polskiego Towarzystwa Filozoficznego we Lwowie,* Lwów, 1931, 2–7.

———. "Zur Geschichte der Aussagenlogik," *Erkenntnis* 5 (1935–1936), 111–131.

———, and A. Tarski, "Untersuchungen über den Aussagenkalkül," *Comptes rendus des séances de la Société des Sciences et des Lettres de Varsovie*, Classe III, Vol. 23 (1930), 30–50. Translation in Tarski, *Logic, Semantics, Metamathematics.*

MacColl, Hugh. "The calculus of equivalent statements," *Proceedings of London Mathematical Society* 9 (1877–1878), 9–20, 177–186; 10 (1878–1879), 16–28; 11 (1879–1880), 113–121; 28 (1896–1897), 156–183, 555–579; 29 (1897–1898), 98–109.

MacHale, Desmond. *George Boole: His Life and Work.* Dublin: Boole Press, 1985.

Mills. *See* Samson.

Mitchell, O. H. "On a New Algebra of Logic," in Peirce, ed., pp. 80–90.

Ore, Oystein. *Number Theory and Its History.* New York: McGraw Hill, 1948.

Parsons, Charles. "A Plea for Substitutional Quantification," *Journal of Philosophy* 68 (1971), 231–237.

Peano, Giuseppe. *Calcolo geometrico.* Turin, 1888.

———. *Arithmetices principia, novo methodo exposita.* Turin, 1889.

———. "Démonstration de l'intégrabilite des équations différentiales ordinaires," *Mathematische Annalen* 37 (1890), 182–228.

———. *Formulaire de mathématiques (Formulario di matematica).* Introduction, Turin, 1894. 2d ed., 1899. 3d ed., Paris, 1901.

———. "Sul §2 del *Formulario,* t. II: aritmetica," *Rivista di matematica* 6 (1896), 75–89.

———. "Studii di logica matematica," *Atti della Reale Accademia di Scienza di Torino* 32 (1897), 565–583.

———. *Academia pro Interlingua. Discussiones,* vol. 1. Turin, 1909–10.

———. "Sulla definizione di funzione," *Atti della Reale Accademia dei Lincei, Rendiconti, classe di sci. fis., mat., e nat.* 20 (1911), 3–5.

Peirce, C. S. *Collected Papers,* Vols. 2–4. Cambridge, Mass., 1932–1933.

———, ed. *Studies in Logic* by members of the Johns Hopkins University. Boston, 1883.

Poincaré, Henri. *Science and Method.* London and New York, 1914.

———. "Les mathématiques et la logique," *Revue de métaphysique et de morale* 13 (1905), 815–835; 14 (1906), 17–34, 294–317. Reprinted with revisions in *Science and Method.*

Post, E. L. "Introduction to a general theory of elementary propositions," *American Journal of Mathematics* 43 (1921), 163–185. Reprinted in van Heijenoort.

———. "Finite combinatory processes," *Journal of Symbolic Logic* 1 (1936), 103–105.

Putnam. *See* Benacerraf.

Quine, W. V. *A System of Logistic.* Cambridge, Mass., 1934.

———. *Mathematical Logic.* New York, 1940. Cambridge, Mass.: Harvard, 1947; rev. ed., 1951.

———. *Elementary Logic.* Boston, 1941. Rev. ed., New York: Harper Torchbooks, 1965, and Cambridge: Harvard, 1966.

———. *O Sentido da Nova Lógica.* São Paulo, 1944. Spanish translation: *El Sentido de la Nueva Lógica.* Buenos Aires: Nueva Visión, 1958.

———. *Methods of Logic.* New York: Holt, 1950; rev. ed., 1959. London: Routledge, 1962.

———. *From a Logical Point of View.* Cambridge, Mass.: Harvard, 1953; rev. ed., 1961.

———. *Set Theory and Its Logic.* Cambridge, Mass.: Harvard, 1963; 2nd ed., 1969.

———. *The Ways of Paradox and Other Essays.* New York, 1966; enlarged ed., Cambridge, Mass.: Harvard, 1976.

———. *Theories and Things.* Cambridge, Mass.: Harvard, 1981.

———. *Quiddities.* Cambridge, Mass.: Harvard, 1987.

———. "Ontological remarks on the propositional calculus," *Mind* 43 (1934), 472–476. Reprinted in *The Ways of Paradox.*

———. "A theory of classes presupposing no canons of type," *Proceedings of the National Academy of Sciences* 22 (1936), 320–326.

———. "Toward a calculus of concepts," *Journal of Symbolic Logic* 1 (1936), 2–25.

———. "On the axiom of reducibility," *Mind* 45 (1936), 498–500.

———. "Truth by convention," in O. H. Lee, 90–124. Reprinted in *The Ways of Paradox;* also in Feigl and Sellars; also in Benacerraf and Putnam.

———. "New foundations for mathematical logic," *American Mathematical Monthly* 44 (1937), 70–80. Reprinted with additions in *From a Logical Point of View.*

———. "On derivability," *Journal of Symbolic Logic* 2 (1937), 113–119.

———. "On Cantor's theorem," *ibid.,* 120–124.

———. "On the theory of types," *ibid.* 3 (1938), 125–139.

———. "Designation and existence," *Journal of Philosophy* 36 (1939), 701–709. Reprinted in Feigl and Sellars.

———. Review of Rosser, *Journal of Symbolic Logic* 6 (1941), 163.

———. "A way to simplify truth functions," *American Mathematical Monthly* 62 (1955), 627–631.

———. "Unification of universes in set theory," *Journal of Symbolic Logic* 21 (1956), 267–279.

———. *See also* Church; Craig.

Ramsey, F. P. *Foundations of Mathematics.* London and New York, 1931.

Roberts, Don. *The Existential Graphs of C. S. Peirce.* The Hague: Mouton, 1973.

Rosser, Barkley. "On the consistency of Quine's 'New foundations for mathematical logic,'" *Journal of Symbolic Logic* 4 (1939), 15–24.

———. "The independence of Quine's axioms *200 and *201," *ibid.* 6 (1941), 96f.

———. "The Burali-Forti paradox," *ibid.* 7 (1942), 1–17.

———. "The axiom of infinity in Quine's 'New foundations,'" *ibid.* 17 (1952), 238–242.

———, and A. R. Turquette. *Many-Valued Logics.* Amsterdam: North-Holland, 1952.

———, and H. Wang. "Non-standard models for formal logic," *Journal of Symbolic Logic* 15 (1950), 113–129.

Russell, Bertrand. *The Principles of Mathematics.* Cambridge, England, 1903.

———. *Introduction to Mathematical Philosophy.* New York and London, 1919.

———. *Logic and Knowledge.* London: Allen & Unwin, 1956.

———. "On denoting," *Mind* 14 (1905), 479–493. Reprinted in *Logic and Knowledge;* also in Feigl and Sellars.

———. "Mathematical logic as based on the theory of types," *American Journal of Mathematics* 30 (1908), 222–262. Reprinted in *Logic and Knowledge;* also in van Heijenoort.

———. *See also* Whitehead.

Samson, E. W., and B. E. Mills. "Circuit minimization: algebra and algorithms for new Boolean canonical expressions," *AFCRC Technical Report* 21, 1954.

Schock, Rolf. *Logics without Existence Assumptions.* Uppsala: Almquist and Wiksell, 1968.

Scholz, Heinrich. Review of Frege, *Zentralblatt für Mathematik* 48 (1954), 1f.

———. *See also* Hermes.

Schönfinkel, Moses. "Über die Bausteine der mathematischen Logik," *Mathematische Annalen* 92 (1924), 305–316. Translated in van Heijenoort.

———. *See also* Bernays.

Schröder, Ernst. *Der Operationskreis des Logikkalkuls.* Leipzig, 1877.

———. *Vorlesungen über die Algebra der Logik,* Vol. 1. Leipzig, 1890.

———. Review of Frege 1879, *Zeitschrift für Mathematik und Physik* 25 (1880), 81–94.

Shannon, C. E. "A symbolic analysis of relay and switching circuits," *Transactions of American Institute of Electrical Engineers* 57 (1938), 713–723.

Skolem, Thoralf. "Logische-kombinatorische Untersuchungen," *Skrifter utgit av Videnskapsselskapet i Kristiania, I. matematisknaturvidenskabelig klasse,* No. 4 (1920), 36 pp. Translated in van Heijenoort.

———. "Über die mathematische Logik," *Norsk Matematisk Tidskrift* 10 (1928), 125–142. Translated in van Heijenoort.

———. "Einige Bemerkungen zu der Abhandlung von E. Zermelo über die Definitheit in der Axiomatik," *Fundamenta Mathematicae* 15 (1930), 337–341.

———, *et al. Mathematical Interpretation of Formal Systems.* Amsterdam: North-Holland, 1955.

Smullyan, Raymond. "Languages in which self reference is possible," *Journal of Symbolic Logic* 22 (1957), 55–67.

Sobociński, Bolesław. "L'analyse de l'antinomie russellienne par Leśniewski," *Methodos* 1 (1949), 94–107, 220–228, 308–316.

Specker, Ernst. "The axiom of choice in Quine's 'New foundations for mathematical logic,' " *Proceedings of National Academy of Sciences* 39 (1953), 972–975.

Tarski, Alfred. *A Decision Method for Elementary Algebra and Geometry.* Santa Monica, 1948; rev. ed., Berkeley: University of California, 1951.

———. *Logic, Semantics, Metamathematics.* Oxford: Clarendon, 1956.

———. "Sur le terme primitif dans la logistique," *Fundamenta Mathematicae* 4 (1923), 196–200. Translated in *Logic, Semantics, Metamathematics.*

———. "Sur les ensembles definissables de nombres reels I," *Fundamenta Mathematica* 17 (1931), 210–239.

———. "Einige Betrachtungen über die Begriffe der ω-Widerspruchsfreiheit und der ω-Vollständigkeit," *Monatshefte für Mathematik und Physik* 40 (1933), 97–112. Translated in *Logic, Semantics, Metamathematics.*

———. "Der Wahrheitsbegriff in den formalisierten Sprachen," *Studia Philosophica* 1 (1935 for 1936), 261–405. Translated in *Logic, Semantics, Metamathematics.*

———. *See also* Łukasiewicz.

Turing, A. M. "On computable numbers," *Proceedings of London Mathematical Society,* Ser. 2, Vol. 42 (1937), 230–266; Vol. 43 (1938), 544–545.

Turquette. *See* Rosser.

Vacca, Giovanni. Review of Whitehead, *Rivista di matematica* 6 (1896–1899), 101–104.

van Heijenoort, Jean, ed. *From Frege to Gödel: A Source Book in Mathematical Logic, 1879–1931.* Cambridge: Harvard, 1966.

Venn, John. *Symbolic Logic.* London, 1881; 2d ed., 1894.

von Neumann, J. "Zur Einführung der transfiniten Zahlen," *Acta Litterarum ac Scientiarum Regiae Universitatis Hungaricae Francisco-Josephinae* (Szeged), *Sectio scientiarum mathematicarum* 1 (1923), 199–208. Translated in van Heijenoort.

———. "Eine Axiomatisierung der Mengenlehre," *Journal für reine und angewandte Mathematik* 154 (1925), 219–240. Translated in van Heijenoort.

Wajsberg, Mordechaj. "Metalogische Beiträge," *Wiadomości Matematyczne* 43 (1937), 131–168.

Wang, Hao. "A new theory of element and number," *Journal of Symbolic Logic* 13 (1948), 129–137.

———. "A formal system of logic," *ibid.* 15 (1950), 25–32.

———. "Arithmetic models for formal systems," *Methodos* 3 (1951), 217–232.

———. *See also* Rosser.

Weyl, Hermann. *Das Kontinuum.* Berlin, 1918.

Whitehead, A. N. *A Treatise on Universal Algebra.* Cambridge, England, 1898.

———. *The Principles of Natural Knowledge.* Cambridge, England, 1919.

———. *The Concept of Nature.* Cambridge, England, 1920.

———. *Process and Reality.* Cambridge, England, and New York, 1929.

———. *Essays in Science and Philosophy.* New York: Philosophical Library, 1947; London: Rider, 1948.

———. "Memoir on the algebra of symbolic logic," *American Journal of Mathematics* 23 (1901), 139–165, 297–316.

———. "On cardinal numbers," *ibid.* 24 (1902), 367–394.

———. "The logic of relations, logical substitution groups, and cardinal numbers," *ibid.* 25 (1903), 157–178.

———. "Theorems on cardinal numbers," *ibid.* 26 (1904), 31f.

———. "On mathematical concepts of the material world," *Philosophical Transactions of the Royal Society of London,* Series A, 205 (1906), 465–525.

———. "La théorie rélationniste de l'espace," *Revue de metaphysique et de morale* 23 (1916), 423–545.

———. "Indication, classes, numbers, validation," *Mind* 43 (1934), 281–297. Reprinted in *Essays in Science and Philosophy.*

———, and B. Russell. *Principia Mathematica.* Vol. 1, 1910; Vol. 2, 1912; Vol. 3, 1913. 2d ed., Cambridge, England, 1925–1927.

Wiener, Norbert. "A simplification of the logic of relations," *Proceedings of Cambridge Philosophical Society* 17 (1912–1914), 387–390. Reprinted in van Heijenoort.

Wittgenstein, Ludwig. *Tractatus Logico-Philosophicus.* London, 1922.

Zermelo, Ernst. "Beweis, dass jede Menge wohlgeordnet werden kann," *Mathematische Annalen* 59 (1904), 514–516. Translated in van Heijenoort.

———. "Untersuchungen über die Grundlagen der Mengenlehre," *ibid.* 65 (1908), 261–281. Translated in van Heijenoort.

Index